*f*P

Also by John Dickie

Cosa Nostra: A History of the Sicilian Mafia

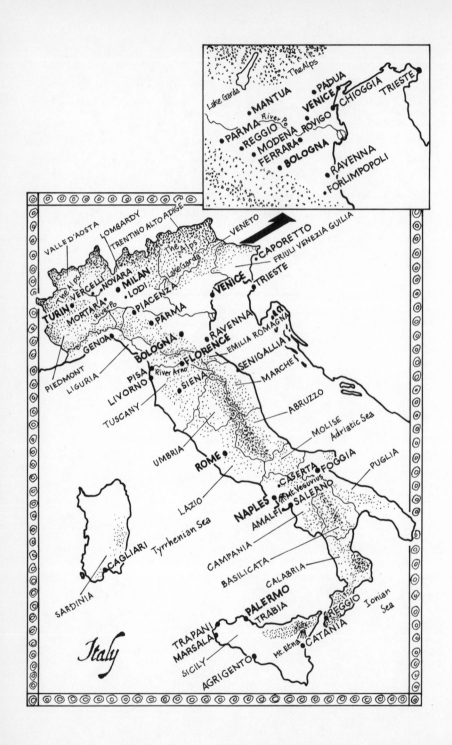

Italy

Delizia!

The Epic History of the Italians and Their Food

JOHN DICKIE

Free Press

New York London Toronto Sydney

Free Press

A Division of Simon & Schuster, Inc.

1230 Avenue of the Americas

New York, NY 10020

First Free Press hardcover edition January 2008

FREE PRESS and colophon are trademarks of Simon & Schuster, Inc.

For information about special discounts for bulk purchases,
please contact Simon & Schuster Special Sales at 1-800-456-6798 or
business@ simonandschuster.com

Book design by Ellen R. Sasahara

Manufactured in the United States of America

1   3   5   7   9   10   8   6   4   2

Library of Congress Cataloging-in-Publication Data

Dickie, John.
Delizia! : the epic history of the Italians and their food/John Dickie.
p. cm.
1. Gastronomy—Italy—History. 2. Food habits—Italy—History. 3. Cookery,
Italian—History. 4. Italy—Social life and customs. I. Title.
TX641 .D44 2008
641'.013—dc22
2007015302

ISBN-13: 978-0-7432-7799-0
ISBN-10:   0-7432-7799-6

PICTURE CREDITS

Archive of the State of Bologna: 135; Archive of the State of Modena:
79; Archivio Touring Club Italiano/Alinari Archive, Florence: 247 (below);
Bridgeman Art Library/Bibliothèque National de France: 50 (above);
Bridgeman Art Library/Galleria e Museo Estense, Modena: 88; Bridge-
man Art Library/Musée des Beaux-Arts, Mulhouse: 150; Bridgeman
Art Library/Osterreichische Nationalbibliothek, Vienna: 33, 50 (below);
Bridgeman Art Library/Vatican Museums and Galleries, Vatican City: 66;
British Library: 49; Courtesy Slow Food, Bra.: 315; Photo by Soldati: 291;
Courtesy of author: 4 (above and below).

For Sarah, Elliot, and Charlotte

Contents

PART V: FASCISTS IN THE KITCHEN

PART VI: THE LAND OF PLENTY

Delizia!

Tuscany

Don't Tell the Peasants . . .

A drive through the country between Siena and the sea in the
sunshine of an autumn evening. The Tuscan hills undulat-
ing past the car window become harsher, shading from vines
and olive groves into pockets of dark forest. The destination is remote,
yet it is a place where you can hear accents and dialects from across
Italy. Here Venetians mix with Neapolitans, Palermitans with Turinese.
In this quiet corner of Tuscany a people divided by ancient local rival-
ries comes to pay homage together at an altar to their common cult of
food.

The building lies in the valley below the perfectly preserved medieval
town of Chiusdino, but it is not easy to find. Not long ago, the track
leading to it was nearly lost in thick scrub. Even now many people miss
the discreet road sign. When the more observant visitors have negoti-
ated a tight, descending corner and nosed over the narrow, parapet-less
bridge, they are rewarded with the sight of a riverside field of Jerusalem
artichokes—yellow flowers craning toward the setting sun.

Then it appears, unwelcoming at first, resolutely turning its worn
back to the outside world, as if hiding its famous face among the poplar
trees. But recognition chimes the moment the corner is turned: a simple brick and stone structure, with a shallow roof and an unassuming
tower; at its flank a mill wheel is gently propelled by the limpid waters

of the river Merce. It was built by monks from the nearby San Galgano Abbey in the early thirteenth century. Even today one can easily imagine a friar emerging from the beamed kitchen with an armful of cheeses and *salami* for his brothers. Or a peasant patriarch, his shoulder bowed by the weight of his hoe, trudging through the surrounding glade at the end of his day's toil. Perhaps the plates and glasses on the table under the pergola were set by his homely wife for their extended family. Dinner is still awhile away, but already the air is laced with appetizing smells.

To the foreign visitor, *Il Mulino Bianco*, the White Mill, seems to typify everything that Italian food should be. To Italians, it is one of the most iconic buildings in the land.

Yet it is also Italy's best-loved fake.

ITALIANS eat lots of biscuits (cookies), mostly for breakfast. In 1989, the leading biscuit brand, Mulino Bianco, was looking for a set for its new advertising campaign. The White Mill shown on the biscuit packets was about to become a real place. The industrialized Po valley—flat and featureless—had distinctly the wrong image, thus ruling out locations in the region around Parma where the biscuits were actually made. Instead set researchers found what they were looking for, abandoned and almost derelict, off the Massetana road near Chiusdino in Tuscany. The old building was given a coat of white paint and a new mill wheel powered by an electric motor. In a short time it was ready to receive its imaginary family of owners. Dad was a square-jawed journalist; Mum, a pretty but prim teacher; their children, Linda with curly hair and a bonnet, and Andrea in slacks and a tie, were as smart-but-casual as their parents; a marshmallow-eyed grandfather completed the group. This, as the company Web site would have it, was a "modern family who leave the city and choose to live healthily by going back to nature." Their story, to be told in a series of mini-episodes, was to embody the second-home aspirations of millions of urban consumers. And to tell it, the agency hired two of the biggest talents in Italian cinema: Giuseppe Tornatore, fresh from winning the Oscar for best foreign film with *Cinema Paradiso;* and Ennio Morricone, famed for his scores to the spaghetti westerns (among other things).

The result, between 1990 and 1996, was perhaps the most successful campaign in the history of Italian television. So successful, in fact, that droves of people from traffic-clogged Naples, Rome, and Milan started to search the hills of Tuscany for the White Mill they had seen in the biscuit ads. Queues of cars stretched back to the ruins of the San Galgano Abbey. Visitors approached the site in reverential silence as if they were entering a shrine. The mill's owner recalls: "There were real processions. Hundreds of people came to visit the mill at weekends. Most of them were disappointed because obviously it wasn't like it was on television. Only the kids were happy: they ran around enthusiastically amid all the plasterboard and polystyrene."

After the last Mulino Bianco advertisement had been filmed in 1996, the White Mill changed again; it was transformed into another, more tasteful manifestation of the Italian rural idyll. The owner spent four years restoring it and converting it into an *agriturismo*—the kind of rustic hotel-restaurant that has become so popular in Italy over the last twenty years or so. The building reverted to its old name, *Il Mulino delle Pile*—the Battery Mill (it used to supply electricity to Chiusdino before the war). A swimming pool was put in and the stonework sandblasted clear of paint. But even if it is now no longer white, the White Mill still answers to the same nostalgia for country food as does the brand that made it famous. It still attracts plenty of people who want to hold celebratory banquets for their weddings, birthdays, and anniversaries where the ads were set. Children still ask the owner whether he is the one who makes all the biscuits.

The rooms in the *agriturismo* Mulino delle Pile conform to an ideal of simple country elegance. The menu in its Old Grindstone Restaurant conforms to current canons of what is good to eat: "authentic, typical Tuscan cuisine, based on fresh, seasonal produce." An *antipasto* of Tuscan sliced *salami* and hams, or *pecorino* cheese with honey. A *primo* of *tagliatelle* with wild boar *ragù*—boar is a speciality. A *secondo* of Sienese entrecôte, or beef braised in Morellino wine, or local sausages with beans. A dessert of Vin Santo and *cantucci* biscuits.

It is not the best restaurant you could find in Italy. Nor is its menu quite as authentic as it claims: there are some concessions to fashion (fillet of beef in balsamic vinegar and green peppercorns), and some

The historical home of Italian food? Known to millions of Italians as the White Mill, *Il Mulino delle Pile* is set in a beautiful valley in Tuscany; its Old Grindstone Restaurant serves delicious local fare. But it is not quite the embodiment of rustic traditions that it claims to be.

national and international favorites, such as *penne all'arrabbiata*, eggplant *alla parmigiana*, and veal escalopes. Maybe the persistent memory of those famous biscuit commercials makes it all just too kitsch. But I can personally attest that the food at the Old Grindstone is, without a trace of doubt or irony, delicious. One can eat twice as well here as anywhere one could find in London for four times the price. The restaurant is evidence of the indisputable fact that gastronomic standards in Italy are as high as anywhere in the world.

How did the Italians come to eat so well? The story of the White Mill has a simple lesson for anyone trying to find a historical answer to that question: it is possible to love Italian food without going misty-eyed about the fables that are spun around it, whether in Italy or abroad. Italy has become *the* model to imitate when it comes to making ingredients, cooking them, and eating them together. Some people believe that our health, environment, and quality of life may depend on whether we can learn some of the food lessons that Italy has to offer. It's all the more reason why we need a less syrupy story about how Italian food got where it is today than the one advertising and cookbooks have told.

The White Mill itself may be unknown outside Italy, but the family of images to which it belongs is all too recognizable across much of the Western world: the *trattoria* in the olive grove; the hams suspended from the rafters of a farmhouse kitchen; the sun-weathered old peasant with a twinkle in his eye; the noisy family gathered under the pergola while *mamma* serves the pasta. These same clichés recur in countless recipe collections, countless ads for olive oil, or those jars of unspeakable pasta sauce. Together they weave a powerful rural myth that finds its favorite setting in Tuscany. What that myth conjures up for us is a cuisine made from a thousand ancient country traditions; it is Italian food as *peasant* food. If the White Mill image of Tuscany has helped give Italian food a respectable claim to being the most popular cuisine in the world, then it has also helped make it the most widely misperceived. The Italian cuisine that the world so admires has surprisingly little to do with peasants.

In Italy, nostalgia for the rustic way of life is a recent development. The success of brands such as Mulino Bianco only came when the vast majority of Italians had left the hardship of the countryside safely behind. In Tuscany, the sharecropping system shielded the peasantry from the worst of the hunger and toil that was the timeless lot of the rural masses up and down the peninsula until as late as the 1960s. But even here, the contribution that dishes of exclusively peasant origin have made to local cuisine is not as great as the recent cult of peasant food would have us believe. The menu of the Old Grindstone Restaurant is not representative of the country fare of yore. Nor is there anything *poor* about quite a few of the recipes one can find in books on *La cucina povera toscana*, including *bistecca alla fiorentina* (a thick Florentine T-bone or porterhouse steak) and liver *crostini* with Marsala wine. The rural masses could only dream of such delights. And even genuine peasant cooking has been the subject of a rebranding exercise. Like the medieval mill near Chiusdino, it has been extensively reconstructed and rethought by contemporary Italians.

Until the middle of the twentieth century, ordinary people in the countryside of Italy ate very badly—countless documents tell us as much. Such, for example, was the uniform conclusion of the many government inquiries into the state of the Italian countryside conducted in the decades after Italy became a unified country in 1861. The poverty of the peasant diet still echoes in a number of proverbs that have been handed down.

When the peasant eats a chicken, either the peasant is ill, or the chicken is. Among the poor of the countryside, chicken was a costly rarity reserved for the sick. Peasants were often only able to eat animals that had died of disease.

Garlic is the peasant's spice cupboard. Spices were essential to sophisticated cuisine from the Middle Ages until at least the seventeenth century. But they were largely unaffordable for the rural masses. Garlic, leek, and onion, by contrast, stank of poverty. This is not to imply that the well-to-do refused to eat these pungent vegetables—just that they looked down on anyone who had no alternative when it came to giving flavor to food.

Saint Bernard's sauce makes food seem good. Saint Bernard's sauce—hunger—was the most important ingredient in the peasant diet for most of the last millennium. Happily the recipe has now faded from memory.

A history of Italian food written as the story of what peasants actually ate would make for a stodgy read. Many pages would be devoted to vegetable soup. There would be a substantial section on porridge. Bread made from inferior grains, and even from things like acorns in times of hardship, would need in-depth coverage. That is not the history I reconstruct here.

Another proverb, a favorite of mine, suggests that we need to look elsewhere for real history of Italian food. "Al contadino non gli far sapere, quanto sia buono il cacio colle pere" (Don't tell the peasant how good cheese is with pears). In other words, don't give anyone any information if they are in a better position to take advantage of it than you are. Or, keep your recipe cards close to your chest. This cynical piece of wisdom can also be interpreted as a simple parable about the imbalance in power and knowledge that underlies Italy's oldest gastronomic traditions. It may have been the country folk who produced the cheese and pears, but the people with the power to appropriate these ingredients, and with the knowledge to transform them into a delicacy by a simple but artful combination, were the inhabitants of the *cities.*

Italian food is city food.

Italy has the richest tradition of urban living on the planet, and the enviable way Italians eat is part of it. It is no coincidence that so many Italian products and dishes are named after cities: *bistecca alla fiorentina, prosciutto di Parma, saltimbocca alla romana, pizza napoletana, risotto alla milanese, pesto genovese, pesto trapanese, olive ascolane, mostarda di Cremona* . . . From early in the second millennium, the hundred cities of Italy hogged the produce of the countryside and used it to build a rich food culture. For centuries, Italy's cities have been where all the things that go to create great cooking are concentrated: ingredients and culinary expertise, of course, but also power, wealth, markets, and competition for social prestige.

So those urban pilgrims to the White Mill are not heading *toward* the traditional abode of Italian food: they are driving *away* from it. Italian food best expresses itself not in the farmhouse, but in the urban market. The real adventure of Italian food is not to be found by trekking off into the Tuscan hills. The point is to roam the city streets savoring the cooking and sniffing out the stories.

ITALIANS sometimes refer to their "civilization of the table." The term embraces all the many different aspects of a culture that are expressed through food: from the agricultural economy to pickling recipes, from kinship ties to the correct technique for spitting an olive stone into your hand. Food itself is fascinating. But ultimately it is much less fascinating than the people who produce, cook, eat, and talk about it. That is why this book is a history of Italy's civilization of the table, rather than just of what Italians put on their tables.

The German philosopher Walter Benjamin once wrote that "there is no document of civilization which is not at the same time a document of barbarism." What he meant was that even our most sacred cultural artifacts, such as Dante's *Divine Comedy,* or Michelangelo's frescoes in the Sistine Chapel, or Pergolesi's *Stabat Mater,* are inevitably marked by the unholy power struggles of the time when they were created. That is not to say that Michelangelo was to blame for the greed, corruption, and brutality shown by the patrons who gave him the resources he needed to make great art. But it does imply that we miss much of the poignancy and relevance of art if we cut it out of its historical frame—if we shut our eyes to the power that makes it possible, and the horrors going on around it.

The same principle applies to cooking. In fact, because it is an art performed with the very raw materials people need to consume in order to live, cooking can be more intimately connected to barbarism than any other civilized activity. There is a dark dimension to the history of Italian food that cannot be ignored. For that reason, there would be something rather bulimic about a history that consisted of nothing but a long pageant of feasts and fine meals, of endless delicacies from days gone by.

The Italian civilization of the table, in short, is a product of Italian history. And Italian history is marked by division and violence as much as it is by beauty and creativity, by barbarism as well as civilization. All of these things are ingredients in what I have written here. Malnourishment, hunger, and famine are an essential part of the story of Italian food. This book also moves between the food of the powerful and the food of the powerless, between everyday eating and elite dining. Put a different way, it combines elements from the history of the Italian *diet* and elements from the history of Italian *cuisine.*

But as the title suggests, this book was a joy to research, and its pages give plenty of space to the delights of eating—mostly other people's, and just occasionally mine. Even though I have spent many years studying Italy and living there, working on this book brought many pleasures I had never tasted before. Like *pane squarato* in Marsala (a deliciously chewy bread that is boiled before baking, like bagels, and then flavored with fennel seeds); or *animelle* in Rome (toothsome sweetbreads, served with artichokes); or *cappellacci di zucca* in Ferrara (pasta envelopes with a pumpkin filling that teeters at the edge of sweetness where a pinch of nutmeg can play to its most subtle and delicious effect). The more one explores Italian food, the more rich diversity there is to discover—and every dish seems to have a story worth telling. So I have inevitably had to resist many temptations. Coffee, wine, and other drinks have been excluded because their history has different laws of motion. I have also tried not to get drawn into foody one-upmanship, into the competition to seek out ever more obscure culinary curios. The focus tends to be on the best-known dishes. So you do not have to know your *caciocavallo* from your *Castelmagno* to enjoy the story.* Pasta is the best-known Italian food of them all, and it provides one of the most important unifying themes in *Delizia!* From the first evidence of dried durum wheat *vermicelli* on Italian soil in the 1150s, to the extraordinary vicissitudes of *tortellini* since the 1970s, the history of pasta and the history of Italian food as a whole move to the same rhythms.

Exhaustiveness is another temptation that I have had to resist. Italian food has become a world food, and comprehensive study of its history would encompass Britain, the United States, South America, and Australia as well as Italy. Many of the stories recounted here go to show that Italian food has been shaped at least as much by its promiscuous traveling as it has by its steadfast roots in the soil of the peninsula. But where Italian foods have traveled so far that they have entered the history of countries other than Italy, I have ceased to chart their path.

The reason for this determinedly Italian focus is that, at its best, Italian food has charisma. And its charisma derives from an almost poetic relationship to place and identity. The main reason why Italians eat so well is simply that eating enriches their sense of where they come from and who they are. Italy's cities are where these links between food and

---

* *Caciocavallo* literally means "horse cheese," but it is more accurately translated as "astride cheese." Rather bland, it comes from the south, and comes in double orbs that are formed by hanging them from a string across or "astride" a stick. *Castelmagno* is a hardish, cylindrical cheese from the northern region of Piedmont; one of its distinguishing features is a tinge of blue mold.

identity were forged. It is no coincidence that cities are also where the diversity of Italian food is made most manifest, or that cities have seen the most dramatic interplay of civilization and barbarism. Thus it is in the cities that the most compelling documentary sources are to be found, sources that show how great Italian dishes have registered the ebb and flow of Italian history. Cities therefore give *Delizia!* its distinctive structure. Following a path dictated by the sources, each chapter in turn tells a self-contained story located in a single city. Together, these slices of urban life build into a single narrative that spans the centuries from the Middle Ages to the present day. The result aims to be both a history of Italian food, and a history of Italy *through* its food.

I

THE MEDIEVAL TABLE

2

$\mathcal{P}$alermo, 1154

Pasta and the Planisphere

"Italian Food Does Not Exist"

Think carefully before you ask for *focaccia* at a Palermo street stall. For, likely as not, the only familiar thing about it will be the sesame seed roll that the stall-holder splits in two to remove the soft center. The filling he places inside, braised and then fried in lard, will comprise slices of veal spleen and strips of lung, topped with the soft cartilage from a calf's throat. A squeeze of lemon is essential: it cuts pleasingly through the fatty juices oozing into the bread to set up the meaty but yielding mouthfeel of the filling.

This *focaccia*, or more properly *pani ca' meusa* (bread with spleen), is the totem of Palermo's venerable tradition of street eating. At the famous Antica Focacceria S. Francesco they offer a convenient *antipasto* sampler of such urban tidbits as: *arancine* (deep-fried balls of rice, peas, and meat *ragù*); *sfinciuni* (thick squares of light but greasy pizza variously flavored with onion, cheese, oregano, olives, etc.); and a miniature *focaccia maritata*—which is *pani ca' meusa* "married" with *ricotta* cheese.

Sicily probably has the most distinctive cuisine in Italy. In a world increasingly habituated to the so-called Mediterranean diet, there is still something unpredictable and lingeringly strange about what Sicilians eat. To eat in Sicily is to appreciate the dizzying variety in Italian food, and to understand why the expression "La cucina italiana non esiste"—"Italian food does not exist"—has become a truism.

There is no feature of Sicilian food more strange than the outlandish colors on display in pastry shops: *cassata*, a sponge cake with *ricotta* cheese encased in stripes of iced marzipan in white and pale turquoise-green decorated with multihued candied fruit; and "Martorana Fruit"—marzipan dyed with garish greens, reds, and yellows and sculpted into the shape of watermelon slices, figs, and prickly pears. To the unaccustomed eye, Martorana Fruit can seem too beautiful to eat, and yet also unnatural and childlike—as if the cakes have gotten into the makeup box and daubed themselves with Mum's lipstick.

Even some of the everyday Sicilian dishes seem exotic. *Pasta colle sarde* is a good example: *bucatini* are dressed with a mash comprising fresh sardines, wild fennel, onion, salted anchovies, saffron, pine nuts, and tiny raisins. Indeed the island's cuisine retains its peculiar allure when it is simple to the point of being self-effacing, as with roast goat, or boiled octopus, or *macco*—dried broad (fava) beans gently boiled and crushed to form a hearty purée. (It is sometimes served with pasta, or made slightly more elaborate with chilies, or the odd ripe tomato, or the clean aniseed taste of wild fennel.)

As one of the peninsula's geographical extremes, Sicily offers a striking example of the enormous diversity of dishes that pass under the label "Italian." How can Sicilian food, with its couscous, swordfish, and citrus salad, possibly belong to the same culinary realm as the subalpine region of Piedmont, with its truffles, rich wine-infused meat dishes, and *agnolotti* (filled pasta parcels)? Many Italians, proud of their own local eating traditions, would say simply that they cannot. In Italy, even something as simple as bread can change from one small town to the next. The widespread notion that Italian food is regional is only a very lazy shorthand for patterns of variation that can be found at a much more local level *within* regions like Sicily or Piedmont, to say nothing of Emilia-Romagna. Generalizing about the way Italians eat is extremely hazardous.

Yet so is saying that Italian food does not exist. The country is *not* a collection of ancient and unconnected microcuisines. Many foods are shared by several regions of Italy, for example *polenta* in much of the north. Other habits apply to the whole country, such as conjugating the courses of a meal according to *antipasto, primo, secondo*, and *dolce*. Eating Sicilian food makes one appreciate what links Italy's many cuisines and gives them a common history.

Couscous, of which Sicilians are so proud, is also known in Tuscany, where it was thought of as a Jewish food because it was brought by the Spanish and Portuguese Jews who arrived in the port city of Livorno in the 1500s. *Pani ca' meusa*—spleen rolls—seem to be a unique local dish that the most intrepid gastro-tourists are keen to tick off their list. Yet these have also been available in Turin, the capital of the northern region of Piedmont, since the time of Italy's postwar economic miracle when thousands of Sicilian workers emigrated there.

Up and down Italy, broad cultural changes have modified eating habits in comparable ways. Many local specialities that were once reserved for particular religious occasions are, in these secular times, year-round treats. *Cassata* is an example: it was once eaten only at Easter. Martorana Fruit has undergone the same shift. The childish impression it makes is not a coincidence because it was originally used as a way of involving children in the Day of the Dead. Mothers would hide small presents around the house, such as fruits, sweets, and sugar dolls, which were supposed to be gifts to the children from departed relatives. Now both Martorana Fruit and *cassata* are nationally recognizable banners for Sicilian pastry chefs.

The Italian peninsula was divided among different rulers until the second half of the 1800s. That history of division carries much of the responsibility for the variety of Italian cuisines. But besides migration and secularization, other historical forces have brought the parts of Italy into gastronomic dialogue with one another—not just in recent years, but for much of the last millennium. It is this dialogue that gives a useful meaning to the term "Italian food." Cities like Palermo, as great centers of exchange, are where the dialogue happened.

To eat in Sicily is also to feel that one is tasting the very beginnings of Italian food's history. The island has been conquered by virtually every dominant Mediterranean power of the last two or three thousand years. Among these various invaders, the Muslims' gastronomic legacy is most often celebrated today—they occupied the island in the ninth, tenth, and eleventh centuries. If many Sicilian dishes are exotic, at least to a northern European palate, it is partly because of their North African and Middle Eastern influences. Some signs of the Muslim legacy on Sicilian tables are obvious, such as couscous, or the jasmine that flavors ice creams and sorbets, or indeed, one even more obvious but rather less exotic dish: spaghetti.

The history of Italian food begins with the arrival of spaghetti, which was brought to Sicily by Muslim invaders. More precisely, the history of Italian food begins when spaghetti enters the food dialogue between the Italian cities, ceasing in the process to be an exotic import. How that came to happen is best explained through the story of one particular Sicilian Muslim, and the map he made—the planisphere. It is a map that provides the first crucial piece of evidence in the history of Italian food, but it is also one of the most beautiful artistic treasures of medieval civilization, and a document of barbarism.

A Diversion for the Man Longing to Travel to Far-Off Places

The planisphere must have been a marvel to the men who first set eyes on it in year 548 of the Hijrah—or 1154 in the calendar of Christian kings: a perfect disk of solid silver, close to two meters in diameter, and weighing as much as two men. Engraved on its polished surface were the contours of the habitable world; it was then the most complete map ever created.

King Roger II, the Norman ruler of Sicily, had ordered it to be made at the zenith of his power. With his enemies either defeated or turned into allies, he gave full rein to his thirst for knowledge—not just of his own kingdom, but of the whole globe. He sent for the foremost geographer of the age, al-Sharif al-Idrisi, and offered him a fortune to produce a cartographic survey that would surpass all others. For fifteen years al-Idrisi studied, and journeyed, and consulted travelers. With a great iron compass, he painstakingly traced longitudes, latitudes, and distances onto a drawing board. When he had finished, the most skillful silversmiths in the realm were commissioned to transfer the resulting outlines onto a specially cast silver disk.

At its western edge the two Fortunate Isles were marked. It was said that on each isle, atop a mound of stones one hundred cubits high, stood a bronze statue pointing to the unknown space beyond.

To the east lay the farthest region of China, where a tree grew in the middle of a river. So convinced were the Chinese that the river flowed toward paradise that praying crowds would gather to watch enraptured men fling themselves from the tree's uppermost branches into the broad waters below.

Sudan, in the south, was made up mostly of sands blown hither and thither by the wind, and its people had skin burned to ebony by the sun.

Set within the Dark Ocean in the far north was the desert island of Scotland. Once, the geographers believed, there had been three towns in Scotland. But they had been abandoned in ruins after their inhabitants had fought one another to near extinction.

Between these outlying points, all the seven seas and the seven climates of the Northern Hemisphere were engraved, with the names of countries, cities, ports, rivers, and roads marked in a handsome Arabic script. Anyone who was not content merely to gaze in astonishment at the world thus displayed, could consult al-Idrisi's great geography book that was kept beside it—its title translates as *A Diversion for the Man Longing to Travel to Far-Off Places*. It contained information on the customs, products, commerce, language, and character of all the locations on the planisphere.

Most of those who first looked on al-Idrisi's silver map would find their eyes drawn toward the western side of the fourth climate. There they could find Sicily—or "Siqilliah" (sih-kee-lee-uh) to the many Arabic-speakers who called the island home. It was known the world over for the fertility of its soil and the excellence of its wares. Chief among Sicily's 130 towns and castles was Palermo, "the beautiful and immense city, the greatest and most splendid residence," as al-Idrisi's book proclaimed it. Only Baghdad bore comparison to Palermo, which stood by the sea to the west of the island, guarded by a ring of mountains. Its two main quarters were bisected by canals, and surrounded by orchards and villas watered by abundant springs. By the port there was the quarter known as 'al Halisah (the distinguished), because it was here that the emir had lived. The other part of the city, Qasr (castle), was a long peninsula crammed with "towering palaces and noble homes, with mosques, baths, warehouses, and shops belonging to great merchants"; its many gardens were irrigated by channels of sweet water brought down from the mountains. At the highest point of Qasr, farthest from the sea, stood the ancient fortress, which had recently been endowed with a shining new citadel. In one of its halls, each decorated with exquisite sculptures, paintings, and calligraphy, the planisphere itself was housed.

The planisphere's creator, al-Idrisi, was born in what is now Morocco in about 1100 and probably educated in Muslim Spain. He had seen both the Balkans and the Bosporus before he settled in Sicily to execute the king's orders. The evidence of his book suggests that he may even have sailed as far as England. (This would perhaps explain the color of what he garnered about the Scots.)

Al-Idrisi was of eminent blood: he could even trace his lineage back to the Prophet's immediate family. Besides being a geographer, he was also a pharmacologist and doctor—an international intellectual star. Yet the surviving sources give only a hazy picture of him, perhaps because subsequent generations of Muslim scholars deliberately suppressed his memory. Their motive, if this theory is correct, was that al-Idrisi worked for an infidel: he was commissioned to create the planisphere by King Roger II.

Roger's father, the twelfth son of a minor nobleman in Normandy, had put an end to two hundred years of Muslim power in Sicily. A child when he inherited his father's realm, Roger proved to be no less remarkable. Like his father, he implemented a policy that mixed generosity to allies with implacable brutality to foes. His influence stretched from the borders of the pope's lands in central Italy, to the Maghreb, and even as far as the Holy Land. He had engraved on his sword: "The Puglian and the Calabrian, the Sicilian and the African all serve me."

Roger shaped his image to impress each of the peoples who became his subjects. He called his most senior officials "emirs," and borrowed the parasol from the Arabs as a symbol of power. His stunning red silk coronation cloak, embroidered in gold thread and set with enamel and hundreds of pearls, can still be seen in Vienna today. From the center of the cloak a palm, the Arab tree of life, spreads its fronds. On either side a heraldic lion attacks a camel, symbolizing the Norman subjugation of the North Africans. Around its border an inscription proclaims Roger's virtues in elegant Kufic characters.

Roger's crown, by contrast, was styled on a Byzantine model, and most of his charters were issued in Greek. The best-known image of the king himself is a mosaic in the Greek style in the Palermo church known as La Martorana: he is shown wearing the ceremonial garb of a Byzantine emperor and has a Christlike beard and long hair.

The planisphere was part of the same policy of asserting Roger's kingship in every possible language, every possible artistic form. Al-Idrisi's work was also meant to proclaim the wealth of Sicily, which the island owed in great measure to the long years of Muslim rule before the Norman conquest. New foodstuffs were one important legacy of Muslim domination. By bringing irrigation techniques that had originated in the Middle East, the North Africans who first arrived in the late 800s diversified agriculture beyond recognition. The Sicily that al-Idrisi recorded was an island of carefully watered orchards and gardens where generations of Muslim technical expertise and commercial know-how had bequeathed a rich agriculture of lemons, almonds, pistachio nuts, cane sugar, dates, figs, carobs, and more.

It is impossible to imagine contemporary Sicilian cuisine without the produce of which al-Idrisi and Roger II were so justifiably proud. For that reason alone, al-Idrisi has an important place in the history of Italian eating. But it is to a few remarkable lines from *A Diversion for the Man Longing to Travel to Far-Off Places* that Roger's court geographer owes the fame he has recently acquired in Italy—remarkable, that is, because they constitute the first and best clue as to the origins of pasta, the most recognizably Italian dish of them all.

Itriyya

Geographically and historically, Italy is a country divided by a common food. Pasta is one of the great unifying motifs in Italy's constantly shifting gastronomic mosaic. But that is not because all Italians have always eaten the stuff—far from it. Pasta takes on varying forms in different parts of the country, and some Italians have only developed a taste for it in recent times.

Many pitfalls, including linguistic challenges, await anyone who endeavors to trace the origins of Italy's pasta habit. The basic meaning of the word *pasta* today is nothing more specific than "paste." It also means "pastry" or "dough." Yet the world knows the word as Italians also use it to mean a broad category of dishes made with a dough that has been boiled after being transformed by any number of methods: rolling, cutting, extruding, filling, etc. Most of these methods were in use by the late Middle Ages. Medieval Italians talked a great deal about *maccheroni, lasagne, vermicelli, ravioli*, and the like—this is when the pasta habit really took hold in the Italian cities. But if you asked a cook in the time of Dante or Giotto to prepare you a plate of *pasta* he would probably just have been puzzled. A separate category of foods called pasta just did not exist. If the term was used, then it embraced all kinds of dough-based dishes, including pastries and cakes. So by the fourteenth century, Italians were certainly eating "pasta" as we use the term, but unfortunately they were not aware that they were doing so.

So the history of Italian pasta begins in the Middle Ages. But the people of that time could not see or name the transformation in their eating habits that was slowly unfolding. Several distinct traditions were coming together to form the genre that would much later be called *pasta*. It helps to think of these traditions as different families who have intermarried to form a broad and diverse pasta clan:

Gnocchi, or dumplings
Lasagne, or sheets
Tagliatelle, or cut strips
Tortellini, or little parcels

First there were *gnocchi*—virtually every food culture has produced some kind of dumpling cooked in water, broth, or stew. Then came *lasagna*. The word is thought to have its origins in the ancient Latin term *laganum*, a sheet of dough that was fried to make a pastry. During the Middle Ages, the *gnocchi* family and the *lasagne* family merged: *lasagne* could now be boiled like *gnocchi*, or cut into strips and boiled like *tagliatelle*. Another great invention of the Italian Middle Ages was the *tortellino*, literally meaning a "little pie"—which was how *tortellini* started life, as tiny pies that were cooked by boiling rather than baking.

There is also a fifth family in the genealogy of the pasta clan. Its historical origins make it something of a renegade, yet it is now the most famous and most characteristically Italian of them all. Many of the offspring of the *gnocchi*, *lasagne*, *tagliatelle*, and *tortellini* families are today grouped under the heading "fresh pasta," meaning that it is cooked soon after being made, when it still contains moisture; many types of fresh pasta also contain egg. "Dried pasta," the fifth family, refers to those packets of *spaghetti*, *penne*, and *fusilli* that now fill supermarket shelves across the Western world. Italians sometimes avoid confusion by using *pasta secca* to refer to this kind of dehydrated product. It is generally made from durum wheat, or "hard grain" as it is known in Italy. "Hard grain" is a variety with a high gluten content that makes it easier to dry and store, and gives it a chewier texture when prepared as pasta even without egg.

Italians also started eating *pasta secca* in the Middle Ages. But once again, they did not make a great deal of terminological fuss about it. *Maccheroni*—spelled in a variety of ways—was the most popular medieval pasta term; it comes from *maccare*, meaning to pound or crush. But confusingly for historians, it was used to refer both to fresh pasta *gnocchi* and to tubes of dried durum wheat pasta. Thus the task of tracing the early development of Italy's distinctive *pasta secca* was made particularly tricky.

So it is easy to understand why the first Italian food historians to come across al-Idrisi's *A Diversion for the Man Longing to Travel to Far-Off Places* fell upon the following passage so eagerly. A few lines after completing his celebration of the glories of Roger II's Palermo, al-Idrisi gives us a description of Trabia, some eighteen miles along the coast to the east:

> West of Termini there is a delightful settlement called Trabia. Its ever-flowing streams propel a number of mills. Here there are huge buildings in the countryside where they make vast quantities of *itriyya* which is exported everywhere: to Calabria, to Muslim and Christian countries. Very many shiploads are sent.

Itriyya is an Arabic word on which we can rely. A medical text in Arabic written by a Jewish doctor living in Tunisia in the early 900s explains that, two hundred years before al-Idrisi created his silver planisphere, *itriyya* already meant long thin strands of dried dough that were cooked by boiling. *Itriyya* produced in Sicily and exported over such distances can only have been made from durum wheat: since the Romans defeated Hannibal, "hard grain" has been the island's most prized crop. After al-Idrisi's time, Italians adopted and adapted the word *itriyya* to label this exotic import: *trie* meant, and still means, thin strips of pasta such as *tagliatelle*. Alternatively, *itriyya* might be referred to with the more down-to-earth Italian word *vermicelli*, meaning "little worms." (*Spaghetti*, meaning "little strings," refers to the same kind of thing but did not become common until the early 1800s.)

Thus it is that al-Idrisi gives us the first ever reference to *pasta secca* on Italian soil. But there is one more enigma. The Muslims brought *itriyya* to Sicily. But does that mean that Arabs invented it? A good few recipe books continue to serve up this story, suggesting that a nomadic people like the Arabs would have found a dried food like pasta as portable as it was nourishing.

The theory undeniably has a romantic charm, but unfortunately is based on muddled thinking. For one thing, pasta's portability only makes it suitable for a nomadic lifestyle if your camels are strong enough to carry the large millstones needed to prepare durum wheat flour. For another, it should hardly need pointing out that not all Muslims, and not all Arabic-speakers, are Arabs. The people who occupied Sicily for two hundred years before the Normans were mostly from the Maghreb. They were Berbers, rather than Arabs. And they were traders, not nomads.

Itriyya, it turns out, is not even originally an Arabic word, but an Arabic transliteration from Greek. To Greek-speakers it referred to something dough-based cooked in liquid—a "something" that is too vague to be given a secure place in the genealogy of spaghetti. So before it reaches Italy, the origins of spaghetti cannot be traced back to one single point in space and time. Whichever route we follow, the prehistory of *pasta secca* takes us back out onto the heavily trafficked waters of the Mediterranean.

The Fate of the Planisphere

Roger II's Palermo was an international crossroads, one of the greatest trading cities in the world. Here the goods of the Muslim Mediterranean were fed into the burgeoning commercial routes of the sea powers on the western coast of Italy. Merchants from Amalfi, Naples, Pisa, and Genoa would come to source the spices, medicines, sugar, textiles, indigo, gold, and precious stones that arrived in Sicily from Spain, the Levant, Egypt, and by caravan across the deserts of North Africa. Al-Idrisi interviewed these polyglot traders as he labored to create the planisphere.

In the royal court that he frequented, Latin, Hebrew, Greek, Arabic, and the dialects of northern France could all be heard. Norman knights mingled with Italian bishops, North African merchants, Jewish craftsmen, Arabic poets, and Greek administrators. It seems highly likely that Roger had Muslim chefs—his successors certainly did.

No wonder Norman Palermo has often been imagined as a grand and happy experiment in cohabitation between different cultures and faiths. But the truth about Roger's reign is more bloody, and less sanguine. In 1153 Palermo witnessed a gruesome event that completely undermines the myth of Roger II's kingdom as an oasis of tolerance.

It features Philip of Mahdiyah, one of Roger's eunuchs—a "completely castrated servant," as one source describes him, meaning that his penis had been cut off as well as his testicles. This drastic surgery was necessary because he was invested with great power over royal affairs. No attachment to lovers or family could come between him and his sovereign.

Many such emasculated administrators worked for Roger II. They were highly educated, multilingual, and ambitious—drawn from across the Mediterranean by the promise of power and gold. Most were also Muslim. But they had to sacrifice even faith for a career in the royal household: Roger forced his eunuchs to convert to Christianity, and did not allow Muslims openly to practice their religion at court. Roger used these talented, rootless, utterly dependent men to free his administration from the influence of overweening barons and their clans. (The barons, as a result, loathed the eunuchs.)

Even among such an elite group, Philip was special. He was both an administrator and a naval chief; he and the king were close—so close, in fact, that it was said Philip had been brought up as a Christian by Roger himself. But during the holy month of Ramadan in December 1153, Philip's Christianity was exposed as a pretense: he had returned to the faith of his birth.

We do not know exactly what evidence the king uncovered. One version of the story says that Philip sent oil to Medina for the lanterns at the tomb of the Prophet. Another says merely that he pleaded too strenuously for leniency toward Muslim captives. Either way, there is no doubt about the vindictive ferocity of Roger's response. Philip was dragged round the palace by wild horses; then, still alive, his broken body was burned.

The execution of Philip of Mahdiyah happened at the very time when engravers were at work on the silver planisphere, and al-Idrisi was bringing his decade and a half of study to an end by writing *A Diversion for the Man Longing to Travel to Far-Off Places.* Since both were members of the royal household, Al-Idrisi must have known Philip, and may well have witnessed the eunuch's fate. Like all the wonderful artifacts of Roger II's court, the great Arabic geography was created in an atmosphere of fear rather than tolerance.

Roger II died within weeks of the planisphere's completion, in February 1154. Seven years later rebellious barons ransacked his palace and slaughtered many of the surviving eunuchs. The knights and their followers then moved out into the city, robbing and murdering its Muslim inhabitants. There was no trace of the planisphere after this massacre. It may well have been heaved, careening, from the palace walls and carried off as booty to be melted down.

The silver planisphere is a sorry symbol of how much of the cultural legacy of Muslim Sicily has been destroyed. Norman rule heralded not just the end of Islamic power on the island, but also the steady eradication of the Muslim population. When Roger's father first arrived, about half of all Sicilians, some 250,000 people, were Muslim. When the last survivors were deported to a colony on the Italian mainland in the 1220s, there were only 20,000 left: pogroms, conversion, and emigration had accounted for the rest. The sophisticated agriculture that the Muslim population created soon went into decline as Sicily returned to its ancient role of providing hard grain wheat for Italy.

Many other aspects of Sicilian Muslim culture shared the planisphere's fate. Only a couple of hundred words of Arabic origin survive in Sicilian today. The architectural legacy is also fragmentary: Sicily has no Alhambra. The buildings in Palermo that show Arabic influences date from the period when Norman monarchs such as Roger II used Muslim craftsmen to further the purposes of their own propaganda.

Sicilian food, like Roger II's Palermo, is often celebrated in a tolerant spirit, as evidence that cultures can mingle in peace. Some Sicilians see a more flattering reflection of themselves in the menu than in the history books. After all, jasmine ice cream and couscous offer a more optimistic image of continuity between Sicily's Islamic past and its Christian present than does the planisphere. But the sad truth is that the turmoil of Sicilian history has reduced the evidence of its food's past to little more than shards. No medical texts, no cookbooks in Arabic survive from Muslim Sicily. One of the few food testimonies comes from a rather haughty Baghdadi visitor to Palermo in the mid-900s, who tells us, mystifyingly, that the locals ate so much onion it clouded their reason. Some of the Sicilian dishes that are often thought to be of Arabic origin have now been shown to have more recent roots. *Cassata* does not derive from the name for a bowl in Arabic, as is often claimed. Much more prosaically, it originates in the Latin for cheese. *Cassata* did not mean a dessert until the late 1600s, and the dessert did not take on anything like its current striped, green-and-white form until the 1700s; the famous decoration of candied fruit came even later. Magical it may be, but the taste of a *cassata* cannot conjure us back to the days of the Sicilian emirs, or tell us what Roger II's Muslim chefs prepared for him. Little documentary trace of the continuity between medieval Muslim cuisine and Sicilian food can be found. The only evidence we have is from our taste buds. But alas, what our taste buds register is often our own wishful thinking rather than the real stuff of history. Whatever flavors and smells characterized Islamic Sicily's civilization of the table, most of them, like the planisphere, have been irretrievably lost.

Rich and Industrious People

Illustrated manuscripts of al-Idrisi's book survive, and give a rough idea of the outlines that were once cut into the planisphere's silver surface. Initially they are hard to recognize. Sicily is huge, occupying about half the area taken up by the Italian peninsula. Sardinia has shrunk and floated off toward Spain. Italy's own famous "boot" outline has a horribly stubbed toe; and instead of jutting diagonally down from the continent it runs horizontally, as if drawn back so as to punt Sicily out toward the mysterious waters of the Atlantic.

Although distorted, al-Idrisi's map offers a cue for some essential introductory reflections on the geographical disunity that has marked Italy's history—and therefore its cuisine.

The Apennines, the peninsula's rocky backbone, are the most obvious feature on any modern atlas. Curving inland from the Gulf of Genoa, the mountains cut diagonally across between Bologna and Florence, almost reaching the Adriatic coast at Rimini before they straighten and plunge down the middle of the peninsula. Toward the south, the line of mountains turns again, through Calabria—the toe of the boot—and out along the northern coast of Sicily.

The Apennines slice the long Italian boot in two from the groin to the toe. In the central and southern half of the country, there are sharp contrasts in relief on either side of the long mountain range. This is a land of short rivers that tend to be torrents in winter and trickles in summer. No town in this central-southern area of Italy is far from the mountains or the sea, and all the landscape features in between. In Calabria, an easy morning's drive from the beach into the mountains can take you from palms, into vines and olives, then up into bright green chestnut woods, to arrive in misty pine forest: the strata of different trees are clearly visible on the mountainsides.

In the northern portion, between the Apennines and the Alps, is the long wedge of flat territory given its character by the sluggish, constantly shifting course of the Po, which at 405 miles is one of Europe's major rivers. The ancient Romans thought of the Po valley as a different country: they called it Cisalpine Gaul—in modern terms, "the bit of France on this side of the Alps." The Po makes the landscape through which it flows unstable; five or six centuries of human labor have been required to adapt the valley for agriculture, industry, and transport. What is true of the Po valley is true of the whole country. Italy is not a naturally rich or fertile country, but a naturally diverse land that has to be worked to produce the fruits of civilization.

Most of Italy's fundamental geographical features were invisible to al-Idrisi. What interested him, almost exclusively, were cities. For that reason, he identified changes that were beginning to give Italy the shape we know. In Sicily and on the southern mainland, the kingdom that Roger ruled from Palermo would last until Giuseppe Garibaldi overthrew it in 1860 and united it to the Italian state. In the north and center, the cities founded and built by the ancient Romans were reviving. Al-Idrisi singles them out for their "remarkable monuments," "dynamic artisans," "thriving markets," and their "rich and industrious people." Brief they may be, but these phrases capture the essence of what was happening to the cities set in the valleys of the Po and Arno while Muslim influence was waning in the south. Since the fall of the Roman Empire, a series of invading powers had struggled to revive Rome's legacy of imperial authority in the peninsula: from the Ostrogoths under Theodoric the Great in the early 500s, through the Byzantines, Lombards, and Charlemagne's Franks. But by the end of the first millennium, central authority in the north and center of Italy had declined to such an extent that the towns and cities were able to assert their independence. As they did so, they became wealthy through industry and trade.

The revival of medieval Italian cities was led by trade, so al-Idrisi's account of the "very many shiploads" of pasta exported from Sicily rings true. Even allowing for a little exaggeration by Roger II's mapmaker, the scale of the *itriyya* business in Trabia circa 1150 is remarkable. Al-Idrisi mentions no other center of pasta-making remotely like it, not even in the North African regions he knew so well, and from which we can safely assume *itriyya* arrived in Sicily. Historians have not discovered any evidence of large-scale pasta manufacture elsewhere or earlier. So the strong likelihood is that it was only *after* it reached Sicily, and after it reached the markets of the eastern Mediterranean, that making *pasta secca* became an exercise in centralized production and distribution for a wider market. Some argue that *itriyya* became so popular in Norman

Delizia!

Sicily because it made such a good food for sailors, that it was a fuel for the "commercial revolution" then overtaking Italian ports. Whether this theory holds or not, Sicily's claim to *pasta secca* preeminence in Italy is irrefutable. Within a century and a half of the planisphere's creation, in the cities along the west-facing curve of coastline from Genoa, through Naples, to Palermo, and up to Cagliari in Sardinia, Italian cooks had adopted *itriyya*, turning it into *trie*, *vermicelli*, and *maccheroni*. These are the places where *pasta secca* begins to be mentioned in the patchy records upon which historians of the origins of Italian food have to rely: a note in a merchant's ledger or last testament, a tiny drawing in the margin of an illustrated manuscript, a passing reference in the life of a saint. Together such documentary scraps proclaim that the history of Italian food was under way.

3

Milan, 1288

Power, Providence, and Parsnips

War Wagons and Parmesan Cheese

What does a *genovese* actually taste when he or she eats *pesto*? Why do Neapolitans find the texture and flavor of their city's pizza so evocative? It only takes a quick search on the Internet to find a recipe for *pajata*. But it surely takes more than the intestines of an unweaned calf, with its mother's partially digested milk still in them, cooked in a tomato sauce, to make *pajata* as a Roman experiences it.

When Italians eat their own food there is always an extra ingredient in it that is imperceptible to outsiders. Corny as it may sound, that ingredient is local pride. Many Italians are, famously, more strongly attached to the town of their birth than they are to their country. They are *bolognesi*, *catanesi*, or *torinesi* first; they are *italiani* second. Food may be the most evocative expression of that historically rooted sense of local belonging.

Pesto, *pizza*, and *pajata* are prime examples of what the Italians refer to as *typical* dishes. What they typify, respectively, is Genoa, Naples, and Rome. *Tipicità*, "typicality," is the Italian word that describes the magical aura a food acquires when local identity is invested in it. *Tipico* has become close to indistinguishable from *buono*—good, wholesome, delicious.

The word *tipicità* is itself a recent invention. But it has its roots in an idea that is far older, and by no means exclusively Italian: certain places are particularly good at producing certain foods. The story of how that simple idea acquired such distinctive resonance in Italy unites many of the chapters of this book.

No product can be typical without a long tradition behind it—the longer the better, in fact. And mere historical evidence is rarely an obstacle to the Italian gourmet's belief that food tastes nicer when it has an aged pedigree tying it to one specific locality. So the Italian gastronomic landscape abounds with food traditions—some of them real, some exaggerated, and some entirely fanciful.

Cassata, the Sicilian dessert mentioned in the previous chapter, is the subject of an invented tradition based on the claim that its roots lie in the Muslim Middle Ages. Many other local food traditions purport to be as old. But of all Italy's many typical dishes, very few can boast genuine medieval origins. One product that certainly can make that boast, however, is the most precious of them all: Parmesan cheese.

Parmigiano-Reggiano cheese is today the food item most often pilfered from Italian supermarkets—according to a recent survey, nearly one piece in every ten leaves the shop without a beep of approval from the checkout scanner. The identification between the city of Parma and a prestigious hard cheese suitable for grating over pasta dates back to the fourteenth century at least. The most famous early mention of *parmigiano* comes from the 1350s and we owe it to the hand of a typical product of the commercial dynamism of medieval Italian cities: Florentine merchant banker's son, Giovanni Boccaccio. In his great cycle of short stories, the *Decameron*, Boccaccio tells us how a wide-eyed painter is duped by tales of a land of plenty where

> There is a mountain made entirely of grated Parmesan cheese. Standing at the top of it are people who do nothing else but make *maccheroni* and *ravioli*, cook them in capon broth, and then throw them down the slopes. The more you take the more you get.

As well as being an important early testimony to the marriage of pasta and Parmesan, Boccaccio's short story also takes us close to the origins of the Italian culture of fresh pasta. The *maccheroni* he refers to were probably small dumplings bound with egg, rather than tubes of hard grain *pasta secca*. Filled pasta envelopes like the *ravioli* Boccaccio mentions were another important early product of that culture. They probably owe their invention to the medieval Italian passion for pies, large and small—*torte* and *tortelli*.

The Parmesan cheese that Boccaccio and his contemporaries were eating on their pasta was the result of something akin to medieval urban branding. In Boccaccio's day, Parmesan was made in a large area of fertile country in the Po valley. But it was sold by urban traders, and distributed through urban markets. And because Italians had a mental map of their land that was composed of cities rather than anonymous stretches of countryside, the cheese became thought of as *Parma* cheese. It seems likely that, as *parmigiano*'s reputation spread, its fame was exploited by merchants who demanded more and more cheese to be made using the same method. So by the time Boccaccio came to write his stories, *maccheroni* with *parmigiano* had become an established favorite across northern and central Italy.

Of course the term "brand" can only be applied very loosely to Parmesan cheese in the late Middle Ages. For one thing, today's sharply defined brands, and the equally tightly managed identity of typical products, only exist because they are protected from cheap forgeries by the law. Today's *Parmigiano-Reggiano* (named after both Parma and Reggio Emilia) is one of an increasing number of Italian foods with European Union DOP status—Denomination of Protected Origin. In Boccaccio's day, the consumer had only a suspicious eye and personal trust in the trader to rely on to ensure that the Parmesan cheese he or she was buying was the real thing. Counterfeit and adulterated goods were a constant presence in the markets of the Middle Ages, and for many centuries thereafter. For that reason, among others, we cannot tell just how similar to the uniform quality of today's hard, granular *Parmigiano-Reggiano* the product mentioned in the *Decameron* really was.

Most typical dishes are much younger than Parmesan. But there is a very real sense in which we do need to go back to the Middle Ages to find their roots. The most emotive facet of typicality, the Italians' pride in their cities, was born in the Middle Ages. Historians tend to refer to it as civic patriotism. As the cities of the center and north of the peninsula began to achieve commercial success in the tenth century, and fight for their political independence in the eleventh, they became very proud of themselves. Their honor came to depend on the competition to build splendid cathedrals, piazzas, palaces, and defensive walls. But when intercity rivalry involved markets and territory rather than architecture, it often turned violent, and the resultant warfare between the city-states gave yet more impetus to civic patriotism. The middle of the eleventh century saw the appearance of the first war wagons, the ultimate symbols of city pride. They began as military standards fixed onto ox-drawn carts. But as more local prestige was invested in them, they grew into mighty mobile ensembles comprising tabernacles, crosses, and portraits of patron saints. Soon, on the battlefield and in civic ceremonies, each city rallied to a war wagon decorated with gilt symbols and brightly colored canopies, streamers, and flags.

Medieval civic patriotism has left its legacy in the way Italians feel about their food today. But the inhabitants of Italian cities in the Middle Ages did not celebrate local dishes in the way that they celebrated their war wagons. There was no edible embodiment of medieval civic identity that stirred a flush of pride as it was carried in ceremony from kitchen to table. The Italians in the cities certainly felt proud of their food, but their pride had different contours.

To trace those contours we need to examine a rare kind of historical source material. The first Italian cookbooks, like the fourteenth-century recipe collection that will come into focus in the next chapter, give us valuable evidence. But in the Middle Ages, they only tell us about the eating habits of the upper classes. Even rarer than early cookbooks are sources that go beyond recipes and tell us about what less wealthy people ate. Rarest of all are documents that allow us to glimpse medieval Italians' *feelings* about food—the feelings that can turn mere nourishment into the stuff of identity. So when, quite by chance in the autumn of 1894, the professor of medieval Latin literature at Milan University came across the only surviving manuscript of *De magnalibus Mediolani* (*The Marvels of Milan*) in the National Library in Madrid, Italian food historians were given something very precious indeed.

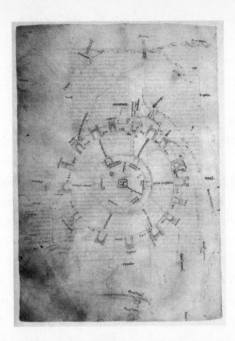

An idealized plan of Milan in the 1300s. According to
Brother Bonvesin da la Riva, the city's "wondrous rotundity,"
just like its rich diet, were the work of divine Providence.

Brother Bonvesin, Milanese Citizen

The Marvels of Milan, written in the late spring of 1288, is one of the
great expressions of medieval city pride. Among many other things, it
contains a detailed description of the Milanese war wagon: wrapped
entirely in scarlet cloth, it was so enormous it had to be drawn by three
pairs of the biggest and strongest oxen; each of these beasts wore a
white caparison marked with a red cross. The wagon carried a long
white banner and a gilded bronze crucifix mounted on top of a mast so
heavy it took four men to lift it into place.

The Marvels of Milan is as overblown as the Milanese war wagon in
its civic patriotism. The book's author, Bonvesin da la Riva, was a good
example of the new types who were asserting themselves in Italian cities.
He was a well-to-do lay member of an order of monks called the *Umiliati*.

"Humiliated" he may have been, but he introduces himself to his readers with his chest puffed out: "Brother Bonvesin da la Riva, Milanese citizen." Bonvesin was nearing fifty when he wrote *The Marvels of Milan*, but a boyish pride seems to burst from every line. Milan, he tells us, is exalted among cities "like the rose or the lily above the other flowers," "like the eagle above birds," "like the lion above quadrupeds." Even Milan's shape is special: "The city's plan is round, in the form of a circle, and this wondrous rotundity is a sign of its perfection." This simple observation (which still holds true today) actually contains an audacious spiritual boast: Jerusalem, the ideal earthly city, was traditionally represented as having the same "wondrous rotundity"—a reflection of the divine order made manifest in the celestial orbs. Nonchalantly, Bonvesin also suggests that his hometown would make the best possible headquarters for the papacy.

These were not words calculated to win friends in Florence, Genoa, or Venice, let alone Rome. Bonvesin is as oblivious as any other patriot to how wearisome one's flag-waving can be to other people. Yet a number of things make *The Marvels of Milan* just as intriguing and informative as it is insufferable. For one thing, Brother Bonvesin marshals an enormous amount of statistical evidence. He instructs us that the city was defended by a rampart and a moat surrounded by a wall that was exactly 10,141 Milanese cubits long. Within that circumference—equivalent to 3.78 miles—there were six monasteries, eight nunneries, ninety-four chapels, and a skyline punctuated by some 120 bell towers.

Amid this mass of figures, Bonvesin's relish for his city's wealth, diversity, and sheer day-to-day hubbub speaks to us across the centuries. The front doors in Milan numbered 12,500. Among the many types living behind those doors (often several families to a building), were 120 lawyers, more than 1,500 notaries, 28 doctors, at least 150 ordinary surgeons, 80 farriers, 440 butchers, 6 lavishly paid public trumpeters, well above a thousand tavern owners, 14 singing teachers who specialized in Ambrosian chant, and in excess of 30 artisans who made a living manufacturing Milan's unique brand of horse bell. "Anyone who reflects carefully on all these things, even if he travels the whole world, will not find a comparable paradise of delights," Bonvesin proclaims. At least he was personally modest enough not to mention that he was one of the city's eight teachers of grammar—meaning Latin. Or, indeed, that he was its one and only writer of note.

For the classical Latin authors that Bonvesin admired, such an out-pouring of data would have been too demeaning to commit to parchment. But numbers were the heartbeat of the busy Italian city-states, because middling people with a head for figures had come to the cities in search of business success. Others arrived, too. Artisans, laborers, and servants found a niche in the urban labor market that commerce helped to diversify. Monks and nuns came to remind their acquisitive fellow citizens of the dangers of greed. The destitute and crippled came to live off alms, ne'er-do-wells to gamble and drink in the taverns, and to scratch a living running messages through the narrow streets. Aristocrats came to remind everyone else that it was they who still represented the lodestar of social status.

In medieval Milan, and any medieval Italian city, these different people lived in a striking physical proximity. They all jostled for space in the streets with pigs, dogs, and chickens, moving to the same rhythm imposed by the cycles of the sun and the tolling of church bells. The house of a successful butcher, for example, would have its ground floor entirely given over to the kitchen and the shop—which was probably little more than a counter open to the street. His household would comprise his wife and children, apprentices, and servants. It was the custom for them all to sleep in the same large bed and, naturally, to share the meals prepared by the master's wife. The butcher would stun and gut animals just outside the house, their squeals and bleating mingling with the cries of the peddlers, the creak and rumble of carts, the clang of farriers' hammers, and the blast from official trumpets resounding from the piazza.

Bonvesin had access to his fund of statistics because his monastic order was integral to the noisy, crowded life of the city. The Humiliated had come to act as a kind of civil service in Milan. In lieu of paying taxes, they looked after the city treasury and gathered import duties on grain and other commodities transported along the city's many canals. Occasionally the Humiliated collected property taxes or ran public engineering projects. At one time, unmistakable in their coarse, ash-gray habits, they were present at almost all the nerve centers of city life. By the time the *The Marvels of Milan* was written it seems that only the lay tertiaries like Bonvesin were involved in the public domain; on the pope's orders, the friars had retired to their monasteries to occupy themselves with matters spiritual. But Bonvesin and his fellows were still vital to the smooth running of the city. His personal speciality was health service management: he tells us that Milan and its suburbs could count ten well-equipped hospitals and three publicly funded surgeons—all devoted to the care of the poor.

The Fruits of Providence

Think about typical Milanese cuisine today and one thinks primarily of meat. Of veal cutlets breaded and fried in butter. Or of *osso buco*—veal shanks braised with a little chopped tomato until the meat softens and separates easily from the bone; the dish is finished with a *gremolada* of garlic, parsley, and lemon zest, and served with a warming, fragrant saffron risotto *alla milanese.* Or of *cazzoeula*: pig's trotter, pork rind, and pork ribs cooked to a sticky consistency with savoy cabbage. If your *cazzoeula* doesn't seem quite porky enough you can also add sausages, *pancetta* (bacon), or even a pig's ear. This is hearty fare, food to keep out the notorious Milanese fog. But you will not find its origins in *The Marvels of Milan.*

Of all the eight chapters of *The Marvels of Milan,* the only one longer than the one on food is devoted to the city's historical and religious pedigree. Yet Bonvesin was decidedly unexcited by meat. In 1288, he notes flatly, *milanesi* ate pigs, sheep, lambs, goats, and "all sorts of other wild and farmed quadrupeds." Nor is he much more forthcoming about fowl: "The city is also abundantly supplied with excellent meat from capons, chickens, geese, ducks, peacocks, doves, pheasant, francolins, coots, larks, partridges, quail, blackbirds and other winged creatures suitable to satisfy men's appetites." On the surface, this parade of birds' names demonstrates only that medieval Italians had inherited the ancient Romans' taste for small, wild birds—a taste that persists today.

Fish generate more enthusiasm. Bonvesin supplies a register of fish-producing streams and lakes, and gleefully notes that more than 264 gallons of prawns are imported into the city every day of the season. Even the city moat, which Bonvesin measured in person and found to be thirty-eight cubits wide, teemed with fish and prawns. Strikingly, Bonvesin prefers freshwater fish to what we call "seafood," a preference that was far from unusual: the idea that freshwater fish was healthier and tastier than saltwater varieties lasted for a long time. So it was no handicap that Milan was far from the sea. On the contrary, its proximity to the lakes and rivers fed from the Alps was a huge advantage.

These days, landlocked Milan is one of the best places to eat seafood in Italy because it is home to the biggest wholesale fish market in southern Europe, but it was not always so. The fish dishes in collections of traditional Milanese recipes are so few—beyond the omnipresent eel and salt cod—that frog's legs and snails are often included, as if they were needed to make up the numbers. Bonvesin was writing long before these Milanese traditions were born. But he enthused about fish for the same reason that frog's legs and snails are categorized with eel and salt cod: heavy religious restrictions on eating meat. When Italy became a Christian land, the Church divided the calendar between "lean" and "fat" days—with meat, lard, and animal products strictly prohibited on the former. Although the rules relaxed over time so that cheese and eggs counted as "lean" cuisine, there were still over a hundred days in the year when fish was the most substantial item the faithful could put on the table. Amid the modern advertising flummery about the ancient traditions of *cucina all'italiana*, it is often forgotten that Italian eating habits now show only residual traces of the religious norms that shaped them until as late as the 1960s, when the Vatican did away with the obligation to eat fish on Fridays. One of those residual traces is the frogs and snails found among traditional Milanese fish recipes and permitted on lean days.

Yet it is not fish, but fruit and vegetables that really feed Bonvesin's civic patriotism. Together with pulses and herbs, fruit and vegetables take up roughly eight times as much space as meat in *The Marvels of Milan*. It is humble produce of the earth such as lettuce and medlars (an acidic fruit a little bigger than a walnut with a pale orange color and a large, smooth stone), pears and sage that bring Bonvesin's fact-collecting to its highest, almost ecstatic, pitch. His long inventories stretch even the fattest dictionaries to their limits. Some of the items he names are highly exotic in Italy today: flat-podded vetch (*cicerchia*), early figs (*fioroni*), Damascene plums (*prugne damaschine*), white horehound (*mar-*

rubio), portulaca (*portulaca*), hyssop (*issoppo*), and even parsnips (*pasti-nache comuni*). (Oddly, the delicious parsnip, a stock ingredient of British Christmas dinners, is impossible to find in Italian greengrocers today.)

Considering that Bonvesin could not possibly have known the many pillars of the modern Italian diet, such as potatoes, sweet peppers, and tomatoes, which had yet to arrive from the New World, the variety of fruit and vegetables that makes Bonvesin proud of Milan is remarkable. It is also a reminder of how ruthlessly modern agriculture has elimi-nated all but a few varieties from our tables.

Another feature of the medieval diet in Milan, as elsewhere, that makes it very different from Italian food today is that it often doubled as medicine. In Europe in the Middle Ages and beyond, there was no clear distinction between nourishment and drugs. To eat was always, insepa-rably, to regulate one's metabolism and counteract disease. Hence Bon-vesin points out in passing that cornelian cherries are good for menstrual pain, that hyssop relieves catarrh, and that pomegranates combat fever.

While compiling his catalogue Bonvesin also stops to offer a few pre-cious hints at how ordinary *milanesi* cooked with the bounty available to them. In winter walnuts were mixed with cheese, eggs, and pepper to make a stuffing for meat. Year-round, they were often eaten at the end of a meal, as were roasted green chestnuts. When dried and ground, chestnuts could also be used to make bread in time of need. A type of millet called *panico* went into *paniccio*—one of the many forerunners of *polenta*. Such porridge-like preparations had been staples since at least ancient Roman times.

That Bonvesin finds such everyday cooking habits worthy of note suggests that ordinarily prosperous *milanesi* like him were not very sophisticated gastronomes. He was enraptured by the city's range of ingredients, but invested little pride in how skillful his fellow citizens were at putting those ingredients to use. Evidently he was no foodie. In fact Bonvesin was a connoisseur of bulk. His overriding message about Milanese food is *quantity:* he wants to wow us with the sheer vastness of consumption—the surest indicator of the city's wealth. Hence he tells us that some seventy oxen were slaughtered daily by Milanese butchers, and that a total of sixty cartloads of cherries reached the city on peak days of the season. The roll of figures accumulates until, by the time he comes to describe the trading activity in Milan, Bonvesin seems to reach statistical burnout: a "stupefying and incalculable" number of buyers and sellers crowd the markets, bringing goods from near and far.

The Marvels of Milan was written in an age when, for the mass of the population of Europe, famine loomed just over the horizon even in years of good harvest. The city Bonvesin loved may have been nearing 150,000 inhabitants; Florence and Venice were not far behind; and only Paris, of all other European cities, could compare in size to the Italian giants. In these large urban communities, the middle-class diet, rich in animal protein, was distinguished by the standards of the time. Butchers, fishmongers, and bakers were men of status who organized themselves into powerful guilds. The lower orders had regular access to reasonably good bread. That is why Bonvesin makes such a plain dish as millet porridge, or *paniccio*, the subject of his civic patriotism. This simple food was common to the ordinary people in both the city and the countryside, but crucially, the citizens had a more dependable supply of it. For Milan to have made such consistent plenty available within its circular walls was indeed a marvel. And proud citizens from many other cities in Italy were boasting of equivalent achievements—Milan was more typical than Bonvesin's civic patriotism would allow him to see.

Political power made those marvels possible. The noble caste who ran the Italian cities attained the ability to determine their own collective destiny in a form of government called the commune. This was an exceptional political development in a Europe dominated by feudal monarchies. As soon as a commune was established, it moved to exercise authority over the countryside around it—an area known as the *contado*. In the minds of the rulers of the cities, the *contado* was a place to levy taxes and conscript infantrymen, to go hunting and hawking, and of course, to source food. Gradually, whether by force of arms, purchase, or treaty, much of the countryside passed from the control of feudal lords and churchmen into that of urban landowners and city officials. In the city's interests, peasants could be told what to grow and compelled to sell their surplus, especially cereals, in the city markets. The reasoning behind this policy was simple: food security in the city was the basis of political security for its rulers. Under the commune's shield, newly wealthy citizens went out and bought up tracts of countryside in order to grow commercial crops or ensure their own private food supply. *Paniccio*, prawns, parsnips, or Parmesan cheese: every mouthful consumed in the Italian cities was the fruit of their supremacy over the land around them.

Bonvesin does not say as much. For him, the city's edible wealth is merely a sign of "the benevolence of the Omnipotent One." Indeed, at the end of his chapter on food he slips easily from lists of produce into the fable of how the city's first bishop, the apostle Barnabas, sowed the seeds of spiritual abundance in the city. "Behold, therefore, the fertility of the fruit that divine Providence has provided for this land!" Perhaps that explains Bonvesin's enthusiasm for vegetables: they are both the most direct evidence of the fertility of the *contado*, and a ready metaphor for his city's special place in the Almighty's plans. To be a Christian and to be a citizen were almost synonymous for many of Bonvesin's contemporaries in Italy. We learn from *The Marvels of Milan* that both religion and civic patriotism gave Italian meals their savor.

Yet the idea of "Italian food" would have meant very little to Bonvesin. Until the Renaissance, Italians were unaware that they were eating in a style that distinguished them from foreigners. Yet without the network of trade links between medieval Italian cities, and without the massive concentration of power, resources, and civic patriotism within them, Italian cuisine would never have come into being.

Eat Not Too Quickly

Among Brother Bonvesin's other works is *De quinquaginta curialitatibus ad mensam* (*Fifty Courtesies at Table*), a long list of pointers on good manners, in verse. Courtesy number 19, by way of a loosely translated sample, goes something like this:

> Don't badmouth the dishes when you dine:
> Just tell everyone that they taste fine.
> In this dire habit I've caught many a dolt,
> Saying "this is poorly cooked," or "this needs salt."

Bonvesin poetically stigmatizes such misdemeanors as eating too quickly, sneezing on the plate, sticking your fingers in your ears or other bodily crevices, and blowing your nose on your fingers. There are also tips on how to behave if you find yourself sitting next to a bishop at dinner. Eminently sensible advice, every bit of it. But what is important about *Fifty Courtesies at Table* is less this list of dos and don'ts than the audience it was aimed at.

Bonvesin wrote *The Marvels of Milan* in Latin, for a limited readership of cultural sophisticates including his own pupils. But he sometimes also wrote in what we could call a dialect—ordinary Milanese. The demands of commerce, and of city life more generally, meant that literacy in Italy was at higher levels than anywhere else. And whereas, elsewhere in Europe, the royal court was the only place where proper behavior really counted, in medieval Italy the city was a key theater of etiquette. So *Fifty Courtesies at Table*, like many other books of advice in Italy, was written in the language of everyday intercourse, for a broader, upwardly mobile urban public. Strictly speaking, Bonvesin was not telling his readers how to be *courteous*, but how to be *civil* and *urbane*. Put another way, he was giving instruction on how *not* to behave *villanamente*—"like a peasant."

Between the rhyming lines of his fifty rules for good manners, Bonvesin gives a glimpse of how people ate at respectable tables in Milan in the thirteenth century. Goblets and wooden platters were shared. That is why sneezing into your plate was forbidden, and why only a clod would fail to wipe his mouth before taking a gulp of wine. Each guest was provided with a spoon (which it was good form to retain between courses), but had to bring his own knife (which it was rude to sheathe before everyone had finished eating).

Bonvesin does not mention forks, although they had been known in Italy for about two centuries. Within a couple of generations of Bonvesin, Italians would begin eating regularly with forks—perhaps the peninsula's single greatest contribution to Western etiquette. In fact the reason Italians took to eating with forks far earlier than anyone else was probably that they were so fond of pasta.

In some of their earliest mentions in Italian literature, forks are used for eating *maccheroni*. One example in the late 1300s comes from the pen of yet another typical product of the Italian cities: Florentine merchant's son, politician, and short-story writer Franco Sacchetti. He tells of one shrewd character, Giovanni Cascio, who was forced to share a table with the famously greedy Noddo d'Andrea. Noddo's favorite trick was to bolt boiling hot food down before his dining companions could even stand to put it in their mouths—a trick that was all the more outrageous when performed on a highly prized platter of *maccheroni* in sauce. On this occasion Cascio, the hero of the story, had only wound the first few steaming strands of *maccheroni* around his fork when Noddo was already halfway through his share and well on the way to eating his companion's, too. (The *maccheroni* at stake here were certainly the long thin tubes of hard grain pasta that today would likely be called *bucatini*.) So for every forkful of pasta that Noddo wolfed down, Cascio tossed one to the dog. Sheer guilt at the waste of delicious *maccheroni* was enough to slow his voracious companion.

The Lack of Concord Between Citizens

Like al-Idrisi's story, Bonvesin's has its dark side. In the pages of *The Marvels of Milan*, the section on the city's abundance is followed by a brief history. But there is something strange about that history: it stops too early. Indeed it stops a whole forty years before the spring of 1288 when Bonvesin began work on *The Marvels of Milan*. Granted, he may have wanted to finish on a high note: in 1248, Milanese troops helped inflict a devastating defeat on the Holy Roman Emperor. Songs of triumph were heard in the city as a captured enemy war wagon was put on display—it belonged to an old rival, Cremona, which had supported the Holy Roman Emperor.

But if Bonvesin omitted to relate the events of the following decades, it cannot have been because they lacked drama. The Milanese war wagon was barely still as the city armies sought to subjugate the surrounding region and intervene in international power struggles. As one historian has remarked, "No one has bothered to count Milan's wars during the third quarter of the thirteenth century."

Domestic events were scarcely less bloody. In 1252 Milanese heretics butchered the Church's inquisitor at a ford in the nearby countryside. When the killers bribed their way to freedom, there was a riot and the governor (*podestà*) was nearly lynched. In 1256 the archbishop and leading noblemen were expelled from the city by their political enemies. For the next half century and more, Milan would be engaged in almost constant fighting against the armies of political exiles. In 1257 the chief tax collector was put on trial, then hacked to death by a mob and his body thrown into the moat to feed the prawns. Like the governor, the unfortunate man was not even Milanese: he had been brought in from Bologna in the hope that he could bring some impartiality to sorting out the city's parlous finances.

In 1259, after a rival was murdered in yet another riot, nobleman Martino della Torre was elected captain of the People, which was the name for the political and military organization of the artisans, tradesmen, and merchants of the city—including those respected bakers and fishmongers, and the 440 butchers listed by Bonvesin. Martino della Torre proceeded to take Milan by force, assume dictatorial powers, and send his enemies into exile. Over the coming years, he would help to maintain the right conditions for trade, and for his own authority, by paving streets, digging canals, taxing the countryside, and ensuring the city's food supply.

In 1263 the new archbishop, Ottone Visconti, led a force of exiles against the city in a bid to take up his post; he failed. In 1266, on three successive days in the churchyard of San Diogini, fifty-four noblemen were beheaded for their part in the savage murder of a member of the della Torre family. In 1277, after a war involving escalating atrocities on both sides, Archbishop Visconti finally defeated the della Torre clan and won his see. The surviving della Torres continued the fight from exile. In their stead, the Visconti family established lordship over the city, expelling factional enemies as they did so. Anyone who found himself sitting next to Archbishop Visconti at dinner would be well advised to mind his manners in the way Bonvesin recommended.

Confused patterns of civil violence like this were repeated across northern and central Italy. Like many Italian city-states, thirteenth-century Milan was divided into a series of fortified compounds. Noblemen and their thuggish retainers presented a constant threat to law and order. They bullied themselves free of both tax obligations and the control of the courts. In response, merchants and artisans fortified their own streets, recruited military muscle, and set mobs loose to mete out popular justice. Anyone who could afford to go about the streets wearing armor did so. On all sides, loyalty to clan or sworn faction ran deeper than civic patriotism.

The communes were too divided to survive. Eventually, opportunistic noblemen, such as the Viscontis, emerged to become the hereditary lords of the cities.

No wonder Bonvesin found it easier to write about food than about history. But his only hint that all was not well amid the plenty available in Milan comes in a few lame words about "the lack of concord between citizens." It is a phrase that has been interpreted as propaganda for the Visconti cause: like all victors, the Viscontis liked the idea of peace and concord. Or perhaps Bonvesin's cheering for his home city was deliberately naïve; it was wise to avoid making political enemies. Either way, the civic patriotism of *The Marvels of Milan* seems strained and shrill—as if Bonvesin was trying too hard to convince himself that he lived in a city of providential plenty. He would not be the last Italian to find consolation at table for his country's troubles.

4

Venice, 1300s

Chinese Whispers

What Marco Polo Found in China

Marco Polo returned home for the last time in 1299, eleven years after Bonvesin wrote *The Marvels of Milan*. The great adventurer was then in his mid-forties, the veteran of seventeen years in China and several more in Genoa as a prisoner of war. He spent the last twenty-five years of his life quietly enjoying his wealth, his new family, and the services of his Mongol slave.

The city Marco Polo had to learn to call home again was an emporium for the world's goods, a teeming city of merchants and craftsmen. Venetians bought and sold in the trade fairs of Champagne and the ports of the Low Countries and England, in Constantinople and on the rivers of southern Russia, in Cyprus, Damascus, and Alexandria. By Polo's time, the Rialto hosted the world's most important wholesale market: at that famous bend in the Grand Canal, silks and medicines from the South China Sea could be traded for Flemish cloth and Cornish tin amid a concert of different languages. The city known as *la Serenissima* stands today as a reminder that the global economy is no novelty. What was once a loose cluster of communities living off the salt pans and fish of the Lagoon had become the greatest maritime power in the Mediterranean. By the standards of any place on earth, it was an extraordinary trajectory.

There are two histories of Venice, two contrasting explanations for its rise. In fact opinions on Venice were radically opposed even at the time. Modern historians continue to be divided along lines established in the Middle Ages.

The first history of Venice's rise is the tale of a city whose beauty, wealth, and power were the reward for a unique partnership between good government and entrepreneurship. Unlike other Italian cities, Venice never fell into catastrophic civil strife and never succumbed to the rule of a despot like a della Torre or a Visconti. The merchant nobility who oversaw that independence were distinguished by their sense of public service, their respect for public institutions, and by their sound environmental policies: the authorities constructed locks, breakwaters, and lighthouses; protected the trees that held the sandbanks together; monitored shipping and refuse; and regulated industrial zones. Venice's long-term future depended on its delicate Lagoon location, which could not be sacrificed to short-term commercial gain.

The other history of Venice is more sinister. The city's commercial dominance owed more to violence than it did to enterprise. Heavily armed galleys compelled nearby lands to bring their wares to Venice, where they could be taxed by its government and traded on by its middlemen: Venice's dependent countryside, its *contado*, was virtually the whole of the upper Adriatic coast. Those same ships engaged in piracy and plunder across the Ionian, Aegean, and Mediterranean seas. The turning point in Venice's fortunes as a trading state came in 1204 when a combined force of Venetians and French mounted an unprovoked assault on Constantinople; they sacked it amid a frenzy of looting, rape, and murder, and the Byzantine Empire's best naval bases fell into Venetian hands.

Venice grew rich on slavery. For centuries, Venetian traders kept much of the Mediterranean supplied with men to be used as mercenaries and laborers, and with girls and boys to serve as domestics and concubines. On this matter, as on others, the Venetian oligarchy was hypocritical even by the low standards of the age. Against the express instructions of the pope, Venice traded in Christian slaves as well as heretics and infidels. It happily supplied Christendom's enemies with weapons-grade timber and metal. The terrible sack of the Christian city of Constantinople in 1204 was perpetrated in the name of a Crusade.

The contrast between Venice's two histories was perhaps never as sharp as it was while Marco Polo was alive. During his time in the east, a revolution in maritime commerce had begun, propelled by innovation. Venetian sailors now used marine charts, traverse-tables (which allowed them to plot a true course despite several changes of direction), and the first compasses. Venice's smarter merchants were monitoring their assets and liabilities across ever-bigger investment portfolios with the revolutionary technique of double-entry bookkeeping. They were also buying government bonds to consolidate their wealth and give the state the financial flexibility it needed.

Marco Polo's return to the city of his birth coincided with tumultuous events that belong very much on the sinister side of Venetian history. In 1308, with typical opportunism, Venice went to war to win control of the nearby city of Ferrara, whose feudal overlord, Pope Clement V, was so indignant that he excommunicated Venice and decreed that its citizens abroad could be enslaved as if they were heathens. The Ferrara crisis exacerbated the tensions between families and factions in Venetian city government. In 1310, in the Tiepolo-Querini conspiracy, Venice nearly went the way of so many other Italian cities when it almost fell under the rule of a tyrant. An attempt to capture the Doge's palace and murder the Doge himself was only thwarted after bloody street fighting in piazza San Marco and the Mercerie. The battle apparently turned when a woman dropped a heavy cooking pot from a high window onto the head of the conspirators' standard-bearer.

During this period of bewildering change, news of Marco Polo's adventures began to spread. While confined in Genoa he had dictated his story to another inmate who was from Pisa. Back in his home city after his release, Polo may well have recounted further details of his time in the service of Khubilai Khan to other amanuenses. Transcriptions and translations of his tales appeared in Venetian, Tuscan, French, Latin, and even German. Much of Europe was gripped; Marco Polo became famous in his own lifetime.

Yet many Venetians were reluctant to believe him. According to a traditional anecdote, children would follow him around shouting, "Messer

Marco, tell us another lie." Some scholars today are as skeptical as those children. It is easy to understand why. No trace of Polo's own version of what he did and saw survives, either in his own hand, or in that of his fellow prisoner. About a hundred and fifty extant manuscripts are third-hand at best, and often markedly different from one another. So Marco Polo's story, as we know it today, is the result of a game of Chinese whispers. That is why, every so often, the academic controversy over whether Polo ever went to China at all reignites: perhaps his adventures are nothing more than hearsay. The manuscripts we have, combine to produce a narrative that is sometimes misleading and often puzzling. Why does he never mention the Great Wall or acupuncture?

Or, indeed, noodles? The story that it was Marco Polo who imported noodles to Italy, and thereby gave birth to the country's pasta culture, is the most pervasive myth in the history of Italian food. The facts of the matter could not be clearer. The Chinese were certainly eating noodles thousands of years before the Italians. In the autumn of 2005, archaeologists excavating at Lajia on the banks of China's Yellow River unearthed an upturned bowl of late Neolithic noodles; they were long, yellow, and made from millet. But however ancient it is, China's noodle culture is nonetheless distinct from Italy's because the Chinese have never cultivated hard grain durum wheat. According to al-Idrisi, *pasta secca* was already present in Sicily at least a century before Marco Polo was born. So the notion that he brought pasta back from the Orient is implausible.

Despite the doubts, it seems almost certain that Marco Polo *did* go to China. The likelihood is that he served as a minor civil servant in the Mongolian administration there, rather than as the influential adviser and emissary he claimed to have been. He became immersed in Mongol culture rather than Chinese—and the Mongols did not eat noodles.

But even if Venice was not the port through which pasta entered Italy, Marco Polo's city did have a huge influence on medieval Italian cuisine. In fact the reason why Venice occupies such an important place in food history, the reason why Venetians found Polo's tales about China so compelling, and the reason why Venetian merchants were inspired to both greed and greatness, are all one and the same: spice.

Pepper, ginger, nutmeg, cloves, and cinnamon had already made the air of the Rialto heavy with their scent even before a seventeen-year-old

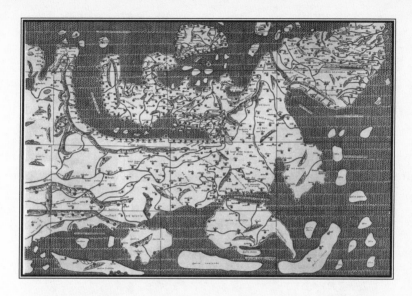

The map that shows where pasta first arrived on Italian soil. Al-Idrisi's
atlas seems upside down and distorted when judged by our conventions.
The triangular island of Sicily is shown at the top.

Marco Polo set off on his adventures. For the city on the Lagoon was
Europe's greatest center of the spice trade. Venice's merchants were
constantly bartering for bales of spices in the markets of Damascus,
Acre, and Alexandria. Even so, the Venetians were only one link in a long
chain that led back beyond the Arab camel drivers who had brought the
spices from the ports of the Red Sea, and the Asian merchants who had
shipped them before that. Marco Polo was the first Westerner to provide
a tempting picture of where the spices actually originated. He found
abundant cinnamon in Tibet and Malabar; saw ginger growing along
the Yellow River; reported a busy trade in ginger, sugar, and galingale
in the ports of Bengal; and witnessed locally grown pepper, nutmeg,
cubeb, and cloves on sale in Java. Somewhere at the origin of Marco
Polo's long line of Chinese whispers lay wealth beyond imagining. By
reading Marco Polo, later generations of European merchants and
conquerors were inspired to follow the spice routes back to the Indian
Ocean and the South China Sea, changing world history and cuisines in
the process.

Women making spaghetti. From a fourteenth-century medical text.

The glamour and prestige of oriental spices. Pepper is harvested and presented to a monarch. From a French manuscript collection of travel writings (c. 1410–1412), including Marco Polo's journey to China.

Book for Cook

Venice's ascent to power followed the rising curve of Europe's addiction to spicy food. The sheer extent of that addiction in Italy is clear from manuscripts that began to spread at exactly the same time that the tales of Marco Polo's exploits were proliferating. The first recipe books to be written in Europe, since late antiquity, started to appear in the late thirteenth century. All told, about a hundred survive, whole or in fragments, from the age before printing.

Two complete manuscript recipe collections, both of which are anonymous, compete for the honor of being the earliest surviving cookbook written in an Italian vernacular rather than in Latin. One of them is in Tuscan, which was the native tongue of Marco Polo's contemporary, Dante. The other is in Venetian, the language that Marco Polo himself would have spoken. The *Libro per cuoco* (*Book for Cook*), as this Venetian manuscript has become known, is difficult to date precisely, but it was probably written in the mid-1300s. *Book for Cook* is a handy little volume, measuring 4½ × 3½ inches—a little less than half the size of a paperback novel—written in a clear, well-spaced script. Its recipes are helpfully arranged in alphabetical order and numbered from 1 to 135. These facts suggest that the recipe collection was designed to be consulted regularly by people who really cooked. Its recipes are generally more precise than those in the Tuscan manuscript; crucially, they specify the amount of each ingredient in such a way that many dishes are easy to reproduce today. So *Book for Cook* offers us one of our earliest and best insights into how food was prepared for those fourteenth-century Venetian slave traders and spice dealers.

Recipe 73 is one of the shortest in *Book for Cook*—partly because its unknown author took for granted that all of its precious ingredients were to be pounded to a fine dust with a pestle and mortar. Yet the influence of recipe 73 is everywhere in the collection. There is no other place to begin when describing the book's contents:

FINE SPICES FOR EVERYTHING

LXXIII

Take an ounce of pepper, an ounce of cinnamon, an ounce of ginger, an eighth of an ounce of cloves, and a quarter of an ounce of saffron.*

---

* Medieval Italians measured their spices, and other things, in ounces. Each city attributed a slightly different value to the ounce, but it was always around thirty grams.

Book for Cook includes spices in about three-quarters of its recipes. In addition to recipe 73 reproduced above, it instructs us how to make two further compounds. Recipe 74, "Sweet spices for lots of good and fine things," contains no pepper—hence "sweet"; and instead of saffron it includes something it calls "leaf," which no scholar has been able to identify for certain, although an informed guess suggests that it may be a kind of patchouli. Whatever "leaf" was, it went to produce a mixture described as "marvelously good," particularly with lamprey and other freshwater fish. The third mixture, "Black, strong spices" (recipe 75), was blended into many different sauces; it combines two ounces of pepper with two nutmegs, an eighth of an ounce of cloves, and two ounces of long pepper. (This last ingredient is a more aromatic variety, originating in India and Malaysia.) Each of the spices in the three mixtures appears in other combinations, and some recipes also use coriander seeds and cardamom, as well as spices that are even more exotic today than they were in fourteenth-century Venice, such as galingale and melegueta pepper. Evidently, the most prestigious dishes in medieval Venice tasted more like chicken korma or lamb dopiaza than modern classics such as liver *alla veneziana* or *risi e bisi* (a soupy *risotto* with peas—the pods can also be used to make the broth even more tasty).

Book for Cook's detailed instructions on how to use spices are unusual in the Middle Ages—most other sources tell us that spices were used, but not *how.* It may seem no surprise to find such careful attention in a recipe collection that circulated in the great spice emporium on the Lagoon. Some Venetians, proud of their food, certainly think that fact significant. Several Venetian cookbooks published since the 1970s cite *Book for Cook* as the starting point of Venice's distinctive food tradition. The suggestion is that, by following the spice trail back to the time of Marco Polo, we can see the first flowering of the gastronomic genius that gives us typical Venetian dishes such as *pesse in saor* (fried fish in a marinade of onion, oil, vinegar—and sometimes also pine nuts, raisins, and a pinch of spices).

The idea that medieval Venetian cooks created a distinctive local style of food around spices is seductive, but it does not withstand an encounter with the historical evidence of *Book for Cook*. Despite Venice's deep involvement in the spice trade, the proportion of recipes that contain spices in *Book for Cook* is more or less the same as in other recipe collections from the 1300s and 1400s—not just in Italy, but across Western Europe. "Fine spices for everything" is as good a one-line summary as one can get of elite cookery at the time. So what is striking and important about this Venetian manuscript is how *medieval* it is, rather than how Venetian. As it turns out, Venice's famed entrepreneurs and captains strove to eat food whose signature flavors were anything but local. That is why its neatly transcribed pages are worth perusing in more detail.

Cooking with Spices

Food historians wearied long ago of demolishing the assumption that all the spices in medieval cooking were there to smother the taste of decaying meat and fish. In Italian cities, fish predominantly meant freshwater species from nearby rivers, lakes, and moats—as we saw in *The Marvels of Milan*—or pickled and salted varieties such as herring and cod that came from northern Europe. Meat, for those who could afford to eat it, was very fresh. Many animals were reared within city walls or close by. Even the beasts that had to be brought in from the country would be driven to market alive, then butchered close to the time and place of consumption.

So if people ate their food heavily spiced it was because they liked the taste. And they liked it for two reasons: first, because they had learned to enjoy what was good for them; and second, because spices were expensive.

Medieval doctors recommended spices as a way of regulating digestion—an idea that had its basis in ancient Roman and Greek medicine, particularly the writings of Galen. A prolific writer and self-publicist, Galen developed his medical theories as a doctor in a gladiator school, and then as private physician to Emperor Marcus Aurelius and his son, Commodus (played by Richard Harris and Joaquin Phoenix in the movie *Gladiator*). Galenic theory revolved around the four bodily humors—black bile, blood, yellow bile, and phlegm. To keep healthy you had to maintain the balance between them, and the principal way of achieving that was to eat and digest correctly. In fact eating and medicine overlapped so much that Galen urged doctors to *taste* their patients' secretions.

Following Galen, medieval dietitians thought of the stomach as being a flesh casserole pot that had to be maintained at the right heat if it was going to keep the humors in order. Moreover, because the humors were derived from the four constitutive elements of all matter—earth, air, fire, and water—you could plot how any edible matter would affect you on a corresponding grid of four qualities: hot and cold, wet and dry. Spices were nearly all hot and dry, so they were the perfect shield against the huge dangers of eating foods classified as cold and wet.

The high price of spices gave them cachet. A costly mortarful of nutmeg and cloves set a dish apart from what ordinary folk ate. Recipe 55 in *Book for Cook* contains a prime instance of the transformative snob value that spices had in the Middle Ages. *Panichata* is a porridge made with the kind of millet that Bonvesin mentions in *The Marvels of Milan*. But the Venetian recipe bestows real status on this humble ingredient by cooking it in almond milk, adding hot fat, then serving it with roast goose and a caramel-colored sauce made from the goose liver pounded with egg yolk, vinegar, and *agresto*—the sour grape condiment known as verjuice in English. The sauce also contains "good fine spices."

The *panichata* is also generously sprinkled with sugar—another expensive foreign commodity that could confer prestige on virtually anything to emerge from a medieval kitchen. One reason why cooks in the Middle Ages and the Renaissance used sugar so liberally was that it masked the taste of salt, which was used in many techniques for conserving food in an age without refrigeration, canning, or vacuum packing. In the winter months especially, saltiness became all-pervading—unless you could afford to use sugar to counteract it.

The kind of sauce eaten with the goose in the *panichata* recipe is a common feature of the medieval European way with meat, whether boiled or roasted. *Book for Cook* tells us how to create some classic sauces, such as *Agliata* (garlic sauce, recipe 3):

GARLIC SAUCE FOR ALL KINDS OF MEAT

Take the garlic and cook it in the embers, then pound it well and add raw garlic and breadcrumbs, sweet spices and broth. Mince everything together and boil it for a while. Serve hot.

"Green sauce" (recipe 81) comprises parsley ground with spices and salt, then diluted with vinegar. Like *agliata*, it was a dipping sauce served in small bowls into which ready-carved bits of meat were dunked by hand.

If spices could give millet porridge class, they could endow that other staple of medieval cooking, the pie, with an aura that was positively regal. Recipe 109 in *Book for Cook* is for "King Manfredi fresh broad bean pie." The filling comprises podded and skinned broad beans that are cooked in milk, drained, then mixed with fried *pancetta*, sweet and strong spices, saffron, and freshly made cheese. The mixture is then layered into the pie casing with slices of soft fatty cheese. In all but the wealthiest Italian homes, such pies would be taken off to the local baker's oven to be cooked.

Book for Cook contains a number of dishes that would be sophisticated even without spices. Recipe 45 is for "Mortarolo," an elaborate pie containing chicken, whole dates, and deep-fried pellets made from pounded cheese, eggs, dates, pine nuts, and *pancetta*. But spices enter every stage of the cooking process for Mortarolo; even the dates are stuffed with ginger, cinnamon, and cloves. "This dish should be yellow and powerful with spices," the recipe concludes—yellow, like white, being a color that connoted luxury.

Pasta recipes are the best measure of what is familiar and strange in medieval cooking compared to what is now eaten in Italy. In recipe 58, "Ordinary ravioli with enhanced herbs," the *ravioli* in question are, like today's ones, small envelopes of pasta. *Book for Cook* advises a filling of herbs which are lightly boiled before being finely chopped and mixed with fresh cheese and beaten egg. The *ravioli* are then cooked in broth and covered with a grating of good cheese to create a dish that could plausibly appear on an Italian table today—except that the filling contains "sweet and strong spices" and "a lot of spices" are also sprinkled over the top before eating. *Lasagne* are another example: prepared for Lent with ground walnuts in recipe 38, they are given the last-minute coating of spices and sugar without which no medieval pasta dish was complete.

It should be made clear that the sugar sprinkled on *lasagne* and *ravioli* did not make them into puddings. Savory and sweet tastes were not yet segregated, and the sequence in which dishes were served had different aims. The praiseworthy goal of the contemporary Italian order of *antipasto*, *primo*, *secondo*, *contorno* (accompanying vegetables), and *dolce* is to separate tastes and arrange them so as to create a familiar and pleasurable sense of progress from the beginning to the end of the meal. In the Middle Ages, Galenic theory dictated the order in which foods were served, as well as the way in which they were combined. The goal, equally praiseworthy, was to balance the hot, dry, cold, or wet properties of the individual ingredients. The medieval meal was made from patterns of humoral opposites rather than a narrative progression of distinct dishes. Some of the combinations of contrasting foods that Galenic cooks recommended are still served in Italy today: for example, Parma ham with melon, or cheese with pears.

Chioggia Salt

Spices were the mark of fine dining, not just in Venice but right across Western Europe. *La Serenissima*, like Milan and other Italian cities, did not invent a gastronomic style for itself until later in its history. The very text of the Venetian *Book for Cook* offers evidence of that fact because it is the end product of yet another game of Chinese whispers. The most exacting scholarly analysis of its recipes suggests that many were copied from originals in Tuscan, some of which were copied in turn from Latin recipes circulating in Naples—a city then ruled by the French House of Anjou. At each stage in this journey, recipes would have been learned by heart, modified, misremembered, recounted to others, then written down again. It is probably hopeless to try to discover exactly when and where any individual recipe was invented. *Book for Cook* is a scrapbook anthology of dishes that mostly lacks the signature flavors of a single place. In fact all medieval cookery manuscripts share the same trait. They are of enormous significance in the history of Italian food—but not because they mark the birth of local culinary "typicality."

Is anything about the recipes in *Book for Cook* characteristically Venetian? Real caution is needed here. Even some of the recipes that look familiar are not as Venetian as they seem. For example, recipe 18 is for a dish called "hare *civiro*": the chopped meat is parboiled and fried in lard before being cooked in a mixture of breadcrumbs toasted until they are black, finely grated onion, vinegar, pounded liver (the hare's, that is), honey, and spices. The mixture of sweet and sour flavors is another typical medieval preference. "When it is well boiled, put it aside to cool and it will be wholesome and perfect," *Book for Cook* advises. A modern version of *civiro*, known as *salmí*, might find its way into a Venetian restaurant today. But it is by no means exclusive to Venice—it is a kind of jugged hare or confit. The same point applies to recipe 80, for a fish sauce, which is similar to the modern Venetian fried fish in a marinade, *pesse in saor*. But *pesse in saor* is itself identical to the *alla scapece* method used in southern Italy, which is identical to the escabeche recipes found in Spain, southern France, Portugal, and North Africa. All of them are equally old, and all originate in a sweet and tangy Persian stew called *sikbāj* that became popular in much of the Muslim world. (Sicily was not the only place in Italy where Muslim culture exerted its influence.)

We are left with just a few authentic hints of Venice in *Book for Cook*. Whoever compiled the collection certainly knew what he or she was doing. For example, some recipes that appear in earlier cookbook fragments are modified to make them easier to follow. One recipe even tells us to add extra salt if the salt in question comes from the pans of Chioggia at the southern end of the Lagoon. (Venice sold Chioggia salt to cities as far up the Po valley as Milan.) The helpful alphabetical arrangement of the recipes in *Book for Cook* is also a novelty. And once the alphabetical list of dishes comes to an end with number 121, "Zuche" (marrows), the Venetian compiler adds a few new recipes of his or her own. One that jumps out as markedly local is recipe 128, for simple biscuits made from a gently baked mixture of egg, flour, and either sugar or honey; they are called "Nun's *bozolati*" *Bussolai*, the contemporary Venetian word that derives from *bozolati*, also means a kind of biscuit that can be made in a variety of ways, some of which closely resemble this fourteenth-century recipe. But then one basic biscuit makes a poor foundation stone for a cooking tradition.

In one sense, by far the greatest share of the food eaten in medieval Italian cities would have been local, produced within the city walls and in the countryside around, as we saw from *The Marvels of Milan*. But today's self-consciously distinctive local cooking styles were far from the medieval mind-set. The merchants of Venice did not aspire to eat Venetian food: they wanted the same healthy, exclusive, spicy tastes as other wealthy Italians. That is why all those contemporary Italian cookbooks that trace the origins of their local food back to the Middle Ages should be taken with a pinch of salt—a particularly large pinch if the salt is from Chioggia.

Book for Cook is nonetheless an exciting taster of the urban food culture developing across much of Italy in the late Middle Ages. It does not represent the food of one particular city, but of a whole *network* of Italian cities. Wealthy urban elites were dominating their cities' hinterland; they were trading with the world and with one another; they were competing for political power and swapping political ideas. The Chinese whispers in the medieval manuscript sources tell us that they were also swapping recipes—most characteristically for pasta dishes. This pattern of exchange within a network of cities is one of the defining characteristics of Italian food culture. Eating tasty, healthy food, and eating it with good manners, was not, as elsewhere, the privilege of a few aristocrats; it was now a badge of success to which broader ranks of citizens could aspire.

II

COOKING FOR RENAISSANCE
POPES AND PRINCES

5

Rome, 1468

Respectable Pleasure

During the Renaissance, Italy's urban food system became wealthier and more sophisticated. Famed as an era of intellectual endeavor and artistic creativity, but also of violence, political scheming, and brash displays of might and wealth, the Italian Renaissance was also in force in the country's kitchens and dining rooms.

The explosion of printed and visual artifacts during the Renaissance provides colorful and detailed documentation of the people and meals that created Italy's blossoming civilization of the table, so the picture of the food world of the elite is clearer, more vibrant—and more familiar. By the close of the sixteenth century, many more of the local specialties for which Italy is known today were in circulation. Moreover, the food network between the cities had produced a fabulous cuisine that was recognizably Italian.

During the Renaissance, moreover, Rome became the center of Italian gastronomy. And there is no more evocative introduction to Rome and its food Renaissance than a stunningly realized painting by Melozzo da Forlì that proclaims the triumph of a pope, a city, and of a conniving, unscrupulous, and clever man named Platina who was also the first and greatest cookery writer of the new era.

The Pope's Librarian

Six men—four of them standing, one seated, and one kneeling—are framed by square pilasters of ornately inlaid marble. Behind them, columns, arches, gilded entablatures, and ceilings inset with azure blue recede in symmetry toward two high windows. This careful geometry makes for a highly theatrical setting; and what the six men are acting out is the very moment when the Renaissance arrived in Rome.

The figure that catches the eye first is the one in the foreground farthest to the right. He sits on a tasseled throne and wears vestments consisting of a diaphanous white rochet and red skullcap: he is Francesco della Rovere, Pope Sixtus IV. His profile is marked by a sardonically arched eyebrow, a thin nose pointing sharply down, and a boxy jaw. Just behind him stand two more eminent churchmen in voluminous ecclesiastical outfits; both are tonsured with Pythagorean precision to a line only just above the tips of their ears. The opposite side of the fresco is occupied by a pair of laymen. Their power and wealth are clear from the heavy chains of office and the ermine lining of their gracefully waisted robes.

Oddly, none of these figures is looking at any of the others. Instead they gaze into some significant nowhere, betraying nothing but absolute self-possession. Their bearing, indeed the whole image, is grandiose beyond mere arrogance.

The sixth man in the ensemble affects a less haughty demeanor. Handsome and graying, with a slight harelip, he is shown kneeling before the pope. The blue-gray watered silk damask of his garment seems to spill out from the picture, close enough to invite our touch. His one visible hand emerges at the end of a long red sleeve; with it he points down at a Latin inscription extolling Sixtus's architectural achievements in Rome: churches, bridges, the Trevi fountain, and, above all, a restored Vatican library.

Through the brush of his official painter, Melozzo da Forlì, Pope Sixtus IV was making a bid for a place in the afterlife—but not of the kind prescribed in the Bible. His wish was to pass into posterity as a glorious patron of scholarship, the arts, and architecture. It is a wish that, we can now safely say, was granted. Before Sixtus was elected pope in

1471, Rome was little more than a cluster of villages where neglected ruins protruded from overgrown hillocks. A Spanish visitor noted that much of the space within the ancient walls was deserted: "There are parts which look like thick woods, and wild beasts, hares, foxes, deer and even . . . porcupines breed in caves." The city had long ago turned its back on its classical past: the Circus Maximus was a market garden. Not only that, but for most of the fourteenth century the papacy had been either resident abroad, in southern France, or contested between rival claimants, so even the most important churches had fallen into disrepair. Martin V's return in 1420 established the papacy in Rome once more. Sixtus, with his mania for lavish building, then began to work a transformation on the city's urban fabric: he paved the streets and built or rebuilt a long list of churches and monasteries. It was he who commissioned the Ponte Sisto—the first bridge across the Tiber constructed since ancient times. He created the Sistine Chapel and had it decorated with frescoes by Sandro Botticelli, Pinturicchio, Pietro Perugino, and Domenico Ghirlandaio. And as the inscription suggests, he was also particularly proud of the project that Melozzo's fresco commemorates: the renovation of the Vatican library.

But for all his efforts to create a prestigious legacy, Sixtus is also remembered for less noble reasons: corruption, ruthless political scheming, warmongering, decadent living, and, above all, nepotism. He bestowed the red hat of the cardinalate on no fewer than six of his relatives, and arranged lucrative positions, estates, and marriages for others. In fact the four big shots standing at the back of Melozzo's group portrait are all the pope's nephews.

The kindest thing generations of chroniclers have found to say about Sixtus's lifestyle is that he did not know the value of money because he had grown up as a Franciscan friar. His relatives were never reluctant to take advantage of this weakness and, naturally enough, dining was one of the most enjoyable ways of spending its fruits. The pope's favorite nephew (or, if some gossips are to be believed, his son) was Cardinal Pietro Riario. In June 1473, Riario gave a six-hour banquet for the daughter of the king of Naples that made the jaws of even world-weary observers slacken in amazement. The cardinal's guest was housed in a wooden palace erected before the Church of the Holy Apostles. This lavish temporary structure was painted to resemble stone and included a courtyard, fountains, a theater, and a vast banqueting hall furnished with tapestries, gold-embroidered carpets, gold brocade, silk, and mountains of silverware. The banquet was the centerpiece of the Neapolitan princess's stay in Rome: more than forty dishes were served including roast stags, herons, peacocks, and even a fully grown bear. Naturally, the menu was as much about show as about consumption: the bread was gilded. In Rome, as in the rest of Italy, the power and wealth that were increasingly concentrated in the hands of a few rulers were being displayed at table.

Magnificent and shameless: like the banquet, Melozzo's group portrait captures the splendor and scandal of Renaissance Rome under Sixtus IV. But it is also the best possible introduction to one of the most enigmatic figures in the history of Italian food. He has received less attention than the della Rovere pope and his nephews over the centuries, yet his story is quite as full of intrigue and scandal as theirs. The greying man with the harelip that Melozzo paints on his knees was the Vatican librarian, a teacher of the humanities—a humanist, as his type later would come to be called—universally known by the Latin name of Platina, which he had coined for himself. Humanists were scholars of classical literature and teachers of grammar, rhetoric, poetry, history, and moral philosophy. But among humanists Platina had a unique distinction: he was the author of the bestselling cookbook of the age. Indeed his *De honesta voluptate et valetudine—Respectable Pleasure and Good Health*—was the first cookbook ever reproduced using the revolutionary new technology of print. *Respectable Pleasure* ran though dozens of editions over the ensuing decades. It was Platina's book above all that would help make Italian food a model to imitate across Renaissance Europe.

Yet there is a sinister mystery at the center of Platina's life, a mystery to which *Respectable Pleasure* supplies most of the available clues. And in order to appreciate its full extent, we need understand how, several years after writing his little food guide, Platina came to be in Melozzo's fresco.

Kneeling or not, a civil servant such as Platina was not usually painted in such august company. Certainly, the librarian had several claims to fame beyond his cookbook and the astute way he managed Sixtus's self-glorifying investment in books. As a teacher he had shaped the minds of some of the most powerful dynasts in Italy. He also had completed the first properly researched history of the popes.

But more than these accomplishments, Platina owed his place in Melozzo's group portrait to the very idea of a "Renaissance." Like other humanists, he sought to convey an understanding and appreciation of the masterpieces handed down from ancient Greece and Rome. But when the humanists transmitted that knowledge it came in a package with a story that was as captivating as it was historically misleading. The ancients had achieved timeless greatness, so the fable went. After the fall of Rome there followed a "Dark" or "Middle" Age of ignorance and barbarism. But now, a millennium later, a miraculous new *rinascita*, or rebirth, was under way. By studying classical literature and following the moral examples it provided, modern men could make themselves as distinguished as the ancients. With artists, architects, and writers to immortalize their deeds, they could also project their reputations far into the future. The humanists, in other words, did more than anyone else to invent the *Rinascimento*, the Renaissance. And what they invented was both a story that men like Platina told about their own place in history, and a promise of greatness that they held out to patrons like Sixtus IV.

Platina's learning, and the idea of Renaissance, had turned a bright boy from a small town in Lombardy, a former mercenary soldier, into a man fit to be painted in the company of cardinals and popes. And it is Platina's finger that points down at the inscription he penned to honor the pope's remodeling of the Eternal City. Platina was the herald of Sixtus IV's immortality.

Platina's *Respectable Pleasure and Good Health* contains some advice that anyone served roast bear meat at one of Cardinal Riario's banquets would have found useful: it is not good for the spleen or liver, but can prevent hair loss. Yet Platina's book is *not* a guide to overindulgence for venal popes and cardinals. Instead, it belongs squarely within the Renaissance humanist agenda of moral rebirth through the study of the classics. In *Respectable Pleasure and Good Health*, Platina had a high ethical purpose: he was making an unprecedented attempt to unite the prestige of ancient learning and moral philosophy with the best of Italian gastronomy.

It is rare to read a historical cookbook that imprints so clear a picture of the author's personality on the mind as does *Respectable Pleasure and Good Health*. Unfortunately, the picture is not endearing: Platina was an intellectual snob prone to jealous sermonizing. (Being touchy and pushy were the professional vices of ambitious humanists like him.)

But there is more to discover in *Respectable Pleasure* than its author's personality. Platina probably finished the book during his summer holiday in 1465, which was fifteen years before he posed for Melozzo, ten years before he became Vatican librarian, and six before Francesco della Rovere was elected Sixtus IV. Much more significantly, it was also three years before the extraordinary events of February 1468, when Platina and the other members of an alleged pagan brotherhood devoted to idolatry, heresy, sexual depravity, and gluttony, were arrested for a plot to murder Sixtus's predecessor, Pope Paul II. Hence the mystery: Was Platina's "respectable" cookbook caught up in this dastardly conspiracy?

Platina, the greatest food writer of the 1400s, is immortalized
in paint by Melozzo da Forlì. Platina is the one shown kneeling
before Pope Sixtus IV and his nephews.

Master Martino's Blancmange

Platina was a professional scholar rather than a professional cook, and he was sensible enough not to pretend otherwise. Some 40 percent of *Respectable Pleasure and Good Health*—the recipes mostly—is actually a word-for-word translation into Latin of a cookbook written in the vernacular by one Martino de Rossi, a veteran chef.

An artisan like Master Martino would likely have been flattered rather than offended that a man of letters like Platina had cribbed his work. The two met in the summer of 1463 in Albano south of Rome, where Platina, an inveterate hanger-on, was a summer guest of Martino's employer—another high-living cardinal. The relaxed atmosphere and the wine of the Alban hills probably helped bridge the cultural gulf between the two and, as they chatted, the idea for *Respectable Pleasure* was planted in Platina's mind.

In Master Martino, Platina found a synthesis of what Italian cooking had become since the cities had begun their return to economic and political prominence in the eleventh century. Martino had served masters from Milan all the way down to Naples. So while Martino supplied all but a handful of the recipes in *Respectable Pleasure*, Platina provided the framework of scientific, medical, historical, literary, and moral knowledge to set them in.

Many of the aspects of medieval Italian eating that we have already encountered are to be found in Master Martino, and thus in *Respectable Pleasure*. There is a similar interest in fruit, vegetables, and freshwater fish; similar pies, porridges, and *ravioli*; similar sauces and, of course, the same spices. Because of its debt to Master Martino, *Respectable Pleasure* contains some marvelous broths, soups, roasts, stews, and egg dishes, making it is the most comprehensive guide for anyone with the patience to *re-create* the flavors of the Middle Ages, rather than write their history.

But the specifically culinary aspects of *Respectable Pleasure*—Master Martino's recipes, that is—need not be covered in any great depth here. Platina himself explains why, in the course of his discussion of blancmange. The *biancomangiare* ("white eating") described in *Respectable Pleasure* is similar to the one that appears in *Book for Cook* a century earlier: peeled almonds and the boned breast of a capon (i.e., a rooster castrated so it fattens) are pounded to a pulp, then cooked in spices and sugar. Often poured over meat, blancmange like this was highly prized across late medieval Europe—Chaucer also mentions it. To achieve the right degree of whiteness, it was prepared with particular attention to cleanliness, sometimes in a separate corner of the kitchen.

Little is original about Master Martino's blancmange, yet Platina is so taken with this dish that, after giving the recipe, he pauses for a highly significant reflection:

> There is no reason why we should prefer our ancestors' tastes to our own. Even if they surpassed us in nearly all the arts, in taste alone we are undefeated.

In other words, the cooking of the Italian cities now outstripped that of ancient Rome. Coming from a humanist, this was the highest praise possible. Italian civilization generally might have been going through a Renaissance, but if blancmange was anything to go by, its civilization of the table was in no need of such an overhaul. In celebratory mood, Platina then took the opportunity to give Master Martino a hearty pat on the back: "O immortal gods! What a cook you gave us in my friend Martino of Como!"

So even though *Respectable Pleasure* is the first Renaissance cookbook, it does not contain any Renaissance recipes. Strictly speaking, in fact, there was never any such thing. Broadly the same range of tastes that made medieval diners salivate continued to have the same effect during the epoch that took its name from the humanists' self-interested agenda of cultural rebirth. Cooking does not necessarily follow the same chronology as other fields of creative endeavor. People did not start eating with more perspective in the Renaissance. Nor, for that matter, did they dine more ornamentally in the Baroque period, or more rationally during the Enlightenment. Nevertheless, before returning to the subject of Platina, there are a couple of aspects of Martino's cookery that were distinctive Italian preferences, and therefore deserve some attention: sugar and pasta.

The enthusiasm for sugar evident in *Book for Cook* is even stronger in

Master Martino: Platina tells us that there is virtually nothing that sugar will not improve. In fact Martino was one of the first to use sugar to make deliberately sweet dishes, such as fritters, rather than simply as a universal seasoning in a similar way to salt. The rest of Europe would soon follow the Italian lead by consuming more sugar, and in a greater variety of ways.

Master Martino is also important in that he gives us some of the earliest instructions on how to make what he terms "Sicilian *maccheroni.*" A dough made from flour, egg white, rose water, and plain water is rolled round an iron rod to create the now-famous tubes. "When they are dried in the sun, they will last two or three years," he explains. *Vermicelli* are made by rolling the same dough into small bits with the fingers.

Martino's serving suggestions for these early forms of *pasta secca* are typical of the age: *maccheroni* and *vermicelli* can be cooked in broth, milk, or almond milk, and are served sprinkled with cheese, sugar, and spices. Also typical of Martino's age, but alarming to ours, are the recommended cooking times: an hour for *vermicelli*, and two hours for *maccheroni*. Martino's dough, with its egg white, probably required longer boiling than the variety with which the world is familiar today. Yet it is clear that Platina's contemporaries liked a very soft consistency to their pasta. The notion of *al dente* was still a long way in the future.

Peacock and Roast Goat

The most obvious thing a Renaissance reader would have learned from *Respectable Pleasure and Good Health* is how to show off his affinity with the classics even while he was tucking into peacock and bear. Platina invokes a range of sources that is intended to impress: from Aristotle to Xenophon, by way of Cicero, Homer, Livy, Ovid, Varro, and Virgil. Pliny the Elder was cited frequently, including on the nutritional properties of bear. From him we also learn that the ancient orator Hortensius was the first man to cook peacocks for a priestly meal. Nothing similar to *Respectable Pleasure* exists today, but the nearest contemporary equivalent would be a bluffers' guide to dropping learned allusions over dinner.

Some pages of *Respectable Pleasure* form a sober contrast to the subsequent lurid goings-on in Sixtus's Rome. The pope's nephews would have choked on Platina's moralizing. The peacock, he warns us angrily, is a "vainglorious" bird eaten for vainglorious reasons by wealthy people who have forgotten that "mere luck and other people's stupidity" are the only reason they are not filling their bellies "in cheap taverns and bordellos" with the rest of the lowlifes.

As his book's full title suggests, Platina was also very interested in the science of good health: early in the book he summarizes Galenic theory on the humors, and he takes great care to comment on how each of a long list of foodstuffs affects the metabolism. Melons, for example, should be eaten with circumspection; they have a chilling and wetting effect on the humors for which wine is a good antidote. Peacocks incur Platina's displeasure for similar scientific reasons: they are indigestible and increase melancholy.

But Platina's main point with peacocks, as throughout *Respectable Pleasure*, is nonetheless an ethical one. Appetite, like any other desire, needs monitoring and controlling through moral education. The issue of how and where to strike a balance between pleasure and self-restraint was a topic of burning debate at the time. Pleasure itself was often considered inherently dangerous. In fact, to many of Platina's contemporaries, *respectable pleasure* was a contradiction in terms. Thus his recipe book had to strike a delicate balance between morality, science, and hedonism.

Platina's bitterness and envy often made that balance extremely precarious. His job as Vatican librarian would later give him a hefty ten ducats a month salary, some servants, a horse, and free food in the dining rooms reserved for the pope's most senior staff. But when he wrote *Respectable Pleasure* he had recently lost his post in the papal civil service—a post he had paid a large sum up front to secure. So despite his moralizing, Platina's anger frequently won out. As did his evident fascination with the high life. Having warned us sternly of how morally and medically dangerous the peacock is, he copies Master Martino's recipe for peacock roasted and served in exactly the way it would be at Cardinal Pietro Riario's banquet—so it still seemed to be alive.

The trick is to kill the bird by slitting its throat, and then to make a shallow incision running right down to the tail. Peel away the skin and feathers in one piece, cutting the legs and head off to keep them all together. The carcass can then be stuffed with herbs and spices, studded with cloves, and put on a spit. The neck should be wrapped in linen, which has to be dampened continually during roasting to prevent the meat drying out. Once cooked, the peacock is reclothed in its own skin and plumage, reunited with its head and legs, and attached to a serving board with concealed nails and wire. Platina goes on to offer a couple of even more outré presentational tips: try dusting the bird with spices and then gilding it, he suggests; or stuff camphor-soaked wool into the beak and set fire to it as you approach the dinner table. Anyone today who wanted to impress his or her dinner guests with this dish would be well advised to practice with a broiler chicken first.

Platina's double standards are there for all to see. He wants to abhor his peacock *and* eat it. He finds it hard to distinguish between morality and a meal ticket. And there are other hypocrisies elsewhere in his writings, as in *De amore*, a treatise on love written during the same summer holiday in 1465 that he spent finishing *Respectable Pleasure*. In *De amore* Platina makes a stolid defense of married love against the temptations of lust. So stolid, in fact, that it prompted one of his friends to write a mocking poem in response that accused him of being a fan of "all-night fellatio" and "vigorous copulation" with "strumpets." Platina, the poem concluded, was as good at writing as he was bad at making love. Even in later life, he was said to have hitched up with a "filthy and monstrously ugly girl." Evidently Platina liked a bit of rough trade.

On sex, as on peacocks, Platina writes like a man with something to hide. In *Respectable Pleasure* he displays an obsession with aphrodisiac foods. He writes of dozens of ingredients and dishes that stir the libido: from pine nuts to partridge, from chickpeas to "Golden Balls" (what we would call French toast). Broad beans stimulate lust because they look like testicles. Onions taken in small doses "arouse sexual appetite, and increase its nourishment with lustful dampness." Oysters are "valuable to the libidinous because they arouse even deadened passion." It is not at all clear whether Platina considers these aphrodisiac qualities dangerous, or useful, or both.

While most of Platina's books were written to impress wealthy and powerful patrons, *Respectable Pleasure and Good Health* was also for his friends. It is full of deadpan jibes and mock-serious praise for the other members of his circle—all of them with Latin names to match his own. For example, the recipe for "Turnip in armour" involves frying slices of boiled turnip and fresh, fatty cheese. With a frankness that some of today's cookery writers could learn from, he describes the dish as "very harmful" and only fit for his greedy pal Domitianus. Another friend, Pomponius, is set up as a paragon of self-restraint for serving only garlic, onions, and shallots at his dinner parties. Callimachus is advised not to eat roast garlic goat because it is bad for the eyesight and good for the libido. The recipe is at least more tempting than that for "Turnip in armour": stud a whole kid with lard and cloves of garlic; then roast it on a spit while basting it in a sauce of crushed garlic, beaten egg yolk, fatty broth, saffron, pepper, and the inevitable verjuice.

Platina and his friends were all members of what he called "the academy." Its figurehead was a charismatic university professor known as Pomponius—the one who apparently served only garlic and onions to his guests. Callimachus, the one advised not to overstimulate his libido with roast goat, was one of the academy's most intelligent and energetic members. Passionate to the point of eccentricity about Latin literature and Roman antiquities, the group would discuss classical authors, comment on one another's Latin compositions, and roam the woods and fields of Rome to visit ruins and dream of their former greatness. They even took to wearing togas and holding uproarious Roman-style dining and drinking parties.

Respectable Pleasure comes straight out of the strange milieu of the Roman academy. It leaves you with the impression of being an outsider at a conversation between old friends: you can sense the air of jollity, but the in-jokes elude you. In short, it all feels a little *conspiratorial*. Which may not be a coincidence, because Platina, Pomponius, and Callimachus were precisely the men charged soon afterward with conspiring to kill Pope Paul II.

The Conspiracy of 1468

Platina's own account of events in the last days of February 1468 is evocative and dramatic. There was a joyful atmosphere in Rome as the Carnival was coming to a close. There had been races run between Domitian's Arch and St. Mark's Church—horses, asses, buffaloes, and men of all ages had taken part, much to the crowd's amusement. There was even a special race for Jews, who had mud and stones thrown at them as they passed. Pope Paul was fresh from presenting money to the winners when he was told that an informer had leaked news of a plot: His Holiness was to be murdered on March 2, the first day of Lent. The plot's ringleader was Callimachus, but other members of the academy, including Platina, were involved. A known revolutionary exile had reportedly been spotted in the countryside south of Rome with an army of bandits ready to storm the papal palace.

The pope, fully aware of Rome's recent history of plotting and revolt, was terrified. The conspirators were picked up one after the other. Papal guards surrounded Platina's house at night and broke down the windows and doors. They found only his servant, who tremblingly informed them that Platina was at dinner with a former pupil, Cardinal Francesco Gonzaga of Mantua. The author of *Respectable Pleasure* was found, dragged from the table, and taken straight into the presence of His Holiness.

It was the beginning of a year of imprisonment, interrogation, and torture for Platina. At one point, he wrote later, "I was seized with such extreme pain, that I would rather have died than endure all the aches of my shaken and battered limbs." From prison he wrote that he was in danger of losing his right arm to the rack. His friends faced a similar ordeal; one young member of the group died of his injuries. Pomponius, the academy's leader, was also thrown into the Castel Sant'Angelo after being extradited from Venice, where he was already under arrest on charges of sodomy. Among the few to escape was Callimachus, the supposed ringleader.

The accusations against the academy members went far beyond conspiracy to overthrow papal rule. Callimachus was alleged to be an astrologer who had made inflammatory predictions of political strife. All the others were said to be deniers of God, Christ, and the Church. They were, it was charged, idolators who worshipped the Roman gods and had changed their baptismal names to pagan ones; Epicureans who were devoted only to pleasure; gluttons who regularly ate meat during

Lent; and sexual degenerates who indulged their carnal appetites with men and women alike.

Suddenly *Respectable Pleasure* became a very compromising piece of evidence. Here was a supposedly moral book about eating that invoked the "immortal gods" far more often than it did Christ, that fervently denounced the eating habits of the Church hierarchy, and gave plentiful advice on aphrodisiacs. It did not offer a very favorable impression of humanism.

Humanists such as Platina had executed a subtle shift in moral thinking in Italy's cities. They played down the importance of sin, and instead offered worldly guides to appropriate behavior based on classical examples that implicitly flattered the powerful. In the harsh light of the 1468 conspiracy, *Respectable Pleasure* seemed to have turned that subtle shift into a dangerous fracture. Had humanist ethics tipped over into heresy and revolt? Friends of Platina's who were lucky enough to escape arrest hurriedly scratched many names, including Callimachus's, from a manuscript copy. They probably destroyed others, including Platina's original. (The first printed versions of *Respectable Pleasure* would only appear in 1470.)

Under interrogation, Pomponius admitted some of the minor sins he was accused of having committed: he sometimes ate meat on lean days for health reasons, and had made the occasional outburst against priests. But he and Platina hotly denied all the other charges. Both prisoners tried to shift the blame onto Callimachus, who was now in Cyprus, out of the range of the pope's emissaries. They said he was a drunken troublemaker who had raved repeatedly about Pope Paul's early demise and the end of Church rule in Rome. They had had no idea that anyone would take him seriously!

Whether it was this scapegoating defense that eventually secured their release, or merely the influence of friends among the senior clergy, is not clear. In fact a great deal about the conspiracy of 1468 remains obscure to this day. It is not even known whether Platina and his friends were thrown into a dank dungeon or put up in a swanky apartment—the round walls of the Castel Sant'Angelo contained both. Some historians suggest there was never a conspiracy at all to murder Paul II. The academy's love of all things Roman had simply got out of hand. The pope, who had always been alarmed by the sexual immorality of many classical poets, just wanted to give Pomponius and his group a bit of a fright. The toga parties had to stop.

Others maintain that the conspiracy was far, far more serious. Callimachus was in league with powerful supporters of none other than the Sultan of Turkey, Mohammed II, who saw himself as the heir of the Roman emperors. Mohammed's armies conquered Christianity's other capital, Constantinople, in 1453, and he had now advanced into the Balkans. Only the Adriatic Sea and the chronically divided forces of the Italian states stood in the way of Muslim rule in Italy—and a Roman empire united once more under the Turk.

Pope Paul II died in 1471. His successor, Sixtus IV, quickly took Platina and the other members of the academy to his bosom, and soon gave them jobs within the Church establishment.

If there had been something shifty about Platina even before the conspiracy of 1468, later on, with the shadow of his time in the Castel Sant'Angelo hanging over his reputation, he became positively devious. He took every opportunity to restate the case for his defense in writing, and began by denouncing his friends in the academy for their lax morals. But in later works he portrayed them as austere scholars unjustly persecuted by a pope who loathed learning. Platina brings his *Lives of the Popes* to a conclusion with a chapter on his persecutor, Paul II. He spends most of it telling the story of the 1468 conspiracy, protesting his own innocence, and besmirching the dead pope's reputation. The author of the first cookbook of the Renaissance writes with vengeful glee about the eating habits of the man who had accused him of gluttony:

> Paul II loved to have a great variety of dishes at his table, and generally ate of the worst; but he would be vociferous if what he liked were not provided. He loved melons, crabs, sweetmeats, fish, and bacon. This odd kind of diet, I believe, caused the apoplexy of which he died; for the day before his death he had eaten two very large melons.

Delizia!

If only Paul II had paid more attention to the warnings in *Respectable Pleasure and Good Health*.

Platina was at the very apex of his career when, in 1480, he was painted with his tortured right arm pointing down at the inscription on Melozzo da Forlì's famous portrait of Sixtus and his nephews. But recent studies have revealed that he was not originally included in the picture: he was painted in over the image of the man who was Vatican librarian before him. Platina also ensured that Melozzo made him look handsome. It was not the only occasion on which he tampered with the historical record. Just how far the members of the Roman academy went in their paganism, debauchery, and gluttony remains a topic for speculation: the shifty pages of *Respectable Pleasure* are the best evidence available. No one will ever know the real extent of the conspiracy of 1468 because almost all of the prosecution documents went missing from the Vatican library—probably in the late 1470s. Probably, that is, when Platina was Vatican librarian.

6

$\mathcal{F}$errara, 1529

A Dynasty at Table

Cauldron and Trowel

During the Renaissance, banqueting joined the arts. Food was combined with theater, music, dance, painting, sculpture, and architecture to indulge all the senses. Florence and its hyperconcentration of artistic talent provide a picture of the way other forms of creativity converged on the dining table.

In the early 1500s Florence produced the era's most imaginative meals. A group of artists who called themselves the Company of the Cauldron held regular gala dinners to celebrate their prowess. Their host was the sculptor Giovan Francesco Rustici. Each member would bring an extravagantly contrived dish to the evening event. On one memorable occasion, Rustici invited the company to dine inside a giant cooking pot made from a wine vat. His contribution to the display of dishes was an ensemble comprising a pastry cauldron and two statues beautifully molded from boiled capons: they represented Ulysses dipping his father into a magic cauldron to rejuvenate him. On the same evening, Andrea del Sarto unveiled a temple that was octagonal, like the Baptistery of S. Giovanni; its eight columns seemed to be made of porphyry but were in fact large sausages topped with sculpted Parmesan capitals and sugar cornices. At the center of the temple's elaborate mosaic floor, made from gelatin, a choir of cooked thrushes dressed in ham cassocks sang from a book made of *lasagne* that was supported by a lectern of cold veal.

Rustici also belonged to another dining club, the Company of the Trowel. Its members were instructed to come to one meeting dressed as workmen. When they arrived, they were shown plans for a building and invited to use their trowels to construct it. But instead of mortar, they were given sugared ricotta, and other cheese mixed with spices and pepper. The bricks, blocks, and tiles were loaves of bread and sheets of *stiacciata*—a kind of sweet *focaccia*. As they were at work, the servants brought a pedestal full of pies and pieces of fried liver, and a column filled with boiled capons and veal. The Company of the Trowel held another of its dinners in Hell—an eerily lit room painted with images of souls in torment. As terrifying screams rent the air, a servant dressed as a demon served the dishes, which were choice meats done up to look like snakes, toads, spiders, and bats.

Giovan Francesco Rustici was an amiable eccentric with a pet porcupine; he was from a noble family, and therefore free to spend more energy on teaching his raven to talk than on taming his creative instincts to conform to the whim of wealthy patrons. The dinners he hosted and attended with the Company of the Cauldron and the Company of the Trowel were inspired by that same ethos of unfettered creativity. But great feasts have always been about power rather than art, as other artists without Rustici's independent wealth had to recognize—for example his friend Leonardo da Vinci who, in Milan in 1489, was enlisted to design sets for the wedding banquet of Gian Galeazzo Sforza and Isabella of Aragon. Such dinners were as political as the marriages they celebrated. A banquet at court was a chance for a ruler to show off his opulence, bounty, grace, majesty, and sense of occasion—his *magnificence*, to use a favorite word of the age.

For that reason, the nights of oddball overindulgence in Florence with Giovan Francesco Rustici and the Company of the Cauldron do not take us to the heart of the Renaissance banqueting experience. Far more significant, because far more *magnificent*, was a banquet that took place on January 24, 1529, in Ferrara, a city that lies north across the Apennines from Florence, amid the wetlands of the Po delta.

The Steward

Ferrara was both fortress and garden. Half of it was tight medieval lanes, half princely avenues and parks. At its center stood one of the most imposing castles anywhere in Europe. Much of Ferrara is still beautifully preserved, and there is no city in Italy whose very walls tell the story of Renaissance despotism, in all its magnificence and shame, in the way that Ferrara does.

As well as being one of the great Renaissance feasts set in one of the great Renaissance cities, the Ferrarese banquet of January 24, 1529, is one of the most minutely documented evenings' entertainment of its time. Fortunately for historians of Italian food, every recipe for every dish was proudly written down. We owe that record to an exceptional creative mind, and one far more important to the art of living at a Renaissance court than that of any painter or sculptor—Cristoforo da Messisbugo, the court administrator and steward to the Dukes of Ferrara.

In 1529 Messisbugo was in the prime of life, at the height of his calling, and confident in the Duke of Ferrara's personal favor. He was from

Cristoforo da Messisbugo, the steward behind one of the most
overindulgent dinners of the Renaissance. The image is taken
from his masterly guide to *Banquets*.

the minor nobility, and with other dignitaries from the Ferrarese court he accompanied the duke on many diplomatic missions. The only existing picture of Messisbugo, an engraving made late in life, shows a strong profile, hollow cheeks, and short hair. Beneath his luxuriant beard, the heavy chain that proclaimed his status at court is clearly visible. Yet at the same time that he moved in elevated circles, surviving records show that Messisbugo kept an almost obsessive eye on even the humblest daily provisions to court, such as chestnuts, candles, and straw. He paid out stipends to the host of servants, officials, and family members gravitating around his duke, all of whom he knew by name: from the footmen, falconers, and musicians, to the baboon and leopard handlers; from the architects, armorers, and upholsterers, to the nuns, dowagers, and bastard sons.

At a Renaissance court there was no separation between the private life of the ruler and the public life of the city. So, no modern job description could ever cover all of Messisbugo's responsibilities at court, his strange mix of menial domestic duties and grand affairs of state. As well as his diplomatic role, he was part quartermaster, part minister of welfare, part majordomo and, of course, part head chef. Grand court dinners offered the chance for a steward, as well as his master, to put all his capabilities on show. Hence when, just before his death in 1548, Messisbugo wrote a book that summarized all the expertise he had accumulated in three and a half decades of service, he called it *Banquets*.

The menu Messisbugo created for the banquet held on January 24, 1529, was a catalogue of dazzling and even disconcerting excess. Yet however fine the ingredients of that famous meal, and however inventively they were blended, the menu in isolation can now make them seem as indistinct as gruel. The problem is not just the obvious one: the tastes, smells, and sights that are lost when food is transferred from table to paper, from reality to history. It is also that Messisbugo's meal was given its real savor by a mix of power and spectacle. To reimagine that mixture we need to combine the menu in *Banquets* with a family portrait of the House of Este, Ferrara's rulers since the thirteenth century when they emerged triumphant from the factional struggles within the commune and established their lordship.

On January 24, 1529, the Duke of Ferrara, Alfonso I, celebrated a crucial rite of passage for his dynasty. To mark it fittingly, Messisbugo's banquet became an idealized picture of court life, a tableau as imposing as Ferrara's fortress, and as uncompromisingly splendid as the parade of dishes. Yet this was a time when the strength of the Italian cities was beginning to fade once more, a time of terrifying instability as well as of sumptuous creativity. So behind the monumental façade Messisbugo created in food lay all the talents, eccentricities, and dark secrets of dynasty, and all the contradictions of an age.

Theater

The festivities for the wedding of Ercole d'Este, heir to the dukedom of Ferrara, and Renée, daughter of Louis XII of France, were unusually protracted even by the standards of the time. The young couple were married in Paris in June 1528. But their departure for Ferrara was delayed—both by an outbreak of plague in northern Italy, and because the king of France tried to keep back some of the dowry as a "loan" to fund his army. So it was only three months later that the newlyweds, with a procession of five hundred rejoicing retainers, set off for home. In November they stopped in Modena to reconfirm their marriage vows in grand style, even though the devastation caused by the recent plague had drawn thousands of destitute peasants into the city. Huge price hikes in basic foodstuffs were causing widespread misery. One witness said that, although the authorities had distributed alms, the poor could be heard in the streets crying "I am dying of hunger," "I am dying of cold"; every day bodies were removed from under the porticoes.

There were ten days of lavish festivities for the young couple in Modena, so December had arrived by the time they reached Ferrara. The citizens were ordered to shed the mourning clothes they had put on for loved ones lost during the plague, and the city streets were decked in red, white, and green—the Este colors. Cannons fired an earthshaking salute, and a triumphal parade was led by a Spanish clown called Diego mounted on a camel, followed by flag-waving children dressed in white, and all the clergy and nobility in their finery. It was the beginning of eight more weeks of celebrations, many of which took place in the *delizie* that were scattered across the Ferrarese countryside. A *delizia* (delight) was a rural place of pleasure, a riverside castle or a villa in a park; here urban courtly life could be luxuriously staged in a setting that was at once Edenic and grandiose.

But it was in the city of Ferrara that the theatrical dimension of Este power was made most manifest. A generation before the banquet, the duke's father, a man with a passion for architecture and theater alike, had refashioned the city. With new loggias, piazzas, and halls the dynasty could display itself to both courtiers and populace. Some of these spaces also served as theaters in a literal sense: in 1487, classical comedies were performed for the first time in the palace courtyard, and new plays were soon being written to capitalize on the success of the experiment. Renaissance Ferrara was where modern, secular European theater was born.

The old duke also extended the mighty city walls to enclose a vast new quarter, primarily for military reasons. To ensure the allegiance of leading courtiers and merchants, he gave permission for this "Herculean Addition" to the city to be occupied by pleasure palaces and gardens. To ensure the allegiance of God, he ordered churches and monasteries to be added, too. With its long, straight roads affording uninterrupted lines of sight, the Herculean Addition was also intended to accommodate grand processions—such as the one marking Ercole and Renée's return from their wedding. But it looked as if the new quarter had been modeled on the optical trickery of a theatrical set. It seemed that, at any moment, at any point in the city, characters from a play by Plautus or Terence might emerge from a doorway or arcade.

The celebrations for the wedding of Ercole d'Este and Renée finally came to an end only at Carnival time, when, as a gesture of thanks to his father, Duke Alfonso, Ercole ordered the faithful Messisbugo to prepare a banquet. Fittingly, a painted city backdrop was set in place in the great hall so that the evening could begin with a play. (Messisbugo was also a theatrical and musical impresario.)

La Cassaria (*The Strongbox*) told the tale of wily servants outfoxing a Turkish pimp on behalf of their wealthy but lovelorn young masters. Although the Company of the Trowel had had *The Strongbox* performed at one of their dinners in Florence, the play suited this Ferrarese occasion even better. For one thing, it contained enough gentle gags about life in Ferrara to amuse the ignorant; for another, it had enough tasteful borrowing from Latin comedies to flatter the cultivated. More important, as far as the politics of the evening's proceedings were concerned, *The Strongbox's* writer and director was Ferrara's own Ludovico Ariosto, the outstanding poet of the age, and thus living testimony to the greatness of Este patronage.

Ariosto was an able courtier, but never an enthusiastic one. He knew and obeyed the reigning ethos of patronage. But he had grown to resent the time he had to spend away from his writing desk, as a diplomat and flunky in the service of the House of Este. Retirement had come as a blessing, allowing him to devote his days to revising *Orlando Furioso* (*Orlando Goes Insane*), the epic poem that had already made him famous. For the banquet of January 1529, he was asked to find a place in the cast of *The Strongbox* for the Most Illustrious Don Francesco, the Duke of Ferrara's youngest son. This spoiled little thespian, only twelve at the time, would grow up to be an impulsively violent character: on one occasion he tore out a functionary's beard with his own hands. He had inherited his temper from his father: Duke Alfonso had once ordered his men to crush the eyes and trample the face of a notary who had displeased him. At a Renaissance court, the threat of capricious violence was rarely absent.

Messisbugo's original plan was to perform a play by Plautus translated into French before the banquet, but, for unknown reasons, there was a last-minute cancellation, and Ariosto was summoned urgently from his retirement home to stage *The Strongbox*. He needed no reminding of whose creature he was.

No sooner had the plot of *The Strongbox* been brought to a happy unraveling by one particularly wily servant than an army of real servants arrived to prepare the hall for the main theatrical event of the evening: the banquet.

Hercules and the Lion

While the 104 guests, "gentlemen and gentle ladies from Ferrara and elsewhere," were entertained by musicians in other rooms, Messisbugo's team covered the great table, nearly one hundred feet long, with three giant tablecloths, one on top of another. Alongside it, they set up five service tables, three for the food and two for the wine. Well drilled, they then suspended forty-eight double candlesticks from the ceiling by wire. For each place setting there was a knife, an ingeniously folded napkin, a soft milk and sugar roll, a *bracciatella* (something like the modern ring-shaped *ciambella* biscuit), a gilded pistachio-based sweetmeat, and some *savonea* (a sticky mixture of starch, sugar, and rose water). The decoration was relatively restrained. Each guest would have some perfumed silk and gold-leaf flowers before them. Running along the center of the table was a series of twenty-five sugar statues, each about two feet high and painted in skin tones; they represented the struggle between Hercules and the Nemean lion, an obvious tribute to young Ercole d'Este. The abundance of costly sugar also displayed the wealth the young man stood to inherit.

The starter course was summoned up from the kitchen and, once everything was in place, trumpets sounded to call the court to table.

STARTERS

104 small pies with a filling of capers,
truffles, and raisin puree

Salad of endive, radish, rampion, and
lemon. 104 small plates.
> *Salads were a popular way to begin meals in Renaissance Italy.*
> *They were thought to open the stomach and whet the appetite.*

104 small plates of anchovy salad

25 large radishes carved into various
figures and animals, with 104 small radishes. 25 small plates.

104 small cream pies dusted with sugar

25 plates of sliced ham, salted beef tongue,

and salt pork loin—all fried and dusted with
sugar and cinnamon

25 pies containing wild boar rissoles
> As well as the rissoles, Messisbugo's recipe for the pie filling
> includes chopped ham, raisins, pepper, orange juice or verjuice,
> and some beef fat.

25 large pork liver sausages in a pastry case
> Orange juice or verjuice and a little beef fat were added to the
> sausage as it was sealed in the pastry before cooking.

50 large, skinned, smoked grey mullet in
25 pies with sweet sauce

15 large salted eels, in 104 cylindrical
cuts. 25 plates.
> Eels were the king of Italian fish in the Middle Ages and
> Renaissance. They could be kept alive for a long time in fresh-
> water reservoirs in the cities, and responded well to salting and
> smoking.

104 soused sea bream, partly gilded, garnished
with laurel leaves. 25 plates.
> Messisbugo's sousing method is essentially the same as the alla
> scapece technique encountered above in the Venice chapter. He
> mixes pepper, cinnamon, ginger, cloves, salt, and saffron into
> his vinegar.

Out in the great hall, the places of honor at the main table were
taken by the groom, Ercole d'Este, and his younger brother Ippolito—
two typical scions of a Renaissance dynasty. Ercole had been given the
best humanist education available, and was as skilled in music as he
was refined in speech and manners. Like all Italian princes, he was well
taught in the arts of war—jousting, swordsmanship, and riding. There
was every prospect that, like his father, he would command a high
price in cash, glory, and political leverage for his soldiering. His brother

Ippolito was not yet twenty, yet he had already been the Most Reverend Archbishop of Milan for nearly a decade. Like many second sons, Ippolito's career in the Church was intended to solidify his dynasty's political position and its moral authority. If he could rise further and become a cardinal, then his rank would equal that of a secular prince.

Foreign ambassadors flanked the two oldest Este brothers. The emissary of his Most Christian King, Francis I of France, was there to be assured that the bride was being treated in a style that befitted her status. The ambassadors from Ferrara's old enemy, the Most Serene Venetian Senate, had to be sent a clear message about Este magnificence. The experienced gaze of these foreign envoys would calculate the price and style of the spectacle, and from their calculations make a diagnosis of the dynasty's strength: showing power and wielding it were one and the same.

FIRST COURSE

Boned capon coated in blancmange,
fried, then covered with fine sugar.
25 plates.

> *Capon and other fowl, especially wild birds, were the favorite meats of the era. Beef and veal, though catching up, were still behind them in prestige.*

104 quails. 104 *tomaselle*. 104 roasted capon
livers in caul. With accompaniments.
25 plates.

> Tomaselle *were liver rissoles made with raisins, sugar, bone marrow, spices, and hard cheese, then wrapped in caul or omentum—a double folded fatty membrane from an animal's lower abdomen that was often used as sausage skin.*

52 roast pheasant with 100 oranges in segments.
25 plates.

Onion *carabaccia*. 25 plates.

> *To make* carabaccia, *onions were boiled with ham in water,*

and then in milk with verjuice and a lump of hard cheese. The cheese was then removed and fresh beef drippings and egg yolks added before a final half hour of cooking. Served with a liberal sprinkling of sugar and a dusting of cinnamon.

25 sweet pine nut pastries. 25 plates.

25 sweet pastry tarts deep-filled with the spleens of sea bass, trout, pike, and other fish.

The fish spleens were cooked in broth and orange juice with raisins, egg yolks, sugar, cinnamon, ginger, cloves, saffron, pepper, and sugar. Caul was stretched over this rich filling to create a cross between a tart and a pie.

25 trout tails, fried and soused, with sliced lemon. 25 plates.

200 fried red mullet. 25 plates.

125 pieces of eel in marzipan. 25 plates.

Cutlets of 50 sea bream in broth. 25 plates.

The court musicians struck up during the first course. Five voices sang to the music of five violas, a double harpsichord, a lute, and two flutes. With every different selection of dishes thereafter, madrigals, choruses, and musical dialogues were intoned to the sound of a new combination of instruments.

Duke Alfonso

Duke Alfonso d'Este was his oldest son's guest of honor at Messisbugo's rolling spectacle. Although able and ruthless in matters of politics and war, Alfonso was a comparatively reluctant practitioner of the other branch of Renaissance statecraft: patronage of the arts. Granted, he employed painters of the stature of Giovanni Bellini, Raphael, and Titian to adorn his private rooms, but he took greater pleasure in practical jokes and practical skills. Older courtiers remembered the day during his father's reign when he had paraded round the city naked at noon. And Alfonso's real love was artillery: he supervised the casting of the guns himself, and gave them macho nicknames such as "Earthquake" and "Great Devil." Back in 1509, his batteries had pulled off the remarkable exploit of sinking the Venetian fleet from the banks of the Po. The most famous portrait of the duke dates from around the time of the great banquet of January 1529; it shows a fiercely bearded man standing in lustrous black armor beside a cannon. With a sword at his left hip and a mace in his right fist, he looks as if he is about to turn around and charge off into the battle shown raging in the middle distance.

Duke Alfonso carried a heavy burden of government. His city's strategic position was almost uniquely delicate. From Ferrara, sited astride the Po, he claimed to rule a saddle-shaped territory. To the southwest, Este dominion extended down to Modena and Reggio. To the southeast,

The guest of honor at Messisbugo's banquet: Duke Alfonso d'Este of Ferrara in a portrait by Dosso Dossi. His right hand rests on one of his beloved cannons.

it stretched across the marshes, streams, canals, and carefully drained fields of the Po delta. Officially, Ferrara itself was the feudal territory of the pope—Duke Alfonso therefore held his capital on authority rented from Rome. The cities of Modena and Reggio, by contrast, were on loan from the pope's rival, the Germany-based Holy Roman Emperor. Both pontiff and emperor were constantly trying to claw back territory handed over to the Estes in earlier agreements. To complicate matters further, Ferrara's northeastern neighbor, Venice, took every chance Fortune offered to take the upper hand over its rival for control of the Po delta. Even in the best of times, the House of Este needed political cunning and military prowess to remain in power. But these were not the best of times.

Messisbugo's dishes were steadily increasing in sophistication.

SECOND COURSE

50 roast francolins. 50 roast rock partridge. 104 meatloaf. 25 plates.

25 fried large white sausages. 104 fried sweetbreads, sprinkled with sugar and cinnamon. 25 plates.

> Cervellati (white sausages) contained a stuffing of milk, egg whites, fatty cheese, starch, sugar, raisins, cinnamon, and pepper. They were boiled and then fried in fat.

25 German-style capons in sweet wine with mace. 25 plates.

> The capon was cooked with small pieces of ham, a sweet wine, whole peppercorns, and raisins. The sauce to pour over it in the last stage of cooking was made from toasted bread crumbs that were soaked in vinegar, sieved, and then mixed with sugar, ground pepper, cinnamon, ginger, cloves, and a little saffron for color.

257 large pigeons in puff pastry. 25 plates.

104 fried Lake Garda trout, sprinkled
with sesame seeds

25 plates of turbot cutlets cooked under
a shallow pan covered with embers

Lobster tails and claws fried and sprinkled with vinegar. 25 plates.

25 trout roe pies

Yellow Neapolitan-style blancmange. 25
plates.

> *This version of blancmange contained the usual pounded
> mixture of almonds, boiled capon breast, and sugar. Once it
> reached a smooth consistency, egg yolks, a little rice flour, cin-
> namon, ginger, and enough saffron to give it color were added.
> It was then tempered with meat or capon broth and cooked
> with verjuice. More sugar and cinnamon were added on top
> for serving.*

104 German-style pastries sprinkled with
rose water. 25 plates.

> *The filling of these pastries comprised a marzipan of both
> almonds and pine nuts, as well as whole pine nuts, raisins, egg
> yolks, butter, and rose water.*

Political turbulence was nothing new to the cities of Italy: they had
been fighting one another constantly since the twelfth century. But at
least they had conducted their affairs with a certain degree of independence from outside interference. By the mid-1400s, the five biggest powers on the peninsula—Naples, Rome, Milan, Venice, and Florence—had
absorbed many of their nearby rivals, and a balance of power had been
established. In the relative calm, a transformation was worked on Italy's
ruling elites: city lords became princes, and leading citizens became
courtiers.

But in 1494 everything changed when the king of France marched an army down through Italy to claim the throne of Naples. No other Italian power opposed his progress, and the Neapolitans welcomed him as their new king. In the wake of these events, the Florentines banished their Medici lords. The weakness of the Italian princes was exposed for all to see. Five years later, a new king of France took control of Milan by force. Spain and the Holy Roman Empire quickly joined the contest for dominance on Italian soil, and mercenary troops from across Europe joined the hunt for the rich booty to be found among Italy's resplendent cities. For two generations, French, German, and Spanish armies inflicted the kind of devastation on Italy that the Byzantines and Lombards had brought a thousand years before. Italy's long history of division, conquest, and bloodshed was entering a new chapter. The countryside was ravaged for supplies. Many towns suffered terrible sieges and occupations. In May 1527 Rome shared their fate. The Holy Roman Emperor's army, which comprised mostly Lutheran Germans, mutinied; it broke through the walls of Rome and began eight frenzied days of despoliation, ransacking churches and monasteries and stripping them of their artistic treasures. Even the tombs of former popes in Saint Peter's were desecrated in the search for loot. Priests were dismembered or hanged by their genitals; captive nuns were swapped in games of dice; cardinals were dressed in women's clothes and abused or tortured until they revealed the whereabouts of concealed valuables. Even citizens who escaped the carnage by heading to the countryside were killed and robbed in the hills by peasants. For ten months afterward Rome lay all but abandoned. Italy's princes could conceive of no more chilling demonstration of how vulnerable their cities now were.

THIRD COURSE

104 roast, boned partridges in a "royal sauce" of sugar, vinegar, and spices. 25 plates.

23 rabbits. 104 doves. Thickly sliced large yellow sausages. 25 plates.
The yellow sausages were made with pork, Piacenza cheese (a

variety of Parmesan) and spices. About eleven pounds of sau-
sage were divided between the 25 plates.

25 boned capons with a Lombard-style
stuffing cooked in broth, with 25 *salami*.
25 plates.

> *The stuffing contained cheese, eggs, herbs, pepper, saffron, lard,*
> *and bread crumbs.*

104 fried pigeons with slices of citron on
top. 25 plates.

200 bone marrow *fiandoncelli*. 25 plates.

> Fiandoncelli *were fried pastries with a filling of raisins cooked*
> *in wine and bone marrow, grated hard cheese, egg yolks, sugar,*
> *and cinnamon. A thick coating of honey and sugar was added*
> *after frying.*

25 plates of large, fresh, roasted eel with
sugar and cinnamon

150 fried goby in sweet sauce sprinkled
with pine nuts and small sweetmeats

> *Italy's history of linguistic diversity, multiplied by its ecologi-*
> *cal and gastronomic diversity, equals many linguistic puzzles*
> *for the historian of Italian food. Fish names often present the*
> *most taxing of them all. Platina faced the additional problem*
> *of translating into Latin, which compounded the difficulties so*
> *much so that he almost gave up: "I had taken the decision to*
> *speak about the nature and properties of all fish, but their con-*
> *fused and constantly changing names defeated me." The goby*
> *mentioned here has several different names in different regions.*
> *Messisbugo's term, gò, is found only in the Venetian and Fer-*
> *rarese dialects.*

25 plates of Comacchio-style trout in broth

> *Messisbugo gives no recipe for this dish. But Comacchio was*

the source of much of Ferrara's seafood, especially the highly
valued eel for which the city is still famous today. Its lagoons
also supplied salt for hunted meat.

25 plates of roast lamprey in its own
sauce
> *The fish was studded with cloves and cinnamon before going*
> *on the spit. The sauce was made from a heated mixture of the*
> *lamprey's blood, vinegar, cinnamon, sugar, salt, and the juices*
> *that dripped from the spit.*

25 plates of chestnut tarts

Bread and Garlic

Duke Alfonso ate at a separate table in the company of his new daughter-in-law, Renée. With them, standing in for his late wife, was his sister, Isabella d'Este, or "The Most Illustrious Marchioness of Mantua," as Messisbugo called her. She was the most famous woman of the Renaissance.

Isabella had turned her husband's city of Mantua into one of Europe's centers of art and scholarship. Perhaps more than anyone else in her era, she embodied the ideal of the cultivated court demiurge. A leader of fashion in clothes, medicines, and cosmetics, she danced, sang, played music, and hunted. She was also a connoisseur of books and codices, tapestries and clocks, jewelry and coins, antiquities and contemporary works of art. Exalted in paint by Leonardo, Mantegna, and Titian, and in words by Ariosto, Bembo, and Castiglione, Isabella was also a skillful politician who had often governed Mantua while her consort was away—and did it much better than he. She took over Mantua again when syphilis led him to an early grave in 1519, and ran the city until her son was old enough to take his birthright.

Isabella also traveled a great deal. She had been in Rome viewing the ruins and trying to secure a cardinal's hat for her second son when German troops overran the city. Besieged in her house for eight days, she had been reduced to eating bread and garlic. The shock, she said, would stay with her for the rest of her life.

Isabella was one of the greatest dinner guests in history, but Messisbugo tells us nothing of her exchanges with Duke Alfonso and Renée, and we have no record of the general rules for conversation at a Renaissance court banquet. Even the most famous guide to good behavior, *The Courtier* by Baldassare Castiglione, who was from Isabella's own city, gives no advice. In fact silence was most likely to have been the order of the day between the three, since Renée had little Italian, and neither Isabella nor her brother spoke much French.

Messisbugo's food continued to arrive, relentless.

FOURTH COURSE

Whole roasted stuffed goats, small.
25 plates.

25 plates of *capirotta* served on a bed of
bruschetta and capon meat

> Capirotta *was a soft paté made from a sieved and pounded mixture of hard cheese, garlic, boiled capon, egg yolk, butter, and fatty broth.*

29 capons pounded to a paste and covered
with small stuffed fried pastries. 25 plates.

104 roast pigeons with a Lombard-style
stuffing covered with French sauce. 25
plates.

> French sauce *was made from apples cooked on the griddle and onions cooked in the drippings from a spit. These were then pounded. Red wine and a little vinegar were added before the mixture was sieved and boiled with sugar, pepper, ginger, cinnamon, and nutmeg. Sliced lemon was added before serving.*

50 pieces of salted pike in yellow imperial
sauce. 25 plates.

Messisbugo tells us that yellow imperial sauce was made with a 2:1 mixture of pounded almonds and bread crumbs pulped with rose water. These ingredients were then cooked with sugar, cinnamon, pine nuts, raisins, saffron, and hard-boiled egg yolks before being pounded again and diluted with sweet wine. It was served liberally sprinkled with sugar.

50 trout cooked in wine Hungarian style.
Served on a bed of bread soaked in broth. 25
plates.

A more sophisticated sousing recipe. The fish was fried in good oil with finely chopped onion. A mixture of sweet wine, water, and white wine vinegar was added and the scum carefully removed as it simmered. Honey, raisins, cinnamon, pepper, saffron, and finely chopped apple were then added.

25 fried turbot covered in three sauces in
Duke Alfonso's colors

The Este colors were red, white, and green. The sauces were a chutney made from spices, mustard seed, and sugar; a white sauce of pounded almonds, bread crumbs, verjuice, rose water, and lemon juice; and the third sauce was unspecified.

150 large fried pilchards covered with
orange slices and sugar. 25 plates.

25 bean tarts

The filling was a pulp of beans, hard cheese, butter, sugar, cinnamon, pepper, ginger, and egg. In this case the tart was made to look like a pie by adding a caul "lid."

104 fried marzipan pastries filled with
Turkish-style rice

Cooking rice Turkish-style involved simmering it in cow's milk and sugar with butter and a little rose water. More sugar was added at the end.

The political and military turmoil made all too manifest by the sack of Rome raised the stakes in dynastic alliances. The great Italian families had once sought marriages among themselves—like Isabella d'Este's bond to the Gonzaga family of Mantua. Duke Alfonso's own late wife, Lucrezia Borgia, was the daughter of Pope Alexander VI (and his lover, according to some reports). But these days, the most politically important brides came from Spain or France. Renée herself had been hawked in the dynastic marriage market of Europe since she was two. Even in the summer of 1527, when negotiations with Ferrara were at an advanced stage, a speculative offer had arrived from Henry VIII of England.

(A much-repeated story has it that one of these international marriages, between Caterina de' Medici and Henry II of France in 1533, brought about the export of Italian culinary expertise to France. Thus, it is claimed, the Italians taught the French to cook. This story has no basis in fact.)

By marrying his son to Renée, Duke Alfonso had pulled off a diplomatic coup. The successful union, he hoped, would bring rich rewards—not just his dukedom secured from the threat of the pope and the emperor, but perhaps even a vast territory for the newlyweds carved from French conquests in northern Italy. The union of Ercole and Renée promised a glorious future for the Este clan. The duke's dynastic hopes explained the celebrations that had begun the previous summer in Paris, and the gargantuan scale of the banquet of January 24, 1529, which brought them to a suitably magnificent conclusion.

But Duke Alfonso's hopes were dashed. Even as he dined, he must already have been aware that he had picked the wrong ally. While the couple were moving in joyful procession back from Paris to Ferrara, French military authority was already crumbling. The Hapsburg Empire, uniting Spain and Germany, was destined to dominate in Italy.

Before the year was out, Duke Alfonso was forced to go to Bologna to pay homage to the emperor and beg for his dukedom. Messisbugo went with him. To ease the critical negotiations, the faithful steward supplied the pope and the emperor with "fish, birds, quadrupeds and other comestibles" during their stay. The emperor made him a count for his services. Duke Alfonso kept his territories, and in return gave up large amounts of money and his alliance with France.

Renée did not take well to this abrupt change in political direction. A shrewd, headstrong woman, she was haughtily proud of her royal French background and the Ferrarese court struggled to integrate her. Within a few months of the banquet, Duke Alfonso would be spitting bile about the reckless spending of Renée's unruly entourage—one historian called them an "unscrupulous mafia." Ercole's new bride would make herself an instrument of French policy in Italy, and her followers a branch of the French court in exile.

Peasantish Things

It is almost impossible today not to be disgusted by Messisbugo's futile banquet. To our taste the doses of sugar in his dishes are giddying, and their mixture of sweet and savory seems an alien hodgepodge—the very thought of salted pike in yellow imperial sauce is emetic. But most repellent of all is the banquet's sheer excess. A rough calculation suggests that if the 104 guests ate their full 104th share of the courses listed above, they would each have consumed the following: eighteen large portions of eleven different fish; three whole birds the size of capons or pheasants; another five smaller birds such as doves; three portions of meat, and four of sausage, *salame*, or ham; fifteen small pastries and pies or portions of large ones; in addition to an assortment of blancmanges, fritters, salads, and so on.

And there were still four more courses to come, as well as a large serving of sweetmeats, and an early morning collation of fruit in sugar and syrup.

The banquet lasted well into the following day. Twice the servants removed the clutter from the table and stripped away the top cloth, leaving a clean one exposed for fresh place settings. New sugar statues arrived, showing more scenes from the Labors of Hercules. There were new entertainments: clowns from Venice and Bergamo; and famous actors dressed as country bumpkins who sang songs and conducted comic dialogues about "peasantish things," as Messisbugo described them. At the end of the meal a raffle was held. Names were drawn from a huge gilded pie case and jewelry and other trinkets awarded to the winners. Then the dancing began.

It is as easy to be appalled by the behavior of the Estes as it is to be disgusted by their food. Their much-vaunted magnificence seems vulgar and morally obtuse against a backdrop of hunger and hardship. The real "peasantish things" on the minds of the rural population in the sixteenth century would have concerned the unstable economic situation. As the burden of supporting court life grew heavier, and ever more grain was demanded from the countryside to keep the vulnerable and politically sensitive city population in bread, the peasant diet worsened: less meat and dairy produce, more *polenta* and bread from inferior grains. The political turmoil also brought repeated episodes of war, famine, pestilence, and flooding to the delicate environment of the Po delta from which Ferrara drew its resources.

But of course the brilliant obscenity of courtly life in Ferrara was not produced solely by the moral failings of those whom it benefited most. Magnificence was a system for governing, and even the outrageous volume of food prepared by Messisbugo was part of it. Each of the guests was seated carefully according to rank, each place varying in the access it afforded to the choicest dishes. Thus even in its most petty aspects, the jealousy between the courtiers—both the old nobility and those who had bought their titles to help pay for the Herculean Addition—was manipulated by the duke. The leftovers from the banquet also served a purpose: they would cascade down to feed relatives, retainers, and servants. Great feasts were the most vivid possible way to dramatize and celebrate the duke's power to hand out favor, the patronage that held together Ferrara and its leading family.

The Estes bore the responsibility for maintaining Ferrara's independent status, but despite their power they had less freedom of choice than we might think. Theirs was a dangerous lot. For instance, in the few weeks that Duke Alfonso spent away from Ferrara to meet his new daughter-in-law in 1528, he survived an attempted coup and avoided an ambush. Indeed in the very first year of his reign, he had uncovered an assassination plot hatched by two of his brothers. At the time of the banquet, twenty-four years later, the two Este conspirators were still bricked up in the castle—within shouting distance of the great hall. The bridegroom's uncles were fed through a tiny aperture in the wall, and their only entertainment was to watch, from the high window in their cell, the guests at state occasions come and go.

Threatened by internal enemies, and pressed on all sides by dynasties that had armies more numerous and treasure chests more capacious than theirs, the Estes had to obey the rules of magnificence or go under. Renaissance princes may have dined in splendor, but they sat on the edge of a precipice.

7

Rome, 1549–50

Bread and Water for Their Eminences

The Pope's Secret Cook

As both a head chef and a courtier in his own right, the Estes' steward, Cristoforo da Messisbugo, was a relatively unusual figure. Cooks are the heroes of the history of Italian food in the late Middle Ages and the Renaissance. Yet unlike Messisbugo, most of them came from backgrounds that were sometimes rural, and almost always humble. They usually remained unknown, too, and so their life stories can now be told only in generalities. Cooks made a living from their appreciation of what the countryside could offer the city, and of what the city's traders and artisans could offer its wealthy classes. They were the great go-betweens of Italian gastronomy. As the seasons, the prices, and their employers' or customers' fancy changed, they would network constantly to find suppliers and discover recipes. They determined the food that left the country to be deployed in the towns. Through them an understanding of good food circulated between poor and rich. The leading cooks were therefore the monarchs of Italy's famed urban food markets; sampling, questioning, and commanding as they strode knowledgeably from stall to stall.

In a world where honor was all, a cook was expected to put his employer's honor, and his own, above everything else. Chefs moved between the social classes, between their employers and their own staff, so they had to be polite to everyone, while trusting none of their underlings. The best chefs were alert, clean, patient, and as sober as possible—given that drink was known to interfere with the natural taste of things. Then as now, tippling was a serious professional hazard for those in the catering industry.

Through years of experience, a cook became a master of every stage of the food preparation process, from butcher's block and gardener's basket, all the way up to the prince's table. A good knowledge of fats and oils was the cornerstone of his expertise. The greener olive oils were best, filtered rather than crushed—we would call them extra virgin. Oils made from almonds, walnuts, and linseed were also used in many parts of Italy, but the elite cooks dismissed them as being better for burning than for eating. The accomplished cook could make lard, *salame*, butter, and fresh cheeses; he could pick the best caviar and knew exactly the shade of pale red that the flesh of a salted eel should be when cut open. The methods for skinning, preserving, and hanging every type of meat were second nature to him. His signature was his particular spice mixture.

A top court cook could expect to have the use of a horse, and to be provided with his own furnished room and a winter supply of firewood equivalent to a gentleman's. Not surprisingly, the cook's food allowance was considerable. Every day he would have three pounds of bread and ample provision of the same wine drunk by the gentlemen of his master's household. The convention in noble courts (apart from those of the popes, emperors, and kings who made their own rules) was that a chief cook was given a daily ration of two and a half pounds of young beef or mutton, plus a chicken or capon—or their equivalent in eggs—and fish on lean days. His personal servant would be given half these amounts. Just as important, the cook had the right to all the waste of the kitchen, such as skins, feathers, bones, ashes, feet and heads, innards, and used cooking fat. There must have been enough cash and calories in these products to support several families. A successful cook was an important figure in the urban community.

The best cooks moved within a network of Italian cities, each of which was located in a countryside offering richly varied produce. The urban network honed the cooks' skills, their professional ethos and expectations, and helped Italian food reach one of its supreme moments of subtlety and sophistication.

Bartolomeo Scappi was undoubtedly the greatest cook of the Italian Renaissance; in 1570 he published a summation of his art, in a mighty six books. As a practical but not a learned man, he gave it a less than imaginative title: *Opera di Bartolomeo Scappi*, meaning *Work by Bartolomeo Scappi*. It is largely thanks to his testimony that we have such a clear idea of the status and values to which professional cooks aspired. The *Work*'s very existence is remarkable—a comprehensive cookery guide and meticulously illustrated monument to one exceptionally successful career, as well as to the careers of those hundreds of nameless cooks who had brought Italian food to such heights. There is nothing like it anywhere else in the world. The sophistication of Scappi's cooking, and the breadth and detail of his culinary knowledge, are breathtaking— vastly superior to what emerges from the first cookery manuscripts, such as the *Book for Cook* of two centuries earlier. Most of what we know about a Renaissance cook's life comes from Scappi. He had a profound influence over Italian eating for centuries, and he is often cited to this day because he left us a picture of a cuisine that can justifiably be called *Italian*—a cuisine, in other words, that drew on ingredients and techniques from most corners of the peninsula.

Born around 1500 in the small village of Dumenza, on the western shore of Lake Maggiore up near the Swiss border, Bartolomeo Scappi came from a background as humble as any of his peers. The few documentary traces show that he was able and shrewd enough to find employment with a senior churchman, a Venetian cardinal, as soon as he could. A career in cookery followed the same upward path as a career in the Catholic Church: its apex lay in Rome, which by this time had become Italy's undisputed culinary capital. Scappi had arrived there by 1536. Over the next three decades and more, he would serve several other cardinals. Then, in 1564, he reached the very top of his profession when he became "secret" (i.e., private) cook to the pope.

Scappi was an old man when the *Work* came out in 1570. He could

How to feed a cardinal at the papal election of 1549. The meals are carried by the men in the center of the picture in decorated containers. To the right, four archbishops check each dish for poison and hidden messages before it is passed through the wheel behind them and into the conclave. From the recipe collection by the pope's "secret" cook, Bartolomeo Scappi.

The ideal Renaissance kitchen. Pie cases are being prepared on the long table in the center. Sauces are being sieved in the foreground to the right. Space on the left is reserved for the specialist blancmange-maker. From Scappi's *Opera* of 1570.

now look back with wistful pride at one particular episode when he was called upon to demonstrate all his skills. In an appendix to the *Work* he wrote a fascinating account of the time twenty years earlier when his cookery had played a key role in the most carefully choreographed yet most politically explosive phase in the life cycle of the papacy: the death of one pontiff and the election, by the Conclave of Cardinals, of another.

As well as being one of the most important documents in the history of Italian food, Scappi's *Work* also affords an unusual insight into a period of cataclysmic upheaval for the Church, and therefore for Italy. In the early and mid-1500s, the weight of earthly power and splendor heaped around the Throne of Saint Peter imperiled its spiritual foundations.

In 1517 Martin Luther began his campaign against the Church's practice of selling salvation through indulgences to cover the colossal cost of rebuilding Saint Peter's Basilica—the sixteenth century's greatest building project. He was excommunicated in 1521, but this only increased his popularity and led him to shape his ideas into a coherent belief system set against Catholic teaching. When Rome was sacked by a largely Lutheran force in 1527, the popes could no longer carry on as if what was now called "Protestantism" were merely a minor heresy. As the city recovered from the devastation, alarms abounded: Protestant teaching was spreading across northern Europe; religiously inspired war and revolt were raging in Germany; Henry VIII's England broke with Rome; and, like Henry, many monarchs clearly relished the chance to make a grab at ecclesiastical property. In a few short years, half of the Western world would detach itself from the Catholic Church.

Pope Paul III, elected in 1534, finally launched a response. Although he was no less personally corrupt than any other Renaissance pope, he set up a Reform Commission that, in 1537, produced a report blaming the ecclesiastical hierarchy for the Church's woes. Paul moved to correct some of the worst abuses, and gave new vim to the campaign against heresy. In 1540 he gave papal approval to Ignatius Loyola's Society of Jesus—the Jesuits. Most important, the Council of Trent, which first sat in 1545, began to work on a doctrinal and organizational renovation of the Church. By the time of Paul's death in 1549, it was already too late for reconciliation between Protestants and Catholics, but the papacy finally seemed ready to begin its Counter-Reformation (as it would later be termed).

The election of 1549 was as momentous as any in the millennial history of the papacy. Whoever followed Paul III would bear a huge burden of worldly and spiritual responsibility. At that time, Scappi worked for one of the cardinals who took part in the election, and his food is best sampled, as the cardinals sampled it, against the background of the Conclave of 1549. His recipes—over one thousand of them—mark a glorious high point in the history of Italian food, but are almost imperceptibly suffused with nostalgia. That nostalgia, and the ironies of Scappi's story, are the first indicators that the gastronomy of Italy's cities was soon to enter an era of stagnation.

With a Key

Pope Paul III did not die until he was declared dead. And as ritual ordained, he was not declared dead until the cardinal chamberlain had hit him on the head three times with a silver hammer, calling him by name with each sharp tap. When no response was forthcoming, the official declaration was made and the fisherman's ring was slipped from the deceased's finger and broken. Across Rome, the bells began to toll in mourning.

From that point on—it was November 20, 1549—ritual dictated every stage of the interval, the *sede vacante*, before a new Vicar of Christ was handed the sacred keys. It was as if time and the motion of the spheres were suspended while the man who would represent divine power on earth was selected. But even as the cardinals were lining up to kiss the dead pope's feet for the last time, even as his white-robed corpse was lying among burning torches in the Sistine Chapel, the buzz of political discussion could be heard playing in worldly counterpoint to prayers and incantations. The papal election was already under way.

It was to manage the uncertain terrain between ritual and politics in papal successions that the set of rules known as the conclave had been drawn up nearly three hundred years earlier, after the difficult election of 1271 in the small town of Viterbo when the College of Cardinals had spent thirty-three months squabbling before it elected Gregory X—thirty-three months in which the unfortunate citizens of Viterbo had to support the heavy economic burden of the Church hierarchy's presence. In the end, the local authorities had blockaded their eminences in the palace, removed the roof to expose them to the elements, and provided nothing more appetizing than bread and water to sustain them. A compromise candidate had rapidly emerged.

After his election Gregory X set out some hard-line regulations for future elections: his 1274 constitution *Ubi periculum* contains the first use of the word *conclave*—from the Latin *cum clavis*, "with a key." *Ubi periculum* placed heavy restrictions upon the cardinals locked up to choose a supreme pontiff. They were allowed only one servant each, for example, and had to live communally so that they could keep watch on one another's movements. On pain of excommunication, they were forbidden to confer with anyone outside. Their only food had to be supplied through a single aperture where it could be searched for messages. Indeed *Ubi periculum* took its cue from the events in Viterbo to prescribe a particularly tough dietary regimen for the conclave. If the cardinals had not reached a decision within three days, they were to be restricted to two meals a day, with only one dish at each. After five more inconclusive days, only bread and water were to be admitted.

In 1353, Gregory's restrictions were amended a little. Those within the conclave could now protect their modesty by hanging curtains across the entrance to their spartan cells, and they had permission to bring *two* servants or clerks as personal assistants. Perhaps more important, they could supplement their two simple meals with a salad or some fruit, a bowl of soup or a little sausage. The proviso was that each cardinal should consume only what was supplied by his own staff.

All of this makes the elaborate arrangements for feeding the College of Cardinals at the Conclave of 1549 particularly captivating. As is clear from the detailed description in Scappi's *Work*, the Renaissance papacy had its own way of doing things.

Scappi describes a garish color scheme within the conclave held in the Vatican. Each member of the College of Cardinals was housed in a large color-coded cell: purple if he had been appointed by the recently deceased Paul III, green if he owed his position to an earlier pontiff.

From the silk trimmings on the cushions, bedspread, and tablecloth, right down to the lantern and chamber pot, all was purple or green—like the bedroom of an obsessive teenage football fan.

More equipment in the same colors was carried by the officials and servants who processed solemnly through the endless corridors of the Vatican to bring each prince of the Church his food. A personal mace-bearer led the way, followed by a steward. Then came two pairs of foot-men walking in line, each lugging a stout pole by one end. Suspended on iron rings from the first pair's pole was a big wooden casket, known as a *cornuta*, which was specially designed to carry hot food into con-claves. Similarly suspended from the second pole was a capacious draw-string bag of embossed leather decorated with tassels. Like the *cornuta*, it was either purple or green and adorned on all sides with the cardinal's coat of arms; it contained cold items such as *salame*, cheese, and sweet-meats. These two vessels were a portable version of the system that Renaissance stewards used at all banquets: cooked dishes were brought to table direct from the kitchens; anything preprepared was kept ready in a *credenza*, a large sideboard, in the banqueting hall. Behind these two important containers in the procession to the conclave came as many as half a dozen equerries with wine racks and jugs of fresh water under the supervision of a wine-waiter.

At the outer gate, the steward's procession encountered a body of Italian and Swiss guards—all helmets, halberds, and breastplates. Over-seeing them were two Roman aristocrats charged with enforcing the conclave's rules. One of these was a direct descendant of the man who had mounted the guard on the first-ever conclave in Viterbo in 1271.

Once through the gate, up two staircases, and into a wide corridor—the conclave's antechamber—the procession was greeted by a papal her-ald who checked it off against a list of those locked inside. (The order in which the cardinals were to be served had been decided by drawing lots the previous evening.) The steward then presented himself to a panel of four archbishops sitting along one side of a table. Under their sol-emn gaze, he unfolded an immaculate napkin to reveal two knives and a fork—cutlery the archbishops would then use to taste every item of food as a precaution against poisoning, and to check for concealed mes-sages. No opaque bottles or jugs were allowed. Pies and whole chickens were banned, too. All table linen had to be opened for careful inspection. In theory at least, the cardinals were to reach their decision in total isolation from the world.

Once the archbishops were satisfied, the food was passed through one of two shuttered turntables fitted into large apertures in the wall to their immediate right—these were the only point of access to the conclave itself. The steward stayed only long enough to be sure that his cardinal did not want any dish changed; then he and his men were escorted away.

This elaborate procedure was performed morning and evening for each of the forty-seven cardinals in attendance, and for each day of what turned out to be, after Viterbo, the longest conclave there had ever been.

In the Kitchen

The teams of cooks, cellarmen, sausage-makers, bakers, and pantry-keepers who worked in the papal kitchens were used to catering for large numbers. They fed the pope's household, as well as the retainers who worked for the cardinals most directly involved in the day-to-day running of the Church administration. Even in normal times, hundreds of meals were served daily in the Vatican's two dining halls, but the population of the Vatican increased enormously for the conclave, so the kitchen staff must have had to cope with nearly intolerable demands.

Scappi provides illustrations of how a kitchen in Renaissance Rome was arranged. At the heart of the operation, against one wall of the main kitchen, there was an open fire large enough to roast a hog; above were mobile iron arms from which cauldrons could be suspended by chains; in front, spits revolved slowly; to one side a screen shielded the spit-turner from the blaze. Hot embers from the fire were regularly transferred to the row of five or six stone burners set at ground level along one wall; pots sat bubbling on grilles placed over each one. High above the burners were alcoves where the boys designated to guard the kitchen at night could rest; theft- and fire-prevention were evidently major concerns in the Renaissance kitchen.

On the opposite wall were two ovens with iron doors, and near them cold water ran continuously into a stone trough. Next to that was the entrance to a lockable larder. In the kitchen's coolest corner stood a solid stone base that came to just below waist height; on top of it was a mortar so large that the cook could barely get his arms around it. These were the days before blenders, and almost every recipe required at least one ingredient to be pounded with a pestle and mortar. Scappi's illustration also shows a bulky bench for chopping meat. As many as ten trestle tables, large and small, were ready to be set up when needed for other tasks. No space was wasted: hams and dried fish hung on hooks from the beams; knives were ready to hand, their handles protruding at all angles from a stuffed bag—like arrows from the body of Saint Sebastian.

Book One of the *Work* contains an interminable list of kitchen tools: every single knife, ladle, grater, colander, cauldron, hook, and stewpot is named and illustrated. The cook in the well-equipped princely kitchen had to know how to use dozens of different pieces, from the *maccaroni* iron (a row of circular blades combined into a kind of rolling pin that could be run over a sheet of dough to cut it into strips), to the new-fangled triple spit-turner.

A secondary kitchen stood adjacent to the main one, with a well, another water trough, a burner much bigger than the ones in the main kitchen, and two more ovens. Scappi's diagram also has a huge side-board with a sturdy lock for precious items such as spices and sugar. Running down the center of the room was a long smooth walnut wood table where two men and a woman mixed, kneaded, and rolled dough. To one side, two men were occupied sieving spices; on the other, a safe distance from any splashes or accidents, the blancmange maker worked away at a large flat pan standing on its own burner.

Scappi's model kitchen also includes a well-ventilated cool room where three cooks are shown working with milk and fresh cheeses, and an exterior loggia where fish were kept ready in open barrels of water, and where knives could be sharpened, pigs flayed, chickens plucked, and dishes washed.

A Diet of Rumors

As these details of kitchen organization demonstrate, Scappi's concerns in the *Work* were primarily practical. The book would come under the glare of the Inquisition's censors, so he could not have reported any of the politicking that prolonged the papal election even if he had wanted to. Yet while he was hard at work, the whole city talked of little else but the stories leaking from the locked rooms in the Vatican.

At the death of Paul III, the cardinals were divided into three factions that reflected the geopolitics of Italy at the time: a French party, an Imperial party, and a more amorphous group mostly comprising the creatures of the recently deceased pope. Many of the Italian cities were aligned with powerful outside monarchies: Florence with the empire, for example, and Mantua with France. But the ambitions of individual cardinals played just as big a part as politics—and so did their greed: some among them scarcely concealed that they were hoping to sell their vote to the highest bidder. The high risk of bribery meant that many dukes and princes felt that they could not rely on their representatives within the conclave, and were thus compelled to keep a close watch on their behavior.

Predictably, then, the long Conclave of 1549 was a vipers' nest of infighting and misinformation. The regulations were flouted shamelessly. Cardinals arrived at the election with more than the maximum of two personal assistants. It was estimated that altogether some four hundred people were locked into the fifty-nine cells of the conclave. Many were spies and minders sent by secular rulers, but some were just relatives or noblemen curious to know what a conclave was like. To accommodate their people, the cardinals erected wooden extensions at the front of their purple and green cells, and put in new windows.

The most egregious breaches of the rules concerned contacts with the outside world. Openings were made in the walls. Emissaries came and went from the supposedly sealed location, their boots stuffed with letters. Ferrara's ambassador complained about how often he had to climb up to the rooftops of the Vatican at night to speak to Cardinal Ippolito d'Este. (We last saw a young Ippolito sitting beside his older brother at the banquet staged by Cristoforo da Messisbugo in Ferrara in 1529. His family's ambitions for him had been realized. Indeed the Estes could now nurture even higher hopes. Ippolito was one of the small band of cardinals considered to be very *papabile*—"pope-able.")

In the early days of the conclave, there were half-hearted attempts to enforce the dietary norms set down all those years previously after the Viterbo scandal. On December 5, 1549, the Gonzaga family's agent wrote:

> The Cardinals are now on the one-dish regimen. The dish consists of a couple of capons, a nice piece of veal, some *salame*, a nice soup, and anything you want as long as it is boiled. That is in the morning. Then in the evening, you can have anything you want as long as it is roasted. As well as some *antipasti*, a main course, some salad and a dessert. The more small-minded ones are complaining about the hardship. If things don't speed up, we'll see how they react when it comes to bread and water.

It never came to bread and water. Soon after the conclave began, the English refugee Cardinal Reginald Pole missed his chance to don the fisherman's shoes by a solitary vote, but as support for him weakened, more candidates emerged. The great question of how the Catholic Church should respond to the Protestant challenge had set further discord among a College of Cardinals already divided into factions. During this period, charges of heresy were lightly thrown, and theological issues were more than usually fraught with political significance. The Imperial faction supported the baleful Dominican theologian, Juan Alvarez de Toledo. Another likely pontiff was Giampietro Caraffa, the Neapolitan nobleman who, as inquisitor general, had spread panic among Church reformers and heretics. Many suspected that a frail cardinal would be chosen to mask the ambitions of the ruthless and abrasive young Frenchman Charles de Guise. As the intrigues multiplied, all the bargaining counters of dynastic affairs—marriages, territory, cash—were fed into the negotiations. The cardinals began to send one another presents of choice dishes, and electoral business was done over banquets lavish enough, as one witness remarked, to satisfy the notoriously debauched Roman general Lucullus.

The teams shuttling between the kitchens and the conclave were clearly made to sweat under the weight of the food. Of the many sins committed within the conclave, gluttony was not the least influential in drawing out the proceedings for so long. December passed, and the conclave carried on into the new year.

Sadly the *Work* does not record which of the cardinals Scappi was working for, or even whether his cell was purple or green. But whoever this mysterious prince of the Church was, his *cornuta* and *credenza*-in-a-bag contained some of the greatest packed lunches ever recorded. Book Four of the *Work* is a calendar of menus that a cardinal or pope might offer his guests, and Scappi tells us that he bore similar spreads into the conclave.

A typical conclave meal might comprise four courses: two cold from the *credenza*, and two carried in hot from the kitchen in the *cornuta*. Each course would itself consist of perhaps eight to ten different dishes. The *Work* recommends a lunch menu for December 15 that is a good example. Like many of Scappi's menus, it includes sweet biscuits in the opening *credenza* course: Pisan or Roman ones served with Malmsey wine, or Neapolitan *mostaccioli*. Scappi gives a recipe for *Milanese mostaccioli*, which are about the size of two fingers, and are flavored with aniseed and a grain or two of musk—a highly exotic ingredient. In Naples today *mostaccioli* are made with grated orange peel and spices—which could be similar to Scappi's version. There were also marzipan cakes and flaky, melt- in-the-mouth butter pastries.

The biscuits and pastries came with a variety of simple cold meats: slices of salted ox tongue cooked in wine; ham cooked in wine and served with capers, raisins, and a sprinkling of sugar; cold venison pie; and boiled capon liberally coated with a mixture of sugar, pepper, cinnamon, cloves, nutmeg, and fennel. A selection of grapes accompanied them.

Although relatively straightforward, these opening gambits of Scappi's menu are bolder in their contrasts than Messisbugo's banquet. But from this point on Scappi's genius really makes itself manifest. His art even shines through the thick shroud of sugar and spices that makes it nearly impossible for us genuinely to appreciate what people in the Middle Ages and Renaissance tasted.

The next two courses come hot from the *cornuta*, and consist almost entirely of meat. Their variety is striking—which is true of all 113 of the sample menus contained in Book Four of the *Work*. Each course offers a purposeful, artful pattern. Like the stanzas of a poem in textures and flavors, it invites us to savor, compare, reflect, and savor again.

Take pies, for example, which appear in both meat courses: pigeon in course two is answered by duck with prunes and dried sour cherries in course three. Then there are the small birds. Course two has thrushes roasted with sausages and oranges in an alternating arrangement on the spit. Course three has starlings stewed with sausage and the stems of edible thistles, and served topped with grated cheese. The poultry also follows variations on a theme: stuffed spit-roast pullet with lemon slices, sugar, and rose water in course two; and in course three, boiled chicken served with small *ravioli* filled with a complex paste of boiled pork belly, veal udder, roast pork, Parmesan, soft cheese, sugar, herbs, spices, and raisins. Distinctive sauces accompany each course, too: with the second, a tangy chutney made from grape must, candied orange peel, and both quinces and crab apples cooked in wine and sugar; with the third, a mixture of garlic and almonds.

This is the menu of an undisputed talent, food that would awaken the coarsest palate to the joys of discriminating connoisseurship. Its rhyming dishes allow the health-conscious diner to plot his own Galenic path through the meal and bring out the strong individual character of other recipes. Course three offers earthier notes with fried hare and Milanese boiled beef, which play against a background of rice cooked in goat's milk and dusted with sugar and cinnamon. Remarkably, in course two, Scappi sets his exceptionally sophisticated recipes alongside what we might think of as inferior fare: fried sweetbreads and goat liver cooked in orange juice, as well as calf's foot that is first boiled and then brushed with egg and fried.

The fourth and final course of the cardinal's lunch on December 15 is a cold, more understated medley, but its notes could not be more expertly plucked. Cardoons with salt and pepper. Truffles steamed with oil, orange juice, and pepper. Pears and apples. Cheeses from Tuscany and the Ligurian riviera. Roast chestnuts and quinces. And two kinds of small pie: a white marzipan pie and one of Scappi's staples, a Lombard pie, which has a sweet pastry case with a filling of green beet leaves, Parmesan, and *ricotta*.

After such a splendid meal, His Eminence would have been forgiven for taking a nap before engaging in a little light electioneering. Then came a dinner quite equal to lunch in its inventiveness, refined patterning, and generous scale. Worth noting is that salads were the dominant item in the opening *credenza* course—as they were in most of Scappi's dinner menus: lettuce and borage flowers, capers and raisins, cooked chicory or carrot. With them came suckling boar pies, salted pork loin cooked in wine and served with orange juice and sugar, and Milanese-style *tortiglioni*, which were cut from a scroll of short-crust pastry rolled over a thin spreading of sweetmeat.

Rome: The Capital of Italian Cuisine

Book One of Scappi's *Work* is addressed to a young apprentice, Giovanni, and contains general advice on the cook's trade of the kind summarized at the start of this chapter. Books Two and Three contain Scappi's recipes for fat and lean days respectively. Book Four gives a calendar of sample menus. Book Five is all about what he calls *pasta*—which still meant pastry and dough, so pies, tarts, and fritters are the main topics of interest rather than *maccheroni, vermicelli,* and *ravioli.*

Scappi reports the catering arrangements for the conclave as an appendix to Book Six, the bulk of which contains recipes for convalescents, who attracted a great deal of attention from cookery writers before the era of consumerism and scientific medicine. In the employ of the Church gerontocracy, Scappi would have been particularly aware of the needs of the sick. He tells us that the Conclave of 1549–50 went on so long that two cardinals died, and another three had to leave because of illness.

Scappi's *Work* cites the produce of nearby papal towns and territories, for example, lamprey and pike from the Tiber, dried figs from Sabina, spring cherries and *mozzarella* cheese from Rome. But strikingly, Scappi's kitchen was also supplied from much farther afield, and not just with the inevitable Parmesan cheese and Comacchio salted eel. The rice Scappi cooked for the Church hierarchy might come from Salerno in the south or Milan in the north. He obtained pickled sardines from Genoa and pickled carp and shad from Lake Garda. So wide is the secret cook's field of reference that he finds himself having to explain the different regional names for the fish he cooks: Rome, Genoa, Venice, and Pisa all had different names for bass.

Scappi mentions Florentine sheep's milk cheeses: the hard and flavorsome *Marzolino*, with its yellow waxy exterior; and the smooth, white *Raviggiolo*; as well as great oval balls of the *caciocavallo* produced near Naples, as it still is today. Many favorite pork products originated, as they do today, in a band of territory across central-northern Italy: from Lucca, Modena, Bologna, and Ferrara. Even humble items could come a long way, such as cabbage and frogs from Bologna. In Scappi's day, as in ours, Italian food was a mosaic of specialties from different areas; gathered in the cities, they were launched from there into the national marketplace.

Olives came from right across this supply network for the rich. Almost every part of the peninsula and its islands sent little green or black offerings to the pope's table. Scappi cites towns within easy reach of Rome, such as Monterotondo and Tivoli, but he also ordered olives from Genoa, Naples, and Sicily; from Cortona in Tuscany and Tortona in Piedmont. They even came from Bologna—a city then famous for olives, but which is today no more associated with olive-growing than are Boston or Chicago. (It is unclear what changed, the weather or taste, to break the connection between Bologna and this particular speciality.)

Olives also came to Rome from Spain, and many other kinds of food products were from abroad: salted salmon and herring from Flanders, eels from Malta, a particularly good fatty cheese from Germany that came preserved in bark.

Recipes are even more portable than barrels of fish and olives and Scappi draws on ideas from across Europe and the Mediterranean. He reserves a place of honor for the all-inclusive Spanish stew known as *olla podrida* and includes a Catalan recipe for spit-roast partridge. Scappi describes a Moorish dish he labels "succussu"—his garbled spelling of *couscous*. From Germany come several ways to cook wild boar and pike, as well as a rich ox loin stew that is simmered for two hours and best served with roasted onions. (Scappi uses dough to seal the lid of the pot and create a gentle pressure-cooker effect.) France's most notable contribution to the papal table is a technique for studding liver and other meat with lardons. But there are no recipes from Protestant England in the *Work*.

All these imports are inserted into a distinctive framework of dishes from across Italy. Scappi's selection of *tagliatelli, tortelletti,* and *ravioli* recipes is in Book Two. (The spellings are his.) His *maccaroni* come in various types: some are dumplings, some are like today's *pasta secca,* and some, like the "Roman style" he describes, are thin strips cut with the *maccaroni* iron from a sheet of dough made of flour and bread crumbs bound with goat's milk and egg yolk. These *maccaroni* are dried for a while and then boiled in water for half an hour. They are then piled into a casserole dish in alternating layers with grated cheese, knobs of butter, sugar, cinnamon, and slices of a local buffalo milk cheese called *provatura.* A final half an hour in the oven with a little rose water melts the cheeses as the taste of the spices pervades them. Other elaborate pasta recipes come from Genoa and Lombardy.

Many of the local dishes in the *Work* are still around today, including some for real cognoscenti, like the Tuscan *berlingozzo* or ring-cake—Scappi associates it with the city of Siena and insists, quite rightly, that it should be eaten warm from the oven. Or the Genoese *gattafura,* which is a delicate cheese and herb pastry that seems to be a direct ancestor of today's *gattafin.* Other local specialties have disappeared. Since Scappi's day, Bologna has lost its reputation not just for olives, but also for herb pies. Milan has ceased to enjoy a fame for the *cervellata,* a sausage made with cheese and the blood, brain, and meat of the pig.

The many typical dishes in the *Work* suggest that, over the centuries since the cities' economic resurgence in the Middle Ages, the Parmesan cheese model was being followed elsewhere. Italy's network of cities had become a system for creating gastronomic diversity and specialization. Yet nowhere but Rome would such a countrywide concentration of produce and knowledge have been possible. The larders of the Eternal City exerted a gravitational pull over Italian ingredients. And like the olives, cheeses, and *salami,* cooks and stewards were drawn toward Saint Peter's from north and south. The same gastronomic cosmopolitanism is already visible in miniature in Platina's *Respectable Pleasure:* following the classical authors he loved, Platina enjoyed citing the provenance of Paduan hens, Viterbo carrots, Neapolitan oranges, and Sicilian honey—among many other foods.

Politics turned Rome into the food hub of Italy. Over the century or so between Platina's day, and the Conclave of 1549 at which Scappi served, the role of the pope as a secular prince had grown more important. Most of his income now came from the land he governed in central Italy, rather than from "spiritual" contributions made elsewhere in Christendom. The power of the Roman aristocrats to influence papal policy was reduced, and the Vatican bureaucracy, the curia, grew in size. As a result, Rome was a city of immigrants with a service economy: more than half of the population originated from other parts of Italy. Merchants, bankers, and an army of small-time traders and artisans came to work for the twenty-five to thirty cardinals resident at any one time. Ambassadors from all the Italian and foreign powers were permanently stationed in Rome, too—all of them employing agents, retainers, and postmen, and all of them spending lavishly on banquets and receptions. Rome's Jewish population, which had been there since before the arrival of Christianity, increased as refugees fled persecution elsewhere. The city hosted crowds of pilgrims and beggars. And its tradition of easy public morality drew in hundreds of prostitutes.

So as Rome became more princely, it also became more Italian, because of course the popes could never be quite like other rulers: for one thing, they were more powerful because their spiritual and political influence traversed Europe; for another, they were weaker because they were elected. That is why, during the Renaissance, the College of Cardinals contained a much higher proportion of Italians than earlier. Princes from across the Italian peninsula were prepared to invest mountains of money and years of diplomatic maneuvers in getting their man a vote in the conclave.

The supply lines along which olives and other goods were brought to the papal kitchens were traced over the paths of ecclesiastical power. Ultimately, the fortunes of both cooks and clerics were made at the conclave. So in addition to Scappi's cooking, the cardinals in the conclave feasted on a glut of scurrilous, politically motivated rumors.

Take the case of poor Cardinal Giovan Maria Del Monte, victim of the most vicious tales, which may have had something to do with his monstrous ugliness: it was remarked that his huge bent nose made his profile "the biggest laugh in the world." But according to the conclave gossip, these unfortunate looks had done nothing to thwart his appetite for fornication. The story circulating in the Imperial faction was that, as a young man, Cardinal Del Monte fathered a hundred illegitimate children. Apparently he had since been persuaded to change his ways by his dying mother. Kneeling by her bedside, he swore an oath that, henceforth, he would only go with boys. Del Monte stuck scrupulously to his vow, it was reported, and now kept a house full of catamites. His favorite was said to be a youth he also employed to train his pet monkey.

In the febrile religious atmosphere in Europe at the time, rumors such as these were bound to spread and grow, which worsened the already dreadful image of the Renaissance papacy. The pontifical court, in effect, generated Protestant propaganda with its many lurid stories. So many were in circulation that historians have found it impossible to sift out fact from fiction. Combined with lax regulations, personal ambition, secular politics, theological controversy, and the generous provision of food, the rumors also helped prolong the conclave through January—and still no candidate commanded a consensus.

Oxtail and Fish Soup

Offal and other inferior meats are central to typical Roman cooking today. *Coda alla vaccinara*, oxtail "butcher's style," is perhaps the totemic offering. That the oxtail should be stewed slowly in wine and tomatoes until it is succulent is the core principle in the many recipes, some of which even contain a little grated chocolate to accentuate the dish's subtle bittersweet edge. Thriving Roman eateries also serve sweetbreads with artichokes, fried slices of bull's testicle, tripe, and many other such delicacies. This is manifestly popular cooking rather than elite cuisine, but it is also unmistakably modern and urban. For one thing, it is part of a tradition that probably grew up around the great nineteenth-century slaughterhouse in the working-class quarter of Testaccio. For another, it dates from a time when beef had acquired the prestige it enjoys today, and when the by-products of the beef industry were consumed by the less well-off.

Coda alla vaccinara was cheap food, certainly, but it was never valueless rubbish; in the late 1800s it was beyond the reach of the poorest Romans. Butchers, slaughterhouse workers, and their families—the comparatively comfortable artisans and laborers who had the best access to offal—drove the taste for delights such as *pajata* (calf intestines). These people, who celebrated such "poor" ingredients, attracted well-to-do gastro-tourists to the working-class areas to sample them. Thus one of the characteristic features of Roman cuisine, but also of Italian cuisine more generally, is a constant exchange of ideas between those on the higher and lower rungs of the social ladder.

It is hard to imagine a wealthier or more exclusive dining club than the Conclave of 1549. Yet even here we can identify tempting traces of the intimate relationship between the diet of ordinary people and the food of the elite. We have already seen how Scappi served calf's foot and sweetbreads alongside some of his most elaborate creations. Elsewhere in the *Work*, there are plenty of recipes for blood, udder, lung, spleen, tripe, head, and tongue. Scappi was the finest chef working in the most gastronomically advanced city in Europe, yet his book shows clearly that he relished cooking with brains, eyes, and testicles.

He puts even more humble ingredients to imaginative use in the *Work*. He suggests cooking leeks and onions in a rich broth, chopping them up, frying them in lard, and binding them with beaten egg, Parmesan, and spices. As with all his vegetable recipes, of which there are very many, Scappi is careful to record when the produce is normally in season, for example nettles and mallow, both of which are best in spring and autumn. There are also dishes made from barley, millet, chestnut flour, broken chickpeas, and even from a recent New World import that was destined for a hugely important and often ignominious role in the history of Italian eating: maize, prepared in the form of a porridge or *polenta*. Scappi gives it flavor with fatty broth, sausage pieces, cheese, cinnamon, and saffron.

But it is not only the ingredients of popular eating that make it to the pope's table. Scappi is not ashamed to admit that many of his recipes have risen as far up the social scale as he has. The sophisticated *ravioli* we saw smothering a boiled chicken in the sample menu for December 15 are a prime example: Scappi points out that the "common people" refer to them as *annolini*. There is also a dish "that the Neapolitans call *pizza*": it is a rich pie whose marzipan crust is filled with mashed almonds, pine nuts, dates, figs, raisins, and biscuits. (The meeting between the word *pizza* and a flat bread or *focaccia* smeared with tomato sauce lay a long way in the future.)

Because Scappi was a Lombard and spent his early career in Venice and Ravenna, the north and northeast of Italy are understandably overrepresented in his choice of dishes. Among these Milanese and Venetian recipes, we glimpse how he built up his expertise through face-to-face encounters with his suppliers. He tells us, for example, that fishermen from Chioggia (the town on the Lagoon where the Venetian salt pans were located) griddle goby over the embers, or put them in a soup with Malmsey wine, water, a little vinegar, and "Venetian spices." The river fishermen of the Po valley have a similar way with barbel. Turbot from the gulf of Ravenna is nicest in a soup. In fact, "the fishermen from Chioggia and Venice make the best soups. They get better results than cooks do because they cook them in the very instant they catch them."

The aromatic, sweet-and-sour fish soups that Scappi learned to make from the fishermen he knew may sound unusual by today's criteria. But regardless of how they tasted, they point to the dialogue between producers and consumers that cooks like Scappi orchestrated. The fishermen of the Venetian Lagoon offered their knowledge of fish, and in return they developed a taste for the sweeter, spice-heavy flavors that since the Middle Ages had come increasingly to dominate elite cuisine.

Royal White Tart

In late January 1550 the overfed cardinals finally saw sense. Their abuses of the regulations were all too plainly the main reason why they had failed so far to elect a new pope, so they set up a reform committee within the conclave, and enforced the Viterbo regimen anew: extensions to cells were knocked down, eighty unauthorized visitors were expelled, weapons were banned, and only one course was allowed at each meal.

Ritual could finally reassert itself over politics and self-indulgence. A week later, on February 7, 1550, seventy-one days after the doors to the conclave had been locked, the papal throne was erected in the Pauline chapel, and the new pope took his seat for the first time. The cardinals were arranged in their usual places before him—this was where most of the negotiating had been done over the last few months. As the master of ceremonies read out a name, each cardinal approached the throne and kissed the pope on the hand, foot, and mouth. The scene was watched over by Michelangelo's freshly painted *Martyrdom of Saint Peter*: it showed the white-bearded fisherman nailed to a cross that was being lowered upside down into the ground; his pale, wiry trunk was twisted so that he could cast an admonishing glare over his right shoulder at both his successor and the men who had chosen him.

Pope Giovan Maria Del Monte announced that he had chosen the name Julius III. One of the many scandalous rumors that had circulated about Del Monte during the conclave was a boast he had made to the effect that, if he was made pope, he would give his lover a cardinal's red hat. Sure enough, a matter of weeks after his election, he elevated his seventeen-year-old monkey trainer to the cardinalate. Personally very pious, Julius III was also bawdy, moody, profligate, and politically indecisive. It turned out that the longest conclave of the Renaissance had elected possibly the worst of its many bad popes.

Yet Bartolomeo Scappi seems to have remembered Pope Julius with a certain fondness. Or at least that is the impression one gleans from the fact that, although Scappi likely worked for him only temporarily, Julius is the only pope with a recipe bearing his name in the *Work*:

TO MAKE ROYAL WHITE TART
AS POPE JULIUS III LIKED IT

Ingredients
2 pounds of *provatura* cheese, freshly made the same day.
   (Then as now, *provatura* was a fresh cheese, made from
   milk that is curdled straight from the buffalo.)
2 pounds of fine sugar
3 ounces of rose water
Either 3 *capi di latte* made that day, or a glass of milk and
   cream. (The nearest modern equivalent to *capi di latte*,
   literally "heads of milk," would be *panna cotta*.)
15 fresh egg whites

Fresh butter to grease the pastry dish, and flour to dust it
Sugar for forming a crust and egg white for glazing

Pound the *provatura* in the mortar until it has the consistency of
butter, adding the fine sugar, the rose water, and either the *capi
di latte* or the milk and cream. Then pass everything through a
sieve. Pour into the prepared pastry dish and cook gently in the
oven, with more heat above than below. (Scappi's directory of
kitchen equipment includes special frames used to put embers
above a pot or dish.) When it is nearly cooked, encrust it with
sugar and glaze it with egg white before removing from the
oven. Served hot or cold, this dish is particularly good in May
because of the quality of the *provatura* and milk.

Why the tribute? There is no obvious explanation for Scappi's gesture in the many reports of Julius's lifestyle: they suggest that the new
pope was given to banqueting, but no more or less than his predeces-
sors. Julius was unusual in that he was fond of garlic and even more
so onions, which were brought specially for him from Gaeta, a coastal
town south of Rome. Given the low reputation that onions enjoyed,
perhaps this was a way to remind people of his humble origins—he
liked everyone to know how far he had risen to reach the papal throne.
(Onions are still used comparatively sparingly in Italy: there is no Italian
equivalent of *soupe à l'oignon*, or indeed of the huge quantities of onion
that the British and Americans tend to like in their pasta sauces and atop
their pizzas.)

Toward the end of his five-year reign, Pope Julius was troubled by
gout and weakened by excess; he reduced his food intake until he almost
passed away from hunger. He finally died in March 1555. It was a sign
that the elite cooks of Rome would soon have to face leaner times,
which may account for Scappi's little gesture of homage in *provatura*
and *capi di latte*—and probably also explains his understated nostalgia
for the Conclave of 1549. By the time he came to write his *Work*, the
election of Julius III must have seemed like the sun's last blaze before
it set on a gloriously exuberant culinary age. For even though the next
pope, Marcellus II, lasted only twenty- two days, it was a long enough

reign for him to inaugurate a more austere regimen in the Vatican by banishing gold plates and silver cutlery from his table.

The pope after that, Paul IV, was feared for his zealotry and gave the Counter-Reformation a fearsome new impetus. He introduced the Roman Index of Prohibited Books and filled the Inquisition's dungeons with heretics. He confined the city's Jews to a ghetto for the first time; they were also forced to sell their property and wear yellow caps, and were banned from working in food retail.

From a cook's point of view, however, Paul IV was not a bad pope. The banquets resumed—for the glory of the Church. However, like many pontiffs who followed him during the Counter-Reformation, Paul was personally abstemious, and a rigid observer of periods of fasting and abstinence.

Pius IV, the next occupant of the throne, made Scappi into his secret cook in 1564. Pius IV was known to enjoy his food, but preferred simple fare, and ate more *polenta* than was good for him. (He was from Lombardy, after all.) Scappi notes in passing that he liked fried frogs dressed with garlic and parsley (another good Po valley dish), and consumed a great deal of barley water—one of the *Work*'s recipes for convalescents.

But the irony of the *Work* is that Scappi wrote it while in the employ of the most self-denying pope of this or any other age. Pius V, who confirmed Scappi in the position that Pius IV had awarded him, wore a friar's rough habit under his ceremonial robes. He abolished the gargantuan annual dinners traditionally held to celebrate the pope's election, and gave the money to the poor. He fasted often, and even when he did eat it was sparingly: a little bread cooked in broth with a couple of eggs for lunch; and for dinner, vegetable soup, salad, some shellfish, and stewed fruit. Silence was observed during these frugal meals, and long prayers recited both before and after. Meat appeared on the pope's table only twice a week. On pain of excommunication, he forbade Scappi to add anything to his soups that would make them more nourishing. As a final insult to the cook's talents, he even stopped him from using spices.

Bartolomeo Scappi had come all the way from Lake Maggiore, and climbed all the way up the long career ladder of Renaissance cookery, accumulating more gastronomic knowledge than anyone had ever done before, only to spend what should have been his glory years doing nothing more creative than making broth for a saint. (Pius V was canonized in 1712.) The greatest chef of the age was left with a lot of time on his hands. He may have been motivated to spend some of that time writing the *Work* out of financial hardship. Given that he was paid partially in food, and in waste from the kitchen, the austere regimen in the Vatican must have reduced his income considerably. Scappi's lavish recipes may also have been a gesture of defiance. One wonders what Saint Pius V would have made of the *Work*'s great compendium of temptations of the flesh.

• • •

The death of Julius III, Pope Del Monte, in 1555 is as good a date as any at which to mark the end of the Italian Renaissance and the beginning of the Counter-Reformation. The abstemious Saint Pius V persecuted Jews, burned books and heretics, waged religious war, and banned debate on theological issues such as the Immaculate Conception. In the pope's domains, ritual and dogma now held sway over inquiry. This was not the way to make Italian culture a model for other countries, and, slowly, Italy moved to the margins of European life. Urbanization proceeded elsewhere and Italy's cities were left behind. Its princes were bested by the great territorial states of France, Spain, and England. Its bankers and merchants—those who had not turned themselves into nobles and landowners—were overtaken by the thrusting new commercial classes of northern Europe.

Italian cooks were left behind, too. The banquets continued, of course. The standard of cooking did not drop. But while the coming centuries brought revolutionary gastronomic change in Europe, Italy was, generally speaking, slow to evolve. The elite European cuisine of the Middle Ages and the Renaissance was surprisingly uniform—the use of spices is the aspect that most marks it out to our sensibilities. Subsequently, between the 1600s and the 1800s, spices underwent a slow but inexorable decline in prestige. From amid the dissolving cloud of pepper, cinnamon, and cloves, the outlines of more distinct national cooking styles appeared. Yet Italian cooks remained attached to spices for longer than their peers in England and France. Italian food also became less "Italian" during the same period: after Scappi, more than three hundred years would pass before anyone else tried to bring the many flavors of Italy to one table as he had.

The seventeenth and eighteenth centuries also witnessed a Europe-wide agricultural revolution that brought new commercial energies, new farming methods, and new crops—the American imports like cocoa, potatoes, tomatoes, and maize without which the modern Western diet would be inconceivable. Partly as a result, the huge gap between the diet of the masses and the diet of their rulers narrowed. Famine gradually disappeared—although hunger remained. Once again, Italy was slower to experience these great changes.

The several centuries after Scappi were an age of relative decline for food in Italy. Foreigners came to sneer and laugh at the very idea of Italian cuisine. But during this time, change did occur; the New World ingredients *were* adopted, which brought Italian food far closer to its contemporary form. Some of the changes that unfolded during the Middle Ages and Renaissance continued, such as the development of typical local specialties and their reputations.

Moreover, after the Renaissance, some important changes in the popular diet were set in motion. At the same time, from the historian's point of view, new kinds of source material create a clearer picture of what food meant to much broader sections of the urban populace. Thus, during the Baroque and Enlightenment eras the history of Italian food was made in the streets and piazzas rather than in the court and the dining hall.

III

STREET FOOD

8

Bologna, 1600s

The Game of Cockaigne

The Banquet of the Underfed

Bologna has been called *la Grassa*—"the Fat"—since the early 1200s. In the 1600s, the century of the Baroque, Fat Bologna also became known as the home of Italy's most illustrious sausage. Just as important, it was one of the places where the strong association between food and city identity took on strange new forms as it encountered a mass audience.

Bologna became *la Grassa* for the simple reason that it was prosperous: for centuries silk, wool, and hemp were its major trades. The city's university played a major part in building its renown, because the number of visiting academics and students helped spread a profitable repute for hospitality and good eating that the Bolognese were eager to maintain.

Thus Bologna was fat long before "fat" became the insult that it is now. To appreciate the polar reversal that the connotations of fatness have undergone since then, we need to recall that until the midpoint in the twentieth century Italians were a people all too familiar with scarcity. The whites and yellows in the meals prepared by the likes of Messisbugo and Scappi stood out all the brighter against an ashen background of hunger and famine. Hunger so insistent that it felt inborn. Famine so frequent that it seemed as natural as the rhythm of the seasons. In this

129

world, meat commanded a higher price if it was heavily streaked with white. Fat carried a halo of wealth, well-being, and security.

But even the fat city of Bologna was not sheltered from the threat of starvation: it was subject to more than a hundred famines in the years between 1200 and 1850. One of the worst began in 1588 and only relaxed its grip with the good harvest of 1597. The population fell by nearly 20 percent. The mortality rate in the surrounding countryside would have been much higher.

How did the hungry cook? The mass of peasants lived at subsistence level and the lowest strata in the city probably fared little better. But how did they prepare food when they had it? Did they have a civilization of the table? The evidence needed to answer those questions is lacking, although the staple ingredients are known. In Emilia, the region where Bologna is located, and in many other places, the peasants and urban poor ate beans, turnips, onions, leeks, and garlic. Chestnuts were a fundamental food, especially in more mountainous parts: they were boiled, roasted, or dried, pounded, and made into *polenta*. But for most of the history of Italian eating, we can only guess at the skills that transformed acorns into bread, and conjured soup out of wild leaves and roots.

The problem, of course, is that for a long time the poor could not write, so even if they had recipes, they could not pass them to posterity. Professional cooks and stewards from Martino to Scappi were literate and prestigious enough to leave firsthand testimonies, thanks to which we, many centuries later, can reimagine how the privileged classes of the cities ate within a whole food-world of feelings, rules, and stories. The food-world of the poor has a wraithlike historical existence by comparison. Any collection of the "literature of the hungry" from the eleventh to the sixteenth century would be a fearfully skinny volume.

This is why the Bolognese popular poet and dramatist Giulio Cesare Croce represents such a novelty in the history of Italian food. A contemporary of Shakespeare, Croce was born a blacksmith's son in the Bolognese countryside. He was first heard plucking away at a two-stringed lute by the aristocratic Fantuzzi family, who were in retreat from the city's enervating heat. They invited him to entertain them, and fed him with leftovers in recompense. In the Fantuzzi villa that summer, Croce evidently saw enough abundance to know that, when autumn came, he would abandon his father's forge and head for Bologna.

Before long, Croce's thin, olive-skinned face was as recognizable as any in the city. Performing in the piazzas, he made himself into the poet of Bologna's daily grind and its great occasions. He celebrated the squabbling of laundrywomen, drinkers, and market traders, and mourned the passing of aristocrats and popes—Bologna was under papal rule during this period. Croce also published his writings in the sheets and pamphlets that first became popular in the second half of the 1500s—a sign of widening literacy in the cities. They told of Bolognese history and Italian current affairs, of street gangs and earthquakes, of executions and the weather, of melons and fleas, of love and debt.

Croce's chapbooks made him famous far beyond his hometown, but they did not make him rich. Perhaps if he had led a less dissolute life as a young man, or if fewer children had issued from his two marriages, his brand of popular verse would have afforded him better security from want. Even in the best of times, he would always have depended on the occasional affluent patron for a glimpse of the good life. As it was, his career coincided with the great famine of the 1590s, and he died in 1609 just as another season of shortage was setting in.

If there had been a cuisine of the poor, it would have left prominent signs in the work of Giulio Cesare Croce, but indications are that this cookery was rudimentary at best. A good example is in Croce's greatest work, *The Cunning Wiles of Bertoldo*, which narrated the adventures of a crude but crafty peasant who finds himself at court. At the end of the story, Bertoldo dies of indigestion because, instead of the humble fare he asks for, the royal doctors give him a meal that is too rich for his primitive metabolism. The king, filled with remorse, engraves the peasant's tomb with lines of praise in gold letters, ending with:

> Death came upon him amid horrible screams,
> For he could not get his turnip and beans.

In his will, Bertoldo leaves the gardener his straw hat as a thank-you for the leeks he brought him for breakfast; he also remembers the cook who made him turnip cooked in the ashes, and pots of bean soup with onion.

These comic lines hardly constitute a documentary photograph of peasant eating habits, but they illustrate the limited implements and techniques that were available to most people: a pot hung over a fire, and ashes used for baking did not permit much creativity. The women cooking in most peasant households were also part of the rural workforce rather than queens of the hearth—bulk and simplicity would likely have been the guiding principles of their cookery. No citizen lived more than a short walk from open countryside, so the resources of the fields and woods were a vital part of everyone's diet. The seasons dictated what was available. Croce wrote several pamphlets celebrating the arrival of spring, and with it the greens that brought relief from the monotony and scarcity of winter. He sang, for example, of the April wedding of the radish and the turnip in a poem that is barely more than a guest list of hundreds of vegetables, leaves, plants, and flowers. Another poem, about May, relates how the herbs all marry one another to create salads. Hunger had clearly taught Croce much botanical lore, as it did to other *bolognesi*, but not a "cuisine."

Thus Croce recorded some of the ingredients that were found on humble tables in his day. But his real value to historians of Italian food resides in other aspects of his work. Like most ordinary citizens, Croce suffered hardship but lived in close proximity to wealth. He knew both numbing hunger *and* the staggering excess of aristocratic dinners. Fears of starvation and dreams of abundance were the poles of Croce's worldview—and of the vast majority of the Italian population over many centuries. What Croce brings across the centuries is not so much the diet of the poor, as their food imagination.

Take the following menu recorded by Croce in the dire famine year of 1590:

Snail's horn relish
Flies' head pie
Hornet meatballs
Wren's tripe
Bee's ribs and kidneys
Midge's foot soup
A quarter of braised wasp with its gizzard, caul, and tripe

Pan-fried fly's liver and flea's brain
Jellied bat's foot
Stewed spleen of spring frog
Cricket's eye soup
Horsefly tongue pie

And so on, through grasshopper's lung in broth to cicada chops, belly of cockroach and mole's pluck fried in leech fat. Not a real meal, of course: it comes from Croce's *The Banquet of the Underfed*, an allegorical play about the wedding of Lady Famine, daughter of Sir Poorharvest, to young Master Sterile. The menu is a parody of upper-class cuisine, the kind of feast prepared by the great Renaissance stewards. Croce's popular audience would have known about such feasts, too—if only by hearsay. He uses the same joke in other works, such as *The True Rule for Staying Thin and Spending Little*, which is a verse catalogue of luxurious foods to be avoided, including capons, pies, and *maccaroni* with lots of cheese. The poem's comic point is that nobody sane would want to stay thin.

Croce's humor suggests that the humblest participated in Italy's rich civilization of the table primarily in their imaginations. When they could not eat, they fantasized. Scappi's many writings show them to be interested in stories, entertainments, and games that allowed them to sample the best that was available—even if only vicariously. Thus in Baroque Bologna, as elsewhere, the food culture of the wealthy often molded the sensibilities of the poor.

The following pages tell two stories from Baroque Bologna that have the hungry imagination as their major theme; they center on the pig, the very embodiment of Bolognese Fatness. One of Croce's primary roles was to play the great city festivals back to the people who had experienced them. Many festivals, notably Lent and Carnival, drama- tized the swing between want and satiety that dominated most people's lives. The uniquely Bolognese Feast of the Suckling Pig, which Croce attended and recounted many times, is the subject of the first story. The second story traces the emergence of a typical food that Croce lionized and that, more than any other, symbolizes Bologna's cuisine today: the *mortadella* sausage.

The Feast of the Suckling Pig

In Bologna, the pig is king, and is venerated in a gastronomic cult. The pigs of the Bologna area have been famous since Roman times. But in the 1500s and 1600s they were very different beasts than the ones one might see on the vast Emilian farms today. They were smaller, darker, and more bristly. But more important, they also *meant* different things. In those days pigs loomed even larger in the symbolic life of the city than they do now. One obvious reason for this was that sausages and hams tend to have a more visceral appeal to anyone on the breadline. But there were many more facets to Bologna's pig culture. The time and place to find out about them was in the city's main square on Saint Bartholomew's Day, August 24, 1597.

In that year, the annual Feast of the Suckling Pig was celebrated with greater fervor than anyone could remember. July had seen the best harvest for a decade, a harvest that seemed finally to have chased the specter of starvation from Bologna's streets. Once the gates had been closed for the feast, everyone in the city felt impelled, at whatever cost to personal safety and comfort, to find a place in Piazza Maggiore. Every order of Bolognese society was present in its appropriate place: from the senior clergy and magistrates, through the guildsmen and confraternity members, down to the general populace. The square became so crammed with carriages, horses, and other animals that people were squeezed onto doorsteps and windowsills, or forced to scramble up to loggias and balconies. On the rooftops the bravest and most agile were rewarded with a vertiginous panorama of the throng from their seats in the crenels or atop the cornices. Luckiest of all were the city's ladies who had reserved places on the wooden stands that had been specially erected around the periphery of the square. Before them, in the center of the piazza, stood a wooden platform about eighty feet square on which an elementary rural scene was laid: a road, a thicket of real bushes and shrubs, a glade; an oak tree stood at each corner of the stage.

At last, barely audible above the expectant din, came the screech and hum of bagpipes and shawms (a precursor of the modern oboe). Countless necks were strained to snatch a glimpse of the festooned ox-drawn cart that had drawn up alongside the stage. Four shepherdesses and

An extravagant setting is constructed in Bologna's Piazza
Maggiore for the annual Feast of the Suckling Pig, 1600s.

eight peasants in identical colored clothes dismounted; those not playing instruments carried baskets of country provisions. As they climbed
the ramp toward the scenery and came into full view of the crowd, they
began vigorously to mime naïve delight at their surroundings. Soon
they settled down for a picnic and a dance in the clearing—as country
people were evidently supposed to do. Their ungainly leaps and weird
rustic gestures drew volleys of laughter from the onlooking citizens.

The laughter was still bouncing off the vast, unfinished façade of the
Cathedral of San Petronio when, from another corner of the piazza,
more noise was added to the cacophony: a pack of horn-blowing huntsmen and their hounds charged straight into the crowd and started to
force a path toward the stage. When they finally made it through to join
the spectacle, a few of their number demonstratively spotted some doves
in the four oak trees, and climbed into the branches to capture them.

The birds had little chance of escape, given that their wings had been
clipped and their feet tied to the fronds. Ripped from their perches, they
were thrown onto the stage, tossed from hand to hand, yanked from fist
to fist, and rapidly reduced to fragments of feather and blood.

As the last tufts of red and white down were landing, the peasants and shepherdesses joined in the jollity and offered a drink to their friends the hunters. But the celebrations were rapidly superseded by the pandemonium of the hunt itself. The animals came in waves. First rabbits and hares, then foxes and other quadrupeds. Following them were chickens, pheasant, peacocks, ducks, mergansers, geese, and quail—all released from trapdoors hidden in the greenery, all with their wings clipped. The company of peasants and shepherdesses, dogs and huntsmen flung themselves across the stage in pursuit. The spectators laughed and cheered.

Once the prey had been netted, throttled, or impaled, the last and most eagerly expected animal of all was released. The Suckling Pig scurried from the bushes to a climactic roar from around the piazza. It enjoyed a respectably long chase around the scenery before it was stopped, speared, and paraded in a musical triumph across the stage.

The players then marched to the Palazzo Comunale, where the fruit of the hunt was presented to the vice-legate who exercised the pope's power in the city, and the other local authorities. As the company returned to the stage to resume picnicking and cavorting, the city elders had all of the carcasses thrown into the crowd to be fought over. Apart, of course, from the Suckling Pig.

In Bolognese folk memory, the next few hours were a gala of public drooling. Croce exclaimed that the aroma emanating from the kitchens of the Palazzo Comunale was good enough to wake the dead. The tantalizing wait came to an end only shortly before sunset. To a fanfare of fifes and trumpets, the source of the smell made its ceremonial reappearance on the balcony under the forbidding bronze statue of Gregory XIII (a Bolognese pope, naturally). Now stuffed with spices, spit-roasted, garlanded with flowers, and mounted on a tray, the Suckling Pig was displayed to the multitude.

A familiar game began. Musicians struck up. The crowd made ready with bags and sheets. The servants holding the Suckling Pig shuffled from one end of the balcony to the other, occasionally making as if to sling their burden over the balustrade, only to pull back at the last instant.

Below them, the dregs of the city, mostly porters or seasonal workers from the countryside, elbowed expectantly for space at the foot of the Palazzo Comunale's huge columned portal. As Croce recorded, these were "low, no-account people of the sort not inclined to look too closely at what they were doing from the point of view of their honor." After they had surged forward in response to one particularly extravagant dummy throw of the Suckling Pig, a cauldron of broth was emptied over their heads. But they knew the traditions of Saint Bartholomew's Day, and took their savory bath in excellent spirit. (The wealthier citizens viewing the scene may well not have been laughing at quite the same joke.)

For a good quarter of an hour the servants feinted, and the crowd surged. Then, at last, the music ceased and the Suckling Pig was tipped into the ragged melee to be torn apart amid flailing fists.

An impressive fireworks display followed: onstage, a flaming serpent launched from the roof of the Palazzo de' Notari ignited a Turkish ship. When the spectacle finally ended, the elders and their guests withdrew into the Palazzo Comunale for a banquet, and everyone else hurried off for their own suckling pig dinner.

Bologna had held a civic festival on August 24 since at least the 1200s. It was thought to be a celebration of a military victory, but its roots may even go back to Roman times. In the late 1500s, its meaning seems to have shifted. In 1568 the authorities threw a roast suckling pig to the crowd for the first time—previously it had been a prize in a horse race. The huge and inventive celebration that marked the end of the long years of famine in 1597 was the first to include a mock hunt and fireworks, which set a pattern for the ever more carefully staged festivities of future years. Thus, in 1597, the Feast of the Suckling Pig that Croce witnessed took a shape it would maintain for the whole Baroque era and beyond. The last one occurred in 1796.

Open-air festivals were common in many Italian cities in the 1600s and 1700s. In Bologna's streets and piazzas, a cycle of elaborate public ceremonies registered the passing of time more surely than the changing seasons. Every year, halfway through Lent, a wooden effigy of an old woman, representing Lent itself, would be sawn in half, then burned or thrown into the Reno canal. Every year, on the night of June 29, a line of penitents hunched under the weight of their crosses would wind its way through the dark streets to mark the feast of Saints Peter and Paul. Every year, on August 14, the authorities would celebrate the city's victory over the Visconti in 1443 with a mounted parade to the sanctuary of the Madonna del Monte. Saints' days and sacred processions, horse races and jousts had turned the calendar into a symbol of political stability, a stability dating back to 1506 when the city had settled into the possession of the pope. In fact Bologna enjoyed a charmed stasis for more than two centuries. Despite the occasional downward lurch caused by famine or plague, the population stayed stable at just below the 70,000 mark until the city joined the Kingdom of Italy in 1859. The layout of the city also remained substantially unchanged. The revelers on August 24, 1597, would have found themselves in familiar surroundings if they had lived long enough to attend the last Feast of the Suckling Pig, 199 years later. Granted, in parts of Bologna, they may have missed a few medieval towers and found the late Baroque and Mannerist churches somewhat overwhelming. But Piazza Maggiore would have been identical: even the façade of San Petronio was still unfinished (as it is today).

Little changed in the city's dramatic social divisions, either: as late as 1840, some 30,000 Bolognese still depended wholly or partly on begging and charity for a living. City politics remained much the same, too: a senate of fifty landed aristocrats, appointed for life, met every Tuesday and Friday throughout the sixteenth and seventeenth centuries. Every two months, with great ceremony, the Senate nominated a Gonfaloniere ("standard-bearer") and eight elders to handle day-to-day government. Every three years the pope would send a new governor, or cardinal-legate, to exercise princely authority by proxy. (His entry into the city with a troop of Swiss guards was yet another occasion for a parade.) Officially, the legate chose the senators and governed with their counsel. In reality, the Bolognese aristocracy, while showing deference to the representative of the Holy Father, quietly did their utmost to make sure that their own power was not unduly curbed.

Compromise, charity, and spectacle were the pillars of Bolognese stability: compromise between its civil and religious rulers; charity and spectacle for the populace. Throwing roast suckling pigs to the rabble may not seem a particularly sophisticated means of government, but Bologna's political stability tells us that it actually worked very well.

The medieval poor dreamed of many marvels: cooking pots that boiled on their own, trumpets that revived the dead, donkeys that shat solid gold. Perhaps the most popular fables of all told of a Land of Cockaigne, a Land of Plenty, in which there were rivers of wine, fountains of oil, and mountains of cheese, and where roast suckling pigs trotted about on their own, ready to be eaten. From the mid-1500s sheets printed with pictures and stories on the same themes became popular in several Italian cities. Soon canny rulers began to see the Land of Cockaigne as a source of propaganda. Hence, among many other innovations, the Feast of the Suckling Pig. The propagandist twist on the old fable was that the animals hurled down to the mob did not descend from some superabundant never-never land, but from the real center of political authority in Bologna. When famine was never far from memory or fearful imagining, the city had to be able to demonstrate to all its ability to provide plenty. To be Bolognese, and to be closed within the city on Saint Bartholomew's Day, was to be entitled to a share in that plenty—even if it was no more than a fragment of roasted pork that you had won in a public fistfight staged for the amusement of more fortunate citizens. Croce tells us that on the evening of the Festival of the Suckling Pig, when the well-to-do went home to their own *porchetta*, the desperate would pawn their cloaks to buy a slice or two at a hostelry. If this was the price for taking part, as a Bolognese should, in the great city festival, then it had to be paid.

Mortadella: **Treble Six**

The mighty edifice that is Bolognese cuisine rests on the single foundation stone of *mortadella*, which has so much "typicality" that it has become synonymous with the city. Often known simply as "Bologna"—hence the American corruption *baloney*—a *mortadella* is a chubby cylinder of cooked sausage in string, generally about the size of a small baby. Sixty percent of it comprises good cuts of pork, triple-minced to produce both a smooth texture and the unmistakable pink color revealed when it is sliced. The meat is evenly speckled throughout with pearly cubes of fat from the pig's throat, which serve to make the taste even smoother and sweeter.

Mortadella is an eminently *typical* dish, but it is not a Bolognese pure-bred. The word *mortadella* came into Italian in the Middle Ages from French and then Tuscan, having originated in the Latin word for the mortar in which the meat was pounded. In Italy the term embraced all kinds of sausages. A recipe for *mortadelle* in the Venetian *Book for Cook* uses boiled pork liver, cheese, and eggs. Platina's *Respectable Pleasure* tells us that Master Martino used to spit-roast *mortadelle* the size of eggs made from fatty veal haunch seasoned with marjoram, parsley, and spices, and bound with egg yolk and cheese. Predictably Bartolomeo Scappi's *mortatelle* (*sic*) are more refined: pork sausages for frying flavored with precise measures of three different spices as well as dried fennel, mint, marjoram, and wild thyme. In short, everyone seems to have made *mortadelle* of one kind or another.

Bologna had long been known for its pork products, although not uniquely for *mortadella*. Yet within a few years of Scappi's death, Giulio Cesare Croce would write, in *The Excellence and Triumph of the Pig*, "What can I say about . . . *mortadella* and *salame*? They are foods for princes and lords. The city of Bologna's boast is that it makes them with all the distinction they deserve." And not long after Croce's death the word *mortadella* would become exclusively joined forever both to the kind of sausage we know today and to the city of Bologna.

What changed? Scappi's *Work* demonstrates that, through the late Middle Ages and into the Renaissance, an increasing range of products were becoming associated with different nodes in the Italian urban network—as happened with the medieval "branding" of Parmesan cheese by its identification with the city of Parma. This same process was subsequently fortified by tendencies in the world economy. As trade grew in the 1600s and 1700s, specialization increased. Various cities in Europe became internationally famous for specific products, like Delft for pottery and Lyons for silk. Cheese from Parma became valued in other countries, too: in 1666, the diarist Samuel Pepys buried his "parmazan" in the garden to save it from the Great Fire of London. By the end of the century, Bolognese *mortadella*, although a comparatively late starter as a local specialty, would be known as far abroad as Parmesan was.

In fact the available documentation suggests that *mortadella*'s rise to prominence marks a significant step toward "typicality" in the modern sense. In the Baroque era, *mortadella* seems to have acquired several of typicality's key components: a precise recipe, protective legislation, an exaggerated ancestry, and a heavy investment of civic patriotism.

First, the recipe. The earliest account of how to make Bolognese *mortadella* dates from 1644. Minus the spices, it is very close to contemporary Bologna sausage.

TO MAKE APPROXIMATELY 100 POUNDS
OF *MORTADELLE*

Ingredients
33 pounds and 4 ounces (i.e., exactly a third) of fatty
  meat from the pig's throat or belly cut into hazelnut-
  size cubes
66 pounds and 8 ounces of choice lean pork, from the
  leg or shoulder, with all the fat, sinew, and membrane
  removed
The part of the pig's intestine known as the "blind intestine" because it has only one opening—rather like a
  single eye. Or other intestines.
6 pounds of salt which has been dried on the fire,
  ground, and then sieved
2 ounces of cinnamon
2 ounces of cloves
2 nutmegs
4 grains of plant musk
12 pounds of whole peppercorns
2 pounds of grated cheese
A little sugar
Malmsey wine, or another good wine

Take the fatty meat and add 2 pounds of the salt. Grind the following spices together with a little sugar: cinnamon, cloves, nutmegs, musk. Dilute the mixture in a little Malmsey wine. Mix everything together and set aside in a large bowl.

Cut and pound the lean meat to a fine consistency, then splash with Malmsey wine. Then add the remaining salt, the peppercorns, and grated cheese, mixing everything together carefully and pounding lightly.

Then mix both portions of meat together well, pounding a little more. Fill the intestine with this mixture, then leave to dry in an oven or hot kitchen. Store in a well-ventilated place until spring, making sure that the *mortadelle* do not touch anything, even each other. They can then be stored somewhere cooler, as long as they are larded and any mold is removed. Some people store them in ashes.

A few years after this recipe was published, the first known law for the protection of a local Italian specialty was issued in order to save the reputation of Bolognese *mortadella*-makers. In 1661, the cardinal-legate who ran Bologna on behalf of the pope issued a proclamation against people "who show so little love for the public good that they arrogate themselves the right to make *mortadelle* containing some beef." This misdemeanor was particularly damaging to "the talent for making exquisitely perfect *mortadelle* that this City has enjoyed *since ancient times* [my italics]." Now the Romans certainly knew and appreciated the qualities of the pigs from the acorn-rich woods around Bologna, but there is no evidence that they knew *mortadella*, too. Thus, ironically, the first historical document to attest to the existence of genuine Bolognese *mortadella* as we know it today was also the first to invent a venerable tradition for the product.

The proclamation of 1661 set strict controls to protect this apparently timeless art and hefty fines for unauthorized producers. The political power of the city's Guild of Sausage-Makers is not hard to detect behind the cardinal's proclamation, which is understandably much celebrated by the modern *mortadella* industry: copies of it can be seen displayed in shop windows.

Baroque *mortadella* counterfeiters were not easy to deter, however. The cardinal-legate's 1661 proclamation mentions that makers of phony baloney were already ignoring existing laws. By the beginning of the 1700s, the Bolognese still had to resort to mystification and secrecy to shield their precious sausage. In the spring of 1706, a French Dominican friar called Jean-Baptiste Labat visited Bologna on his way home from more than a decade spent in France's Caribbean territories. His curiosity was immediately aroused by the city's most famous product. He had eaten Bologna sausage in the Americas, and found it even more appetizing on its own home turf. But how was it made? Some *bolognesi* told him that *mortadella* was made with the meat of newborn donkeys. (He dismissed this as a joke at his expense.) Others, that the main ingredient was boar. (Probably another red herring, he surmised, because all the wild porkers in the Americas would not have sufficed to make the mountains of sausage exported from Bologna.) More reliable informants told him that the domestic pig was the main ingredient, but he was also inclined to believe those who said that beef or veal entered the mix as well. "It is evident that the Bolognese are wise enough to make a mystery of its composition," he concluded. "And they are right to do so, because everyone would like to imitate them, and if they did, in the end, the trade in these meats would collapse entirely."

Given that Bologna's sausage was so commercially important, and had an international reputation to compare with that of the mighty Parmesan, considerable civic patriotism was attached to it, as is clear from one of the more unusual pieces of evidence in the history of Italian food: a Baroque board game.

Board games became popular in the 1600s. In the territories of the pope this was partly because dice and card games had become a source of tax revenue and an object of official censure. As one law issued in Rome in 1588 stated, "Ancient experience demonstrates how pernicious gaming is. It gives rise to the loss of private wealth and the ruin of whole families." Board games were explicitly excluded from the law's provisions.

Some of the games invented to take the place of cards and dice were accident-filled races akin to snakes-and-ladders. Others involved penalties and rewards handed out according to the throw of dice. Players had to follow instructions written on the square of the board that corresponded to the number they had thrown. Some numbers won money; others lost it. Some numbers brought an embarrassing forfeit, like blowing a raspberry at everyone in the room; others might bring the power to impose forfeits on others.

Giuseppe Maria Mitelli was Baroque Bologna's great designer of board games. He was born in the city in 1634, the second son of a successful painter. Much to his frustration, his own artistic efforts did not meet with the same acclaim as his father's, so he became an engraver, and made quite a career from this lesser, cheaper art. Prints reached a much broader audience than oils and frescoes since even the illiterate could enjoy them. Mitelli's prints were satirical, but always soundly based on official morality (his brother was, after all, a Jesuit).

Mitelli engraved thirty-three board games, including the Game of Cockaigne (1691). The illustrated squares correspond to specialties from different Italian cities. Throw fifteen, and you get bread from Padua. Throw eleven, and you get Genoese *gattafura*—the cheese pastry that Scappi mentions. Throw nine, and you get the almond biscuits from Pisa known as *cantucci*—now to be found on the typical Tuscan dessert menu at the Old Grindstone Restaurant in the White Mill. Throw seventeen, and you win another typical product that is still around today: nougat from Cremona—but you are only allowed to suck it. The most

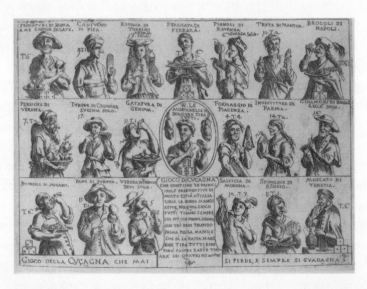

Board game in which players throw dice to win specialities from Italian cities, including Neapolitan broccoli, sausage from Modena, and Piacenza cheese (which would now be called Grana Padano—one of the varieties of Parmesan). But it takes a treble six to win the top prize: Bologna's *mortadella* sausage. Bologna, 1691.

delicious prizes await players who throw three dice with the same number. Hence a treble two wins Milanese tripe; a treble four brings Rome's fresh buffalo-milk cheese, *provatura*; and a treble six, needless to say, wins the greatest reward of all. In the central square of the board, a man is shown standing between two suspended sausages as big as his head: "Long live the *mortadelle* of Bologna," the caption reads. "You win everything."

The Game of Cockaigne has its basis in a popular Bolognese patriotism, and in the spread of the idea that Italy was a land of local specialties. But it also displays the same playful moralising as Mitelli's other engravings. "Nobody ever loses and everyone always wins in *The Game of Cockaigne*," the motto on Mitelli's board says. But as he must have known, only in a game or a public festival could Italy's urban Land of Plenty, its Cockaigne of typical dishes, be so effortlessly available to all.

• • •

Bologna was not the only city in which the myth of the Land of Plenty took on new forms and acquired a new political importance. Indeed, the most famous example was the *Cuccagna* in eighteenth-century Naples. The *Cuccagna*, or Cockaigne, was a multistory wooden structure decked out as a hill, a palace, a city, or such. On four successive Sundays at Carnival time, a *Cuccagna* would be erected in one of the city's largest squares. It would be stuffed with food and drink, then live chickens, geese, and other birds were crucified to its exterior. Once the king had given the signal, a mob of paupers would attack it, fighting with one another and climbing to the very top to gain possession of the bounty on offer. The deaths and injuries that resulted were all part of the entertainment.

In the 1700s Naples also acquired a ritual representation of plenty that could be enacted every day: eating *maccheroni*. By the middle of the eighteenth century, the city had firmly established its reputation as Italy's *maccheroni* capital. It was in Naples that *pasta secca* first became what it is now—a dish of the people, the crowning glory of the everyday Italian diet.

9

Naples, late 1700s

Maccheroni-Eaters

An Egg, a Frog, and Bad Wine

The eighteenth century was the era of the Grand Tour, when wealthy young gentlemen, most of them English, came to Italy to view the sites of the classical past—and, of course, to carouse. Their journals and letters provide a lively, but heavily biased commentary on the state of Italian food.

Almost every page written by Grand Tourists betrays a serene arrogance. The Italy they visited was merely the backdrop for the ruins that ancient Rome had left behind. Visitors from England generally contrasted the Italians' poverty and provincialism against the glorious standards set by the ancient civilization that had built the Colosseum and the Pantheon. Plainly, Italy had squandered its imperial inheritance, thus forfeiting the right to be Rome's true heir. No one could deny that Italy was beautiful, but even nature became evidence of Italian decline: such an incomparably fertile land was considered wasted on such slothful, ill-disciplined people.

To English tastes, Italian food offered the most alarming evidence of how nature's bounty had been spoiled. Most Grand Tourists agreed: with honorable exceptions like *mortadella* and Parmesan cheese, Italy's food was generally poor, and eating in the Italian countryside was often a disgusting experience. Forewarned, many travelers ate as little as possible of the local fare, and gravitated toward city inns run by English people, or at least by Italians trained in proper English cooking: bacon and cabbage, boiled mutton or beef, bread pudding.

On returning home, Grand Tourists outdid one another in their tales of how badly they had been fed. For a century London seems to have hosted an informal competition to find the worst Italian eating experience. One person reported paying a fortune for meals cooked so that "a Hottentot could not have beheld them without loathing." Another complained that "when eatables were found, we were almost poisoned by their cookery." The meals set before the English in Italy included "mustard and crows' gizzards," "an egg, a frog and bad wine," "a soop [sic] like wash, with pieces of liver swimming in it; a plate full of brains, fried in the shape of fritters." One traveler said he had had to eat "the water of a cistern full of tadpoles" mixed with wine "that resembled treacle much more than the juice of the grape. While I held the pitcher to my lips, I formed a dam with a knife, to prevent the little frogs from slipping down my throat." But the competition's winner was probably one Lady Miller, who in a village near Ferrara was offered "a pork soup with the bouillée in it, namely a hog's head, with the eye-lashes, eyes, and nose on; the very food the wretched animal had last eat of before he made his exit remained sticking about the teeth."

It is difficult to know whether such accounts are a true reflection of Italian food. Italian agriculture was certainly backward in some regions by comparison with British, and life in the country was undoubtedly harder. Yet there is clearly snobbery and literary fashion in play here, too. Moreover, English food had a different geography. During the eighteenth century the English cooking tradition took its characteristic form, and at that time it was the country gentry who were thought to be the bearers of the values that produced good English eating: they were as hearty, wholesome, and unfussy as game pie, a good ham, or a nice joint of beef. The prestige that country life enjoyed in England probably generated mistaken expectations about *where* one should eat in Italy. Many Grand Tourists had the wrong map of Italian food—a rural map. All the same, when they arrived in the right place to eat—in the cities, that is—they then provided sometimes insightful and vivid testimonies.

"From Leaf-Eaters to *Maccheroni*-Eaters"

Paroxysm gripped Mount Vesuvius at exactly the right time. The Grand Tourists had understandably avoided Naples during the terrible famine and pestilence of 1763–64, when the city stank of death and seethed with rebellious anger. But when it was all over, they returned in greater numbers than ever. The journey to Italy was part of every wealthy young Briton's education, and Naples was now that journey's almost obligatory final destination. After Rome, whose ruins held such sober lessons, the sunny gaiety of Naples made for a suitably relaxing next stop. As James Boswell confessed, for example, "During my stay at Naples I was truly libertine. I ran after girls without restraint. My blood was inflamed by the burning climate, and my passions were violent." So, perhaps sensing the Grand Tourists' need for release, Vesuvius obliged them by erupting no fewer than eight times in the 1770s. The spectacle could not have been better calculated to impress pictures of the city in to northern European minds: the cone smoldering in sunshine above the blue curve of the bay; hellish fire streams glowing by night; the lustrous greens of the land when the rain washed it clean of a gray-black pall of ash.

Vesuvius aside, the city seemed made to be captured in prints and paintings. Such was the conclusion reached by the greatest German polymath of the Age of Enlightenment, Johann Wolfgang von Goethe, who visited Italy in 1786–87 to escape from the stresses of political office. His response to the sights of Naples was ecstatic: "Every time I wish to write words, visual images come up, images of the fruitful countryside, the open sea, the islands veiled in a haze, the smoking mountain, etc., and I lack the mental organ which could describe them."

Challenges to the mental organ lay on all sides of Naples. To the west, there were the Roman ruins and unearthly, steaming exhalations of the Phlegraean Plain. At the volcano's base, segments of the embalmed cities of Pompeii and Herculaneum were first opened to visitors in the 1750s. Farther down the coast Paestum became a popular tourist attraction in the 1770s; its uncannily well preserved Greek temples stood amid idyllic countryside—the very definition of a picturesque scene. Near the city center, visitors could take a moonlit promenade along the

Chiaia. And when Goethe saw the rays of the setting sun creep into the entrance of the Grotto of Posillipo he wrote, "Now I can forgive anyone for going off his head about Naples."

With a population of around 400,000 in the late 1700s, Naples was by far the biggest city in Italy, because unlike all the others it was the capital of an entire kingdom, embracing both Sicily and the southern part of the Italian mainland. (This was the latest incarnation of the realm founded centuries before by the Norman kings of Sicily.) For the Grand Tourists, the city's swarming populace made for as quaint a spectacle as the surroundings. Goethe was not alone in thinking that Neapolitans were "happy by nature," content to live permanently outdoors, enjoying the bounty effortlessly provided to them by their paradisiacal homeland. They delighted in noise, music, and above all color: display was essential, especially in food. In Santa Lucia, fishmongers framed their rock lobsters, oysters, clams, and mussels in special baskets on beds of leaves. Butchers even gilded the lean parts of the quarters they hung up for sale.

The very epitome of this sunshine existence, of the Neapolitans' "intoxicated self-forgetfulness" (Goethe again), were the city's curious paupers, the *lazzari* or *lazzaroni*. In the late eighteenth century, hardly any account of a journey to Naples fails to mention them. They were famous for being incorrigibly lazy. It was not just that they were reluctant to work; it was said that they regarded fecklessness as a badge of honor, and physical labor as an insidious threat to their dignity. The *lazzari* were a different caste than the underclass of London or Paris. They were highly superstitious and religious, and subscribed unquestioningly to the cult of Saint Gennaro, whose dried blood, kept in a glass vial, would protect the city from harm by liquefying miraculously every so often. Most distinctively, the *lazzari* were neither drunken nor given to riot or rebellion. In fact they were thought to possess such innocent joy that, in them, even filth and malnourishment acquired an impish charm. Ragged, bony, and cheerful, they seemed to be everywhere, sprawling, catlike, in any available patch of sunshine, or sucking down fruit with all the hedonistic braggadocio of Roman emperors.

The *lazzari* were never more cheerful than when eating pasta. Indeed, a meal of *maccheroni* seemed to be the central goal of their existence, the very definition of *lazzarone* bliss. As one French observer noted, "When a *lazzarone* has earned four or five coins to have some macaroni for the day, he no longer worries about tomorrow and stops working." The sight of the indigent of Naples eating pasta became one of the most recognizable street scenes in Europe: little men in tatters, heads tipped back and mouths agape like newborn chicks, feeding themselves handfuls of *maccheroni* they have just bought from a cauldron. It is an image most familiar to us from countless nineteenth-century photographs; at one time, it was almost as big a cliché of Naples as the view of Mount Vesuvius. Like so many other clichés about the *lazzari*, and about Naples in general, it has its origins in the second half of the 1700s, when pasta was consumed in huge quantities by the Neapolitans, often at open-air stalls. Goethe discovered that ready-cooked *maccheroni* could be "bought everywhere, and in all the shops for very little money."

So Goethe and the other Grand Tourists were witnesses to one of the most important developments in the history of the Italian diet: pasta's transformation into a dish for the masses. What visitors to Naples were

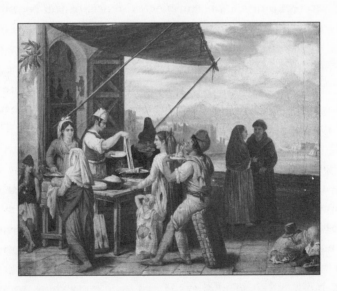

In eighteenth-century Naples, pasta became a dish of the people. Here the poor buy *maccheroni* from a street vendor and eat it with their hands. Vesuvius can be seen in the background. This kind of scene, taken from a French painting of the early 1800s, became a cliché of life in Naples as viewed by visitors.

not to know was how recently that transformation had occurred. Neapolitans had not always been so in love with *maccheroni*. Back in the 1690s, if you had thrown three threes while playing the Game of Cockaigne, Mitelli's board game of city specialties, you would have landed on the square labeled "Neapolitan broccoli." Until about that time, the city under the volcano was known for its passionate fondness for a small group of broccoli and cabbage varieties—frequently referred to simply as "leaf," and eaten with bread as an accompaniment to meat. For most of the sixteenth and seventeenth centuries, the Neapolitans were called "leaf-eaters" or, more pejoratively, "leaf-shitters." They were rather proud of this association. As one of the city's dialect poets exclaimed in 1621,

> *Oh leaf so tasty! Oh leaf so sweet!*
> *You are our magnet, and our treat.*

By the time Goethe arrived, the diet had changed so much that the Neapolitans had usurped a nickname that until then had belonged to Sicilians: they became *mangiamaccheroni*, "*maccheroni*-eaters," or even just *maccheroni*. So in the eighteenth century, dried durum wheat pasta became the emblem of a popular urban identity, and Naples became Italy's capital of *pasta secca*—a title it still enjoys today. Just as importantly, the pasta gobbled in such great quantities in the streets of Naples carried not a trace of cinnamon or sugar. It was now a *savory* dish, cooked in water containing a little salt and pork fat, and sprinkled with grated cheese and perhaps pepper before serving.

Several things conspired to wean the metropolis from its leaf habit. Agriculture in the kingdom became dominated by large estates where grain was the most economically rational crop—especially given the high demand from the capital. Perhaps even more important were technological improvements in manufacture: in the early 1600s, the city witnessed the arrival of the first screw presses for squeezing dough through perforated plates to make *maccheroni*. Pasta became cheaper and more plentiful, and offered a neat solution to the problem of feeding Naples.

The reputation of the Neapolitan screw-press pasta extruder even reached the United States in the late eighteenth century. Apart from being the principal author of the Declaration of Independence, the third president, and the greatest American polymath of the Age of Enlightenment, Thomas Jefferson was the first person to import a *maccheroni* machine into the United States. In 1789, the year after Goethe had left Italy, Jefferson asked a protégé who was due to visit Naples to bring back a pasta press. The young man wrote to explain that the contraption he had successfully procured was actually a miniature: "I went to see the macaroni made. The machinery for pressing as used at Naples is enormous."

It was as if Jefferson had asked his friend to bring a tractor back in his luggage; evidently the great man had failed to appreciate the scale of the pasta industry in Naples. The largest Neapolitan pasta workshops were outside the city, and out of range of the city's guilds. The satellite towns of Torre Annunziata (between Herculaneum and Pompeii), Castellammare, and Gragnano (where the Sorrento peninsula joins the mainland) built their success as centers of pasta production on a centuries-old milling tradition. The screw presses in these workshops were not the only enormous equipment: kneading was done with a giant lever, rather like one arm of a seesaw—the pasta-maker would sit on its farthest end, springing and crouching to bring the beam down on the dough.

Dried pasta was also made on a proto-industrial scale elsewhere in workshops along the Ligurian coast from Genoa. In fact Jefferson need not have bothered sending anyone to Italy to get a pasta press, for the machines were in use a short carriage ride away from his temporary home in Paris (where he was American minister plenipotentiary in France at the time). The best guide to late eighteenth-century pasta manufacturing techniques was published by Parisian baker and pasta-maker Paul-Jacques Malouin in 1767.

Malouin's guide is comprehensive and even advises on the best lubricant for a pasta press: boiled cow brains, mixed with a little oil. More important, Malouin offers an interesting insight into the dramatic effect that the new technology was having on the shape of dried pasta. The three major pasta shapes produced in both Paris and Naples were *vermicelli*, *maccheroni*, and *lasagna*, which owe their prominence to an earlier era of pasta technology, and to the methods used by medieval and Renaissance cooks. But by the second half of the eighteenth cen-

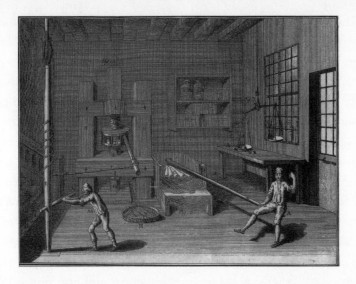

Pasta manufacture in the Age of Enlightenment. The man bouncing on the seesaw-like contraption in the right half of the picture is kneading durum wheat dough. To the left of him, *vermicelli* (marked G) can be seen emerging from the bottom of a nine-inch diameter screw press.

The more detailed images below show the molds inserted into the screw press to make different kinds of pasta. Tubes of *maccheroni* (marked X) are created by squeezing dough through the ingenious mold marked A (top view) and C (underside). The fan (Fig. 14) is used to cool the pasta as soon as it is made. From a guide published in Paris, 1767.

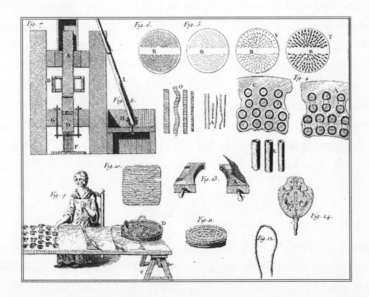

tury, the giant new presses had begun to liberate the imaginations of pasta-makers. Malouin had almost certainly learned his trade in Naples, where, he tells us, thirty different shapes were in production, such as *trenette*, *Pater Noster*, and *stellette*. Assuming these names meant the same as they do today, *trenette* were a kind of spaghetti with an oval cross-section; *Pater Noster* were very short ribbed tubes; and *stellette* were little flat six-pointed stars.

But of course that assumption is rather risky: naming pasta shapes was almost as haphazard then as it is now. A recently compiled online *World Directory of Pasta Shapes and Names* lists 141 different pasta types— for just the ones beginning with the letter *C*. In fact there is something futile about the very idea of a directory of pasta shapes. Probably no mathematical limit can be placed on the variety of threads, tubes, grains, ribbons, twists, shells, bows, nests, ears, curls, and hoops into which dough can be molded, rolled, squeezed, and cut. So it will surprise no one to learn that Italy has no unified system for cataloguing them. Identical shapes have a variety of different names: identical names denote varying shapes. Naples may be the capital of pasta, but Babel also has a good claim to the title.

So in the eighteenth century, pasta became more popular, more widespread, and more varied in its forms. Population growth, agriculture, and machinery all played their part in making those changes particularly manifest in Naples—in turning the Neapolitans from leaf-eaters to *maccheroni*-eaters, in other words. Yet the blunt forces of demography, economics, and technology are rarely all there is to any historical transformation. *Maccheroni* were not just identified with Naples, but with the *lazzari* in particular. And as the more perceptive Grand Tourists found out, the *lazzari* were a mysterious group. Discover who they really were, and we discover a rather more bizarre and more Neapolitan side to the story of *maccheroni*.

Lazzari

Travelers rarely see everything there is to see in the places they visit. They arrive with a hefty baggage of prejudices and expectations; their gaze is attuned to the bizarre and picturesque. So foreigners in Naples in the late 1700s were often biased in their view of the city, and of its poor in particular—the *lazzari* provoked some very strange theories and reflections. Most visitors assumed that *lazzaro* was merely another word for a member of the city's barefoot underclass, numbering as many as 40,000. Others surmised that the *lazzari* were actually a special, restricted elite among the poorest of the city, a kind of plebeian aristocracy. One English lady who visited Italy in 1770–71 reported to her mother that the *lazzari* "govern themselves by a point of honor, which is strictly observed," and which impelled them never to betray a trust, or steal from anyone who asked them to carry valuables. A less sympathetic view was that they were all filthy, lazy criminals. As a disgusted English visitor wrote, "The Lazeroni [*sic*] are such miserable wretches as are not to be seen in any other town in Europe. . . . They are suffered to sun themselves, a great part of the day, under the palace walls, where they lye basking like dirty swine, and are a much more nauseous spectacle." To add to the confusion, there was the widespread belief that they actually formed a community, a semi-independent republic of loafers. A friend of Goethe's who was in Italy at the same time suggested that they were a philosophical sect devoted to a simple credo: *Do nothing. Think nothing. Be happy.* Other stories about the *lazzari* were just as far-fetched. Wolfgang Amadeus Mozart was only fourteen when he was taken to perform in Naples in May 1770, so he can be forgiven for reproducing one of the wilder rumors in a letter to his sister:

> I do not know whether Naples does not surpass London for the insolence of the people; for here the *lazzaroni* have their own general or chief, who receives twenty-five silver ducats from the King every month, solely for the purpose of keeping them in order.

Goethe was more skeptical. In his less enraptured moments, he was curious enough to observe the poor with care and began to doubt the received wisdom. Whatever the *lazzari* were, Goethe noted, there were not nearly as many of these professional idlers as most visitors thought. Any porter pausing to catch his breath, or any fisherman sitting out a contrary wind could be mistaken for an exemplar of the famous *lazzaro* by the incurious traveler. Perhaps, Goethe concluded, the *lazzari* were entirely mythical creatures, an invention of northern European prejudice.

Thus Goethe was one of the few Grand Tourists self-aware enough to question his own presuppositions, and seek out the real Naples that lay behind the stunning landscape, the fabulous classical ruins, and the eye-catching street life. His coolly rigorous approach to the enigma of the *lazzari* marks him out as one of the most perceptive minds of the age. Unfortunately, however, he got it wrong. He would have been better off listening to Mozart.

The key to the identity of the *lazzari* lies back in the days when Naples was ruled from Spain, and peopled with leaf-eaters. At that time, it was not thought of as a city of sunlit hedonism, but as a hot-bed of revolt. In 1648, the world had been astounded to see a fish-monger, known as Masaniello, lead a popular uprising against heavy taxes on food; not only that, he even ruled the city like a king for ten days, dispensing orders and instant justice to widespread acclamation. Masaniello's power base was in the main marketplace, Piazza Mercato. The most organized wing of his revolution was a gang of young pro-letarians from the same area of the city who wore red caps and were armed with butcher's hooks. The Spanish authorities dismissed them as *lazàros,* meaning beggars or lepers. But the insult became a banner for the self-styled *lazzari.* Long after Masaniello had died and the *lazzari* militia had disbanded, the memory of 1648 caused a flush of pride in the poor quarters around Piazza Mercato, and a shudder of fear among the city elite. The *lazzari* remained the most tight-knit and recalcitrant group within the vast Neapolitan rabble.

The famine of 1763–64 that temporarily scared the Grand Tour-ists away from Naples was a turning point in the story of the *lazzari.* Months of bad weather brought poor harvests in 1763; flour and fruit grew scarce in the markets of Naples. But what turned a serious situa-tion into a disaster was that the authorities proved entirely incapable of responding efficiently to the shortage.

Since the Middle Ages, all Italian cities had provisioned themselves at the countryside's expense through a system known as the *annona.* At its simplest, it involved the city government in buying up grain when times were hard, and selling it to citizens at fixed prices. But many *annona* systems became fiendishly complex as the different political factions within the city wrestled over the power to distribute food: there were depots and distribution centers, inspectorates and tribunals; there were grain quotas and regulations on the precise size of a loaf of bread; in some places, storing corn in the countryside was banned. Bakers, merchants, and *annona* officials became powerful vested interests.

In Naples, the *annona* was in the hands of a cabal of corrupt city magnates and nobles, and the royal government was too weak to counter their influence. Indeed some government initiatives only made things worse. When emissaries from Naples went about the kingdom begging or buying more wheat, provincial landowners and dealers began to hoard supplies and speculate on the rapidly rising prices. As hunger became more widespread in Naples, a military force was sent out to commandeer what could not be bought peaceably. It was a familiar scenario: the kingdom was being starved to feed its capital. No wonder Naples was often compared to a grotesquely swollen head on top of an emaciated body. But in 1763 the cartloads of precious grain that arrived in the city were soon followed by some 40,000 peasants, driven from the land to beg for food in the streets and piazzas. The hungry urban proletariat now had rivals in the struggle to survive. Even when officials tried to buy grain in foreign ports at vastly inflated prices, they were frequently cheated by unscrupulous merchants. The grain they did manage to obtain fed the profiteers rather than the citizens of Naples. For months on end bread was either impossible to find, or made from flour so heavily cut with ashes or grit that only the starving could bring themselves to swallow it.

In August 1763, infuriated by the authorities' incompetence and greed, a crowd of women in Piazza Mercato surrounded King Ferdinand, who was still only a boy; they demanded the head of the official they blamed for the famine, and reminded their young sovereign that his duty was to guarantee plenty. Through the autumn, as the tension in the city rose still further, famished mobs began to raid bakeries and shops. By December, the *lazzari* were acting out mock executions and carrying threatening placards. Everyone waited for the city to explode.

Yet it never did. The relative calm in Naples during the famine was as bizarre, in its own way, as Masaniello's revolution had been more than a century earlier. The king's ministers helped a little, by setting up a highly visible distribution center in Piazza Mercato from which good flour could be bought at a protected price. But the *lazzari* also knew how to help themselves, and how to turn famine into good business. With the tacit collusion of the authorities, the most violent and best organized of them seized control of bakers' ovens and shops, and started to sell flour at inflated prices to the hard-pressed middle classes of the city. They also used their muscle to monopolize sources of charity from religious institutions and prevent the peasant immigrants taking food from the mouths of the urban masses. More than one historian has compared the *lazzari* in 1763–64 to the *camorra*—the Neapolitan mafia that would emerge in the nineteenth century. (Strictly speaking, the comparison is anachronistic. If the *lazzari* were a mafia, then so, too, were all the other vested interests within the *annona* system—indeed so, too, was anyone within *ancien régime* society who had power that the king's ministers coveted.)

Without political leadership from the *lazzari*, the poor of the city remained calm until plenty returned—even during the epidemic that killed so many hunger-weakened citizens in the spring and summer of 1764. The poorest and weakest died vomiting both blood and the grass that they had been reduced to eating. Between 30,000 and 50,000 people are thought to have succumbed in Naples, and many more in the provinces. Yet foreign ambassadors noted with amazement that, rather than blame the authorities, the masses believed the priests who told them that the catastrophe was not a governmental scandal, but a divine scourge. Rather than attack the palaces of the mighty, they went on penitential processions through the streets and begged Saint Gennaro for relief. It was a sight that, once food supplies had been restored with the harvest of 1764, worked a radical reversal on the reputation of the Neapolitan proletariat in general, and the *lazzari* in particular. In European opinion, Naples was transformed almost instantly from being a powderkeg of revolt into a natural paradise by the sea. From being volatile rebels, the *lazzari* became the ragged *bon viveurs* who so fascinated the Grand Tourists.

In short Mozart was right and Goethe was wrong. The *lazzari* certainly did exist, and they did have a leader, or *capo-lazzaro*, and it is entirely plausible that he took money from the king in return for keeping order among the impoverished masses—when it was the *lazzari* themselves who were the likeliest cause of trouble. It was a protection racket, as we might, rather harshly, term it today. While Mozart was in the city, he and his father mixed in court and ambassadorial circles where this business was an open secret. A French aristocrat in exile who also had access to the Bourbon court would later claim, "The King is the protector of the *lazzaroni* so that they, in turn, protect him, because they make the government tremble. They are kept in check by favouring their laziness and never letting them go without bread, macaroni and, in summer, ice."

The chief of the *lazzari*, the *capo-lazzaro*, when both Mozart and Goethe were in Italy was a man called Nicola de Sapato—he had probably held the post since the time of the famine. He had some unusual privileges, if the available sources are to be believed. A French testimony, which claims to be based on informers at the court of Ferdinand IV, tells us that the *capo-lazzaro* had the right to make representations to the king and was treated with great respect by senior ministers. His presence was expected at the drawing of the highly popular lottery, and at certain court ceremonies, most notably when the queen gave birth: he would take the royal baby in his arms, kiss it, check its sex, and then show it to the populace from the window. During Carnival, the *capo-lazzaro* would be admitted to the king's presence to make a speech of praise just before the assault on the *Cuccagna*, the artificial food mountain that was erected on four successive Sundays in the square in front of the Royal Palace. Like the Feast of the Suckling Pig in Bologna, the Neapolitan *Cuccagna* was a public show of abundance that guaranteed calm. The *lazzari* had come to expect certain symbols of plenty as privileges of their station: the *Cuccagna* during Carnival, ice in summer, and *maccheroni* all year round. Although the poorest might only consume it on special occasions, pasta was nonetheless a daily sign of an accord between the throng and the throne.

No one was more conscious of this accord than the king himself, Ferdinand IV: dubbed the *Lazzarone* King, he was well known for his passion for *maccheroni*.

Ferdinand was an unusual-looking man. Around the time of Mozart's visit, he was described as thin and stooping, with his knees permanently flexed; a long nose and heavy bottom lip protruded from beneath a mop of light brown hair. His aristocratic genealogy was as cosmopolitan as any in Europe: his ancestors, the House of Bourbon, had originally been the rulers of Navarre, in France; his mother was from a long line of dukes of the northern Italian city of Parma; his father, Don Carlos, was the king of Spain's son. Don Carlos had won Naples for the Bourbons by chasing the Austrians from the city in 1734. Twenty-five years later, he resigned the throne of Naples to become king of Spain, leaving his eight-year-old son, Ferdinand, to inherit the Neapolitan crown. Ferdinand was the boy king surrounded by women in Piazza Mercato during the early days of the famine in 1763.

Like many European rulers, Carlos longed to centralize authority in royal hands, to create an absolute monarchy unrestrained by the feudal powers of Church and aristocracy. Before leaving Naples, he gave instructions that Ferdinand should be kept away from the influence of any ambitious nobles during his upbringing. As a result, the young King Ferdinand became more comfortable in the company of valets and servants than princes and duchesses, and more at home in Neapolitan dialect than any other language. For the rest of his life, according to the ambassador from London, he would share his pleasures with "people of the very lowest class" and imitate their coarse manners. This scion of a cosmopolitan dynasty became as earthily Neapolitan as the commonest urchin.

The reports filtering out from the Neapolitan court portray the *Lazzarone* King as something of a street entertainer. He loved nothing better than practical jokes, and would often slap or kick his courtiers' backsides. He was once seen with his breeches around his ankles and his chamber pot in his hands, chasing after his retainers and bawling at them to inspect its stinking contents. He delighted in playing with guns, and was given to groping his Austrian wife, Marie Antoinette's sister, in public. One of his favorite pastimes was fishing in the Bay of Naples: he would reportedly then sell his catch in the market, shouting and haggling as enthusiastically as any stall owner. And of course, like all good *lazzari*, the king devoured *maccheroni* with a feral greed. As one Irish guest of Ferdinand's recalled:

> He seized it in his fingers, twisting and pulling it about, and cramming it voraciously into his mouth, most magnanimously disdaining the use of either knife, fork, or spoon, or indeed any aid except such as nature had kindly afforded him. . . . This exhibition, I honestly confess, surprised me most of any thing I had ever seen either of a king or a subject.

Ferdinand was even known to scarf down *maccheroni* in this way in his box at the sumptuous San Carlo Theater, in full view of the audience.

Many of these anecdotes about Ferdinand obviously have some political spin. The enemies of the Bourbon monarchy had every interest in portraying him as an oaf, and in linking his name to the much-derided *lazzari*. Ferdinand was made out to be a lazy, ignorant king for a lazy, ignorant mob. The truth is more subtle. To his friends, the Bourbon king was a man in tune with the people, and his *maccheroni* eating sealed an unlikely entente between one of Europe's greatest dynasties and the hungry masses of one of Europe's biggest cities. Through *maccheroni*, Ferdinand bridged the gulf between the extremes of Neapolitan society, and made the rabble into a source of support.

The Head of Mouth Services

Tomato sauce is now more recognizably Italian than the tricolor or the Leaning Tower of Pisa. It is the lifeblood of Italian food—some would even say of the Italians themselves. It is a national religion: its Holy Trinity is Fresh, Canned, and Paste; and its Jerusalem is Naples. Jeanne Caròla Francesconi's *La cucina napoletana*—the best guide to the city's food today—combines pasta with around fifty different sauces containing tomatoes.

Yet while the 1600s and 1700s were a time of rapid change in the consumption of pasta, its predestined partner, the *pomodoro*, dawdled in relative obscurity. Indeed, despite the glorious destiny that awaited it, tomato sauce made a very muted first entry into the historical records.

SPANISH TOMATO SAUCE

Take half a dozen ripe tomatoes and place them on the embers to toast. When toasted, carefully remove the skins and cut into tiny pieces with a knife. Add finely chopped onion to taste, thyme, *piperna* [an aromatic herb—something like marjoram], and some finely chopped hot pepper. Mix well with a little salt, oil, and vinegar.

Apart from its lack of complexity or ambition, the striking thing about this, the first ever tomato sauce recipe in Italy, is its date: it appeared in a cookbook called *The Modern Steward*, published in Naples in 1692. By that time, nearly a century and a half had passed since the little red or yellow *pomo d'oro*—golden apple—had reached the Spanish territories in Italy from the Spanish territories in South America. Evidently, after all that time, the tomato had still not acclimatized. *The Modern Steward*'s author, Antonio Latini, was as oblivious to its potential as the rest of his contemporaries. He suggests perfunctorily that it makes "a very tasty sauce for boiled meat, or other things," and never mentions it again. Unsurprisingly, this lukewarm endorsement failed to set the Neapolitan gourmands' passions ablaze.

Nor did much change for the tomato in the next eighty years. The Grand Tourists who witnessed *lazzari* eating *maccheroni* in the 1770s and 1780s did not see them flavoring their favorite food with tomato sauce. In 1773, Vincenzo Corrado, who would subsequently become "Head of Mouth Services" to the court of the *Lazzarone* King, published a recipe book called *The Gallant Cook*. Corrado tells us that tomatoes can be stuffed with pulped veal or sweetbread, or with rice cooked in milk, butter, sugar, and cinnamon. They can be cut lengthways, filled with anchovies, garlic, oregano, and parsley, and then covered with bread-crumbs. They can be chopped into small pieces, mixed with butter, eggs, and ricotta, then shaped into croquettes for flouring and frying. Clearly tomatoes were becoming more acceptable. Nevertheless, only occasionally are they made into a *salsa* or *sugo*. *The Gallant Cook* gives just one tomato sauce recipe: it contains vinegar and spices, garlic and rue, and is recommended as an accompaniment for mutton. The taste of the other ingredients, especially pungent rue, which was thought to be good for flushing worms from the body, must have been overwhelming. Clearly, it was not thought gallant for a Neapolitan cook to prepare tomato dishes that actually tasted of tomato.

In fact, only in 1844 did *vermicelli con salsa di pomodoro* appear in a Neapolitan cookbook. And even then, the tomato sauce in question was rather unorthodox by today's standards, made with reconstituted dried tomatoes and cooked with butter or pork fat rather than olive oil.

Thus, in the age of the Enlightenment, tomato sauce was still a long way from its modern Neapolitan apotheosis atop a plate of spaghetti. Yet plenty of foods did feel the influence of the new climate of reason.

The Bourbon monarchy brought a certain Enlightenment spirit to the government of Naples and the Kingdom of the Two Sicilies, as it became known. Carlos and his *lazzarone* son, Ferdinand, gently sponsored a new Neapolitan patriotism, and an ethos of public service. They helped free their capital from the oppressive atmosphere of the Counter-Reformation and turned it into a center of intellectual life. Neapolitan thinkers challenged old orthodoxies in religion, agriculture, economics, and feudal law. Reform was on the agenda—even though the crown rarely had the authority to drive it through. After the famine of 1763–64 there was talk of abolishing the *annona* and introducing a free market in grain. (One of the few concrete results of these debates was that part of the state-controlled grain supply was earmarked for *maccheroni* manufacturers.) In 1779, Ferdinand's ministers did succeed in abolishing the ransacking of the *Cuccagna*, which was now viewed, in classic Enlightenment fashion, as merely a barbaric spectacle rather than a delicate tool for governing the piazza.

The reforming intellectual atmosphere reached the royal kitchens. Great changes were afoot in the elite diet of Naples, as is clear from a further comparison between the two cookery writers whose tomato sauce recipes were cited above: Antonio Latini, author of *The Modern Steward* (1691), and Vincenzo Corrado, who wrote *The Gallant Cook* (1773). *The Modern Steward* still repeatedly refers to Galen, the gladiators' doctor whose theory of the humors had had such an influence on the European diet since the Middle Ages. There is nothing modern about *The Modern Steward*. But by the late eighteenth century, Galen was out of date. In 1781 Corrado wrote a small guide to what he called "Pythagorean" food—meaning a vegetarian diet—based on recent scientific research into the benefits of fruit and vegetables. Corrado styled the book a guide to appropriate eating habits for "nobles and men of letters." For the first time since the Renaissance, intellectuals and the elite were combining to refine Italy's civilization of the table.

The mood of gastronomic renewal also embraced the imports from the New World, many of which were still treated with suspicion and eaten by those who had little choice. *On Pythagorean Food* has a short section on sweet peppers, which Corrado says are a "rustic, vulgar food" that quite a few people like anyway. The pepper recipes include a particularly tempting creation with pine nuts and *bottarga* (dried fish roe) in lemon juice and oil.

Corrado's *Treatise on Potatoes* (1798) sought to help increase tuber consumption in the Kingdom of Naples. "Served simply," he writes, potatoes "are an excellent food for the poor because they are very nourishing and very cheap." This, of course, was the entire secret of the potato's European success. Along with maize, it would make a huge contribution to ridding the continent of famine. But like maize, and in fact to an even greater extent than maize, potatoes would struggle for acceptance even among the hungriest Italians. Whereas a porridge or *polenta* made from cornmeal was a staple in northern and central Italy by the time Corrado was writing, potatoes did not become a regular part of the peasant diet until the mid-1800s.

Unlike some other Enlightenment writers, Corrado was less interested in the potato's ability to fill the bellies of the poor than he was in its potential to excite more refined palates and more inquiring minds. The Kingdom of Naples was so fertile, he argued, that it hardly needed yet another vegetable in its repertoire. Nonetheless, genteel curiosity had turned its attention to the potato. "As a new food among us," he writes, "it has awakened and aroused men's sense of taste, and they are eagerly carrying out research into it." The result of Corrado's own research is a list of magisterial recipes. The *Treatise* has suggestions both elementary (potato salad dressed with chopped capers, anchovies, and rocket) and extremely elegant (potatoes with a sauce of toasted almonds and caviar). Corrado often recommends cooking them in white wine—as in one recipe where they are then sliced thickly, interleaved with grated Parmesan, and put in the oven smothered with a dense, sieved coulis made from fatty ham, parsley roots, parsnips, toasted bread crumbs, and broth. Needless to say, this was avant-garde cookery, far ahead of its time—and in some ways, still ahead of ours.

But the most distinctive development over the course of the 1700s was the decline in the use of spices. The direct trade between Europe and the Far East that had first been inspired by Marco Polo's adventures had brought down the price of spices, and so decreased their value as a marker of social distinction. Also, Galen's theory of digestion as a secondary cooking process had lost scientific credibility. Now that cold and wet foods were no longer thought to dampen the bodily casserole pot, they no longer needed to be counteracted with hot and dry spices. *The Modern Steward* was written more than a century after the era of Messisbugo and Scappi, but its recipes contain almost as many spices as theirs. Vincenzo Corrado, by contrast, was more of an innovator, as *The Gallant Cook* demonstrates: he was not averse to frying fresh anchovies in oil and simply flavoring them with salt, pepper, and lemon juice. Other fish dishes show his willingness to complement the most delicate tastes with herbs rather than muffle them with spices. Sea bass and sea bream, for example, can be simmered in water and wine, dressed with lemon, parsley, onion, and oil, and served with lobster roe or caviar. Or they can be poached in water, salt, herbs, and butter and served with a butter and sorrel sauce. But Corrado had not yet reached the point of throwing out his nutmeg and cloves: he also suggests stuffing sea bass and sea bream with a *ragù* of sweetbreads, veal kidneys, ham, herbs, truffles, *and* spices. And although the *Treatise on Potatoes* is radical in some respects, it is conservative in others: he makes fritters from a mash containing veal fat, *provatura* cheese, egg yolk, spices, and "a little sugar," for example. Some of his potato recipes involve sauces made with fish livers, truffles, Malmsey wine, prawns, frog meat, sea urchins, and much else besides—all containing spices, as they would have before the "earth apple" reached European shores. Nonetheless, with ingredients that are slightly less bland than the potato, Corrado shows a tendency to let them speak for themselves. Even something as simple as marrow is dressed only with oil, lemon juice, garlic, mint, and pepper in his "Pythagorean" recipe for "Marrow *all'italiana*."

The Neapolitan Enlightenment did not reach quite so happy a conclusion in the street as it did in the dining room. In 1789, the French Revolution raised fears about the new intellectual and political climate, to which the government of the Kingdom of the Two Sicilies responded with more censorship and a rapprochement with the Church. Then, in 1799, a French invasion reduced Naples to terror and chaos. The king fled the city for Sicily and the protection of Britain's Royal Navy. A Neapolitan Republic was set up by young men galvanized by Enlightenment ideals of constitutional government, impartial justice, and rational reform. French troops marched toward Naples to act as "protectors" of the new republic—and it was from the *lazzari* that it needed protecting. Even while Ferdinand IV was still in the city, they were committing atrocities against suspected "Jacobins"; a hapless Piedmontese tourist was mistaken for a Frenchman and lynched. When the French army arrived it was met with fanatical resistance from the *lazzari*. There were three days of street fighting before the *capo-lazzaro*, a man known as Michele il Pazzo ("Mad Mike"), was captured; he was treated with great honor by the French general, who wrote in his report that, "the *lazzaroni*, these astonishing men, are heroes."

When the Neapolitan Republic was overthrown a few months later, the revenge of the *lazzari* was just as astonishing. Any man with Republican short hair was butchered in the street; women with "Jacobin" sympathies, or even just a bit of money, were publicly raped and murdered. The republic's "Liberty Trees" were burned, and many Republicans thrown half alive into the flames. *Lazzari* were heard boasting that they had eaten the roasted flesh of their enemies.

10

Turin, 1846

Viva l'Italia!

Lorenzo Valerio's Toast

Turin, it is often said, is Italy's drawing room—*il salotto d'Italia*. Its *palazzi*, regular in their features, are set out in a sensible rectilinear grid; its porticoes and piazzas have a sober grandeur. In the pedestrianized areas of Piazza Castello you may feel out of place for wearing shoes instead of slippers. Other Italian cities can look either showy or untidy by comparison. Naples might be on the other side of the world.

As well as being Italy's drawing room, Turin was also its first capital city, and the capital of the Risorgimento, the movement of cultural and political nationalism that culminated in Italian unification. On March 17, 1861, a famous one-line law was passed by both houses of parliament: "King Victor Emmanuel II assumes the title of King of Italy for himself and for his successors." By virtue of that law, Italy became a united state for the first time in history; Turin became its capital; and Victor Emmanuel of the ancient House of Savoy became its hereditary monarch.

Even just a few years earlier, absolutely no one had expected such an outcome. Indeed the diplomatic and military story of Italian unification is so familiar that it is sometimes difficult to recall what a surprise it was at the time. In 1858, the prime minister of the Kingdom of

Piedmont-Sardinia, Count Cavour, struck a deal to win French support in a war to drive Austria out of its territories in northern Italy. In 1859, following the shockingly bloody battles of Magenta and Solferino, Austrian armies retreated eastward from Milan, allowing Lombardy to join with Piedmont. As the Austrians withdrew, uprisings farther south soon brought cities like Florence, Parma, Modena, and Bologna into Victor Emmanuel's realm. The next stage of Italian unification was the most surprising of all: in May 1860, Giuseppe Garibaldi landed at Marsala, on the westernmost tip of Sicily, with a volunteer force of 1,088 men and one woman. After less than six months of fighting, Garibaldi met Victor Emmanuel at Teano, north of Naples, and presented him with sovereignty over what had once been the realm of the *Lazzarone* King.

Historians have long argued over what made these remarkable developments possible. Perhaps the single most important underlying cause was the spread of a new idea: that "Italy" should be a *political* concept and not just a geographical or cultural one. Italy was to be a *Patria*, a fatherland of freedom not despotism; it should undergo a *Risorgimento*, a "Resurgence" or "Resurrection," after centuries of division and shame. With the ideas of Patria and Risorgimento came a craving for national symbols and rites. Educated young men from the cities were usually the first to feel it. In the name of Italy, they mourned at the tombs of long-dead poets, took blood oaths, exchanged secret handshakes, and brandished conspiratorial daggers. This romantic patriotism inspired some young Italians with almost suicidal panache, such as the Bandiera brothers, Attilio and Emilio, who tried valiantly to spark an Italian revolution against the Bourbon dynasty in far-off Calabria in 1844. They were quickly betrayed, caught, and shot. Such exploits became symbols in themselves, acts of national martyrdom.

But by the time the Bandiera brothers had been executed, the ideal of an Italian Patria was becoming more respectable. Even some men of power, rank, and property began to align themselves with the Risorgimento cause. As they did, the craving for national symbols spread further: Italian hearts were stirred by patriotic operas, and Italian eyes moistened before patriotic paintings. There were patriotic history books and even patriotic statistics. Wearing tricolor clothes could become a gesture of defiance against the enemies of the Patria, as could sporting facial hair in papal Rome, or refusing to smoke in Austrian-controlled Milan, where the Vienna government held a monopoly on tobacco. In Risorgimento Italy, it seemed, anything could come alive with Italian feeling.

Anything, that is, except food.

It is often said that, today, food and soccer are the only things that inspire Italians with national pride. No one would disagree that *la cucina* is fundamental to Italian identity. Yet during the Risorgimento, the period that saw the birth of the Italian nation, the almost total *absence* of national pride at table is striking.

Many different kinds of people contributed to the Risorgimento: writers and generals, exiles and spies, monarchs and conspirators, idealists and statesmen. Their thoughts and deeds over two generations fill countless yellowing pages in Italian libraries and archives. Yet hardly any of those thoughts and deeds concerned food.

Take Vincenzo Gioberti, the eccentric Turinese theologian who wrote a highly influential book about why Italy is great. *On the Moral and Civil Superiority of Italians* (1843) tells us that Italy is the "creator, preserver and redeemer" of European civilization. Italians are best at theology, philosophy, experimental science, political theory, history, literature, art, music, and language. Italy is the most cosmopolitan and universal of nations because, in the diversity of its various provinces, it mirrors the diversity of Europe. For hundreds of stultifying pages Gioberti extols the virtues of Italy and the Italians. But not once does he mention food.

Or consider Giuseppe Mazzini, the Genoese "prophet" of Italian unification. He spent most of his life plotting from exile for a new Italy, but does not seem to have been nostalgic for Italian or even Ligurian dishes. All that we know about his feelings for food from his vast output of letters and tracts is that he quite liked chocolate, and that he once sent his mother a recipe for almond cake—which he had learned from a French-speaking Swiss girl. "I'm no expert on cooking," he explained.

Giuseppe Garibaldi, the very embodiment of romantic patriotism, was another Italian hero with higher things on his mind than eating. Perhaps the only dish that commemorates the swashbuckling spirit of the great *condottiere* is the Garibaldi biscuit, a thin sandwich of short pastry and chopped currants that could hardly be less Italian: it was invented in a factory in Bermondsey, South London, in 1861. The manufacturer, the company Peek Frean, baptized it "Garibaldi" to cash in on the general's fame.

In short, during the Risorgimento, the Italian Patria and the Italian palate failed to forge a bond. The craving for patriotic symbols was not matched by a hunger for food that symbolized Italy.

For one brief moment, however, the Risorgimento and the history of Italian food *did* converge—in a toast. Granted, it was not a particularly dramatic moment, not a tale of self-sacrifice and daring that ranks with the Bandiera brothers' expedition to Calabria in 1844, or with Garibaldi's defense of the Roman Republic in 1849; the toast did not inspire a patriotic legend. But it is among the few episodes in the Risorgimento that actually had a menu, one that tells us a surprising amount about the history of Italian food, and about Turin's crucial place in it.

On September 12, 1846, at the closing banquet of the congress of the Subalpine Agrarian Association, it fell to the secretary, Lorenzo Valerio, to propose a toast.

Stern-featured, with a very short neck and broad, rounded shoulders, Valerio rose from his seat at the top table and looked out on the hall. The congress had been an undisputed success. Besides discussing the usual issues, such as model farms, cattle insurance, and crop rotation, the members had paid a fascinating visit to some silk mills in nearby Vigevano. All this fit very well with Valerio's version of patriotism: his goal was to get the Risorgimento message across through philanthropy, education, and practical advice; in other words to bind together the ideals of Patria and progress. Even silk cocoons and mutual aid funds could contain a promise of the nation to come.

Valerio could also take pride in the venue. The Subalpine Agrarian Association was based in Turin. But rather than host the event in the Piedmontese capital, Valerio had brought the members to Mortara, a small town close to Piedmont's border with Lombardy, a region then under the control of the Austrian Empire. Among the four hundred faces that Valerio could see craning expectantly toward him were many

Lombard farmers and landowners. He raised his glass, and proposed a toast he knew would be highly controversial:

> To our brothers from Lombardy.
> May this union of agricultural interests herald a much more important union. I hope that everyone will join together in drinking to Italy.
> *Viva l'Italia!*

Viva l'Italia! was echoed by hundreds of voices from the floor. But the dignitaries sitting with the secretary showed only silent dismay. The association's aristocratic president, pale with fright, immediately brought the banquet to a close and abandoned the hall. At the top table, Valerio was left alone to brood on his act of patriotic provocation.

Rumors of what had happened at Mortara raced back to Turin. Under the arcades of Piazza San Carlo, in the cafés and clubs, it was even said that Valerio had hailed the king as the leader who would drive the foreigners out of Italy. Only a few months before, the Subalpine Agrarian Association had been denounced to the monarch as a "den of revolutionaries," and Valerio had been summoned before the throne. The association had only been allowed to continue operating with a loyal nobleman as its president, to make sure that, amid all the farming talk, nothing incendiary was said—like Valerio's toast. Around the whist tables, and in the crowded Caffè San Carlo-Vassallo and the Madera, Turin's opinion-formers watched to see how the authorities would react.

Nothing happened. Valerio's provocation went unpunished, an unmistakable signal that royal sympathy for the Risorgimento was growing. And within eighteen months, the Piedmontese king would lead an army against the Austrians. The battle for Italian independence had begun in earnest.

Lorenzo Valerio's toast was a small turning point in the story of Italian unification that reflected a striking change in the atmosphere in Turin, where Italian unification would be officially proclaimed. Once the capital of the most oppressive of all the Italian states, it enforced an absurdly rigid censorship. Even in 1844, two years before the Subalpine

Agrarian Association's banquet, newspapers were not allowed to print the words *Italia*, *Patria*, *Nazione*—"Italy," "Fatherland," and "Nation." So Valerio's *Viva l'Italia* was more daring than it might seem. In fact not even recipes were exempt from the stroke of the censor's pen. In 1843, the chef to the British ambassador tried to publish a domestic science magazine called *The Families' Friend*, which was banned on the grounds that giving advice to servants (i.e., "families," in the language of the day) might undermine the authority of their masters.

Things changed rapidly from around the time of Valerio's toast. Another indicator of that change was the publication in Turin of the menu for the Subalpine Agrarian Association's banquet in Mortara. Indeed the man who published it, the cook on that day in Mortara, was the very same chef to the British ambassador whose recipes in *The Families' Friend* had been deemed so subversive only three years earlier. His *Healthy, Economical and Elegant Cooking* came out in four 150-page volumes, one for each season of the year. The preface to the first in the series, "Winter," is remarkable: it appears to be nothing less than a manifesto for a gastronomic Risorgimento. Italy is called a land "favoured by Heaven." Nowhere else has "tastier fruit and vegetables, finer oils and dairy produce, better poultry or more succulent butcher's meat—to say nothing of its copious and exquisite game, and both salt- and freshwater fish." All that Italy lacks are "great kitchens and pantries where cooks can perfect by experiment and maintain by practice the right methods for preparing and combining ingredients and dishes."

"Autumn," the last of the four sections of *Healthy, Economical and Elegant Cooking*, includes the menu for the association banquet, proudly placed at the head of a list of meals for special occasions. What better opportunity than such a stage-managed patriotic event to put the delights of Italian food on display? After all, the members of the Subalpine Agrarian Association had actually produced the "tasty fruits and vegetables" and "succulent butchers' meats" that made Italy a land "favoured by Heaven." Here, then, is what Lorenzo Valerio and his colleagues ate:

MENU
Du dîner maigre donné à la réunion de 400 personnes de
l'Association Agraire à Mortara

1. *Potage.* Crème aux Pistaches.
2. Brunoise à l'essence de Poissons.
3. *Assiettes hors-d'œuvre*, Beurre, Anchois, Cornichons, Olives, Œufs et Thon.
4. La friture de pain de Riz, Croquettes de légumes, petits Vols-au-vent de Clovisses, huîtres gratinées, filets de Perches.
5. Les gros Poissons de mer à la Hollandaise, Turbots, Loups, Dentiches, etc.
6. Les filets de Soles aux Truffes blanches, Sauce piquante.
7. Les Truites à la Financière.
8. Les pâtés de Thon à la gelée de Poisson.
9. Les Champignons en Croustade au vin de Madère.
10. Les Œufs brouillés aux Truffes.
11. Les Tanches rôties.

And so on, through to "Les Mousses au Chocolat" and "Assiettes de Fromage doux." It is not just the language of the menu that is French: its structure is French, with a soup starter and hors d'œuvre; its prestigious sauces are French, such as Hollandaise and Financière; so, too, are its classic recipes, such as *vol-au-vents,* oysters *au gratin*, and *Gâteau de mille feuilles.* The "Parisian Salad" seems designed to mock the Italian *insalata* as it was conceived by the great Renaissance cookery writers. Among its constituents are chicken, ham, salted tongue, boiled eggs, whitebait, and prawns, and the heavy dressing contains garlic, anchovies, sage, cayenne pepper, white wine, honey, parsley, and oil.

Even as the members of Valerio's association were loudly toasting their country's liberation from foreign dominance, the food on their table was quietly confirming what no one would have disputed: that Italian cuisine was subservient to its transalpine neighbor. Lorenzo Valerio may have shouted *Viva l'Italia!* but the menu said *Vive la France!*

The menu's creator, François Chapusot, born just west of Dijon in 1799, certainly would not have challenged the philo-French orthodoxy. Despite the optimistic note he strikes about Italian food in the preface to *Healthy, Economical and Elegant Cooking*, French influences shine through every other page of his book. In fact, although the opening "manifesto" quoted above may sound initially like a call for a Risorgimento in Italian kitchens, on closer inspection it seems more like a program for turning Italy into a French gastronomic colony. Italian cookbooks, he writes, "present nothing more than an indigestible hotchpotch of recipes for food that is frequently coarse and almost always greasy, overwhelming, and nauseating." Chapusot's disdain carries echoes of the Grand Tourists' beliefs in the previous century: Italy was naturally fertile, but the ignorant Italians did not know how to take advantage of what nature had bestowed on them.

In Chapusot's day, the preeminence of French gastronomy was an accepted fact. The influence of French food on modern fine dining was and is so profound that one would struggle to write its history without recourse to French words such as _cuisine_ and _gastronomy_. (I have not even tried to do without them in this account of Italian food through the ages.) The origins of its preeminence can be found two hundred years before Lorenzo Valerio's toast.

Perfected in Paris

Modern French cookery developed along a historical path beaten by a number of key recipe books, starting with François La Varenne's _Le Cuisinier François_ of 1651, to which French haute cuisine can trace back some of its key features, such as reductions made from the concentrated cooking juices of meat, or a _roux_ of fat and flour as a thickener. François Massialot's _Le Cuisinier roial et bourgeois_, first published in 1691, shows that rich sauces made from a base of fat and particularly butter were replacing the sour-sweet tastes that had been integral to European cooking since the medieval period—indeed since ancient Rome. Verjuice was finally falling from favor, as were spices. Vincent La Chapelle's _Le Cuisinier moderne_ (1733) and François Marin's _Les dons de Comus ou les délices de la table_ (1739) mark further advances: natural fresh tastes were prized; sweet flavors were kept until the end of the meal, while precise and delicate _recipes_ challenged simple boiled and roast meats as the most prestigious moment of the dining experience. Marin himself summed up the new criteria of taste:

Modern cuisine is a kind of chemistry. The cook's science consists
of separating tastes out then absorbing them and distilling their
quintessence; it consists of drawing out their juices, which are both
nutritious and light, and then mixing and blending them together
in such a way that no single flavor is dominant and they are all per-
ceptible.

One historian of French food has described these changes as a shift from
the medieval and Renaissance cuisine of *mixtures,* to a new cuisine of
impregnation—the description itself is a fittingly French reduction.

But more important than the strictly gastronomic novelties contained in these cookbooks is the fact that they formed a self-consciously
innovative tradition. In the late 1730s, an energetic but confused debate
about *nouvelle cuisine* began in Paris. There was little agreement about
what this *cuisine* was, or indeed what was particularly *nouvelle* about it: in
that sense the debate generated "more smoke than roast," to use an Italian expression. But the controversy was more significant than the con-
clusions, because it was triggered by the most recent wave of chefs who
claimed that all previous cooks were so vulgar and out-of-date that it was
embarrassing to be seen eating their dishes. Food, in other words, had
begun to move to the accelerated rhythms of fashion; it has not stopped
doing so ever since. France's culinary fashion system began to generate
constant invention—or at least constant publicity about how inventive it
was. Yet at the same time, from within the competitive melee, a canon
of classic dishes formed: from *bœuf à la mode* to *béchamel.*

Unlike Italy, France in the seventeenth and eighteenth centuries had
a single center from which tastes radiated out to the rest of the country:
the court in Paris. Thus French cuisine was dominated by a metropolis, and it increasingly became a focus for national pride. Italian food,
by contrast, was the product of many cities, and the pride it generated
was local rather than national. Moreover, whereas French cooks were
armed with a uniform terminology—*coulis, hors d'oeuvres, potage*—their
Italian counterparts spoke a variety of mongrel food dialects. Absolutist
France offered a political model to monarchies across Europe: all Italy
could offer was a parable of political decline. In any contest for prestige
between the two food civilizations, there was only one possible victor.

From the late 1600s, the great French recipe books, whether in the original language or in translation, were imported into Italy in ever greater numbers. The gastronomic invasion from across the Alps virtually extinguished the indigenous tradition of food writing. After 1694, no Italian wrote anything significant on food for three-quarters of a century.

The silence was only broken in 1766 by *The Piedmontese Cook Perfected in Paris*. Published anonymously in Turin, and hugely successful elsewhere in Italy, *The Piedmontese Cook* is, as its title suggests, a recipe collection in thrall to French taste. In fact it is even more in thrall than it lets on: a more appropriate title would be, *The Piedmontese Cook Who Has Directly Copied the Vast Majority of His Recipes from the Best-Selling Recipe Book in Paris*. Apart from the insertion of a few pasta dishes, and a few local ingredients such as truffles and Aosta cheese, the book is little more than a translation of Menon's *La Cuisinière bourgeoise*, which was first published in 1746 in an effort to popularize a simplified version of cutting-edge Parisian cuisine.

But translating sleek Gallic food terminology into Italian is no easy task, and the "Piedmontese" cook frequently botches it. *Coulis* becomes *sugo*—the generic word for "sauce." Sauce *à la provençale* becomes *salsa alla provinciale*, meaning that the sauce in question, instead of hailing from the region of Provence, is just plain provincial. "Quite so!" the metropolitan sophisticates of Paris would have sneered. Often French terminology is so impregnable that translation is futile: the Italian for *au gratin* is . . . *au gratin*. But even the simple process of copying French vocabulary sometimes goes awry. *Soufflé* is wrongly transcribed as *soufflet*, which means something very different: thus the exquisitely light Parisian *soufflé au chocolat* becomes a "chocolate slap" in Turin. The Piedmontese cook may have perfected his cooking while in Paris, but not his command of the French language.

Translation howlers notwithstanding, in the 1700s Turin became the major channel through which French culinary ideas penetrated the length and breadth of Italy. In the eighteenth and nineteenth centuries the nobility of southern Italy and Sicily employed a *monsù*, a *monsieur*, that is, to do their cooking. Piedmontese chefs, many of them trained in France, were most in demand to fill this role in northern and central Italy—they were the next best thing to the Gallic original.

It is not hard to see why the Piedmontese capital performed such a role. On a good day, Alpine peaks gleam clearly at the end of the city's streets; over the mountains, a mere fifty miles away from Turin at the nearest point to the west, lies France. For much of its history this was the direction that Turin faced: west, toward France and the source of the river Po in the Alps, rather than east, down the Po and into Italy. The House of Savoy, the feudal dynasty whose fortunes were tied to Turin from the 1100s, ruled a territory that traditionally straddled the Alps and included Gruyères, Geneva, and Chambéry. For centuries, as the fortunes of war and diplomacy turned, bits of Savoyard territory were swapped back and forth between Paris and Turin.

The Revolution of 1789 did not break Paris's hegemonic tradition of gastronomic creativity. This was the period that saw the rise of the restaurant, which quickened the pace of fashion by freeing a number of cooks from the constraints imposed by their aristocratic patrons. The distinctively French cult of reductions and essences was pushed to further extremes: two or three pheasants sacrificed to supply a tiny quantity of sauce. The chain of great chefs continued with confectioner extraordinaire Antonin Carême.

In the aftermath of the French Revolution, the political culture of France remodeled Italy even more profoundly than its cuisine. Once again Piedmont was the region most receptive to that new influence—Napoleon even annexed it to France in 1802. With the post-revolutionary French conquest came a whole series of innovations that were to change Turin, among other Italian cities, for good: a new bureaucracy, primary schools, conscription, the metric system, Jewish emancipation, and street numbers. Moreover, just like Italy's taste in modern food, its new taste for patriotic symbols was also a French import: liberty trees and liberty caps, national flags and national anthems. In other words, the Italian Risorgimento was born in Paris. Italians also imitated the French by holding patriotic banquets at which citizens could dine together fraternally. Yet the documents that have survived from these grand occasions confirm that the food was never smothered in a glaze of national pride: nobody in early nineteenth-century Italy seemed to care whether or not patriots ate food symbolic of Italy. Thus Lorenzo Valerio's 1846 banquet was one of many occasions where the Risorgimento cause manifestly did not embrace *la cucina italiana*.

After the Risorgimento had reached its surprising conclusion, with the proclamation of the Kingdom of Italy in Turin, the gastronomic picture remained unchanged. The French influence on Piedmontese cuisine, and Italian elite cuisine, continued to be strong. The diplomatic architect of the new Italian state, Count Cavour, was a redoubtable trencherman who would later have several dishes named in his honor. But he sent his own chef to be trained in Paris.

An 1869 guide to Turin for Italian visitors provides a striking insight into the local gastronomic culture. It devotes little space to the city's eating habits, mentioning a couple of local specialties which evidently are not considered the basis of a distinctive Turinese food style: *grissini*, the bread sticks that are now as much a part of the place settings in Italian restaurants around the world as knives and forks; and *agnolotti*, Piedmont's typical meat *ravioli*, which in 1869 were "prepared with sovereign artistry." Yet the guide's conclusion is unequivocal: "Turinese cuisine has a good reputation among gastronomists. It is not original, but rather the result of the deep study undertaken by Subalpine cooks, some of whom, like Chapusot and Vialardi, have published treatises." Chapusot we already know from the Subalpine Agrarian Association banquet. Giovanni Vialardi was chef to King Victor Emmanuel—a monarch who was much more comfortable conversing in either Piedmontese or French than in the language of the country he now ruled. Vialardi was just as heavily influenced by French gastronomy as Chapusot. In fact the Italian royal household's eating habits remained markedly French throughout the 1800s: it would take more than forty years after unification for menus for court occasions to be written in Italian.

By that time, another French innovation had further restructured how wealthy Italians ate by rearranging the order in which food was served: the medieval practice of loading the table with a buffet of multiple, contrasting dishes was replaced in the mid to late 1800s by the so-called *service à la russe*, or "Russian service," with separate courses on single plates brought individually to each diner. The sequence of courses in *service à la russe* was much longer than the progression from *antipasto* to *dolce* today, but the principle is undeniably the same. Thus the Italian *menu* (another term brought in from across the Alps) is yet more testimony to Gallic gastronomic power.

The legacy of the long era of French supremacy in the kitchen is still with us today: Italian food would not be Italian food without the French. Understandably enough, the transalpine influence is strongest in Turin and Piedmont, as evinced in the region's great fricassees as well as its *fonduta* (a cousin of the Franco-Swiss fondue), its *ratatuia* (ratatouille), and even its chicken Marengo, the dish of chicken browned then cooked slowly in tomatoes, garlic, and white wine and served with fried eggs and crayfish—it seems that this recipe was improvised in 1800 by Napoleon's adjutant before the Battle of Marengo (which took place in Piedmont).

But the history of Italian food in the 1700s and 1800s is not entirely about French triumph. Even at the apogee of Gallic dominance in the kitchen, the value of local produce and specialties survived and developed across the divided regions of the peninsula. Vincenzo Corrado, the *Gallant Cook* and "Head of Mouth Services" to the king of Naples, furnishes a good example of the local cuisines that slowly developed in Italy during the late 1700s and early 1800s as the cult of spices faded. It was local identity, rather than national identity, that found expression in Italian food. In Naples, that meant fish from the bay and cheese, meat, and vegetables from the kingdom—and, of course, *maccheroni*. Neapolitan pride in *maccheroni* and other local foods reached down into the streets. During the Carnival of 1768, when the city guilds performed their traditional procession before the ransacking of the *Cuccagna*, the pasta-makers handed out leaflets insulting the wealthy for adopting French eating habits. The flame of civic patriotism at table had not been extinguished.

After unification in 1861, the history of Italian food is the story of the relationship between these proud local food cultures, and the dream of bringing all of Italy's many traditions to one table to create a national cuisine to rival that of France. The dream would not prove easy to realize. Restarting the gastronomic dialogue between the cities was a difficult task partly because of poor communications within the new kingdom: at unification, the whole of southern Italy was without railways, apart from a few miles in Naples. Moreover, political conflict, hunger, economic backwardness, and war left their mark on the history of eating in the new Italian state. The sheer poverty of many inhabitants closed them off from the civilization of the table; integrating them fully would take most of the next century. Yet after 1861, however hesitantly and painfully, for the first time since the Renaissance, the phrase "Italian food" began once more to acquire a real meaning.

IV

FOOD FOR THE NEW NATION

II

Naples, 1884

Pinocchio Hates Pizza

Gusto **and** *Disgusto*

To the Italian palate, the American way of eating is a cornucopia of horrors. The gastronomic culture clash begins over breakfast. In the morning, the Italians gently coax their metabolism into activity with coffee and a delicate pastry. The very notion of frying *anything* so early in the day is enough to make stomachs turn. So the classic American breakfast is an outrage; among its most nauseating features are sausage patties and those mattresslike omelets into which the entire contents of a refrigerator have been emptied. Grits defy belief. And anyone in Italy who tried serving a steak before the early afternoon would be disowned by their family.

Such crimes are compounded by another national pathology: the compulsive need to have everything on the same plate. Bacon with hash browns. And pancakes with maple syrup and cherry topping. And applesauce. And eggs. And a salad garnish. And a heap of fruit. Why not—it might occur to an Italian to ask—serve it all in a bucket and pour some of your edifying cereals in milk over the top, too?

A people like the Italians, brought up to savor the way *antipasto, primo, secondo, contorno,* and *dolce* make for an evolving pattern of distinct tastes and textures, experiences shock and pity when confronted with brunch. The Americans can only have invented it to allow their lust for mutually contaminating tastes to descend into savagery.

Italians also find it distressing that Americans eat on the move. In Italy, ice cream is the only thing that can be enjoyed absolutely legitimately while walking, but even then the cone should be wrapped in a napkin, with another napkin ready to dab at the mouth, and the maximum permitted speed is a gentle amble. Italy has many street food traditions, ranging from Rome's simple and omnipresent pizza squares and *supplì* (a deep-fried rice ball with a melting heart of *mozzarella* cheese), to the more demanding Florentine *lampredotto* (a bread roll filled with succulent strips of boiled gut topped with oily parsley and chili dressings). But consuming even these ready-to-go delights is an experience to be savored, an experience worth framing with rules. Hence the napkin etiquette: skin and food should not come into contact. Hence also the fact that Italians eat things like *panini* and *tramezzini* (rolls and little crustless sandwiches) either standing at a counter, or perched on a stool by a shelf. To do anything as purposeful as walking at the same time would be disrespectful to the understated artistry of the cook, and it would cross the line that distinguishes eating from mere feeding.

The Americans—at least in Italian eyes—are innocent of such refinement. They munch burritos in cars. They stride to work sloshing brothy "coffee" into spongy mawfuls of industry-standard muffin. In fact the Yanks eat anything, anywhere, at any time: they slurp Chinese takeout while tapping at a keyboard between meetings, and masticate their loveless, overladen "pizzas" in front of the TV.

Then there is the salad question. A typical Italian salad is spare and simple, designed to complement a meal rather than compete with it: at most two different kinds of leaf, dressed with good oil, salt, and a hint of wine vinegar. The absurd, all- singing, all-dancing American "salad bar," with its bacon bits and croutons, would perhaps attract only detached curiosity or amusement from an Italian—were it not for the dressings. Thousand Island, honey mustard, blue cheese, ranch. Revolting, every one of them. Some of these swills actually contain buttermilk. On salad. *Ti rendi conto?*

All you can eat. Any style. To the Americans, phrases like these seem to hold out the promise of abundance, choice, and freedom. In an Italian, the mere sound of them causes the stomach to tighten in anticipatory repugnance. Four thousand varieties of the same muck is no choice at all. After all, the richest, freest nation on earth has proved itself incapable of making edible bread.

The Italian dread of American food expresses itself in many stereotypes, but it also reveals a truth about the most visceral of human emotions: we are defined by what disgusts us. As we shiver with revulsion, our bodies vibrate in tune with our sternest prejudices. A rule has been violated and we feel it physically as much as we perceive it mentally. Perhaps more compellingly than any other sensation, disgust shows who *we* are. Because *we* don't do things like *that*.

When it comes to food, Italians are as sedulous in their disgust as they are discerning about good eating. Taste and distaste, *gusto* and *disgusto*, are inseparable partners in the Italian civilization of the table. It has always surprised me that the upmarket cookery courses hosted in so many Tuscan villas these days do not begin with lessons in *disgusto all'italiana*.

What is true now was also true in the past. Whenever Italian gastronomy has been strong, then Italians have had a fine sensitivity to what is repugnant, and a finely articulated code of manners. But the rules of repugnance have changed over time. In the Middle Ages and the Renaissance, garlic stank of poverty. Yet many contemporary dishes, from *pesto genovese* to *spaghetti alle vongole* (with clams), would be unthinkable without it. Medieval and Renaissance chefs boiled their pasta until it was very soft, but overcooked spaghetti repels today's Italians more violently than any other kitchen misdemeanor. So it should not come as too much of a surprise to discover that, early in its history, in the late 1800s, pizza was disgusting. Today, pizza is almost certainly the most widely eaten food on the planet, a blazon of Italian identity. Yet only just over a century ago, in the city where it was born, pizza would as likely have provoked a screwed-up nose as a salivating mouth. It is time to delve into the bowels of Naples.

Pizza Margherita

There are few hard facts in the history of pizza. The word probably shares its origins with the Greek *pitta* and the Turkish *pide*, which tells us that it belongs to a wide, ancient Mediterranean family of flatbreads. Many dictionaries of Neapolitan dialect from the late eighteenth century onward tell us that *pizza*, at its simplest, was merely a generic word for all kinds of pies, and for what would be called *focaccia* or *schiacciata* elsewhere in Italy, that is, a flat piece of dough dappled with fat or oil and cooked quickly in a hot oven. This is such a commonplace recipe that it would be pointless to try to seek out its specific origins.

For a long time, from Scappi's 1500s until the end of the nineteenth century, *pizza napoletana* denoted a sweet tart containing almonds. But by the early 1800s, *pizza* had also come to refer to something like its modern form. One of the earliest pizza sightings was made by the author of *The Three Musketeers*, Alexandre Dumas (*père*), who visited Naples in the 1830s and observed the *lazzaroni* eating pizza—largely because it was much cheaper even than *maccheroni*.

> The pizza is a kind of *talmouse* [triangular cheese pastry] like the ones they make in Saint-Denis. It is round, and kneaded from the same dough as bread. . . . There are pizzas with oil, pizzas with different kinds of lard, pizzas with cheese, pizzas with tomatoes, and pizzas with little fish.

Given the pizza's sketchy history, it is perhaps no wonder that Neapolitans in search of certainties about their famous contribution to the way the world eats have latched eagerly on to one episode in June 1889. At that time, Margherita of Savoy, the queen of Italy, was making a monthlong visit to Naples. Although from Turin, she was eager to try pizza, so she sent for the renowned local *pizzaiolo*, Raffaele Esposito, who worked in a pizzeria tucked into a corner between the cramped alleys of the Spanish Quarters and the grand open space of Piazza del Plebiscito. Esposito was set to work in the kitchens of the hilltop palace of Capodimonte where the queen was residing. He made three pizzas: one with just oil; one with whitebait; and one with tomato, mozzarella cheese, and a couple of torn basil leaves. The queen preferred the last of the three, and it was duly baptized *pizza Margherita* in her honor. Esposito's shop, now called the Pizzeria Brandi, still proudly displays the letter of recognition he received:

Household of Her Majesty

Capodimonte
11 June 1889

Mouth Office Inspectorate

Most esteemed Mr Raffaele Esposito. I confirm to you that the three kinds of Pizza you prepared for Her Majesty were found to be delicious.

Your most devoted servant

Galli Camillo
Head of Table Services to the Royal Household

There seems little reason to doubt the authenticity of this document, although I can find no reference to Queen Margherita's pizza experiment in the press of the day. Yet still the story suggests far too cozy a picture of what pizza meant to nineteenth-century Naples. Understandably, many Neapolitans assume that their disk of baked dough flavored with tomato sauce and cheese is so unquestionably a good thing that it only needs to be discovered to be loved. But in reality pizza traveled a much harder and slower road to popularity. Italians had to *learn* to like pizza. Not only that: they had to learn not to loathe it.

One person who manifestly hated pizza was Carlo Collodi, the cook's son from Florence who finished writing *The Adventures of Pinocchio* six years before the queen's visit to Naples. After *Pinocchio,* Collodi's next venture, published in 1886, was an account of a young Tuscan boy's journey around Italy that often reads like chunks of a Baedeker tourist guide as retold in a twelve-year-old's letters home. All the same, it ran rapidly through fourteen editions, and sold particularly well in schools. When the boy in question reaches Naples, he finds a city of sunshine, happiness, and singing. The *lazzari* are now just a memory and, we are assured, the famous *maccheroni* with tomato sauce are eaten with a fork rather than with the hands. But the breezy mood is broken when it comes to describing pizza:

Queen of hygiene. Margherita of Savoy, shown in 1889—
the year the pizza Margherita was named after her.

Pizza is a *focaccia* made from leavened bread dough which is toasted in the oven. On top of it they put a sauce with a little bit of everything. When its colors are combined—the black of the toasted bread, the sickly white of the garlic and anchovy, the greeny-yellow of the oil and fried greens, and the bits of red here and there from the tomato—they make pizza look like a patchwork of greasy filth that harmonizes perfectly with the appearance of the person selling it.

Collodi was a hidebound Tuscan, so his evident revulsion could arguably be dismissed as just regional chauvinism. But Matilde Serao, a bustling, extroverted young Neapolitan journalist, is a different matter. In 1884, she wrote a series of reports on the poorest areas of her home city that were published under the title *The Bowels of Naples*. Like Collodi, Serao's description of pizza shows her explaining a custom that was as yet unfamiliar to the great majority of Italians; it also shows her distaste:

Pizza is made from a dense dough that burns but does not cook, and is loaded with almost raw tomato, garlic, pepper and oregano. If a pizza-maker has a shop, he makes a great number of these round *focacce* during the night. He cuts them into so many slices worth one *soldo* each, and gives them to a boy who goes off to sell them from a portable table at some street corner. The boy will stay there almost all day, while his *pizza* slices freeze in the cold, or turn yellow in the sun as the flies eat them.

A prominent writer at a time when women in any kind of public role in Italy were still very rare, Matilde Serao was also profoundly fond of Naples, and knew how hard life could be there; in her early twenties she had made ends meet by doing piecework in a telegraph office. So what was it about pizza that provoked aversion even in her? Fundamentally, it was not the quality of the ingredients or the dubious methods of the *pizzaiolo*; it was not even the flies. The problem with pizza was Naples; and the problem with Naples was cholera.

Cholera is a uniquely revolting disease. The *Vibrio cholerae* bacterium is carried in food and water contaminated by human excrement; when it is ingested it becomes attached to the wall of the intestine. The symptoms of cholera result from the immune system's attack on the bacteria and from their breakdown, which releases a powerful toxin that reverses the normal flow through the intestinal wall, allowing the fluid components of blood to drain into the guts, and out of the body in a characteristic "rice-water" diarrhea. The most severe cases of cholera can bring about an instant, fatal collapse. Even slower progression can reduce the human body to a corpse-like, wrinkled pallor within a few hours. Death is frequently brought on by severe shock, and is preceded by violent gas, vomiting, diarrhea, suffocating chills, agonizing thirst, paroxysms of abdominal pain, and uncontrollable writhing caused by muscular spasms. The torment is made more dreadful by the fact that the shrieking victims stay conscious and mentally alert throughout. Even those lucky enough to survive this initial, aggressive phase of the disease are usually too weak to make it through the quieter but more insidious stage that follows. Eerily, the corpses of cholera victims often continue to twitch for some time after death.

Nineteenth-century Naples had eight outbreaks of this fearsome malady in the half century after the *Vibrio cholerae* first reached Europe from its endemic home in India in the 1830s. At the time, Italian doctors were still unsure of what caused cholera, and why Naples was so vulnerable. The most widely accepted hypothesis was that its germs lurked in the fetid subsoil of the city, a theory that magnified visceral fears about the notorious filth and squalor of the Neapolitan slums.

With nearly half a million souls, Naples was still by far Italy's biggest city, and Europe's most crowded when Collodi and Serao wrote their descriptions of pizza. London could then count, on average, one inhabitant for every ninety-four square yards of the city's surface area; in Manhattan, there was one for every fifty-eight square yards. The average Neapolotan had markedly less room to move: nineteen square yards. And in the three most densely packed quarters of Naples, the figure reached one person every nine square yards. This was the dark and terrifying "low city" near the seafront, the stinking belly of Naples where no outsider would venture without a revolver. Entire families with their hens and chickens lived in single tiny rooms with barely enough space for everyone to lie down—"kennels," the chief of police called them in 1869. Six-, seven-, and eight-story stacks of these hovels were built around handkerchief-sized courtyards, along alleys so narrow that the tenements sometimes touched one another at the top.

A Swedish doctor called these buildings "the most ghastly human dwellings on the face of the earth." There was no plumbing. Soil pipes and sewers, when there were any, were often cracked or blocked. Cesspools and latrines overflowed and leaked, their contents seeping into wells and water tanks. Excrement and rubbish of all kinds collected in dunghills in the courtyards, or was simply trodden into the unpaved, uncleaned passageways where rivulets of fetid water ran.

Desperate poverty was the norm in the low city. In *The Bowels of Naples*, Serao explains how the indigent majority in the low city ate mostly in the street—even rudimentary cooking was difficult in the "kennels." The cheapest dishes, at one *soldo*, consisted of a slice of pizza, or four or five fritters made from bits of cabbage stalk and fragments of anchovy, or nine boiled chestnuts swimming in a reddish juice. Two *soldi* might buy a plate of snails in broth with a biscuit, or a small portion of *maccheroni*, or some octopus boiled in seawater and flavored, like most other poor dishes, with chilies. These foods, sold by peddlers from trays or small stalls, supported a fragile service economy that was one of the few sources of employment in the worst areas.

A population living in these conditions, on this diet, was inevitably small, thin, sickly, and very susceptible to a bacterium such as *Vibrio cholerae*, whose effects are usually nullified by the juices in a healthy stomach. The cholera outbreaks had taken a huge toll in the low city, and a dread of the disease set its roots deep into the popular psyche. Many tourists shared the same fears, and avoided Naples during the cholera era. Mark Twain did visit in 1867 to climb Vesuvius and wrote a grimly witty evocation of the city's permanent state of apprehension:

> "See Naples and die." Well I do not know that one would necessarily die after merely seeing it, but to attempt to live there might turn out a little differently. . . . The people are filthy in their habits, and this makes filthy streets and breeds disagreeable sights and smells. There never was a community so prejudiced against the cholera as these Neapolitans are. But they have good reason to be. The cholera generally vanquishes a Neapolitan when it seizes him, because, you understand, before the doctor can dig through the dirt and get at the disease, the man dies.

Countless more serious-minded commentators thought that conditions in Naples said something profoundly disturbing about the Italian nation. The enthusiasm that had followed unification in 1861 rapidly faded as the scale of the problems facing the new state became apparent. The Risorgimento, it was now clear, had been the affair of a tiny minority. Concerned patriots turned their attention to exposing the poverty and backwardness of the majority—those for whom the word *Italia,* if it meant anything at all, meant taxes on basic foodstuffs, conscription, and heavy-handed policing. There was a series of investigations, both private and official, into banditry in the countryside, agriculture, illiteracy, the mafia, and other areas of social concern. But of all the problems that exposed the frightening divide between the state and the people, between "legal" Italy and "real" Italy, the low city of Naples was perhaps the most alarming. According to one Tuscan writer, who entered the low city, revolver in hand, in 1877,

> Here you can forget about the Fatherland, Italy, nationhood. They are Neapolitans and that's that. To them, all other Italians are either Piedmontese (to the north) or yokels (to the south). Besides, these people do not even show any noble affection for their own dens, and have no greater ambition than to enjoy their miserable poverty in peace. If they are left alone to roll around in their own filth, and given cheap snails and *maccheroni* to eat, then they will never ask what kind of government is running their country.

Despite this and other impassioned pleas, nothing was done, until the early autumn of 1884, when cholera returned once more to Naples, culling the vast proportion of its victims in the low city. Anyone who had the means to abandon Naples did: 150,000 fled in all—virtually the entire aristocracy and middle class. Sulfur bonfires were lit because they were thought to purify the atmosphere of noxious exhalations. But the infernal fumes rendered the air even worse than normal—some people with breathing difficulties choked to death. In early September, hundreds of tenement dwellers were expiring from cholera daily; the shrieking of the victims and the wailing of the bereaved was incessant; bodies were left uncollected for days. More than 7,000 people are thought to have died in little over a month. Panic and rage took hold, and rumors spread unchecked: it was said that cholera was a poison concocted to exterminate the deprived; doctors and officials were pelted and beaten because they were suspected of deliberately spreading the disease. European public opinion looked on in horror at what the *Times* of London called "a people steeped in ignorance and superstition, and overwhelmed by sorrow and fear." Initially, only penitential processions and the parading of saints' images seemed to keep the seething mass in check. The press at home and abroad lined up to thunder belated denunciations: Naples was a disgrace to humanity, to civilization, and to Italy.

It was then that King Umberto took the initiative. Natural disasters, such as the floods in the Veneto in 1882 and the earthquake on the island of Ischia in 1883, were becoming an important showcase for a monarchy that was still unsure of its role, and for a king who was an insipid and rather dim character. When news of the raging epidemic reached Umberto, he resolved to go to Naples in person. As well as a politically astute move, this was also a very brave one. There was not just the cholera and popular tumult to face; when Umberto visited the city for the first time, soon after inheriting the throne in 1878, an anarchist cook had tried to stab him to death. But this latest royal stay in Naples was greeted with almost universal relief and approval: according to *The New York Times*, Italy went "almost crazy with enthusiasm for the King." His presence settled the nerves of the populace and gave new courage to the overwhelmed authorities. He visited the hospitals, accepted petitions, gave out money, and even went on a personal tour of the poorest boroughs—without, it can safely be assumed, sampling pizza.

Whether it was Umberto or his prime minister who said "Naples must be disemboweled!" during that stroll through the low city is not certain. Nevertheless, the phrase became the slogan of the long-term government response to the crisis: the city's putrescent innards had to be ripped out, the tenements demolished, and new clean and airy quarters constructed. This was also the phrase that provoked Matilde Serao to write *The Bowels of Naples*, and her description of pizza. She, like many Neapolitans, had a well-informed fear of cholera—she said even the thought of it gave her an upset stomach—so she stayed in her adopted home in Rome during the outbreak and wrote her vivid account of the low city from memory. Its success helped propel her into a hugely successful career as a novelist, gossip columnist, newspaper editor—and professional Neapolitan.

The plan to "disembowel" Naples produced some very concrete results that are still visible today: notably Corso Umberto, the long boulevard that slices straight through the four city quarters worst hit by the 1884 cholera outbreak. To inaugurate the reconstruction work, King Umberto went back to Naples in June 1889. The queen went with him and during this visit the *pizza Margherita* acquired its name.

After the king's heroics in 1884, the cult of the monarchy was particularly strong in the city. The royal household had clear ideas about how "impressionable" the Neapolitans were, and how well they responded to royal charisma—the memory of the *Lazzarone* King's early popularity played a part. Margherita, who was blond, forthright, and personable, was far more loved than the doughty Umberto. Matilde Serao, a conservative monarchist, was one of the loudest trumpeters of the queen's virtues. The leading ladies' fashion magazine carried Margherita's name, and fawning biographies turned every aspect of her lifestyle into a model for Italian women. She was an exemplar of beauty, elegance, charity, and *hygiene*—a buzzword of the era that embraced everything from washing and exercise to medicine and diet. Thus "hygiene" brought health and eating into a new relationship; but the smooth working of the digestion was still the great measure of well-being, as it had been in the Galenic era. According to one Neapolitan biographer, the queen hygienically balanced what she ate with her "digestive power," by preferring chicken and game birds, rice, boiled vegetables, eggs and milk products, and by taking an ice cream and a black coffee after her meals—everything was calculated not to "disturb the digestion." Her rigorously French formal lunches were also modest and hygienic, typically consisting of a *consommé*, a couple of *hors d'oeuvre*, two *entrées*, *a sorbet*, a roast, vegetables, and *entremets*.

The water supply in Naples was certainly much cleaner when the royal couple returned in 1889 than it had been in 1884. But whether the queen of hygiene had the courage actually to *taste* the pizza named after her is open to doubt—the letter in the Pizzeria Brandi offers no conclusive proof either way. All the same, her gesture of bestowing royal approval on this, the poorest dish of the poorest city in Italy, made political and human sense: it can be thought of as a late-nineteenth-century equivalent of the moment in 1987 when Princess Diana embraced an AIDS patient. Through pizza, Margherita took her own journey into the bowels of Naples.

In the name of hygiene, Naples was the subject of much undeserved snobbery from farther north in Italy. Commenting on the royal inauguration of the "disembowelling" in 1889, the Florentine newspaper *La Nazione* expressed the patronizing hope that the Neapolitans would learn to correct their old habits, which were "certainly not very hygienically correct." But even a Neapolitan could not disguise that pizza was so unhygienic that it was potentially lethal. The chances of exporting this sample of squalor outside Naples were close to zero. Serao's *The Bowels of Naples* tells the story of a small-time Neapolitan entrepreneur who tried to set up a pizza outlet in Rome. In theory, there should have been a ready market: many Neapolitans had taken the opportunity to move away when the Italian seat of government was transferred to Rome in 1870. The entrepreneur offered the full range of products: tomato pizza, pizza with *mozzarella*, pizza with anchovies, pizza with garlic, oil, and oregano. But the business flopped. As Serao rather daintily put it: "Pizza, when taken away from its Neapolitan environment, seemed out of place; it was indigestible." The word *pizzeria* is not recorded in an Italian dictionary until 1918. Even in 1947 a Neapolitan journalist, describing his city for a national audience, used the word in quotation marks—he clearly thought outsiders might not be sure what it meant. It was not until the 1960s and 1970s that most of the rest of Italy found pizza not only digestible, but delicious.

12

Florence, 1891

Pellegrino Artusi

Mutton Chops

Pellegrino Artusi's *Science in the Kitchen and the Art of Eating Well*, published in 1891, is the most influential cookbook in Italian history. For much of the twentieth century, it was virtually the only book in many Italian homes, its much-thumbed pages bulked out with handwritten notes and recipe variants. Artusi's rules and suggestions became axiomatic: even today, Italians discover that their grandmothers' recipes are often, in reality, Artusian formulae that have seeped unattributed into the fabric of family lore.

Artusi commands a respect that can even cut through Italians' friendly disdain for the opinions of foreigners in matters gastronomic. Any non-Italian who has dined with a group of Italians has experienced becoming suddenly invisible and inaudible when the conversation turns to food—as it almost invariably does. The sense of isolation increases the longer the other guests continue to exchange stories, precepts, and lapidary opinions: "There is only one way to make a *castagnaccio* [a flat chestnut flour cake] . . ." or "Where have all the old *osterie* [cheap eateries] gone?" Short of undressing or setting themselves alight, there is nothing that outsiders can do to attract their companions' attention, let alone grapple a way back into full membership of the conversation. Nothing, that is, except to wait for a lull and utter the words, "Secondo l'Artusi . . ."—"According to Artusi . . ." In Italy there are two kinds of foreigner: those who know nothing about food, and those who have read *Science in the Kitchen and the Art of Eating Well.*

Pellegrino Artusi not only brought together and codified many of the recipes that are still the mainstays of the peninsula's cuisine, but he also turned those dishes, for the first time, into a template of Italian national identity. He was the first since Scappi, the pope's "secret" cook in the 1500s, to try to bring Italy's different food argots into dialogue with one another. Firmly but politely, he was also the first to fight against French domination in the kitchen, nonchalantly observing that "Italian cuisine rivals French, and in some points betters it." With *Science in the Kitchen*, Italy emerged from under the gastronomic shadow of its transalpine neighbor.

Pellegrino Artusi was one of those rare people for whom no one has a bad word. Generous and avuncular, he was a model of comfortable propriety, yet endearingly unashamed of his own gentle eccentricities: he dedicated *Science in the Kitchen* to his two white cats; he wore a frock coat, top hat, and massive muttonchop whiskers that were out of fashion even at the time.

Artusi's easy manner proved to be the key to his cookbook's triumph: "with this practical manual you only need to know how to grab hold of a ladle and you'll muddle through." Much of the charm of *Science in the Kitchen* is in its anecdotes, many of them from Artusi's own life. On one occasion, when discussing roast peacock, he digresses so far that he even forgets to put in a recipe—he knew that food tastes better for being seasoned with a story. At the beginning of the entry on stuffed bread rolls he makes an aside that reveals something fundamental about his cooking, and about Italy's:

A good cook in a great city is more or less like a general in a vast theater of war who has at his disposal legions of battle-hardened troops in well-dug trenches—in other words, everything he needs to show his bravado. It is not just that big cities are ever more bountifully provisioned with all sorts of fine ingredients. They have people

The father of contemporary Italian cuisine, and
Forlimpopoli's favorite son: Pellegrino Artusi in his
unfashionable muttonchop whiskers.

whose job it is to supply you with the tiny things that may have little
intrinsic importance, but which help make your handiwork varied,
elegant and precise. Thus in a city one can find bread sticks for slic-
ing and putting on a spit with birds, and there are rolls the size of
apples specially baked for stuffing.

There could be no clearer account of why, after unification, Italy's food
continued to be city food. Without Florence, without its markets, its
restaurants, its artisans, its thriving literary milieu, and its sense of bourgeois respectability, the greatest Italian cookbook of them all would
never have been written. (The bread rolls, incidentally, have most of
their soft interior removed through a plug cut out of the crust; they are
then dampened with milk, dipped in egg, and fried before being filled
with a mixture of chicken livers, sweetbreads, and other meat in a gravy
flavored with truffles.)

Yet as anyone who heard his accent could tell, Artusi was not born
in Florence. Nor was his cooking Florentine—although many Tuscan

favorites appear in *Science in the Kitchen*. Artusi came from Forlimpopoli, a small walled town on the other side of the Apennines in the Romagna region—then one of Italy's poorest—and always kept some land near Forlimpopoli, even when he lived in Florence. The Romagnol influence on his recipes is even more pronounced than the Tuscan.

Artusi called his cookbook's triumph a "Cinderella" tale. *Science in the Kitchen* was initially snubbed by the literary establishment, but became a publishing phenomenon when he had it printed himself. When fame found Artusi, he was already an old man—seventy-one when his cookbook first came out. The Cinderella tale of *Science in the Kitchen* itself resulted from the coming together of a number of other stories: of a man, his roots, his travels, and his adoptive city of Florence. Forlimpopoli is where all the stories that go into the making of *Science in the Kitchen* begin. The decisive moment that brought out all Artusi's good qualities and instigated his journey from the lawless Romagna countryside to the city of Florence had come forty years before he wrote *Science in the Kitchen*. On January 25, 1851, the Artusi family found themselves caught up in the most infamous brigand attack of the age.

The Ferryman

A deadly calculus of notoriety ruled the life and death of a brigand. The more successful and terrifying his robberies, the more his reputation grew, cowing potential enemies and firing the greedy loyalty of his gang members, friends, and relatives. The more outrageously he was known to spend booty and celebrate triumphs—with generous gifts, garish clothes, whoring, and the playful torture of captured traitors—the farther that shudders of fear and expectation spread through the countryside. And as his fame accumulated, so, too, did the political embarrassment he created for the authorities, the price they placed on his head, and the number of uniformed men they sent out from the cities to hunt him down.

When the Ferryman, protected from the drizzle by a large green umbrella, knocked at the gates of Forlimpopoli on the evening of Saturday, January 25, 1851, he probably sensed that he was about to propel himself much further down a road that would bring both great fame and an early and violent death. His spies inside the town's medieval walls had told him that five of the garrison of twelve gendarmes were away on patrol. Better still, five more were on duty in the theater where the performance of a tragedy, *The Death of Sisara*, had just begun. The situation could hardly have been more convenient, or better set to create a brigand legend: all of Forlimpopoli's wealthy citizens, dressed in their finest, were sitting in neat rows in the theater ready to be robbed.

The Ferryman was not yet twenty-seven years old, but his deeds had already made him unmistakable. His waistcoat shone with gold watches, chains, and pins, and strained under the weight of the coins and jewels sewn into its lining—the garment was both his savings bank and his insignia. Countless judicial proclamations had described the youthful, syphilitic pallor of his face, his sparse black beard, and the spray of gunpowder pinpricks that a misfiring weapon had tattooed under his left eye. Born Stefano Pelloni, he owed his nickname to his father, who had supported Stefano and nine older children by piloting a barge across the Lamone at Boncellino, inland from Ravenna. On this boggy terrain traversed by flood-prone rivers, the peasants huddled in shacks made from sticks or reeds.

Although the Ferryman would sometimes flee to the mountains above Faenza, and strike out at targets north and south, he found sanctuary and constructed his notoriety around the village of his birth. In Bagnara, Cotignola, and Brisighella, the Ferryman and his band perfected their technique of taking over whole villages. First, they threatened the gendarmes into giving up their uniforms; in this new disguise, with its characteristic yellow breeches, some of the bandits would then take over an inn as their base. From there they spread out through the streets, tricking or intimidating their way into their victims' homes before returning to the inn to eat, drink, sing, and pile high their plunder. As stories of the brigands' exploits spread, anyone who could do so fled the countryside for the safety of the cities.

Not even Forlimpopoli's medieval walls could prevent the gang's technique from producing its most spectacular results that Saturday night. The theatergoers first noticed that something was wrong during the interval after the first act, when they heard shouting and scuffling at the tiny theater's side door. Before the seated burghers could react, seven or eight men strode onto the stage and leveled their rifles at the audience. With a flourish, the bandit leader removed his gendarme's kepi and announced that he was the Ferryman, and that this was a robbery.

A musician from the orchestra was summoned to read out a list of names supplied to the bandits by their spies. As each name was called, a member of the audience stood up so that a couple of the criminals could lead him home; there they beat him until he revealed the whereabouts of any secret stores of money or valuables. Back at the theater, while they waited for their companions to return and add to the mounting heap of booty by the stage, the outlaws laughed and drank; as they drank they ordered the orchestra to play and began to pull terrified women from the audience to dance. Several hours passed before they finally made their getaway.

As news of the Ferryman's Forlimpopoli escapade spread, some of its more mundane particulars were quickly embellished. The gang had not marched onto the stage through the stage door, it was said, but had appeared in two chorus lines as the curtain was raised for the second act. The Ferryman had not mugged his victims willy-nilly, but, like Robin Hood, had taxed them according to their wealth.

Less than two months after the attack on Forlimpopoli, the Ferryman was dead. Fittingly, and typically, an anonymous informer made sure that the bandit paid the ultimate price for his terrible renown. Bedraggled and exhausted, Pelloni was spotted by a vagrant near where his father had once moored the ferry. When gendarmes arrived, he tried to run and was shot in the back. To prove to the pope's subjects that the dreaded Ferryman was no more, his corpse was taken all the way to Bologna on a tumbril.

Feasting had been an important ingredient of the Ferryman's fame. Even after Forlimpopoli, hounded as never before by the gendarmes, he still managed to celebrate Carnival in true brigand style. In a hideout near Traversara, the story went, he and five of his companions dallied with ten whores while they ate "*maccheroni* and *gnocchi*, lamb and chicken, mutton and *focaccia* studded with pork fat, biscuits and ring-cakes with *rosolio* and *zabaglione*, jam tart and whipped cream." In the peasants' hungry imaginings, gluttony on this scale was, quite simply, heroic—vicarious revenge for a life of hardship and shortage.

Yet historians of Italian food have a reason to remember the Ferry-man that is more important than this last blowout. Among the houses raided from the theater on that damp, misty night in Forlimpopoli was the home where Agostino Artusi, the town's grocer, lived with his wife, Teresa, their six daughters, and their only son, Pellegrino—the man destined to write *Science in the Kitchen and the Art of Eating Well*. Soon after eight, the father of the house was summoned by the voice of an acquaintance to open his front door. No sooner had he done so than he fainted with shock at seeing several bandits push their way past him, yelling threats.

With his father unconscious, Pellegrino—a shy, shortsighted, hemor-rhoidal bachelor of thirty—tried to save the family. Spurning the chance to escape, he stepped forward to assure the outlaws that nothing valu-able would be kept hidden. But even as he tried to reason with them, the situation spun dangerously out of control when his mother threw a cooking pot out of the window to raise the alarm. Then she made for the front door but was quickly kicked to the ground. From within their room on the floor above, Pellegrino's three younger sisters began to shriek in terror. The brigands hacked a hole in their door with an ax. One of the gang had to be restrained before he could fire his gun through the gap; rape, he was persuaded, was surely a more tempting prospect than murder. Now Pellegrino bore the brunt of their anger. Bellowing "kill him," they pistol-whipped him to the edge of uncon-sciousness. One older sister who came out to put herself in the way of the blows felt a stiletto-point gash open her head.

Recalling why they were there, the bandits then set about smash-ing open every drawer and box in the house in their hunt for booty, keeping a keen eye on the clock as they did so. Once satisfied, most of them returned to the women upstairs only to find the bedroom empty. Two of the youngest Artusi sisters had managed to hide themselves in a large fireplace. The third, Geltrude, who according to her brother was "beautiful, with delicate and graceful features," had fought a desper-ate struggle with some of the intruders; after being "manhandled and contaminated," in Pellegrino's words, she escaped through a dormer window and out onto the Forlimpopoli rooftops; her screaming could now be heard across the town.

The bandits took their loot and left.

The next day the family was reunited. Once he had shed tears of relief that no one had been killed, Pellegrino found the resolve to announce to his parents that he was going to move to Florence for good. Dismayed by the robbery, they decided to sell what they had and follow him. Their son was now head of the household. For the next twenty years, Artusi's overriding concern was that his family's security and dignity should never be threatened again.

Spinsters in the House

Florence in 1851 still stood within the same walls built to enclose it at the start of the fourteenth century—long before the Medici family had decided to give up farming and try their hand at banking, politics, and art patronage instead. Within those crumbling city walls Florence had not remained entirely untouched by the moves to rationalize town planning that had spread across Europe in the mid-nineteenth century. The cholera outbreaks of 1835 and 1855 and the Arno flood of 1844 had produced some piecemeal improvements. A miserly system of gas street lighting was introduced in 1846—the lamps were left unlit when there was a full moon. But even the newer, more salubrious quarters lacked proper sewers. Peasants would come in from the countryside at night to fill barrels with fertilizer from the Florentine cesspools.

The Artusis quickly found a home in Via Calzaiuoli, within the shadow of Brunelleschi's cathedral dome. Pellegrino's career began soon afterward when he took over a wholesale silk business in the same street, relying on his father's contacts in the Romagna for supplies. Just behind Via Calzaiuoli stood the Old Market, a quarter so squalid that visitors routinely called it medieval. Except, of course, that in medieval times the area had been the wealthy heart of Florence, a place where some of the city's most famous families, including the Brunelleschis, had built their homes. As Florence fell into decline, these glorious towers, palaces, and loggias were whittled from within and encrusted from without. Slowly they became a damp, sunless maze of hovels, shops, and semipermanent stalls. By the early 1800s, the overcrowding, dirt, and din of the alleys and tiny squares of the Old Market were infamous.

The most notorious part of the quarter was the old ghetto, where the Jews had first been confined in 1571. Here cramped apartments in blocks eight or nine stories high teetered over two tiny squares, shutting out air and sunlight. The Jews moved out as they were granted rights in the first half of the nineteenth century, and their places were taken by the most desperate of Florence's lowlifes: the old ghetto was the first place the police looked for any robber.

Petty crime was not the only problem harbored in the Old Market. Members of the city's bourgeoisie, such as Artusi, turned up their noses at the smell of cheap popular food. Arno fish and salt cod, zucchini flowers and artichokes, apple fritters, *gnocchi*, sweet rice dumplings, and hot blood sausages—all were tallow-fried to take away. In wood-fired urns, potatoes, *cavolo nero* (a kind of kale), broccoli, and other cheap vegetables were boiled then displayed on huge copper dishes. There was every kind of butcher, including *testicciolai*—specialists who would scald and peel sheep's heads before their customers' eyes. Cheap meats were piled high on tables: pork rind, veal hoof, and tripe. Preserved fish—pilchards, herring, tuna, and anchovies—were sold from open barrels. The Old Market stank of a "medieval" world that comfortable, progressive-minded Florentines wanted to leave behind.

Despite these disturbances, over the next two decades Artusi's life was mercifully free of any shocks to compare with the one that had caused his move to the city. But it was not without incident. The quirky autobiographical notes he penned late in life make slightly shamefaced reference to a good number of sexual adventures. Not that he was a libertine: "I have always broken through doors that were already open, and I have always respected friendships," he wrote in his own defense. Marriage, however, never appealed to him: "Indissoluble vows are Medieval dogma, obligations that run counter to nature and have no reason for existing in the rational, progressive environment we find ourselves in." He would remain a bachelor, and a happy one, for the rest of his days.

The greatest sadness in Artusi's new life was the fate of his poor sister Geltrude. She lost her wits after being abused by the brigands in Forlimpopoli. In 1855 she was diagnosed with mania and admitted to an asylum; there she would spend the rest of her life, unable to recognize the brother who paid for her keep. When his mother passed away in

April 1859, Artusi was so grief-stricken that he was ill for weeks. From his bed, he heard the demonstration that caused Grand Duke Leopold II to flee and that brought Tuscany into the Kingdom of Italy. Artusi's other duty was to provide for two of his sisters who were getting on in years and manifestly craved the comforts of a husband. ("Anyone who has experienced what it means to have a spinster in the house will say what a torment it is to put up with them.") The problem was resolved by the simple expedient of increasing their dowries. Both sisters, he reported proudly, made faithful wives.

In 1870, commerce, investment, and these well-meaning double standards in the management of his domestic affairs had made Pellegrino Artusi rich enough, and free enough of responsibilities, to retire to a new, spacious house on the edge of the city. At the age of fifty, he could finally indulge in his greatest pleasure: intellectual pottering. He frequented libraries and lectures, developing a passion for anthropology and literature. He wrote two books on poets: a life of Ugo Foscolo and a commentary on some of Giuseppe Giusti's letters. The introduction to the second work, published in 1881, evinces a modesty that does Artusi credit, but can have done nothing to improve sales: "May God save you from yawns," he wished his readers. Neither book made any impact whatsoever. Piqued by these failures, he began to conceive of a book that, with its humble and practical subject matter, would allow him politely to thumb his nose at the literary circles he had failed to impress: *Science in the Kitchen and the Art of Eating Well.*

Piazza Massimo d'Azeglio

Hitherto, Artusi's years in Florence had been unremarkable. But at the same time, the city on the Arno had gone through profound changes. *Science in the Kitchen* was a mirror of that urban transformation.

In September 1864 astonishment greeted the news that Florence was to become the capital of Italy. A couple of years earlier, when the dashing novelist and statesman Massimo d'Azeglio had suggested that Florence would make a good seat of government, he was greeted with scoffing. But his argument acquired momentum by a process of elimination: Turin, the capital since unification, was too northern; Naples, still the peninsula's largest city, was too far south and far too chaotic; Rome, which almost everyone thought of as Italy's natural capital, still belonged to the pope and was protected by a ring of French bayonets.

Florence's total population then stood at about 100,000. Thirty thousand politicians, bureaucrats, journalists, lawyers, and hangers-on would now have to be squeezed in, as well. Residential streets, covered markets, wider bridges, barracks, and a station were hastily planned. Progress demanded hygiene, light, air, and a healthy segregation of the social classes who still lived in uncomfortable intimacy in the old center. Italy's respectable citizens wanted to sit in spacious cafés and theaters, to gaze into the sparkling windows of new boutiques, to stroll along tree-lined avenues—without bumping into a footpad or a fish seller. The Old Market and the ghetto were marked for demolition. Twenty years before Naples, Florence was "disemboweled."

The hygienic transformation of Florence did not go entirely according to plan. In 1870, France withdrew its troops from Rome, and the Italian state apparatus was soon transplanted from the Arno to the Tiber. Much of Italy rejoiced, but Florence was left teetering on the brink of financial catastrophe by a fall in property prices. In 1878 the council finally gave up the struggle, resigned en masse, and declared the city bankrupt. But in fits and starts, the reconstruction work continued. The Old Market square was replaced by a spacious new piazza with a mounted statue of the king at its center. The medieval walls on the right bank of the river came down, and a broad boulevard took their place. And just inside the boulevard, at what was then the city's eastern edge, a soberly elegant square was built over the messy orchards of the Mattonaia quarter. At its center, crisscrossed by paths of gravel, was a garden where children could play under their parents' or nannies' supervision. This was Piazza d'Azeglio, where Pellegrino Artusi came to live.

Today a plaque marks the spot where *Science in the Kitchen* was written: Artusi's retirement home at number 25, Piazza d'Azeglio. The name turned out to be appropriate because Massimo d'Azeglio was not only the man who first suggested that Florence should shoulder the patriotic duty of becoming capital, he was also the author of the most-quoted phrase in Italian history: "Now Italy is made, we must make the Italians." In other words, Italy had a state, but the Italians were not yet a united people. D'Azeglio's dictum soon came to encapsulate the nation-building zeal that influenced every aspect of life in the new country. Bourgeois Italians found a multitude of ways to spread the patriotic gospel: school books and monuments, shooting clubs and street names. One bourgeois, Pellegrino Artusi, gave a less jingoistic and more lasting contribution to making the Italians than anyone else. *Science in the Kitchen* is a product of the ideals made concrete in the rebuilding of Florence, it is to cooking what Piazza d'Azeglio is to town planning. With Artusi, the urban middle classes became the architects of the national cuisine.

The early pages of *Science in the Kitchen* include advice on hygienic principles such as living in a light, ventilated home and taking gentle exercise—all delivered with Artusi's cheery good sense: "Some hygienists recommend that you drink water throughout lunch, keeping wine until the end. Do it if you have the courage, but to me it seems like asking too much." The bourgeois diet was to be moderate, varied, and consistent: only brigands and aristocrats swung wildly from bone-gnawing hunger to gut-stretching binges. In his usual breezy way, Artusi explains who is meant to use his book:

> Obviously what I have written here is addressed to the comfortably-off classes of society. People less favoured by fortune are forced, in spite of themselves, to make a virtue of necessity and take consolation in the thought that a frugal and active life maintains good health and keeps the body robust.

Between the crude, indigestible cooking of the masses, and the pretentious, Frenchified cuisine of the nobility, *Science in the Kitchen* develops an ethos of respectable eating for the bourgeois households now living in Piazza d'Azeglios up and down Italy. Artusi is practical, homely, and humorous throughout. He gives handy tips: put a few drops of turpentine in your chamber pot after eating asparagus for dinner and the indecorous smell of asparagus-infused urine will be instantly transformed into an aroma of sweet violets. The cost of prepared dishes is always on his mind, for waste is as vulgar as ostentation. Some dishes are "not for presentation to anyone outside the family," for example, *pollo in porchetta* (a whole chicken butter-roasted in a casserole dish after being stuffed with ham, garlic, a few tufts of fennel, and the odd peppercorn), or lamb's head stewed in tomato sauce and broth. Others "won't make a bad impression," such as a soup made from the orange-colored Caesar's mushrooms that grow in the hills around the city. Artusi recommends frying a pound of them gently in about two ounces of bacon fat and two ounces of butter with a little chopped parsley, before simmering them in broth for ten minutes, and finally mixing in a whole egg, a yolk, and a handful of Parmesan; a few croutons add the finishing touch.

By the time Artusi moved to 25 Piazza d'Azeglio, he knew more of the territory of the new Italian state than the vast majority of his compatriots did. His commercial traveling, both with his father and in his own right, had taken him far afield. As early as 1847 he had made the weeklong carriage journey from Forlimpopoli to Rome, where he spent two months, and made a further ten-day visit to Naples. Later, Italy's new railways made his trips to such places as Padua, Milan, and Turin much faster and easier. The area Artusi knew best, where he had been to numberless *osterie*, *locande*, and *trattorie*, was a wedge of central Italy from Rovigo down to Senigallia on the Adriatic, and then over the Apennine mountains to Livorno on the coast of Tuscany. Crucially, he felt particularly comfortable in the culinary powerhouse of Bologna where he had been a student; as he would write in *Science in the Kitchen*, "When you hear Bolognese cuisine being mentioned, you should bow deeply and respectfully, because it deserves it."

Gastronomically speaking, Artusi straddled the Apennines—the mountain range is a food fault line. He was brought up on the Emilian and Romagnol culture of pork, ham, lard, and fresh pasta, but he also understood the oil- based cooking of Tuscany, with its fondness for beef, fish, legumes, and vegetables. These two distinct cuisines provided an excellent template onto which other regional dishes could be added.

Writing *Science in the Kitchen* systematized all this raw culinary knowledge. So in the kitchen in Piazza d'Azeglio, Artusi began to test recipes: his two faithful servants, Marietta Sabatini, from northern Tuscany, and Francesco Ruffili, from Forlimpopoli, cooked them to his instructions. Thus, through memory and experiment, *Science in the Kitchen* began to assemble a portrait of Italy in food. From the interior of his own

Romagna came *passatelli*—a worm-shaped fresh pasta made by squeezing a dough of bread crumbs, Parmesan, egg, and bone marrow through a colander or a special grid ("there are very few families in the Romagna who don't have one," Artusi explains). From Livorno and Viareggio, on the Tuscan coast, come two recipes for *cacciucco*, a fish soup. The coastal towns on the opposite, Adriatic coast provide a mullet broth. From near Rovigo, in the estuary of the Po, comes a thick, hearty chicken-and-rice dish—Artusi learned the secret of this meal-in-one plate from the proprietress of a hostelry when he was on his way to a trade fair. Some classics merited detailed attention: there are three separate recipes for Milan's typical saffron *risotto*. There are Sicilian *maccheroni* with fresh sardines and wild fennel. From Lodi in the flat expanses of the Po valley southeast of Milan, Artusi takes some simple cheese and *polenta* fritters. There are purple Roman broccoli, which are first boiled, then seasoned and turned in hot fat, and then flavored by adding white wine and boiling it off. Some ingredients are given many treatments taken from different places: salt cod can be done in a Bolognese or Florentine style, among several others. There are old favorites, such as Comacchio eel and Neapolitan pizza—meaning, of course, the almond pastry rather than the disease-bearing disk of dough with tomato and cheese.

Artusi's panorama of the state of Italian eating tells us that tomato sauces, from their beachhead in Naples, had now spread into every corner of Italy. The potato, too, had full citizenship by his day, and was used in dishes like potato *gnocchi*. And the allure of spices had vanished. Italy's civilization of the table had entered the contemporary era.

Yet looking back at *Science in the Kitchen* from today, it is all too easy to show how distorted and partial Artusi's map of Italy's foods is. Some areas are overrepresented, notably the Romagna, Tuscany, and Bologna. Other places, such as Sicily, receive only token treatment. Others still, notably Sardinia and the mainland south outside Naples, simply do not exist. Artusi's writing also betrays little regional biases at every turn. Compare his respect for Milan's way with veal shank, or *osso buco* ("the Milanese make it best, so I intend to describe it without any pretensions for fear of being teased"), with his much less reverential attitude to Neapolitan *maccheroni*, which he rather dismissively says will appeal particularly to "people who like swimming in tomato sauce." As a young man in Naples, Artusi had also struggled to come to terms with *maccheroni* dressed only with pepper and sharp cheese, and had sought out what he called a "refined restaurant" where they were served in a nice *béchamel*—hardly a Neapolitan practice. In fact, Artusi does not disguise that his food knowledge of the whole of Italy south of Tuscany is largely restaurant-based. For instance, *saltimbocca* (literally, "hop-in-the-mouth") is one of Rome's best-loved dishes: thin veal cutlets, with half a sage leaf and a slice of Parma ham sewn on top with a toothpick, sautéed in butter—for longer on the veal side so that the *prosciutto* does not become hard. Artusi's recipe is perfect, but it begins with what today reads like a confession: "I have eaten them in Rome, at the Trattoria Le Venete, so I can describe them exactly."

But in such a new and diverse country no one could be expected to reflect the entire range of cooking in the different regions. Given the circumstances of his time, Artusi's achievement was monumental. Almost single-handed, he restarted the long interrupted food dialogue between Italy's cities. In his own sensible, conservative way, he was a gastronomic visionary who put the civilization of the table back at the center of national life.

The trouble was that nobody seemed to notice.

The Cinderella Tale

Writing *Science in the Kitchen* had not cured Artusi of his craving for approval from the people who counted in Florentine cultural circles. He first showed the recipe book to a literature scholar who looked down his nose at it. He sent some Florentine publishers the manuscript and invited them to lunch. "It might work if Doney had written it," they complained—Doney being the owner of the city's best-known restaurant, café, and patisserie in Via Tornabuoni. Then as now, a recipe book would struggle without a celebrity name on its cover. The pile of rejection letters continued to grow until Artusi stubbornly had a thousand copies of the book printed at his own expense. Even then he suffered further humiliation: he sent two copies to be given away at a charity raffle in Forlimpopoli, but the winners bartered their prizes for tobacco.

Salvation came in the form of Italy's foremost academic sex symbol, anthropology professor Paolo Mantegazza, whose uncanny physical resemblance to Buffalo Bill was remarked upon during the legendary cowboy showman's visit to Florence in 1890. Mantegazza had made his name by exploring the wild frontier of hygiene: such titles as *The Hygiene of Beauty* (1870), *Forms of Human Ecstasy* (1887), and, above all, the international bestseller *The Hygiene of Love* (1878) habitually drew a large female audience to his public talks. He also recommended that cocaine would give the working classes more vim, and wrote about the hygiene of eating. When Mantegazza received a copy of *Science in the Kitchen* from Artusi, he immediately recognized its merits, sympathized with its modernizing spirit, and enthused about it during a couple of his lectures. *Science in the Kitchen* had the celebrity endorsement it needed; Mantegazza's support triggered an exponential growth in sales.

Artusi handled everything from home: to buy the book, you had to write to him personally, and each copy was signed as a guarantee against cheap imitations. He only entrusted a publisher friend with distribution when the operation outgrew the house in Piazza d'Azeglio and his servants could no longer keep pace with packing the hundreds of copies being dispatched across Italy. By the sixth edition, in 1902, the hundreds of copies had become thousands. Smart old businessman that he was, Artusi steadily drove down the price he paid to the printers, and drove up the percentage he received from the distributors; he expanded sales through newspaper advertising and by sending free copies to women's societies. As he entered his eighties, Artusi was busy making himself a second fortune.

With each new edition of *Science in the Kitchen*, the number of recipes also grew. This expansion had a commercial logic, since it made older editions obsolete. Artusi's servants joked to one visitor that "we're stuck in front of these ovens almost the whole day, and sir is driving us mad with his continual experiments."

The recipes on which the servants worked so hard were often sent in by readers, mostly women who had been won over by Artusi's amicable and even flirtatious tone—his preface began with the words, "Cooking is a little minx . . ." So *Science in the Kitchen* is a multiauthored work— and that is one of the most historically significant things about it. Before 1891, women cookery writers were rare. The culinary knowledge of middle-class women and their domestic cooks was transmitted orally down through the generations, or shared in private letters because it was simply not considered worth discussing in public. After Artusi, female cookery writers took an increasing share of the market until they reached a dominant position in the 1920s and 1930s. Artusi's contribution to that transformation was immense. After all, in his time, Italian women were legally prohibited even from subscribing to a newspaper without their husbands' permission.

A lady from Parma wrote in with a recipe for the city's semicircular filled pasta parcels called *anolini* that were reserved for Christmas and Easter; the filling includes four or five spoonfuls of the juices produced by sautéing a piece of beef studded with bacon fat in butter, and then simmering it in broth for eight or nine hours in a covered casserole dish. "I declare myself obliged to the aforesaid lady," Artusi owns. Among the other recipes for which he was obliged to his female fans were artichoke "cutlets" fried in *béchamel*, fried folds of cognac-infused pastry called "booklet pizzas," a simple *soufflé* with Gruyère cheese, and some chocolate biscuits specially designed to restore strength to women who have just given birth. The French influence on this little sample of middle-class mothers' specialties is manifestly strong, suggesting that, in the centuries since the gastronomic invasion from over the Alps, comfortable Italian households had adopted the Gallic innovations and shaped them according to their own environment, to the rhythm of their families' lives, and to local food preferences.

Science in the Kitchen includes quite a few French recipes—even the "chocolate slap" recorded more than a century earlier by *The Piedmontese Cook Perfected in Paris*. There are also Germanic dishes, such as *Sauerkraut* and *Krapfen* (doughnuts). And there is even a generous helping of English classics like roast beef (two recipes), pigeon pie, plum pudding, and toad-in-the-hole. So although Artusi permitted himself a gentlemanly chuckle about the name "toad-in-the hole," he was no gastronomic xenophobe. It is refreshing to note that the word *tradizione*, which is now often used in an exclusive way, to reject foreign dishes from the supposedly timeless roll all of genuine Italian products, is never used by the founder of contemporary Italian cuisine.

All the same, Artusi was a patriot. He made plain his distaste for the English way of eating vegetables—"boiled, with no dressing or with a knob of butter at most"—and who can blame him? Artusi's particular concern was that the demanding foreign tourists and their much-needed money were erasing the distinctive qualities of Italian food. For example, his entry on *tagliatelle* gives the recipe in a couple of lines, but devotes a page and a half to explaining the value system that surrounds them. Long strands of pasta of this kind, he insists, "must preserve the character of the nation because they are special to Italy"; it simply will not do to cut them up small "to conform to foreigners' tastes." If Artusi had read the authoritative Baedeker guide to southern Italy, published in 1896, he might have had even more cause for worry: "the Maccaroni of Naples is much esteemed," it advises, "but is generally hard, and should therefore be ordered *ben cotti*"—meaning well cooked. (The Italian habit of eating pasta *al dente* had spread from Naples in the early 1800s.)

But it is on the issue of language that Artusi really goes into battle for Italian food. In one of the early recipes he declares that he will reject high-sounding French labels; for the sake of Italian dignity, he will instead use "our beautiful, harmonious language." But the real challenge he faced was that this "beautiful, harmonious language" had not yet been invented. At table, the country was still split between French—used at grand banquets, at high-class tourist restaurants, and in cookbooks—and the many regional dialects that the overwhelming majority of Italians spoke around the table at home. The compiler of the most important dictionary of the Italian language written during Artusi's lifetime thought that it was impossible to write a book on cookery in Italy because the words did not exist. The legacy of Scappi and other Renaissance cooks was not enough: Italy had no shared vocabulary in which a Venetian and a Neapolitan could come to terms with pots-and-pans issues.

Even for the minority of Artusi's compatriots who actually knew it, Italian was a second language, a written language, a language of public affairs and literature. But in two places, Italian was routinely spoken in more everyday circumstances: Rome, the city of the Church where constant immigration had long since turned Italian into a *lingua franca*; and Tuscany, where Italian originated in the language used by Florence's supreme medieval writers Dante, Petrarch, and Boccaccio. If there *was* to be a book about cookery that would be accessible across the whole of Italian territory, then Rome and Tuscany were the only likely sources of its vocabulary.

As an immigrant to Florence, Artusi was in the ideal position to write that book: he knew how Tuscans talked about food, but his travels had endowed him with a feeling for their dialect, which would sound alien to Italian-speakers in the rest of the country. Thus *Science in the Kitchen* contains a short guide to Tuscan terms used in the book, but that might be obscure to people from elsewhere. A sample gives a sense of how basic the language problem was: *lardo* (lard), *cotoletta* (cutlet), *tritacarne* (mincer). These terms are all in common use today.

Tuscan dialect could not offer all the linguistic solutions Artusi needed. In some cases he just reproduces the regional name for a dish; in others he gives alternative words for the same thing: for example, cardoons, which can be either *gobbi* or *cardi* depending on where in Italy you happen to be. French imports were another problem that did not permit a single solution. In some cases, the French word is clear enough to be left as it is: *sauté*, for example, or *gâteau*. In other cases, by the time Artusi came along, Italian had already absorbed the French word and made its spelling more familiar: for example, the French veal fricassee, *fricandeau* had become *fricandò* in Italy. More often, Artusi takes plea-sure in giving no-nonsense Italianizations: hence the grand Gallic *Sauce Ravigote* becomes just another "green sauce."

Italian did not absorb all the words that Artusi used. He tried to render the French *béchamel* with the charming invention *balsamella*—roughly meaning "delicate little balsam." Italians today use the more prosaic *besciamella*, which is the sound of the French word transposed into Italian with an extra *la* stuck on the end to give it a more homely ring. However, Italians largely have Artusi to thank if they do not have to go armed with a large dictionary every time they eat in a restaurant outside their own hometown.

In 1903 Pellegrino Artusi wrote a short autobiography. Although its occasional outbursts of bitterness show that it was not intended for pub-lication, it was mostly frank and engaging, as befit the man. He wept as he recalled the Ferryman's attack on Forlimpopoli which had brought such tragedy and upheaval to his life. The autobiography contains very little information about food, which is not a surprise, since *Science in the Kitchen and the Art of Eating Well* had already told that part of his life story to thousands of readers. By the time he died in 1911, at age ninety, his cookbook had reached its fourteenth edition, and contained a grand total of 790 recipes—315 more than the first edition of 1891. As a sign of his affection for the place of his birth, he left the bulk of his estate to fund a home for Forlimpopoli's least fortunate inhabitants. The future royalties from *Science in the Kitchen* went to the two dedicated servants, Marietta Sabatini and Francesco Ruffili, who had labored so long on his vision of Italian cuisine.

Artusi's legacy to his country was the template for a properly Italian cuisine based on respect for local food traditions. The problem was that many people could not afford to eat most of the items on the national menu. In fact, for the underfed millions, the only way to start eating like an Italian was to leave Italy altogether.

13

Genoa, 1884–1918

Emigrants and Prisoners

Emigrants: Aboard the *Nord America*

For the previous two nights, the streets that sloped toward the port of Genoa had been full of fitful forms huddled protectively around their worthless luggage. Many of the emigrants now lining up to have their passports inspected had been forced to sleep in the open. They had come from all over Italy. Families from the Venetian mainland driven off the fields by debt, taxes, and a diet of onion broth and *polenta*. Peasants from the countryside around Mantua; to survive each winter they were forced to cross the Po and supplement their *polenta* with tasteless black tuberose. Workers from the fever-cursed rice paddies of lower Lombardy—where moldy bread, rancid bacon fat, and *polenta* were the only reward for long days spent with arms and legs immersed in slimy water, backs beaten by the sun. There were southerners in the line, too: Calabrians who made their "bread" from wild lentils, which clung in the mouth like mud and sawdust; and ploughmen from Basilicata who slept in sties and never tasted meat from one year to the next—unless disease killed one of their animals. From Puglia came the estate workers who stood in line each evening to eat what their landlord offered: the remains of a flat black loaf in a ladleful of hot brine with a few drops of oil.

The small groups that emerged from the customs building and crossed the quay knew they were the lucky ones. Others had not made it so far. Some had been swindled by emigration agents and forced to return home to beg for a living. Others had failed the medical inspection. Reddened and swollen mouths, discolored and peeling skin, trembling hands, poor vision, melancholy, memory loss, idiocy: it was hard to disguise the symptoms of pellagra, the illness caused by the niacin deficiency of a diet based on maize porridge, *polenta*.

Mi emigro per magnar. In whichever dialect it was spoken, the reason for embarking on the steamship *Nord America* that day was the same: *I'm emigrating so I can eat.* Over the gangplank lay a future that might not be better, they told themselves, but could hardly be worse.

Later, as dusk fell and the *Nord America* backed away from her moorings, the third-class passengers gathered at the prow. The city known as *la Superba* stretched out in a wide semicircle above them. Just after Italian unification, Genoa's civic leaders dedicated a huge marble statue to their city's most famous son. He looks out seaward and leans on an anchor; a naked maiden wearing a feather headdress kneels meekly at his feet—she represents America. The inscription reads:

He divined a new world,
and bound it to the old with everlasting benefits.

To Christopher Columbus
The Fatherland

Since the statue was completed, Genoa had grown stronger on the "everlasting benefits" of the Americas. Its outskirts had begun to climb into the hills. The port was reaching farther out into the sea as barge-mounted cranes lifted mighty blocks into place to extend the New Mole. More and more transatlantic merchandise was passing across these quays: American cotton and grain, Brazilian sugar and coffee . . . and Italian emigrants.

From on board the *Nord America*, an old Tuscan peasant in a battered green overcoat looked back at the lights of the urban amphitheater and shook his fist in impotent, sarcastic anger: "Viva l'Italia!" he shouted.

• • •

Exporting hungry peasants was a peculiar way for Italy to launch its food on the journey to worldwide popularity. The Irish, another rural people driven to mass emigration by hunger, have not had remotely the same influence on America's way of eating, or the world's. One might expect that, like the Irish, the Italians who arrived in the New World would have chosen ways other than food to express themselves. Yet largely because of mass emigration to the Americas, today pizza and pasta are virtually ubiquitous. *Pesto*, Genoa's most famous contribution to Italian cuisine, has become almost as widespread. Some Italian foods are now world foods.

In 1884, the year the *Nord America* sailed to Montevideo, 50,000 emigrants passed through Genoa on their way to Brazil, Uruguay, and Argentina. Although Genoa would remain Italy's leading departure point, the numbers of emigrants would increase enormously in later years. In 1913, at the peak of the exodus, outward migrants from all Italian ports were officially recorded as numbering 872,000 for the year, with the United States now the principal destination. In all, between 1876 and the First World War, more than seven and a half million Italians shipped to the New World.

Why did those who arrived in the New World from the different regions of Italy eat in such a distinctively Italian style? Good flavors are only one part of the explanation. Ultimately it is the profound bond between identity and eating that turned those "huddled masses" of ill-fed emigrants into the pathfinders for Italian food on American shores. In other words, feelings explain the success of *la cucina italiana* on the other side of the Atlantic as much as do the brute socioeconomic facts. But we should not forget that most of the people who emigrated did so precisely because they were *excluded* from Italy's civilization of the table. *Polenta* and other dishes of the poor were miserable daily reminders of that exclusion. Food certainly shaped the identity of peasant emigrants from Italy, but envy, anger, and ambition—not nostalgia—marked their attitudes to eating when they departed, and those feelings turned food into a badge of who they were once they arrived.

Edmondo De Amicis, the writer to whom we owe the account of departing emigrants with which this chapter began, was a curly-haired former soldier. Soon to become Italy's bestselling author, he recorded the embarkation of 1,600 men, women, and children on the *Nord America* on the evening of March 10, 1884. Three weeks later he landed with them in Uruguay. His passionate portrayal of the emigrants' plight during that journey was destined to set the pattern for Italy's response to the exodus from its shores.

As a canny author of sentimental travelogues, De Amicis was drawn most powerfully to the emigrants' story by the enigma of their feelings, which often escape the sociologist's gaze. His skill lay in turning his report on their voyage into a human comedy with larger-than-life characters, tear-jerking scenes, and a patriotic payoff. But this very penchant for sentimentality made De Amicis unusually sensitive to how the passengers aboard the *Nord America* felt about food.

On the Ocean, as De Amicis' travelogue was called, was reprinted ten times within two weeks of publication. It chronicled a grim, pan-Italian kaleidoscope of undernourishment on board the *Nord America*, but sex also kept the pages turning—a theme established soon after the steamship weighed anchor. The foulmouthed Genoese captain announced a rigid moral code for all passengers, rich, and poor. He had a catchphrase: "Porcaie a bordo no ne véuggio"—*Filth*: I don't want any of it on board." He even ordered an elderly hunchbacked sailor to separate couples and guard the entrance to the female third-class dormitory after dark. It was to prove a futile gesture.

As the *Nord America* sailed from the Mediterranean into the Atlantic, it became ever less a ship, and ever more a microcosm of a nation divided between rich and poor: between the emigrants crammed into every available space at the prow and around the funnels, and the first- and second-class passengers who took the air in a secluded part of the quarterdeck. Gastronomically speaking, there were two Italys aboard the *Nord America*: one a people who ate hardtack and soup from mess tins on their laps; and the other an elite that dined on *maccheroni* with the captain.

In the confined proximity of the crossing, there could hardly fail to be tensions. Strolling uneasily among the third-class passengers, De Amicis heard them relishing the prospect of what the mass departure of labor would do to their former bosses: "When we've all left then they'll die of hunger, too." The old Tuscan in the green overcoat, it turned out, was something of a rabble-rouser, and food was the subject of his finger-wagging harangues. Now and again he would hurl his mess tin away in disgust, shout abuse in the direction of the galley, and proclaim that anyone who carried on eating had "sold out." When an old Piedmontese peasant died of pneumonia, the Tuscan troublemaker claimed that the deceased man had been given dishwater instead of broth. As was habitual on such transatlantic crossings, the restless souls in third class were intermittently pacified with a portion of fresh meat—the steamer had its own livestock on board for just that purpose.

The green-coated Tuscan radical had a kind of alter ego in first class—a chubby Genoese foodie with only one eye and a beard like a horsehair brush. For De Amicis he embodied the upper classes' self-satisfied disregard for the poor. He passed hours in the stores and galley, inspecting the ingredients and swapping tips with the cooks. He took pride in being the first to announce what was for dinner every night: chicken breast in Madeira wine, liver pie, *maccheroni al sugo*. His greatest delight at table was laying down judgment on the chef's repertoire: "rather too reliant on stews," "strong on sweets," "those mixed fried meats last night—oh dear!"

As the ship neared the tropics, and the heat, boredom, and gossip all intensified, so, too, did the tensions both alimentary and sexual. The *filth* in first class was as bad as it was in third: from the shy newlyweds who kept half the ship awake by "reciting Spanish verbs" in their cabin at night, to the opera tenor who cruised the lower decks for peasant beauties, to the Swiss-Italian woman in black silk stockings who gaily betrayed her bookish husband with the Argentinian politician, the Tuscan adolescent, and the opera tenor. As the old hunchback commented in despair, "Se e' porcaie pesassan, saiescimo zà a fondo"—"If filth was heavy, we'd be on the bottom already."

A few days out from Montevideo, a violent storm struck the *Nord America*. The one-eyed Genoese foodie, undeterred by the pitch and roll of the decks, sneaked into the kitchens for a couple of slices of ham or cold roast. The ship bucked and he was thrown against a beam, cracking his head open: the gastro-bore's comeuppance.

The Tuscan militant was restless, too: he organized a petition signed (after a fashion) by forty-seven third-class passengers and demanding "a more varied supply of meat dishes." De Amicis certainly did not admire the subversive cheek of this aging Oliver Twist. His only comment was a snide one: the piece of paper the petition was written on showed that everyone who had signed it had an "instinctive abhorrence of the wash tub." He did not need to point out that the dirty peasants who were now demanding a more varied meat diet had probably not seen fresh animal protein more than a handful of times in the year before they boarded the *Nord America*.

Having survived torrid heat, a ferocious tempest, frayed tempers, a food rebellion, and a tide of *filth*, the *Nord America* finally neared the Uruguayan coast. As it did, the emigrants' thoughts turned to what lay in store. The pessimists among them spread alarming rumors. The Tuscan peasant in the green overcoat told everyone to avoid the government shelters where they put a special poison in the soup—it made you so stupid you would sign any employment contract, however exploitive. The optimists countered that American earth sprouted green as soon as you touched it with a plow, and that meat cost only fifty *centesimi* a kilo. "Viva l'America!"

There was much concern about customs duty. A crowd gathered outside the purser's office in search of information and favors. De Amicis listened in pity as the wide-eyed peasants invoked the gifts they were taking to the Americas: "a bottle of local wine, a *caciocavallo* cheese, a *salame*, a kilo of pasta from Genoa or Naples, a liter of oil, a box of dried figs, even an apron-full of beans, but beans from home, from some special corner of the vegetable patch that their relative or friend would surely remember."

The poignancy of these presents is that they meant so much even though they were so humble. That, at least, was what De Amicis thought. But perhaps, on this occasion, he was being a little *too* sentimental and overestimating the peasants' nostalgia for foods they had left behind—those beans from the special corner of the vegetable patch.

Most of these gifts would bring *prestige* to an immigrant's table, not wistfulness about the simple tastes of home. A can of olive oil or a *salame* was a small status symbol rather than a memento. Traveling with one of these treasures meant bolstering a kinship network that stretched across the Atlantic. They were investments as much as gifts; they bore more aspirations than they did nostalgic memories.

In the miniature society that was the *Nord America*, food was far from being a symbol of a common Italian identity. An appetite for *filth* was about the only thing that united all the decks. At the final first-class dinner, while elsewhere grumbling emigrant stomachs were being placated with pork chops and potatoes, De Amicis was informed by a whisper that even the morally rigid captain of the *Nord America* had been up to *filth* with the Swiss-Italian woman in black silk stockings. But unlike sex, food staked out drastic divisions between fellow countrymen, between those who could afford to cultivate their gastronomic connoisseurship and those who had to protest or emigrate in order to fill their bellies. For them, food could trigger resentment; it could trigger ambition. But it did not trigger a shared sense of Italian identity.

As the *Nord America* steamed into the immense, dirty yellow mouth of the river Plate, De Amicis gazed for the last time over the poor families he had come to know during the crossing. Seeing them assembled on deck to be counted like cattle by Uruguayan officials, he could not help comparing this pathetic scene to the noisy jingoism of patriotic rallies in the piazzas back home; his eyes smarted with pity and shame. These mixed emotions about emigration would resonate from the pages of *On the Ocean* and spread across Italy as the tide of emigration increased. The poor Italians who boarded steamers in Palermo, Naples, and Genoa left behind a country that could not decide how it felt about them. Would the emigrants cease to be Italian on the other shore of the Atlantic? Or would the distance finally teach them to love a homeland that had been so neglectful? Should Italy be ashamed at failing so many hungry people? Or alarmed that its lifeblood was draining away? Or moved at the sight of the downtrodden taking their destiny into their own hands? These dilemmas about identity generated politically volatile emotions; they were first distilled for a broad Italian public in the pages of *On the Ocean*.

Italy's mixed emotions about mass emigration gave rise to a minor flood of reports and inquiries from the Italian officials who followed the migrants into America. Today, such documents are the source to which food historians turn first when they want to understand how Italians ate in the New World. Although De Amicis did not seek out what happened to the passengers on the *Nord America* once they had disembarked, the feelings he recorded in *On the Ocean* provide the key to making sense of the government documentation.

At the time of the *Nord America*'s voyage, many emigrants ended up working on the Brazilian plantations, or *fazendas*. Here the unluckiest colonists would find themselves far from roads and other facilities, unable to buy or sell anything through anyone but the same *fazendeiro* who used violence and debt to tie them to the land. Campaigners denounced the situation as one of near slavery. Yet the Italian consul in the state of São Paulo reported that even the worst-off Italians, the ones he found living in mud huts, ate much better than they had done at home. They now consumed beans, rice, potatoes, fresh vegetables, as well as maize and a highly impressive annual average of 1,256 pounds of pork, beef, and chicken per family.

These observations chime with what peasants related in the stilted letters they sent home to their relatives. The sheer quantity of food in the Americas was the dominant note: "Here everyone, from the richest to the poorest, lives on meat, bread and soup every day," one peasant in Argentina wrote to his former boss in the Veneto. One returned migrant from Piedmont told his son that "meat in Argentina is what *polenta* is here." The vision of abundant meat was a strong lure to poor Italians, many of whom had previously been obliged by circumstances to be almost entirely vegetarian. The regular presence of meat on the table constituted a radical break with the eating habits of the past.

A similar study conducted in the United States in the early twentieth century found that, unlike their peers from Germany and Hungary, Norway and Finland, immigrants from different regions of Italy were reluctant to take on the American lifestyle. They kept themselves to themselves—so much so that some employers had to provide separate accommodation and food outlets for them. Indeed employers were often glad to do so, since Italians of all regions ate far more cheaply than other workers. In 1907 the U.S. Department of Labor found that it cost an employer $18 per month to provide food and shelter for each non-Italian. The equivalent for an Italian was only $6.90. No wonder that the peninsula's manpower was in such demand on America's building sites and railroads. But even on this meager budget, an Italian could regularly afford such items as *salame*, cheese, sardines, lard, salt beef, tea, coffee, and beer. For many peasants in the old country these would have been rare or unknown luxuries. Even the most exploited Italian laborers had a much richer diet than before. Many would have had their first taste of the great Bolognese *mortadella* sausage in a railroad workers' camp in the United States.

Workers like these maintained a sense of their distinctiveness by eating together. For some, thrift was the strongest force influencing this choice: they did not want to fit in with Americans because their intention was to save as much as possible to take back home with them. It was an unsentimental outlook: Italian workers preferred to buy *maccheroni* made in the United States because it was cheaper than the stuff brought all the way from Naples or Genoa.

The Italians who ate *maccheroni* and *mortadella* together in labor camps, boardinghouses, and tenements in the early years of emigration to American cities had few precursors in the history of Italian eating. They were inventing new food habits. The same could be said of the men and women who set up myriad pasta workshops in the "Little Italies" of the United States, or sold fruit, vegetables, olive oil, *salame*, and cheese from handcarts. Small food businesses were many Italian immigrants' first step toward prosperity—the Genoese, who were among the first waves of emigrants, had a head start on the rest.

But it is striking that, even though these immigrants reinvented the way they ate, they did so along recognizably *Italian* lines. Their diet in the New World was a collage of the kinds of food that marked out the social differences on board the *Nord America*. Wherever they could settle in sufficient concentrations with sufficiently good communications—in the cities, in essence—Italians of different regions chose to eat things like *salame*, cheese, olive oil, pork chops, homegrown vegetables, and, of course, *maccheroni* with a rich sauce. This was not peasant food, but the food of peasant ambitions. Eating in this way told the world they had joined the upper deck—and sent the same message to the folks back home even more clearly than gold teeth and good shoes. This food tasted, among other things, of a sweet settling of old scores: with full stomachs, they could think back and laugh at the landowners who had kept them hungry.

Few, if any, immigrants retained an attachment to *polenta* or black bread in brine. As soon as economic circumstances permitted, Italians in the cities of the New World rejected the dreary staples of the Italian countryside. In their stead, they created a kind of fusion cuisine whose components came from different regions of Italy: squeezed into close proximity in the tenements of United States cities, for example, Sicilians and Neapolitans, Tuscans, and Piedmontese quickly began to exchange kitchen know-how in a way that only the bourgeois readers of Pellegrino Artusi had been able to do back home. They intermarried, joined the same benevolent societies, and attended the same churches and street festivals. Their fusion cuisine began to accompany all these significant community occasions. Between the wars, increasing prosperity saw the emergence of Italian-American housewives—the housewife was a rare figure indeed among the peasantry of southern Italy in particular, since women were integral to the workforce. Female artistry in the kitchen became a way for families to proclaim their status. The immigrants were inventing a new Italian civilization of the table in America.

If there is one dish that encapsulates the emerging Italian-American food culture, it is spaghetti with meatballs. Pasta and meat: two symbols of prosperity in the old country were combined to make an edible celebration of life in America. Spaghetti with meatballs carries no trace of any specific regional provenance; it is not Lombard, or Calabrian, but joyously, anonymously, uncomplicatedly *Italian* in a way that was only possible in the United States.

Spaghetti with meatballs also constituted a bridge between the Italian-American enclaves and the mainstream diet of the United States. The dynamic immigrant business elite promoted the dish actively. On October 15, 1929, the *Macaroni Journal*, the Minneapolis-based organ of the National Macaroni Manufacturers Association, published a fine recipe intended for non-Italian use:

ITALIAN SPAGHETTI AND MEATBALLS

One pound of ground meat
½ pound spaghetti
1 bay leaf
1 clove of garlic
1 cupful of bread crumbs
1 cupful of tomato paste or concentrated fresh tomatoes
1 small onion
2 cloves
2 grains allspice
Salt and pepper

As commercial tomato pastes vary, if a very thick paste is used dilute it with a cupful of strained canned tomatoes or ¾ cupful water. Heat slowly, add salt to taste, spice, bay leaf, and garlic, chopped very fine. Barely simmer for an hour, keeping the vessel tightly covered to retain all the flavor. Chop the onion very fine and mix well with the meat and bread crumbs, add salt and pepper to season well, and shape in small balls about an inch in diameter. Add these to the sauce, replace the lid and cook slowly for 1½ hours. Cook the spaghetti, without breaking, until tender, drain, rinse, and arrange a layer in a hot baking dish. Remove the meat from the sauce and arrange on a platter to serve. Cover the layer of spaghetti with the sauce, sprinkle lightly with grated cheese, add another layer of spaghetti, sauce, and cheese, and continue until all materials have been used. Serve at once.

The same issue of the *Macaroni Journal* published a tongue-in-cheek short story that explained the historical origins of America's favorite Italian dish. This rather crude piece of advertising turned out to be unimaginably successful and gave rise to the most widespread of the many myths about Italian food. The anonymous author of "A Saga of Cathay" relates that pasta was discovered in China by a Venetian called Spaghetti, a sailor on Marco Polo's ship. While on land looking for water for the rest of the crew, seaman Spaghetti happened across a native village.

His attention was drawn to a native man and woman working over a crude mixing bowl. The woman appeared to be mixing a dough of some kind, particles of which had overflowed the mixing bowl and extended to the ground. The warm, dry air, characteristic of the country, had in a short time hardened these slender strings of dough, and had made them extremely brittle.

Seaman Spaghetti was sharp enough to realize that these strings would make a fine meal if boiled in salted water. Not only that, he uncannily presaged the National Macaroni Manufacturers Association's own marketing puff for the new food:

> He discovered its energy producing qualities, its ability to remain fresh and wholesome for long periods of time, and noted the acclaim with which it was received by his shipmates and other Europeans to whom he introduced it.

The *Macaroni Journal* notes that the copyright for "A Saga of Cathay" belongs to the Keystone Macaroni Manufacturing Company in Lebanon, Pennsylvania—a firm founded in 1914 by an immigrant from Reggio Calabria, one Girolamo Guerrisi.

Hollywood picked up on the fable nine years later, in 1938, when Gary Cooper played the title role in the howlingly bad movie *The Adventures of Marco Polo*. Cooper makes the Venetian adventurer into a craggy ladies' man. When he arrives in China, he is welcomed into the home of a kindly old gent who offers him a dinner of what he calls *spa ghet*. Polo is so taken by *spa ghet* that he takes some of the dehydrated strands to show his friends in Venice when he gets home. Thus Marco Polo may not have introduced spaghetti to Italy as Girolamo Guerrisi and Gary Cooper would have us believe, but he certainly helped introduce it to the United States.

The process of inventing Italian-American cuisine, and of making it acceptable to other Americans, would take until after the Second World War. The end result of that process is foreshadowed in *Italian Cooking for the American Kitchen*—a wonderful, creolized 1953 recipe collection by a former U.S. Army hospital cook, Garibaldi M. Lapolla. As if to stress how new this kind of cooking was to the United States, Lapolla provides translations for his approximately spelled Italian dishes: Fish Sauce Venetian, Tortelli Bologna Style, Consommé Romana (*Straciatella*), Basic Tomato Sauce (*Salsa alla napolitana*), Green Sauce Lucania (*Salsa verde alla lucania*), Lamb Tongues Agrigento. The recipe for Veal Cutlets Parmesan recommends using "1 pound of mozzarella, Swiss cheese, Wisconsin muenster, or Grueyere." *Pesto genovese* is not included, although there is a "Ground Basil Sauce Piemontese" (*Salsa di basilico pestato*). Piedmont is the region just north of Liguria, the home of *pesto*—for Garibaldi M. Lapolla that was evidently close enough.

But the most significant recipe in *Italian Cooking for the American Kitchen* is *polenta:* Lapolla serves thick slices of it smothered in butter and grated cheese, or with steaming ladlefuls of fish sauce or meat *ragù*. Seventy years after the *Nord America* set sail, the memory of peasant hardship was now so distant that even *polenta* could be given the spaghetti-with-meatballs treatment.

Interlude in Ravenna: Theodoric's Boast

On the eve of the First World War, archaeologists digging in a vegetable garden in Ravenna made an intriguing, evocative discovery.

On the opposite side of Italy to Genoa, close to the Adriatic coast, Ravenna was famous in ancient Roman times for its turbot and for the asparagus that grew so well in its sandy loam. Little about the pretty, sleepy town remained the same in 1914. The silted deposits of the Po delta had long since put the Adriatic Sea out of sight; it now took a huge effort of the imagination to recall that this was once one of the most dynamic military ports of the Roman Empire. Ravenna also guarded the major roads and Apennine passes that linked ancient Rome and its northern Italian dominions. In the fifth century, Ravenna became both the empire's final redoubt and its graveyard, the capital city of both the last Roman emperor and of Italy's first Gothic king. And in the year 493, Ravenna became associated forever with the mightiest Goth of them all: Theodoric the Great.

In that year Theodoric captured Ravenna and brought to a climax his conquest of Italy. He held the throne until his death thirty-three years later—a reign that would later be remembered as a time of peace, prosperity, and justice. Theodoric, one chronicler recorded, "attained the highest possible degree of wisdom and manliness." It was the last time that the whole of Italy would be under a single government for more than 1300 years.

Theodoric's soft-eyed features are known to us today from a splendid mosaic on the west wall of the Ravenna church called S. Apollinare Nuovo. Another famous mosaic there shows Theodoric's Royal Palace itself, all that now remains of the home and center of government that Theodoric planned. The mosaic depicts a large central porch flanked on each side by a long colonnaded gallery. With what seems like childish pride, the word PALATIUM (palace) is spelled out in large letters across the top. The arresting beauty of this mosaic is enough to tell us that the hub of Theodoric's realm must once have been an awe-inspiring sight. One of his ministers was certainly impressed: "Lo! a glittering house! the type that rich India admires, gem- adorned Persia visits often and noble Spain stands agape at."

After Theodoric's death, his Royal Palace vanished, torn apart by Italy's constant wars. By the early twentieth century the site had become an under-cultivated vegetable garden, but when excavated, it revealed the structure's drains, foundations, and floors. The most exciting discovery was the Gothic king's dining room. Here, it is thought, guests ate beneath a large portrait of Theodoric on horseback holding a spear in one hand and a shield in the other. The mosaic floor represented the four seasons in nine square panels. In the center a rectangular sign held by winged cherubs read, "Autumn, spring, winter and summer: Take what the sequence of seasons brings in the whole earth's renewal." The gastronomic world, and the gastronomic calendar, were to be laid out before Theodoric's clients. One faithful minister explained the theory behind the boast: "A private person may eat only the produce of his own district, but it is the glory of a king to collect at his table the delicacies of all lands." Power conquers the culinary constraints of space and time; it brings the foods of all seasons and of all regions to one table.

At the dawn of the twentieth century, the earth's most technologically advanced peoples were coming close, for the first time in history, to fulfilling Theodoric's boast—not just for the powerful few, but for the masses. In much of Western Europe, hunger had already become history as the food revolution of the 1700s and 1800s reached its conclusion. Modern agriculture and fishing had created the possibility of permanent surplus. Steamships and railways were turning the world into a single marketplace. New preservation techniques such as canning and refrigeration surpassed the ancient methods of smoking, salting, and drying, to make local seasonal foods available everywhere, year-round. In their preserved forms, canned and concentrated tomatoes extended their popularity into every region of Italy during Artusi's lifetime.

When the food did not move, the people could. Many of the Italian emigrants who went to the Americas found their dream of plenty. But the years of mass emigration before the First World War were also years of profound change in Italy. The departure of such a large proportion of the rural workforce drove up wages in the countryside. The many migrants who returned brought new wealth even to the isolated rural hill towns of the south. Government investigations recorded how indignant many men of property were that the peasants they called *americani* were getting above themselves. The mayor of Belvedere, a small seaside town in Calabria, lamented, "Consumption is up. The peasants are less sober; they eat meat, which was unknown to them before, and they dress decently. Emigration has brought moral disorder to their customs." That "moral disorder" was beginning for the first time in centuries, to change the way ordinary Italians ate.

These dietary developments were associated with progress in other aspects of Italian life. The money that emigrants to the United States hoarded so carefully through their hard work and frugal eating habits also provided a substantial supply of capital for Italian business: the northwestern "industrial triangle" of Milan, Turin, and Genoa made rapid leaps into the age of heavy industry—the age of hydroelectric power and motorcars, of sulfuric acid and fertilizer, of steamships and beet sugar. (The last two were Genoese specialties.) The cities expanded, and urban habits, such as taking coffee at a bar, were adopted by new sectors of the population. Through canning and refrigeration, the bounteous meats of Argentina and Uruguay became known even in Italy. The country also took its first difficult steps into the era of mass democracy.

But the promise of a society without hunger was not to be fulfilled—not for nearly another half century. In fact the history of the Italian diet between the 1700s and the 1950s is the history of how hunger's demise was repeatedly postponed. For many Italians, the food revolution kept failing to happen. After unification, Italy's economic and political difficulties kept its people hungry. And then, after the progress made during the years of mass emigration and industrialization in the early 1900s, the most terrible military conflict the world had yet seen plunged them into renewed hardship.

Prisoners: *Offiziergefangenenlager, Celle, Hanover*

Since 1861, some politicians and intellectuals on the right had been arguing that only a hard and bloody war could turn the Italians into a nation. These bellicose voices grew louder during the bitter political tussles of the early twentieth century. Then, in the spring of 1915, the bloodbath arrived when this divided, rapidly changing country was pitched unexpectedly, and against the will of the majority of its population, into the Great War. But such were the horrors of mass, industrialized slaughter that the conflict's effects were the opposite of what the warmongers had hoped: the Great War came close to tearing Italy apart, and put an end to its nascent democracy. But amid the carnage and the violent political divisions, the war of 1915–18 also produced a sublime moment of gastronomic creativity in the improbable circumstances of a German prison camp.

The war proved traumatic for the peasant masses who were conscripted in the millions to fight among the trenches and escarpments of the Alpine foothills. The national war aim, to win the "unredeemed" Italian lands still under Austrian occupation, was mystifyingly remote. Officers were haughty, noncommissioned officers were few, and discipline was severe even by the standards of the day: men were sent over the top on well-nigh suicidal charges with machine guns aimed at their backs; the summary execution of "cowards" was commonplace; and it was an accepted practice for units deemed to have performed dishonorably to be decimated—literally—one man in every ten was chosen by lot to be shot in front of the rest. Soldiers spent months at the front without relief or leave because the Supreme Command feared that too much contact between the army and "defeatists" at home would undermine the war effort. Meager, inconsistent food supplies to the troops were a major cause of poor morale, and soldiers who had experienced life in the United States were often the most articulate in their discontent. As one man wrote desperately to his family in Ohio in May 1917, "I can tell you it's terrible here and we're dying of hunger and we haven't eaten for five days and it's like living in a slaughterhouse."

In October 1917, after two and a half years of inconclusive carnage, the underlying weakness of the Italian forces was exposed when the Austrians and Germans broke through near Caporetto. Poor organization and leadership quickly turned the defeat into a catastrophe: exhausted, bewildered troops abandoned their weapons and trudged down from their hilltop positions. The enemy threw back the Italian line more than ninety miles, driving a host of military stragglers and civilian refugees before them. Only the flooded river Piave prevented the advance from penetrating even farther, and allowed the shattered Italian army to regroup and create a new defensive line.

The news of the Battle of Caporetto was greeted with panic, dismay, and shame among Italian patriots; there was a wave of suicides in its aftermath. Some 11,000 Italian troops were killed—a relatively small total compared to the wholesale butchery of the Somme or Passchendaele. But many Italians were mortified less by the total of dead and injured than by the numbers who seemed to have given up: 300,000 Italian soldiers were taken prisoner—twice as many as had been captured during the entire conflict until then. The sorry plight of these men is in every way symptomatic of the callous way the war was fought. In the hunt for scapegoats that followed the rout, POWs took much of the blame for the national disgrace. Stamped as deserters by the military authorities, they were abandoned to starve.

Italy's allies recognized early in the war that food parcels dispatched to individuals by their families would not adequately feed the unprecedented numbers of POWs: it was simply too logistically inefficient. Soon, in Great Britain and France, the state took on responsibility for preventing its citizens in foreign captivity from dying of hunger. Italy had no such policy. Thus, for most of the war, a highly unreliable supply of parcels from home coordinated by the Red Cross was all that supplemented the desperately meager rations in the Lagers scattered across the Austro-Hungarian Empire. Only in the final weeks before the armistice, when a few token wagonloads of government-funded hard-tack were sent as an experiment, did the Italian state make any material contribution to internees' welfare. It is difficult not to share the conclusion that the Italian government was guilty of a campaign of collective extermination by neglect—a campaign aimed at its own men. Italian soldiers in captivity suffered an even higher mortality rate than at the front. One-sixth of them died—the vast majority from hunger-related diseases such as tuberculosis and famine-dropsy, which is a ghastly swelling of the limbs and face caused by protein deficiency and subsequent organ failure. Countless testimonies tell how many Italian POWs were reduced to the state of walking skeletons with only tatters to protect them from the cold. In conditions where some would risk being shot to inch closer to the perimeter fence for a mouthful of grass, prisoners often concealed the bodies of dead fellows so that there would be a spare ration of watery soup to share around.

Officers received special treatment and died much less frequently than did enlisted men. But even they experienced the agonies of famine during the terrible winter of 1917–18. After Caporetto, the flood of new prisoners overwhelmed the German and Austro-Hungarian infrastructure. The Italian military authorities placed a total ban on sending parcels to "deserters." Defeated and imprisoned by the enemy, forsaken by their homeland, isolated from their loved ones, the officers would have struggled to maintain any self-esteem even without the sheer physical hardship of captivity. Their diaries and memoirs have a dull ring of enervated hysteria: "Desperation, hunger, guts tortured by hunger: continual wasting away." Every unnecessary physical effort was relinquished; between meals, all that many could do was huddle in their bunks and wait. In this enforced inactivity, food became a gnawing obsession. "The continuous hunger meant we only thought about eating, eating, eating; we talked about it, thought about it, remembered it." "Little by little, hunger became a kind of delirium: we talked of nothing but eating, and waited only for the moment when the miserable bowl of slops was distributed."

In these dehumanizing circumstances, in January and February 1918—the very bleakest months of Italy's war and the POWs' ordeal—one junior officer decided to compile a recipe book. Second Lieutenant

Giuseppe Chioni was captured after Caporetto and held in an officers-only Lager in Celle, a town of picturesque half-timbered houses near Hanover in Germany. He called his collection *Culinary Art*, and it begins with an apologetic preface, one of the most moving documents in the thousand-year history of Italian food. Only those who have suffered with us, he writes, can really understand.

> Long periods of fasting force us to stay curled up so that the cramps of hunger feel less strong, and to remain motionless for whole days so as to waste less energy. Bear this in mind, and it will seem natural that, in our need for the home hearth, each of us has remembered the exquisite meals and appetizing sauces prepared by the delicate and caring hands of a far-distant mother or wife.

The strong impression is that Lieutenant Chioni feels ashamed of the "very strange psychological phenomenon" he has undergone—as if he and his fellow prisoners have been unmanned by "the metamorphosis that has turned us from warriors into cooks." *Culinary Art*, which has never been published, is handwritten on the cheap, loose-textured paper of a small flip pad; but as a response to an overwhelmingly bleak predicament it reads as if it is carved in stone.

Starvation took men's respect for themselves and for one another. One infantry colonel, also confined in Celle Lager, observed:

> There are continual disputes over trifles: there are cries against injustice when an extra piece of potato falls into someone else's bowl. A tiny bone is a huge stroke of luck for anyone who finds it at the bottom of their soup. The man favored by fortune sucks it first. Then, with a timid, "may I?," his neighbour picks it up and sucks at it in grateful bliss.

Culinary Art seeks to build a mental refuge from these daily degradations, to re-create identity step-by-step as if it were a familiar delicacy, to bring comfort through the simple solidarity of sharing all there was to share. As Chioni writes, "This collection of recipes has arisen from the memories, regrets and desires we have exchanged with one another."

His and his fellows' suffering speaks all the more loudly for the quiet care with which *Culinary Art* is constructed. Its hundreds of recipes are lovingly transcribed in eleven sections: *Antipasti*, Sauces, Soups and Pastas, Pizzas, Fish, Meat and Game, Omelettes and Eggs, Polenta, Bread, Vegetables and Beans, Sweets and Jams. Each section begins with a touchingly amateurish drawing of the foods in question: a couple of lemons, a can of sardines, and a little jug of oil for the *Antipasti*, for example; a joint on a spit and a casserole dish for Meat and Game. The recipes in *Culinary Art* have the same sketchy but painfully evocative quality. They rarely give details of how much of any given ingredient is required—nostalgia needs no such precision. Yet it is striking that only a few of the recipes are abnormally enriched. One case is "Extravagant soup," a starving man's hallucinatory concoction of toasted bread soaked in lard with bacon and ham. It is much more often the case that the recipes are recalled with measured care, with the several ingredients meticulously recorded, as if each separate flavor held out its own promise of home.

Chioni's home was in Genoa; he was born on the outskirts of the city in 1895. So *Culinary Art* gravitates around the flavors of the Ligurian capital. A prime example is his recipe for *pesto*, which opens the Sauces section of the book; it gives a clue to the historical development of the port city's fêted condiment:

> 1). *Pesto alla Genovese.* Basil, garlic, parsley, a little scattered onion, spices, Sardinian *pecorino* cheese. Grind everything in the mortar and reduce it to a pulp. To use, add raw oil.

Pesto prepared as Lieutenant Chioni dreamed of it would provoke consternation in Genoa today. The parsley, onion, and spices would be deemed minor heresies. But it is highly unlikely that Chioni's famished memory was deceiving him. For *pesto* is an example of how recently some of even the most famous typical dishes have taken a definitive form.

Genovese *pesto* today is a pulp of basil leaves, cheese, garlic, pine nuts, and olive oil. But according to the earliest dictionary definition, which was first published in 1844, *pesto* was a condiment made from a pounded mixture of garlic, oil, cheese, and *either* basil, *or* parsley, *or* marjoram—a far more liberal range of herbs than would be admitted today. Pine nuts were not mentioned. Neither pasta: in 1844, it seems, *pesto* was a flavoring most often used in soup. Even in a region like Liguria where *polenta* was not common, and in a pasta-exporting city like Genoa, ordinary people would have eaten *minestrone* far more frequently. An 1876 edition of the same dictionary showed no significant changes.

By 1910 a Genoese dialect dictionary described a *pesto* that contained basil, and basil alone. Crucially it was also at this point that *pesto* was identified as a sauce for pasta: the 1910 *Dizionario moderno genovese-italiano* cites *taggioen co-o pesto*, (*tagliarini* [thin strips] with *pesto*) as a commonly used phrase. There were still no pine nuts—as there were not in Lieutenant Chioni's *Culinary Art*, written eight years later. The POW's recipe is also evidence that the exclusive preference for basil was still far from becoming an orthodoxy.

After the Second World War, lexicographers started to get finicky and set out strict *pesto* rules: one 1955 dictionary stresses that the ingredients must be pounded in a marble mortar with a wooden pestle—as do today's most authoritative recipes. Yet there were still no pine nuts.

Giuseppe Chioni knew all about *pesto* in 1918, just as the Genoese crew of the *Nord America* did back in 1884. But they were far less fussy about the way it was made than many are today. There are plenty of other Genoese classics in *Culinary Art*. One example is *tocco*, which is a rich *ragù*, or "Stockfish [air-dried cod] with broad beans"—the chief components are combined with potato, garlic, oil, and salt to make a simple, succulent warm salad.

Yet the truly impressive thing about *Culinary Art* is not how local it is, but how national. A brief comparison with Artusi's *Science in the Kitchen* shows the scale of Lieutenant Chioni's achievement. Liguria and Piedmont, in northwestern Italy, were both underrepresented in *Science in the Kitchen*. *Culinary Art* rectifies the imbalance, including recipes such as Piedmont's wonderful garlic and anchovy dipping sauce for vegetables, *bagna cauda*. Artusi's own stamping ground, the central belt of Tuscany and Emilia-Romagna, is very well represented. But Lieutenant Chioni does not copy anything from Artusi, giving distinctive touches to all of the dishes common to both recipe collections. More impressively still,

Chioni brought together recipes from places that had been nothing more than points on the map for the charming old bachelor from Forlimpopoli, such as the Abruzzi, the region that lies east across the country's Apennine backbone from Rome; and Puglia, the heel of the "boot," which gives Chioni the relatively unknown but highly characteristic dish *marro. Marro* is rather like a haggis, made from lamb's gut stuffed with chopped innards enriched with boiled egg, *salame*, parsley, and ham and cooked by roasting in the oven or on a spit. Sicily is more convincingly present in the POW's recipe book than it is in *Science in the Kitchen*: there are *cannoli*, the tubes of crunchy deep-fried pastry filled with sweetened ricotta cheese and flavored with candied fruit and chocolate chips; there is also a more city-specific local Sicilian dish, baked pasta from Catania, the town at the foot of Mount Etna in the east of the island.

Lieutenant Chioni's recipe collection is even more inclusive than *Science in the Kitchen* in another sense: the officers' hunger liquidates any trace of snobbery toward dishes that smack of poverty. *Culinary Art* includes the refined French-influenced fricassees and *fricandòs* of Piedmont, but also as unassuming a northern staple as *polenta* with boiled leeks—for which Chioni provides an entire recipe. *Culinary Art* also tells us how to make stuffed roast hedgehog: pieces of *pecorino* cheese rind are the secret ingredient in the stuffing. Tomato pizza is another instance: Chioni not only rescues it from the ignominy to which the squalor and disease of Naples had relegated it in the 1880s, but places it where it should be—at No. 1 in the section devoted to pizzas.

When Italy went to war in 1915, the idea that a national cuisine could be depicted through a mosaic of local specialties in this way was still a novelty. Pellegrino Artusi had paved the way—the definitive edition of his *Science in the Kitchen* was published shortly before he died in 1911. Italy's first avowedly regional cookbook was only published in 1909 and its title alone betrays how innovative, how new, was the idea behind it: *The New Cuisine of Regional Specialties.* The book, which contains about twelve dishes each from nine cities and regions, is a rather skimpy, tentative affair: it copies some of Artusi's formulae, but other recipes are unconvincing—its *pesto* contains "Dutch cheese." Even a tolerant *pesto* maker like Lieutenant Chioni would probably have balked at including Edam.

Culinary Art is a far superior, more representative compendium of Italy's gastronomic riches than *The New Cuisine of Regional Specialties.* Indeed the remarkable and poignant fact is that the starving POWs in Celle Lager managed to produce a serious rival to Artusi's *Science in the Kitchen* as the best Italian cookbook yet written.

Where else could such a great cookbook possibly have been created? Since the foundation of the Italian state in 1861, recruits to the new nation's army were assigned to units made up of men from a variety of regions, a policy designed to forge peasants into Italians. So for many soldiers, army life involved meeting their countrymen from distant provinces for the first time. During the Great War, in POW camps across the territory of the Central Powers, there was even more interregional mingling. Among the officers, at least, the culinary dialogue between the cities that had taken Italian food to such heights in the Middle Ages and the Renaissance was now re-created in miniature among the wooden huts of an internment camp in faraway Saxony.

Culinary Art was a collaborative venture. Lieutenant Chioni, with his assistant, Second Lieutenant Luigi Marazza (about whom nothing is known), obviously wrote down what they were told by their brother officers from other parts of Italy. Some recipes contain telling little echoes of their discussions, of the play of accents and dialects from up and down the peninsula. One of Chioni's brother officers must have been from Rome, where *spaghetti all'amatriciana* is a favorite: the sauce takes its name from the small town of Amatrice in the mountains to the northeast of the capital, and it comprises tomatoes and chunks of fatty bacon topped with the salty tang of Roman *pecorino* cheese. Chioni gets the recipe right, but transcribes its title wrongly as *alla madrigiana*—which is how it sounds to a northerner when pronounced in a Roman accent. *Culinary Art* is also a faithful document of Italy's great anchovy divide. In the north and center, these versatile little fish are called *acciughe* (achoogeh), whereas in the south they are *alici* (aleechee). The two second lieutenants dutifully copy down northern recipes using *acciughe*, and southern ones with *alici*.

However authentic the regional recipes in *Culinary Art* were, the Italy fondly re-created in food by Lieutenant Chioni did not exist in reality.

Such a national feast could only be conjured up in the memories of famished men far from home.

Remarkably, Lieutenant Chioni was not the only prisoner of war to find consolation in writing about food. In fact he was not even the only one in Celle Lager to do so. Giosuè Fiorentino was from Palma di Montechiaro near Agrigento on the southern coast of Sicily. He was another second lieutenant captured in the aftermath of Caporetto who was taken to Celle and collected recipes in captivity. Although his cookbook is less extensive and less elegantly presented, it has many of the same characteristics as Chioni's: it mixes elite dishes with popular dishes, and reproduces recipes from all over Italy, ranging from Sicilian *arancine* or rice balls, to Sardinian *culingiones* (pasta envelopes filled with fresh cheese and vegetables); from Roman *maccheroni* with *pajata* (veal intestines), to Milanese breaded veal cutlets. Indeed the Sicilian's recipes betray their varied origins even more clearly, as they are all written in the hands of different men—his fellow internees in hut B98.

There is no obvious sign that Chioni and Fiorentino had any contact with each other while compiling their collections, which are very different. Celle Lager was a big place. It may just be that in the same camp at the same time, these two starving young men from opposite ends of Italy arrived independently at the same way of easing the pangs of want and homesickness. If so, it is telling evidence of food's place in Italian national identity. There is no way of knowing how many more of the hundreds of thousands of Italian prisoners scattered across Germany and the Austro-Hungarian Empire reacted in the same way to their ordeal.

After the armistice, Giuseppe Chioni returned to Genoa in 1919. He married his fiancée the same year and went on their honeymoon in Tuscany before returning to his job as a deputy stationmaster. His cookbook remained secret for two generations, but is now a family treasure. Giosuè Fiorentino also survived the war, gained a degree in engineering at the Milan Politecnico, and became socialist mayor of his Sicilian hometown. His niece recently transcribed his recipe book for the rest of the family.

The land to which these men returned had achieved victory in the end, but triumph quickly turned it into a country of food riots and fighting in the streets. The weak political system had suffered fatal blows to its credibility during the Great War. In 1922, Mussolini's Blackshirts imposed themselves on the crisis, and established the world's first fascist state. But although Italian cuisine would continue to develop during the two decades of dictatorship, the problems of the hungry remained unsolved. The food revolution was to be postponed once more.

V

FASCISTS IN THE KITCHEN

14

Rome, 1925–38

Mussolini's Rustic Village

Fascists were not supposed to like food. There was something fundamentally unfascistic about eating in any other than the most rapid and functional way. The early Blackshirts preferred to eat their "rations" on the go—a preference that fit with their aim of bringing the discipline of the trenches back into Italian life after the Great War. Benito Mussolini liked to assert that no one should spend more than ten minutes a day at table. Once the Duce's dictatorship became established, adulatory biographies emphasized his frugal, self- disciplined eating habits: nothing but warm milk for breakfast; a late lunch of steak, or fish, or an omelet, with boiled vegetables; and nothing more substantial than milk and a piece of fruit for dinner. Propaganda photos rarely showed him sitting, let alone eating. In fact he had poor manners and was averse to dining in company. This may well have been because a nasty gastroduodenal ulcer, first diagnosed in 1925, led to his being put on an unusual diet— hence all the milk and fruit. Anyone sharing a meal with him would thus have been privy to one of the regime's most embarrassing secrets: that the Duce, supposedly a muscular dynamo, was often unwell.

In the mold of Mussolini, or at least of the Mussolini fashioned by propaganda, fascists were supposed to be tough and aggressive with a youthful disdain for comfort. There was something dozy about the very idea of dinner. In one of his most important summations of fascism's muddled doctrine, published in 1932, Mussolini declared,

> Fascism declares that the materialistic conception of "happiness" is not possible. . . . In other words it denies the equation well-being=happiness. That is an outlook that would convert men into animals with only one thing on their minds: being fed and fattened.

The regime's propaganda in the 1930s accordingly targeted its enemies' lethargic greed: the United States was a "beefsteak civilization" and the English were the "five meals a day people."

Mussolini styled himself an abstemious athlete, an image that conformed to a cliché about the Italian national character that had been around a long time before he espoused it: Italians were frugal and sober, it was often said, with a natural tendency toward vegetarianism. This was a useful myth, because it made a virtue out of the chronic poverty that priced meat out of the diet of many peasants. But fascism inserted this convenient commonplace into a whole ideology based on the cult of the countryside and the Roman Empire. One of the regime's central tenets was that Italy had to be "ruralized," because life in the industrial cities was undermining the nation's virility—"sterilizing the people"—and thus depriving the country of its future fighting men. Italians were a rural stock who, like the farmer-legionaries of ancient Rome, would march to Mediterranean hegemony on little more than bread and the occasional grape.

The moves to put Italian food on a permanent war footing began quickly after Mussolini dismantled democracy. The Battle for Grain was proclaimed in July 1925—it was the regime's first major propaganda campaign. Duties on imported grain were raised, and home production encouraged, with the aim of making Italy self-sufficient in wheat (and, it should be added, of bolstering the regime's support among the land-owning classes in the Po valley). The people were exhorted to eat only homegrown products such as rice, fish, and cheese. In particular, bread was officially venerated. The Duce even penned a sloganeering poem on the subject. It began, "ITALIANS, LOVE BREAD":

HONOR BREAD
Glory of the fields
Fragrance of the earth
Feast of life

But fascist lionization of the loaf faced a fundamental snag: there was rarely enough to go around. In the end, Mussolini could not free Italy from what he called the "slavery" of foreign bread. The Battle for Grain was a failure: its headline effect was that less wheat was available, and at a higher price. Almost all other foodstuffs became harder to obtain during fascism, too. Hence the revealing final verse of Mussolini's poem:

DON'T WASTE BREAD
The Fatherland's wealth
God's sweetest gift
The holiest reward for human toil

Italians could love bread as much as they wanted—they just couldn't *eat* very much of it. A combination of austerity and propaganda continued to characterize Italy's food through the two decades of fascist rule. As circumstances became harder, Mussolini continued to demand more and more sacrifices from his people in the cause of creating a new Roman empire.

So even when fascism was in its pomp, the mass of Italians ate worse than they had done before. Estimates of the average calories consumed daily by workers in the cities show a decline from 2,954 in 1926, to 2,476 in 1936. And this was when nutritionists were arguing that a man engaged in moderate physical work needed a *minimum* of 3,000 calories per day. Peasants were portrayed by regime propaganda as the healthiest and most virtuous of the race, but they generally had a tougher lot. It was ever thus. The history of mass nutrition throughout the fascist epoch tells the same old story of rural hardship. If that story lasted far longer in Italy than it did in other Western European countries, then twenty years of totalitarianism were partly to blame.

Fascism's myth of frugality was so strong that the regime tried only intermittently to associate itself with the riches of Italian cuisine. One important instance was in 1938, when an exhibition of regional foods was held in a highly unusual village—one that contained no less than seven characteristic local *trattorie* from different parts of Italy. But even in this perfect embodiment of the fascist rural ideal, the urban imprint of Italian food could not be disguised: for one thing, the *trattorie* represented cities like Turin, Florence, and Naples; for another, the "rustic village," as it was termed, had been specially built in what was left of the Circus Maximus, where ancient Rome held its chariot races.

Mussolini inaugurated the exhibition on May 24, and took the time to wander around while apparatchiks of the state leisure organization dressed in traditional peasant costumes danced around the pretty fountain in the village square. The Neapolitan restaurant was decorated with a mural of Vesuvius smoking in the distance over the bay. Its chef sang in a plaintive baritone to the sound of a mandolin, then broke off to prepare *vermicelli* with clams, steak *pizzaiola*, and *mozzarella* "in a carriage"—little cheese sandwiches battered and deep fried. When Mussolini turned up, he was immediately surrounded by the chef's fifteen children. Manifestly pleased by this proof of reproductive hyperactivity, the Duce passed an envelope of cash to their father.

In one corner of the village stood a Ligurian hostelry where make-believe sailors and fishermen ate *minestrone* or *trenette* with *pesto* amid coiled ropes and lifebuoys. "You can really breathe the air of the sea and ships," one journalist in the Duce's entourage exclaimed. "It's just as if you are down in Genoa's little alleys by the docks."

The huge Florentine restaurant could feed 200 diners with a daily total of 330 pounds of steak *alla fiorentina* and 88 pounds of *fagioli all'uccelletto*—ivory-colored cannellini beans in a tomato and garlic sauce. Rome was represented by an old winery where, around a painted log fire, visitors could eat spaghetti *all'amatriciana*, tripe, oxtail, and unweaned lamb.

The Venetian La Fenice tavern was on a first-floor loggia set over an arch—all that was missing was the canal to flow beneath it. Here one of the city's leading chefs cooked up rice with peas (*risi e bisi*), liver *alla veneziana*, and *polenta* with "escaped birds"—which are not birds at all, but rolled slices of pork loin and bacon flavored with sage. The restaurant was supplied daily with fish brought in by airplane from the Lagoon.

Eating on the march. Mussolini (at the head of the table)
and early Fascist Blackshirts munch their "rations."

An intimate moment of gastronomic nostalgia for the Duce. Mussolini
visits a *trattoria* from his own Romagna region—it was specially
constructed in the Circus Maximus in Rome for a 1938 exhibition.

But of all the local eateries in the rustic village, Mussolini was understandably most drawn to the Trattoria La Romagnola, for, like Pellegrino Artusi, he was from the Romagna. On his approach, comely housewives from Forlì and Imola made a deeply symbolic presentation: a large round loaf from his native region. The cook paused from his job of throwing *tortellini* into broth and cooking *piadine* (flatbreads) on a circular earthenware hob. "Where are you from?" he was asked. "Castel Bolognese," came the reply. "Then we're almost fellow villagers!" beamed the Duce.

Mussolini's "rustic village" was one of Italy's first examples of pastoral gastronomic kitsch. It served only to emphasize how, despite all fascism's efforts to ruralize Italy, the cities remained islands of relative prosperity and good eating. But under Mussolini, as throughout the history of Italian food, the cities were also centers of gastronomic innovation, places where the nation was made and remade through food.

15

*T*urin, 1931

The Holy Palate Tavern

Anyone who visits Turin in search of its many gastronomic attractions should take a moment to pause and give thanks at no. 2 via Vanchiglia. The site is tucked away just off the stately arcaded slope of Piazza Vittorio Veneto. It was, until recently, a travel agency, and is now being converted into a pizza parlor, but for a short time during the fascist years, Italy's most famous restaurant, the Taverna del Santopalato ("Holy Palate Tavern"), stood here. Supposed to be the headquarters of a culinary revolution when it was launched in 1931, it served meals that were, according to their designers, the edible equivalent of the discovery of America or the storming of the Bastille. In the end, the revolution at 2 via Vanchiglia turned out to be a tired charade, a sorry sign of the times rather than a moment that changed food history. And for that, lovers of Italian food across the world should be grateful.

For weeks before it opened, the Holy Palate was the subject of a publicity barrage, which even the most chic metropolitan restaurants of today could never hope to emulate. When its name became known, a leader in the local newspaper announced that the restaurant would make Turin into "the cradle of another Italian Risorgimento—a gastronomic one." A Roman paper was only half joking when it wondered whether there ought not to be a nationwide 50 percent discount on rail tickets—that way Italians could go to Turin en masse to sample the tavern's startling cooking. The restaurant's creator, known as Fillìa, intended to "kill off the deeply rooted old habits of the palate." "Artusi's time is up," he proclaimed.

The Holy Palate was set to open on Sunday, March 8—a date, according to the restaurant's own publicity, that would remain "imprinted in the history of culinary art." On that day, the journalists invited had to wait in the cold until nearly midnight to be admitted. When they finally got in, they were dazzled by the interior created by the architect Diulgheroff: from floor to ceiling it was aluminum, with large lamps set into the walls. The food, served without knives and forks, had a great deal to live up to.

Intuitive Antipasto

A basket made from a hollowed-out orange containing several kinds of salame, butter, mushrooms in vinegar, anchovy, and whole green chilies.

The green chilies contained mottoes appropriate to the occasion, like "Live dangerously."

Aerovictuals

Black olives, fennel hearts, and candied bitter orange (on a single plate set down to the diner's right).

Sandpaper, red silk and black velvet (on a rectangular pad to the diner's left).

Wagner (issuing from hidden speakers).

Each customer was instructed to bring the foods directly to his or her mouth with one hand, while repeatedly stroking the rectangular pad with the other, and having perfume applied to the back of the neck by the head waiter. The multisensorial results, according to one reviewer, were "dumbfounding. Try it if you aren't convinced."

Carneplastico

A large cylindrical meatloaf made from roast veal is stuffed with eleven types of cooked vegetable and set vertically on the plate. A thick cap of honey sits on the top, and the base is encircled several times by a long sausage tube. Three spherical chicken nuggets, fried golden, are arranged around it.

This tribute to Italy's different landscapes was Fillìa's signature dish. Before the restaurant opened, a famous surgeon announced that he was so interested in the effects of *carneplastico* that he would perform a free abdominal operation on the first person to eat it.

Equator + North Pole

Raw egg yolks, dressed with salt, pepper, and lemon, are used to create an "equatorial sea." At its center there rises a conical meringue island studded with orange segments and topped with pieces of black truffle cut into airplane shapes.

A recipe that endeavored to bring the heroic age of airplane exploration to Italian tables.

Ultravirile

A shelled lobster tail, covered with green zabaglione, and set on geometrically arranged prawns and slices of veal tongue. The plate is decorated with hard-boiled eggs (halved), cocks' combs, and a cylinder formed from slices of lemon, truffle, and fried testicle.

This dish was reserved for women. Although the even more masculine *Aroused pig*—a peeled *salame* jutting out from a sauce of espresso coffee and eau de cologne—was available to both sexes. (Though not on the menu, it was brought to the guests anyway.)

The opening night at the Santopalato finally concluded at 4 A.M.

Despite the hair-raisingly experimental nature of the menu that evening, in the days that followed it was the conspicuous absence of pasta that attracted the attention of most journalists. For the Holy Palate Tavern was the first and only Futurist restaurant. It was here that the principles announced in the "Manifesto of Futurist Cooking" were put into practice for the first time. The most important, most sensational of those principles was not stroking sandpaper while eating, or mixing incongruous flavors, or making phallic symbols the centerpiece at dinner, but the abolition of pasta. For the Futurists, pasta was "Italy's absurd gastronomic religion." It was too weighty and bulky for the speed and dynamism of modern life. It stifled the enthusiasm of Neapolitans in particular, making them skeptical, ironic, and sentimental. Worst of all, it induced pacifism. Its abolition was first announced in November 1930 by the main speaker at the opening of the Holy Palate: the Futurist movement's founder and leader, Filippo Tommaso Marinetti—often referred to as FT. The Holy Palate Tavern was an aluminum megaphone for FT's ideas.

A forceful, glamorous Egyptian-born poet with a private income, FT had founded Futurism back in 1909. The turning point in his career came when somehow he managed to persuade the leading Parisian newspaper, *Le Figaro*, to publish the Futurist manifesto on its front page on February 20. At the time, the Futurist movement did not exist, but in its manifesto, the first of many, FT called for a revolution that went far beyond art and poetry to embrace every aspect of Italian life. Aiming to blast Italy out of its fixation with the past by demolishing museums and libraries, Futurism celebrated all that seemed new in industrial society: the cities with their seething crowds, stations, and workshops; and above all the speed, noise, and violence of machines. Italy's buildings, its politics, its manners, its most intimate daily habits were to acquire the tempo of a hurtling automobile:

> We want to glorify war (the world's only hygiene), militarism, patriotism, the libertarians' destructive gesture, beautiful ideas one dies for, and scorn for women. . . . We want to exalt aggressive move-

ment and feverish insomnia, running and leaping, the slap and the punch.

This Parisian publicity coup helped make Futurism the most influential Italian art movement since the Renaissance. FT attracted a small legion of acolytes. The Futurists toured Italy's theaters declaiming their writings, presenting their paintings, and showcasing their own take on music and clothing. At these performances, they rejoiced in being pelted with fruit and vegetables by Italians of all classes, and "exalted the slap and the punch" by fighting with members of the audience. FT became an international art celebrity.

Two decades later, the FT who spoke at the opening of the Holy Palate cut a very different figure. A paunchy fifty-four years old, he habitually wore a suit and bow tie, which went well with his toothbrush mustache and baldpate. Of course, even in middle age FT still had his nose for publicity. Hardly a newspaper in the Western world failed to report the end of spaghetti—there could be no surer measure of how widespread pasta now was. But Italy had long ago become accustomed to Futurist shock tactics. The Manifesto of Futurist Cooking felt scarcely more dangerous and exciting than FT's clothing. It is doubtful that the Italian press would have been so indulgent to the idea of abolishing pasta if FT had not been a personal friend of the Duce.

The two had become acquainted early in 1915 when they were both arrested at a Futurist demonstration in Rome in favor of Italy's joining the Great War. After the war, as Italy's fragile democracy began to enter its terminal crisis, FT was a supportive presence when Mussolini founded fascism in Milan's Piazza San Sepolcro in March 1919. A month later, Futurists and fascists together raided and ransacked the headquarters of *Avanti!*, the Socialist Party newspaper. These were tempestuous years in which only a hazy line separated avant-garde art and violent politics. But as the rigors of the struggle for power imposed their disciplines, and as FT proved too creative and too contrary to fit in with the fascist program, he and Mussolini fell on either side of that line.

While Mussolini was setting the legislative and political basis for dictatorship after 1925, FT tried to exert some leverage over the fascist leadership by making noises about the conservatism of the regime's art bureaucrats. It worked to some extent: the Futurists were placated by being included in the Venice Biennale in 1926. But the needs of the regime and the aesthetics of Futurism were drifting apart. FT failed to make Futurism into an official artistic doctrine. State patronage tended to go to a monumental, neoclassical modernist style instead— fascism's myth of ancient Rome and the countryside won out over the Futurist myth of the industrial city and the machine. But for all that, Marinetti settled into being a semidetached member of the Italian art establishment.

Historians of Italian food, like students of Futurism, are almost unanimously unimpressed by Futurist cooking, and it is difficult to disagree with them. Fillìa, the twenty-six-year-old driving force behind the Holy Palate Tavern, was typical of the artists who were attracted to FT's banner in the mid-1920s: he was young, mediocre, and desperate to raise his profile. He called for Futurists in Turin to produce work in tune with the "mechanical spirit" of the motor city. The interior of the

The man who tried to abolish pasta. FT Marinetti is snapped by friends while failing to live up to his own rigorous dietary principles. He wrote an ironic dedication on the back of the photo: "It is pointless trying to mock me! The conspirators from Bari have had their pasta liquidated."

Holy Palate was the perfect example of what he wanted. This "pulsating aluminum structure" looked less like a restaurant than something that might have been seen speeding around the famous rooftop test track at Fiat's Lingotto factory. But all in all, Lingotto was a far more impressive statement of the mechanical spirit than either the restaurant or the food it served.

The story of the Holy Palate shows how domesticated the avant-garde had become under Mussolini. FT and Fillìa had the freedom to propose a new industrial cuisine that was, in some respects, at odds with the regime's rural image of what it termed the "Italian race," but in the *Futurist Cookbook* (1932), they were careful to echo the war cries of fascism's Battle for Grain: "Remember that the abolition of pasta will free Italy from expensive foreign wheat and support the Italian rice industry." Fascism expended a great deal of energy on promoting rice, and even distributed free samples to southerners, who had never had much of a taste for it.

The dishes on offer at the Holy Palate also pandered to the myth of Italian parsimony. They were meant to answer the call for "the abolition of volume and weight in the way we think of and value nourishment," and to prepare Italians for the day when they would not only listen in to the Duce's broadcasts, but actually be nourished by radio: the ultimate realization of fascist propaganda over the airwaves.

16

Milan, 1936

Housewives and Epicures

Living Well in Difficult Times

Mussolini had a dream woman, and celebrated her in propaganda films and medal ceremonies. Broad-hipped and prow-bosomed, from lusty country stock, she was a thresher of wheat, a tender of chickens, and a breeder of little legionaries. The Duce's model *italiana* was a Rural Housewife.

In the early 1930s, three million women joined the "Rural Housewives"—the section of the Fascist Party created to make peasant women more closely resemble Mussolini's ideal. The gastronomic aims of the movement were predictably limited. One typical recipe was published in the organization's monthly newspaper in 1935. It described the perfect meal for a Rural Housewife to serve to her sons just returned from war: a "patriotic omelette" made from home-produced eggs, tomatoes, and greens so that it had the red, white, and green of the national flag. Through such an omelet, women could show that "without leaving home and hearth their hands are working and their hearts beating for the Nation."

In the early 1930s fascism moved to reconstruct the whole of Italian society in its image through totalitarian organizations like the Rural Housewives. But ironically, it was primarily women from the urban bourgeoisie who carried forward the regime's drive for more spartan eating habits. The new Italian middle classes of the fascist years were eager to learn about food, and a new generation of female cookery writers taught them, dominating the expanding market for cookbooks. Typically, these writers were upper middle class, and their readership several rungs below them on the social ladder. In tones that were often condescending, Italy's *grandes dames* were teaching the ladies of the *petite bourgeoisie* about the virtues of frugal housekeeping.

Fernanda Momigliano, for example, was the very opposite of the Rural Housewife. A petite, smartly dressed, forty-something author of romantic fiction, she lived with her ailing mother in the very center of Milan, and rarely stepped beyond the bounds of the city's canals. Despite the occasional suitor, she never married. If she had been a man, she would have had to pay the Duce's bachelor tax as punishment for depriving the nation of her progeny. Her wider family was remarkable for the number of leading intellectuals it included: two historians, a philosopher, and a literary critic. Fernanda Momigliano was also unusual in that she was one of Italy's 45,000 Jews.

Momigliano's first book, *Living Well in Difficult Times: How Women Face Up to Economic Crisis* (1933), is a classic of its type: it shows how Italian housewives created good food in tough circumstances. Italian cuisine has a justified reputation for being delicious without being pretentious, complex, or expensive—a reputation that is one of the secrets of its success in homes and restaurants across the Western world. Those values were first integrated into Italy's civilization of the table not by peasants, but by the middle classes of the peninsula's many cities, by people who did not have money to waste but who valued good food and the social status they had struggled so hard to achieve.

The first pages of *Living Well in Difficult Times* exude a genteel paranoia as they depict a domestic scene menaced by the bugbear of economic crisis. The crisis has the whole world in its grip, Momigliano points out to her female readers. Think of how it affects your husband, she advises. The husband finds that the crisis creeps into every conversation in the bar, at the tram stop, or in the office. Even the thought of it is insidious: it creases worries into his brow and slopes his shoulders with despondency. Now imagine what happens when he turns the key in the front door and finds a clean table, shining place settings, and the aroma of a modest but elegant lunch. His mood lifts; he has found a sanctuary. His wife, smiling with the confidence that only sturdy principles of domestic economy can bring, restores his faith in the family's future. He can breathe confidently once more. While she watches over her little realm, the crisis will be kept at bay.

> Girls! Kindly mothers! Women of Italy! You who have had the strength to overcome moments of tragedy. You who have filled heroic pages in our history. You can easily show the world that the crisis has not set foot in your home!

The book was published in 1933, when Italy was still feeling the effects of the crash of 1929. But Momigliano's lessons, and the sense of domestic propriety she advocates, would become even more relevant in the years to come: during the sanctions imposed by the League of Nations following Italy's invasion of Ethiopia in 1935; during Mussolini's policy of autarky, or economic self-sufficiency, after 1936; and during the succession of disasters that shaped Italy's experience of the Second World War. The latter years of fascism were one long crisis.

The Italian home's main rampart against this relentless threat and the housewife's chief weapon in the perpetual hand-to-hand combat with waste was *minestra*. Whether it came in the form of soup, rice, or pasta, a first course or *minestra* was almost all a woman needed to cook in order to fulfill her domestic duty. *Maccheroni* with *ragù* or ham, potato *gnocchi* with butter and cheese, saffron *risotto*, chickpea soup, a vegetable *minestrone* thickened with rice: the ideal Italian housewife's first courses were endlessly varied and unfailingly reassuring. A *minestra* at every meal allowed a family "to live in tranquility, without sacrifices, and with a certain degree of elegance." The second course was a secondary concern: meatballs, liver, or butter-fried eggs during the week; roast chicken and roast potatoes on Sundays. Women like Fernanda Momigliano placed a filling *primo* at the heart of a new model for Italian domestic existence.

Momigliano also gives her readers a portrait of an archetypal, respectable family; helpfully, she calculates this ideal family's expenditure right down to the last penny. The husband, who works in an insurance company, brings home 1,300 lire per month—a sum that is well above the middle-class average earned by the bureaucrats in the expanding state sector of the fascist economy. This family can afford for the mother to stay at home and for her daughter to take piano lessons; they pay the stipend of a domestic servant, and take a holiday in the countryside every August. Yet even with all of the scrimping that Momigliano counsels, even with *minestre* like bread crumb soup or rice and dried peas, this ideal family still spends more than a third of its total income on food. The vast majority of Italian households were spending much, much more.

Leafing through the model menus in *Living Well in Difficult Times*, it is striking how closely they resemble everyday Italian home cooking today—when Italy is one of the most prosperous countries in the world. *Pasta* with fresh tomato sauce, a salad of raw vegetables, then a piece of cheese. Minestrone followed by breaded veal cutlets. Mushroom *risotto* and carrots dressed with parsley. Of course, much has changed, too: Italians sit down to fewer stews and more quick-cooked steaks and chicken breasts than they once did. *Salame* and canned tuna are now commonplace, whereas Fernanda Momigliano saw them as dangerously wasteful and liable to let the crisis in through the back door. Nevertheless, it is clear that, even when times became less difficult, the mass of Italians would choose to eat as if they were *Living Well in Difficult Times*.

Wandering Gluttons

While bourgeois women like Fernanda Momigliano were at home writing cookbooks and guides to domestic thrift, their male equivalents were out creating a role for themselves as roving gourmands.

Devoted to celebrating the glories of the country's landscape, promoting foreign tourism, and producing maps and visitor guides, the Touring Club Italiano was founded in Milan in 1894, three years after the first edition of Pellegrino Artusi's *Science in the Kitchen*. One of its early achievements was Italy's first system of road signs. In the seventy or eighty years since the young Artusi had crossed central Italy by carriage and on horseback, travel had become considerably easier. For the middle class, at least, journeys of discovery to different cities and regions were now fun—and patriotic, too. Touring Club Italiano members explored the peninsula by bicycle, at first, and then by automobile and even airplane. Under fascism, membership touched half a million. To be middle class in Italy, it has been suggested, was to be a member of the Touring Club.

In the process of getting to know Italy, the middle classes discovered edible treasures of all kinds. In 1931 the Touring Club turned its attention from mountains and ruins to food with its *Gastronomic Guide to Italy*—a 527-page cornucopia that was sent to all members. Some of the tastes it catalogues were familiar, such as the seasoned sweetness released by a slice of Parma's rich red *culatello* ham. Others were strange but marvelous dishes from hitherto obscure regions, especially the rural south, such as a fried wild rabbit served with a bittersweet mix of eggplant chunks, olives, capers, celery, honey, and roasted almonds—the recipe was discovered near Agrigento, on the far coast of Sicily.

The Touring Club Italiano's guide filled in the gaps in Artusi's patchy culinary map, and extended its reach to every corner of the country. More and more of Italy's great food mosaic was becoming available to those who could afford to find it. In fact, for that lucky caste, eating became integral to the experience of travel. Unfamiliar landscapes, exotic dialects, rough and heady wines—all evoked a unique sense of place that was concentrated most intensely in the local specialties. To know Italy was to know its food.

As other publications in the same vein followed, and newspapers picked up the cue, a novel kind of connoisseurship was taking shape. It was given its definitive form in 1935 by the Modenese journalist Paolo Monelli. With his copy of the Touring Club's *Gastronomic Guide* in hand, Monelli undertook to eat his way along the entire length of the peninsula and write a series of reports for a Turin newspaper. Monelli's manner, rather than his itinerary or the dishes he tried, insinuated its way into Italy's civilization of the table. In a monocle and slicked-back hair, bantering with cooks and waiters, Monelli came across as cheerily opinionated and gently cynical. His reports, which were published in book form as *The Wandering Glutton*, gave Italian epicures a persona to adopt. What he wrote can hardly be translated, so full is it of literary allusions, wine-fueled philosophizing, and overblown similes. In the Alpine region of Val d'Aosta, for example, he samples a *carbonata*, "a beef stew in a violaceous sauce that had the color of Vesuvian ashes, and the sadness of lost clouds," but which was "a thing of the utmost sapidity, bathed in onion and cooked wine, redolent with innumerable pastureland flavors." Just down the coast from Genoa a hostess with a face "sculpted from a sea crag" serves him *pesto:* "Pesto speaks Ligurian. Only take a smell, and your ears will pick up the vernacular: it is both harsh and tender at the same time, built from drawled noises, whispered syllables, grim vowels."

In Rome, the city's "tasty, aggressive, polychrome" cuisine is incarnated in "the gargantuan matrons of Trastevere, with their alley-blocking buttocks." In the hills south of the capital, Monelli eats "spaghetti *all'amatriciana* imbued with the aroma of a herd's dusty descent from the mountain," and ends his meal with peaches "like a young priest's cheek." The prose was overindulgent, but it was based on the old but powerful Italian connection between places and tastes. The wandering gluttons of fascist Italy gave the idea of typicality a new swagger and a new poetry.

Goose and Eggplant

In 1936, Fernanda Momigliano, author of *Living Well in Difficult Times*, was moved to write a second book, *Eating Italian*. Much less typical of its time, it is yet far more poignant, showing how one woman sought to remodel the image of her country's food and uncovered a crucial dimension of its history in the process. And she did so just as the darkest forces within fascism were being unleashed against herself, her family, and her friends. *Eating Italian* is the first attempt to integrate Jewish dishes into an Italian national culinary tradition. A plea for tolerance and inclusiveness written in Italy's favorite language, food, it is all the more powerful for being delivered from the very edge of tragedy.

There has never been an Italian-Jewish peasant; nor was there a significant community in the south, after the Jews were expelled from Spain's territories in Sicily, Sardinia, and southern Italy in the late 1400s and early 1500s. During the fascist era, some of Italy's Jewish communities were from provincial centers such as Casale Monferrato or Pitigliano; most were from places like Venice, Ferrara, Livorno, and of course Rome—where the old ghetto by the Tiber housed the largest and poorest group. They were generally secularized and well integrated. Some Italian Jews—proportionally as many as other sectors of the population—became fascists. Many more were patriots: it was, after all, Italy's national Risorgimento that had opened the ghettoes, emancipated Jews, and taken papal dogma out of politics. Prefascist Italy was beset by many problems, but institutional intolerance toward Jews was not one of them.

The political climate harshened in the late 1920s, as Mussolini sought a rapprochement with the most powerful conservative force in the country: the Vatican. The Duce made an unnerving request for "clarification" from the Jewish community. Where did their loyalties lie? Were they a nation or were they a religion? In 1929, Catholicism was made Italy's religion of state for the first time; its values were to be taught in schools.

Fascism's decisive turn toward racial oppression came in 1935, at the apex of the regime's popularity, when Italian forces mounted a brutal conquest of Ethiopia. Poison gas was used against the members of an "inferior race," and new laws prohibited interbreeding between colonists and natives. As the League of Nations condemned the invasion and imposed sanctions, Mussolini moved closer to fatal alliance with Nazi Germany. Italy's Jews were well aware of what was going on under Hitler: they had offered aid and refuge to those persecuted by the Nuremburg laws of 1935. But they generally tried not to believe that the same kind of laws could be promulgated in their own country. After all, they said to themselves, the Duce himself had had a Jewish mistress for years, and he often stressed that he did not believe in the existence of "pure races."

At this uncertain, anxious moment, Fernanda Momigliano wrote her second collection of recipes. More than a cookbook, *Eating Italian* is a calibrated political gesture, its cover marked in patriotic red, white, and green. Momigliano's message of frugality and wifely conformity is proclaimed even more loudly than it was in *Living Well in Difficult Times*. Women may never be great chefs, she writes, but they can be proud of bringing a practical and economizing spirit to every meal they make. They can pass the sternest tests when they are spurred on by love of the

Fatherland and family. Home produce is best, especially rice: we don't eat enough of it.

In the highly sensitized circumstances of early 1936, Momigliano had to make her cooking as conformist as it could possibly be—without endorsing the regime. The absence of any reference to the Duce or his dogma among the recipes is notable. Momigliano could not stomach kowtowing to fascism; her family was all too aware of its repressive nature. Her older brother Eucardio was a successful lawyer and Radical Party politician. Back in 1924, in two separate incidents, black-shirted thugs had smashed his legal offices and savagely beaten him up at a Milan theater. He was banned from practicing his profession, and forced to fall back on writing historical biographies that the Italian press refused to review.

Eating Italian meant using the "good and varied produce of our land," preparing simple classic dishes from the peninsula's cities, such as Novara's marinated and deep-fried frogs, Neapolitan spaghetti with tomato sauce, Bolognese *tagliatelle*, rabbit Trieste-style, or *pesto alla genovese*. By 1936, this was a familiar program—all Artusi's female heirs had followed it. But Fernanda Momigliano created one crucial, courageous difference: *Eating Italian* also meant eating sixteen recipes that were explicitly labeled *all'ebraica*—"Jewish style." They range from pieces of carp cooked in white wine, onion, and dried mushrooms, to a saffron *risotto* that Jewish families prepare on the eve of the Sabbath: "Jewish *risotto* is exquisite, and it can be appreciated by everyone, whatever faith they profess!"

The history of Jewish-Italian cooking is centuries older than *Eating Italian*. In fact Jewish food through the ages in Italy has reflected all the diverse experience of Italy's Jews themselves: their varied origins, their varied readings of religious taboos and norms, their changing relationship with the society around them, and their different economic fortunes. But amid all the variety, two distinct Jewish cuisines emerged between the Renaissance and the 1800s; each can be encapsulated by one particular dish. The Po valley, from Piedmont to Venice and Ferrara, was goose territory. Geese came to occupy exactly the role in Jewish-Italian cuisine that the pig did for Christians: its fat was used for frying, its flesh for making sausages and *salami*, its skin for making crackling. South of the Apennine curve, by contrast, in Tuscany and particularly among the ancient community confined in Rome's grim ghetto, the archetypal Jewish foods were vegetables, particularly artichokes and eggplants. No account of Roman cuisine would be complete without *carciofi alla giudia*: since at least the 1500s these deep-fried whole artichokes have stood in neat rows, crown down, in Roman roasting tins.

Fernanda Momigliano shows those two traditions fusing. She includes Roman artichokes *alla giudia* and six different eggplant recipes. But she is also hugely enthusiastic about goose, explaining how to make ham, for example, by placing boned goose breast with the skin still on it in an airtight container with plenty of salt for around ten days. Once removed from the salt, the breast is hung somewhere cool and dry until it goes dark—it is then ready to be pared into deliciously filmy slices.

As a predominantly urban population, Italy's Jews have had an influence on Italian food civilization that is out of all proportion to their numbers. This is despite the anti-Semitism that led to a series of attempts at food segregation, and to the widespread notion that goose and eggplant were inferior, dirty foods. In 1560 in Counter-Reformation Bologna, the papal legate issued an order preventing Jewish butchers from selling their meat to Christians. The civil authorities annulled it on the grounds that "the people of Bologna proclaim themselves more satisfied by Jewish meats, which are excellent, than by meats from Christian butchers." The more sophisticated hygiene involved in kosher slaughtering practices probably had something to do with this.

Some of Italy's best cooks through the centuries appreciated aspects of Jewish food culture. During the Renaissance, the Este dynasty of Ferrara relied on the financial skills of the city's well-established Jewish banking community to fund its magnificent lifestyle. Jewish culinary traditions also influenced the Este's steward, Cristoforo da Messisbugo, whose penultimate recipe in *Banquets* is for a "Hebrew-style meat dish": a kind of Scotch egg, formed by wrapping ground beef flavored with raisins, herbs, and spices around hard-boiled egg yolks; Messisbugo recommends cooking and serving them in broth with a slice of bread. Bartolomeo Scappi, the pope's secret cook, liked to make paté with the livers of geese raised by Jews.

In the late 1800s, Pellegrino Artusi included some Jewish food in his

Science in the Kitchen. He had many friends in the Tuscan Jewish community, and learned how to cook couscous from two of them. He was also a lover of eggplant, which gives him pause for a typically jocular aside:

> Forty years or so ago, eggplant and fennel were rarely seen in the market in Florence. They were thought of as vile, Jewish food. Which goes to show that on this question, as on other more important ones, the Jews have always had a better nose than Christians for what is good.

A nose gag: undoubtedly gauche. But those otherwise harmless words would later become a sign of terrifying change. When Artusi's *Science in the Kitchen* was republished for the umpteenth time in 1939, the passage quoted above was deleted—clearly it was not appropriate to praise national enemies for their good taste. The previous year Mussolini had implemented Italy's own racial laws: Jews were banned from the professions, from owning property, from attending state schools, and from marrying or employing "Aryans." All pleas for tolerance and inclusiveness, in whatever language they were expressed, were set aside. Fascist Italy was now a racist state. In June 1940, when Mussolini joined the Second World War on Hitler's side, non-Italian Jews were interned. Anti-Semitic vandalism and violence occurred in several Italian cities, especially Trieste. In May 1942 all Italian Jews were compelled to register for forced labor. In September 1943, Italy capitulated to the Allies; the Germans overran the country and quickly implemented a campaign of arrest, deportation, and genocide.

There are many survivors' stories among Italian Jews, stories of shrewd moves, courage, and blind luck; of unexpected help and betrayals averted. Fernanda Momigliano could tell one of those stories. On October 16, 1943, the first large-scale Nazi roundups of Italian Jews took place in major cities. In Rome more than 1,000 people from the ghetto were deported to Auschwitz. Many of Milan's Jews, including Fernanda Momigliano, were already in hiding by that date, but still 200 fell into the clutches of the SS, who raided addresses on lists they had inherited from the Italian authorities. The next phase of the Holocaust saw Italians doing the Nazis' work for them: police and fascist militia, or members of freebooting gangs that operated with full approval of the Germans' puppet Italian government; many were just ordinary citizens corrupted by the rewards offered for Jewish victims. Against this background, with exceptional bravery, Fernanda Momigliano went to Busseto, between Milan and Parma, to warn her sister Bianca and save her from deportation. Bianca's husband was not so fortunate, and was gassed. Their mentally ill mother was hidden in the new Niguarda hospital in Milan. Fernanda saved her, too—by explaining to the nurses that she was not Jewish, just insane. Many uneducated Italians had little idea what a Jew was.

In the end, the author of *Eating Italian* owed her own survival to the help of non-Jewish friends. The Italian police used a ruse to try and catch her. While she was in hiding, she was told that someone had called at her apartment claiming to have a message from a deported relative. Just as a shopkeeper she knew was explaining this episode to her, a man came in and asked to see her. Fernanda pretended to be a customer while her friend explained that she was nowhere to be found. The man was later followed—all the way back to police headquarters.

The Second World War saw Italy invaded from the south by the Allies, and from the north by the Germans; its territory was contested in a savage civil war between the Resistance and recalcitrant fascists; its cities were bombed, its infrastructure destroyed, and its people went hungry. In the areas where the fascist writ still ran, the system of rationing was hopelessly inefficient. In the Allied-controlled south, illegality was so widespread that food aid rarely reached its intended recipients. Even the age-old food polarity between the city and the country was reversed: farmers could command eye-popping prices by funneling their produce into the urban black market. It all seemed like a terrible echo of the privation and destruction wrought by foreign and domestic armies since the fall of the Roman Empire. Italy, along with its civilization of the table, had all but collapsed.

VI

THE LAND OF PLENTY

17

Rome, 1954

Miracle Food

The Food Revolution, at Last

And then everything changed. Italy's "economic miracle," which centered on an unprecedented surge of industrial growth between 1958 and 1963, turned a nation of farmhands into a nation of factory operatives.

Statistics tell the story of the miracle with stark efficiency. In 1951 Italy manufactured 18,500 refrigerators; by 1957, it was making 370,000 of them; and in 1967 a massive 3,200,000 were trundled off the lines. Production of cars, radios, washing machines, typewriters, and other domestic consumer goods accelerated at a comparable rate. Italy became an exporting giant: brands like Vespa, Fiat, Candy, Zanussi, and Olivetti were now familiar in households across the new European Common Market.

For Italians, modernity meant mobility. Between 1955 and 1971, more than nine million people moved between regions. From 1958 to 1963, the hottest years of the great transformation, 900,000 people left the south for other, richer, parts of Italy. By the end of the 1960s, the northern motor capital of Turin housed more southerners than any southern city except Naples and Palermo. Up and down the country, there was a mass exodus from the land, and the cities burgeoned. Rome's population jumped by half a million between 1961 and 1967. In the northeast, a region of poverty and *polenta*, the percentage of workers employed in the countryside dropped from just under a half to just over a quarter in not much more than a decade.

During the miracle, Italy's long-delayed food revolution finally arrived. The Land of Plenty had been a feast-day mirage for most Italians since time immemorial. Now it was a quotidian reality. As the emigrants to the New World had done before them, Italians in the miracle abandoned staples that smacked of past hardship—*polenta*, above all. In the early 1950s, on an average measured over the whole national territory, each Italian man, woman, and child was eating more than two ounces of yellow maize meal every day, even though at the time *polenta* was massively concentrated in the north and parts of the center. Yet in the late 1960s, that figure had dropped by two-thirds. By the early 1980s, the national average consumption of *polenta* was too small to register statistically.

Again, just as the emigrants to the Americas had done in the early twentieth century, Italians in the 1960s turned to meat with a relish born of age-old hunger. In the year that the unified state was founded, 1861, the average consumption of meat was estimated to be a mere twenty-six pounds per person per year. This amounts to 1.2 ounces per day—equivalent to half the weight of an egg. A century later, in 1960, that daily total was still only just over 2.1 ounces. In the first four months of 1963 alone, imports of quality meat quadrupled. By 1975, the daily consumption per person was six ounces. By 1989, Italians were more fond of meat than the British, Mussolini's "five-meals a day people"; and, proportionally, they even ate three-quarters of the massive quantities consumed in the "beefsteak civilization" of the United States. Regional dietary imbalances began to vanish, too. In 1964 southerners only consumed meat at half the rate northerners did. A decade later, they were up to 80 percent of the northern level—*and* they consumed three times as much fish.

The miracle set in motion a panoply of changes that are still unfolding today. The average Italian was an inch and a half taller in 1972 than she or he had been in 1951: it was a clear physiological sign that, in the brief space of a few years, the peasant dream of meat every day had come true. Plenty, variety, and choice—privileges without which a food culture cannot flower—were available to all.

Mobility and leisure combined to multiply the forms of culinary transformation. As bicycles and carts were replaced with scooters and cars, millions gained the freedom to zip into the city center and meet friends at a *pizzeria*, or to take the family out into the country for Sunday lunch. The age of mass motorization profoundly changed the Italian culture of the table, introducing wholly new food experiences such as driving to the seaside in August to eat spaghetti with clams, or stopping for a bite at an Autogrill—a highway service station.

During the miracle the number of people who actually grew what went into their meals declined rapidly. Instead, Italians became infatuated with products from the food industries. Their infatuation has increased over the years. Less and less time is devoted to preparing food. The meaning of eating has undergone a metamorphosis: no longer merely a biological necessity or even a collective ritual, eating is a form of entertainment like going to the cinema or watching a football match. Strange new habits, such as snacking and dieting, were adopted and special foods created for novel subcategories of consumer, from babies to bodybuilders. Day-to-day food responds to urgent bulletins from the frontiers of science, and to the convulsive dictates of fashion. The marriage between television and advertising radically changes the meaning of food for millions. Humble goods like ham, pasta, and oil are enveloped in the magical aura of capitalist merchandise. Consumers no longer eat food: they eat icons of desire, promises of love and success.

It would be possible to compose a history of Italian eating since the economic miracle entirely from such icons. There is the rise and fall of chicken, for example. In the 1950s and 1960s, a roast chicken was a family's way of saying it had arrived. By the 1990s, a skinned, grilled breast was the glum incarnation of self-restraint for millions of dieters. The same arc of time could be traced by changing technological must-haves: first the refrigerator and then the electric whisk, to be followed in sequence by the rotisserie oven, the pressure cooker, and the microwave. Consumer foods have come to characterize decades in the same way that pop records do. Thus Italy's 1950s were defined by cans of pink Simmenthal meat in gelatin, stock cubes, and Cirio canned soups. The 1960s meant Ritz crackers and packet cheeses—whether ready-sliced, or prechewed and squirted into silver paper triangles for spreading. In the

Pasta advertising, 1915.

1970s, all pasta sauces were made with ultrahigh temperature cream, and children feasted on Day-Glo Popsicles. The 1980s saw the arrival of whole wheat pasta, and the great yogurt explosion. The dishes that defined the '90s were frozen ready meals for busy single people, such as pasta or *risotto* from the untranslatable *4 salti in padella* brand (literally, it means "four hops in the frying pan"); the packet suggests you add "a personal touch" such as a sprig of parsley or a drizzle of olive oil.

Italy is not the timeless land of *mammas*, *nonnas*, and priests that is portrayed in so many cookbooks and ads. It has plenty of supermarkets and fish farms. Its citizens are every bit as enthusiastic as anyone else about consumer gewgaws and every bit as susceptible to advertising. In a couple of postwar generations, Italy has gone from being a rural society, to an industrial society, to a postmodern information society. The Italian diet has reflected that head-spinning transformation.

Milan has certainly been in the vanguard of this half century of dietary revolution. As "the citiest city in Italy," the capital of industry, finance, fashion, commercial television, advertising, and shopping, it was the earliest to manifest many symptoms of consumerism. The first supermarket opened there in 1957, and the first Italian fast-food restaurant, a Burghy, arrived in Milan in 1982. Yet the changes of the last fifty years are so numerous that no single Italian city can encapsulate them all. At the same time, almost *any* city illustrates the modernization of the Italian diet as well as any other—all that varied was the pace of change. For these reasons, the remaining chapters of this book will range rather wider than has been the case so far.

But a history of Italian food since the economic miracle that comprised only chiller cabinets and Nutella spread, in-store bakeries and Findus frozen pancakes, would be dispiriting and, more important, not distinctive to Italy. Such products and services are the props of a story that the whole developed world has lived through. The *real* miracle of Italian food makes for a different tale, albeit one that could never be separated from the relentless advance of consumer capitalism. The great mystery and virtue of Italy's food in the last half century is that a civilization of the table with its roots in the age of Boccaccio and Bonvesin, of Marco Polo and Master Martino, has remained recognizably itself despite the advent of refrigerators, packet *minestrone*, and juice bars. That, after all, is why the world loves it. And the story of how that happened begins in Rome, in 1954, with just one meal.

An American in Rome

A young man returns home late at night to a flat in the old Trastevere district of Rome. He has been out on his own watching a Hopalong Cassidy movie, so he enters the kitchen backward, pointing two imaginary six-shooters from his hips and muttering lines in a mixture of pseudo-American English and a thick Roman dialect: "You double-crossed me! I'm gonna take you down!" His dress is a childish version of Hollywood machismo: a baseball cap that is a couple of sizes too small; a long-sleeved vest that looks like the top half of a pair of long johns; dark jeans; a wristband, a belt, and a pair of cowboy boots all made from the same studded leather. Turning around, he sees the supper that his despairing parents have left on the table: a bottle of wine in a straw casing stands beside a covered plate. With a long-practiced gesture, he spins his nonexistent guns, holsters them, and looks to see what the plate contains. There is a prolonged intake of horrified breath. *"Mack-a-rownee! Mack-a-rownee!* This is cart drivers' stuff! I don't eat *maccheroni.* I am American, I am!" He pushes the plate to one side.

Thus begins the best-loved food scene in Italian cinema, a movie moment that has acquired a life independent of the film, *An American in Rome (Un americano a Roma,* 1954), starring Alberto Sordi. It launched its protagonist into the special place in public affection that is reserved for comedians who embody a nation's most endearing and infuriating character traits. Sordi's *maccheroni* scene also betrays contemporary Italians' most cherished culinary values. It embodies a narrative about food that underpins the Italian civilization of the table, keeping it stable in the face of the constant upheavals of the consumer epoch.

An American in Rome satirizes postwar Italy's fixation with all things Uncle Sam. In the 1940s, the United States military had saved Italy from fascism and Nazism. The Marshall Plan had saved it from starvation and communism. A vast back catalogue of Hollywood films, which had been banned in the last years of Mussolini's regime, were dumped on the Italian market to create a phantasmagoria of automobiles, skyscrapers, western horizons, and Rita Hayworth's satin-glove striptease. Reconstruction Italy dreamed in an American accent.

Sordi plays a character called Nando Moriconi whose little bedroom is filled with the bric-a-brac of American popular culture: football pennants and Charles Atlas posters, cowboy comics and photos of Betty Grable. Our hero's obsession extends to the fake cop's uniform he wears while riding his motorbike; he tries to dance like Gene Kelly and swing a bat like Joe DiMaggio. The plot revolves around the moment when he climbs to the top of the Colosseum and threatens to throw himself off unless someone pays his passage to New York. *Everything* about him speaks of the same infatuation with the United States. Yet in one corner of his psyche, in spite of himself, he draws an uncrossable Italian line.

Back in his parents' kitchen, Nando, assembles the ingredients of a better meal, talking to himself all the while:

The Americans eat jaaam! *This* is American stuff.

Yogurt. Mustard. *That's* why the Americans always beat the Apaches. Americans don't drink red wine. They drink milk. That's why they never get drunk. Have you ever seen a drunk American? Me neither.

The Americans are strong.

Turning his chair around the wrong way to sit at table, he mimes slapping the plate of pasta, and threatens, "I'm gonna take you down!" He then proceeds to spread all of his American ingredients onto one slice of bread: jam, yogurt, mustard, milk. "This is what Americans eat. Healthy, filling stuff."

Soon after he has taken the first bite, Nando's chewing becomes slow, openmouthed, and spasmodic. He gags, then rolls the ball of bread around his mouth and spits it out loudly. An untranslatable Roman drawl issues from his mouth: "Holy shit! What filth!"

But the break in his deluded self-confidence lasts only for a couple of beats before he says, "*Mack-a-rownee.* You riled me, now I'm gonna take you down!" The scene closes as Nando chomps eagerly on a cheek-stretching fork load of spaghetti and swigs wine straight from the bottle.

At a time when the United States embodied wealth, success, modernity, and glamour in every facet of life, not even a starstruck half-child could fool himself into believing that American food was better than Italian. If pasta had not already been a symbol of Italian identity before 1954, then Alberto Sordi's comic genius would have turned it into one. We may sometimes be naïve, backward, and even a little vulgar, *An American in Rome* is saying, but we've always known how to eat, and that won't change.

Even before the economic miracle really got under way, the *maccheroni* scene provided a catchy argument for *tradition*. It portrays Italians as rather stuck in their gastronomic ways, viscerally averse to foods that are newfangled, inauthentic, and foreign. There was unquestionably a great deal of truth in that national self-image in 1954. In fact *An American in Rome* came out in a significant year for *maccheroni*, statistically

The most famous food scene in Italian cinema: Alberto Sordi
just can't help himself in *An American in Rome* (1954).

speaking. *Pasta secca* was a great emblem of Italy's new prosperity. It was one of the first foods to register the effects of postwar economic growth: in 1954, as northerners were able to indulge their preference for *pasta* over polenta, national annual per capita consumption reached sixty-one pounds—about three-quarters of a bowl a day, in other words. It has stayed at pretty much the same level ever since. Precisely 800 years after al-Idrisi first reported the presence of *pasta secca* on Italian soil in *A Diversion for the Man Longing to Travel to Far-Off Places*, Italians were finally eating all the *maccheroni* they wanted.

Half a century after *An American in Rome*, Italians are still wary about imported and artificial food practices. France, the United Kingdom, and Germany today have between eight and eleven times as many fast food outlets as Italy. A few foreign drinks, such as soda, champagne, and whisky, have had lasting success in the Italian market; almost no foreign foods have. Italians buy a quarter of the amount of frozen products that Brits do. They have continually resisted the allure of American-style breakfast cereals. Fifty percent of Italian food spending is still accounted for by unpackaged goods. Any tourist to Naples, Rome, Florence, or Milan can see that there are far fewer foreign restaurants than there are in British or American cities of comparable size.

As soon as postwar Italians became prosperous enough to eat what they wanted, they mostly chose to follow homegrown examples of what was good—examples that were concentrated in the network of cities that covered so much of Italian territory. Since the miracle, Italy has been a nation of food conservatives. As always, the good tastes of Italian food provide some of the reasons for this conservatism, but not all. Other reasons are political.

Among the many casualties of the catastrophic fascist era was a unifying idea of the nation. After the war, Italian patriotism became just another word for bombast, hardship, war, and desolation. One of the few nonfascist symbols of the common Fatherland, the king, had been entirely discredited, too: the monarchy was abolished in a referendum in 1946 when Italy became a republic. Between the birth of the republic and the fall of the Berlin wall in 1989, Italian democracy was dominated by the contest between two parties: the ruling Democrazia Cristiana (or DC) and the opposition Partito Comunista Italiano (or PCI), neither of which was patriotic, in a conventional sense. The DC drew its overarching ideology from the Catholic Church, whereas the PCI's code of higher values derived from the historical mission of the working class to make the world a better place. Both the DC and the PCI were more than just parties, they were ways of life in many communities, particularly the Catholic or "white" regions of the northeast, and the "red belt" across the center. Each party sponsored a rich subculture of organizations, such as parish cinemas and youth leagues, and agriculture was a particularly fertile terrain for both Catholic and communist associations. The red and white value systems left little room for the nation in any aspect of Italian culture.

Food was perfectly suited to fill the nation-shaped gap in Italy's symbolic life. Its cuisine reflected the country's diversity and unity. It had a long and honorable history that could easily be rewritten to play down its elitist moments. And it could be the focus of a homely, almost self-effacing kind of pride. The table was one of the few places where Italians could find images of what they shared. No wonder Alberto Sordi's irresistible revulsion for "American" foods and his comic addiction to spaghetti struck such a chord.

Italian food also resonated in the red and white political subcultures, both of which were averse to American-inspired consumerism. The Catholic Church regarded overindulgence as materialistic, an insidious concession to the mirage of earthly happiness. The PCI's leaders had cut their teeth on the black bread of farm laborers or the slops of fascist jails, and had a stern self-denying streak. Revered party chief Palmiro Togliatti was known to dine only on bread, *mozzarella,* and the occasional fried fillet of salt cod in the cheapest Roman eateries. Both political subcultures liked to frame eating in a collective rather than an individualistic setting: the family or a religious festival for the Church; and the Festa dell'Unità for the PCI—these annual communist fairs were held to fund the party newspaper, *L'Unità,* but cheap barbecues, *spaghetti,* and local specialties were their major attraction. Thus, despite the Cold War antagonism between them, both the white and the red subcultures shared an antipathy toward consumerism, and helped entrench those values in the national civilization of the table. A profoundly divided country had a united ethic of good, simple eating.

An American in Naples and Bologna

The year 1954, which saw Alberto Sordi's *mack-a-rownee* scene capture the public's imagination, was historic for Italian food in another sense—one that gives an ironic twist to the gastronomic xenophobia that *An American in Rome* encapsulated. For in February, March, and April of that year an American citizen paid a visit to Italy that would ultimately shift the foundations of the Italian diet and save countless lives in the process. His name was Professor Ancel Keys, pioneer of cardiovascular disease epidemiology and inventor of the Mediterranean diet.

Keys had already made his mark on the history of food, and on the Italian psyche, before he visited the peninsula. The K rations eaten by U.S. troops during the Second World War were designed by him—the *K* stood for Keys. Portable, ready to eat, and high in calories, K rations included dried biscuits and canned meat, as well as the chewing gum, chocolate, and hard candy with which children across liberated Europe were charmed.

After the war Keys noticed that the prosperous, well-fed businessmen of Minneapolis, where he worked, were dying young, and dying of heart attacks. This ran entirely counter to dietary common sense that more calories meant better health. Yet anecdotal evidence and pilot research suggested that cardiovascular disease was not nearly as common in the impoverished city of Naples. Keys conducted a field study in 1954 to test a hypothesis he had developed to explain this apparent contradiction. The hypothesis had two planks: fat in the diet influences cholesterol concentration in the blood; cholesterol concentration in the blood is related to the furring of the arteries that is the cause of cardiovascular disease. Fat was about to lose its centuries-old association with wealth, health, and well-being.

Keys's study was conducted on sample groups of men: Neapolitan steel workers, council clerks, firefighters, and members of the Rotary Club; and, by way of a comparison, Bolognese policemen. In the capital of *maccheroni*, around 20 percent of the population's total intake of calories was accounted for by fat. Unsurprisingly, in the home of the *mortadella* sausage, the proportion was close to 30 percent. True to the Keys hypothesis, the respective levels of blood cholesterol concentration accurately echoed these proportions, as did the incidence of degenerative heart disease: thus the southern clerks had healthier hearts than the Po valley policemen. In fact only the well-to-do members of the Naples Rotary Club had cholesterol levels similar to those in "Fat" Bologna. But even the Rotarians and the Bolognese fared markedly better than white-collar workers from urban Minnesota, who ate fat equivalent to 40 percent of their total calorie intake, had high serum cholesterol levels, and were succumbing to coronaries at an epidemic rate.

Keys argued that "middle-aged men in the United States should be able to enjoy at least as good cardiovascular health as Italians," and he would devote the rest of his long life to developing his research and making that prediction come true. His field trips to Naples and Bologna fed into a gigantic "Seven Countries" study, comparing the same variables in Italy, Japan, Greece, Yugoslavia, Holland, the United States, and—unhealthiest of the lot—Finland, where the people even spread butter on their cheese. In 1959, together with his wife, he published *Eat Well and Stay Well*, a cookbook based on his findings. Among the Italian dishes it included were liver *alla veneziana*, potato *gnocchi*, and *risotto*. Although it was freighted with a hundred pages of rather indigestible introductory science, *Eat Well and Stay Well* was an enormous success: a family holiday villa near Naples was bought on the proceeds.

Eat Well and Stay Well was translated into Italian in 1962, but its message initially struggled for acceptance in Italy, where northerners were unlikely to be impressed by the proposition that they should eat more like the firemen and petty bureaucrats of Naples.

Later, in 1975, Keys would come to call his recommendations "the Mediterranean diet," explaining that it was a "relatively new invention" and not what the peoples of the Mediterranean had always eaten—otherwise pig meat and pork fat would have been among its central ingredients.

> The heart of what we now consider the Mediterranean diet is mainly vegetarian: pasta in many forms, leaves sprinkled with olive oil, all kinds of vegetables in season, and often cheese, all finished off with fruit, and frequently washed down with wine.

In this more familiar-sounding formulation, the Keys regimen proved more acceptable to Italians. They did not all become vegetarians, of course—the memory of near-vegetarianism enforced by hunger was too recent for that—but from the early 1980s, they embraced the Mediterranean diet as if they had known it was a great idea all along. As a direct result, lard and butter were driven out of their ancient strongholds in the Po valley, and olive oil, the good fat, became as much a national favorite as pasta.

Genuine Foods

Italian food conservatism expressed itself in other ways. One of the most influential was nostalgia. In the very years when they were taking their first steps as consumers, Italians also discovered that the authentic ingredients and dishes of days gone by were endangered. Just as hunger was finally disappearing from the peninsula, Italians were told that good food was a thing of the past.

One of the most captivating early expressions of Italian food nostalgia was a series filmed during the same year, 1957, that saw advertising first appear on Italian television. The twelve episodes of *In Search of Genuine Foods: A Journey Along the Po Valley*, were a major undertaking for Italy's RAI-TV, which itself had only been in operation for three years: the camera and sound crew was fifteen strong, and they traveled in a six-vehicle convoy, including a truck and minibus. *In Search of Genuine Foods* was made and presented by Mario Soldati. Apart from being a novelist, screenwriter, and filmmaker, Soldati was also Italy's most eloquent "wandering glutton" in the tradition established during the fascist era by Touring Club Italiano and Paolo Monelli. Soldati's idiosyncratic, opinionated style is stamped all over his program. He looked like a movie director who had hired himself from central casting—beret, tortoise-shell glasses, neat little mustache, sports jacket, and an eyepiece worn around the neck—and stood in his jeep at the head of the convoy, ordering his film crew around with peremptory blasts on a whistle. His interviewing style involved rarely allowing anyone else to finish a sentence. It all made for superb entertainment, and a remarkable document of the changing face of Italian food.

Soldati's aim was to seek out what he called "genuine gastronomy." Some of his program's earliest sequences, shot in his home region of Piedmont, show most clearly what he had in mind. By a mountain torrent below the snowy, pyramid-shaped peak of Mount Monviso close to the source of the Po, Soldati films a man fishing with a rod and line for trout no longer than his hand. Down in the plain near Chieri, he interviews a peasant about the cardoons he grows: after being buried to their tips for eight days to acquire the right pallor, they are sent just up the road to Turin, where they are used to dip in *bagna cauda*, the city's typical warm garlic and anchovy sauce. In the seventeenth-century town of Cherasco, Soldati examines the local "horse rump bullocks," which are fed a special diet including eggs to accentuate the distinctive shape and taste of their haunches. In Turin itself, Soldati sees *grissini* bread sticks being made by hand, and visits one of Italy's oldest and grandest restaurants, just across from the building that accommodated the country's first parliament. Back in the studio, he introduces a countess in a twinset and pearls who demonstrates how to make a fondue topped with truffle shavings, and explains that "social tragedy" is the fate of any housewife who serves her guests a fondue that is stringy rather than creamy. This was an image of Italian eating that could easily have been painted a century earlier.

But perhaps the most telling moment in Soldati's journey is when he finds himself amid the huge steel tubes, enameled vats, and gleaming domed inspection hatches of a giant cheese factory near Lodi, southeast of Milan. Here the boss is not a landowner but an entrepreneur in a double-breasted suit, and his key employees wear white coats and spend their time taking readings from gauges. The milk comes from cows reared on concentrated soya-based feeds from Japan. Looking around him, Soldati removes his beret and gives his head a demonstratively downhearted scratch. Then, talking direct to camera in a resigned tone, he concedes that there is no other way adequately to feed the masses:

> The great majority of what we eat is industrialized. So if I had had to limit my search for what is genuine only to things that are artisanal, handmade, and traditional, I would have ended up showing you, the viewers, a gastronomy that would be out of reach in most cases. Unless you wanted to die of hunger.

At the end of the tour, however, the genuine and the industrial are reconciled when Soldati takes a stroll in a warehouse where some of the factory's 50,000 *Grana Padano* cheeses are slowly maturing. He ends the program at table, extolling the time-honored virtues of *Grana* and *Parmigiano-Reggiano*, the two varieties of Parmesan. Recalling an ancient piece of Italian wisdom, he recommends that the "king of cheeses" be eaten at the end of a meal with "the queen of fruits," the pear.

The curious thing about Soldati's search for genuine foods is his uncertainty. He never quite makes up his mind where to draw the line between what is genuine and what is industrial. Part of him wants to restrict "genuine" to the man fishing for trout in the Alps. Another part of him is less wistful. Even Soldati would have to admit that some of Italian food's most genuine traditions center on such products as cheeses, hams, *salami*, and *pasta secca*; originally designed for preservation, transport, and trade, they therefore lend themselves very well to industrial methods. Telling the difference between genuine and artificial is not always as easy as choosing a plate of *maccheroni* over a foul concoction of jam, yogurt, mustard, and milk.

Soldati's uncertainty has run through the history of Italian food since the economic miracle. Italy is still a country "in search of genuine food," a country permanently nostalgic for the dishes of yesteryear. The meaning of *genuine* has never been particularly clear—it is too misted with nostalgia, too vulnerable to being appropriated by advertisers. Yet the word retains its magical aura. Despite the confusion surrounding it, a belief in what is genuine, combined with a regret for what has become industrial or artificial, has been written into the statutes of Italy's civilization of the table. It has become an article of the Italian gastronomic faith.

Italians only take foods to their hearts that have a claim to being "genuino," "tipico," "autentico," or "tradizionale"—words that have the same vague and evocative appeal. The contemporary era is the era of national foods, dishes that, for the first time in history, have united culinary Italy from north to south, and from the top to the bottom of the social scale. All of those national foods have a sound pedigree in one or another region of the peninsula; yet all are made on an industrial scale. *Panettone* is one instance: the deliciously soft, light cake with candied fruit was originally a Milanese speciality. But by the time of *In Search of Genuine Foods*, shrewd marketing had turned it into a Christmas treat for all.

Other national dishes, such as *pizza* and *mozzarella*, came from the south to conquer the north. Soldati sees *provolone* being made at a factory in Lombardy, but this melon-shaped cheese was brought up to the Po valley in the early 1900s by southern entrepreneurs in search of a more fertile commercial terrain. The factory owner tells Soldati that 70 to 80 percent of *provolone* is now made in the north.

The mass migration of the economic miracle had much to do with this nationalization process. Southerners took their favorite foods to Turin, for example, and in time they also learned to like *bagna cauda*, just as the *torinesi* learned to like pasta with tomato sauce. (However, in the early years, prejudiced locals sneered that "dirty southerners" grew tomatoes in the bathtub and basil in the bidet.)

Since the 1950s, the spread of national dishes has gathered speed and, in the process, the confusion surrounding what is genuine has become ever greater. In most of Italy, it is not traditional to eat arugula, balsamic vinegar, and buffalo milk *mozzarella*, yet these foods became national crazes in the 1980s and 1990s by selling themselves as authentic products, hallowed by the ages. (Shortly afterward, of course, the craze swept through supermarkets in the rest of the world.) Italian food can only reinvent itself by pretending it has stayed the same. Change only comes in the guise of continuity; novelties must be presented as nostalgic relics. This food conservatism is a cultural quirk that makes for a great deal of misunderstanding and cant. But it is, underneath it all, the Italian civilization of the table's saving virtue in the age of mass production.

From the Cauldron to the Tureen

One of the best and most remarkable features of the Italian love of food today is how democratic it is, how egalitarian. Before the Second World War, hungry day laborers from the most backward regions of the south lived on a different alimentary planet from the bourgeoisie of the cities. Now their children and grandchildren are likely to share the same knowledgeable appreciation for tasty cooking. In Britain, teenagers from deprived inner cities are so habituated to fast and packaged foods that many of them are unable to recognize a carrot in its natural state. In Italy, even preschool kids from poor families can tell an eggplant from a bulb of fennel—as British celebrity chef Jamie Oliver discovered in 2005 during his highly popular *Jamie's Italy* series. Italy does not suffer nearly as much as other countries from a great divide between *cuisine*, the art of fine eating cultivated by the few, and *diet*, or the foods that most people feed themselves on a daily basis. *Simplicity* is frequently cited by Italians as one of the characteristic merits of the way they eat.

Italy's respect for simple peasant dishes is one of the strongest signs of the country's comparative freedom from food snobbery. That respect is so strong that it often topples over into credulity: the surest way to get a product moving off the supermarket shelves is by putting "peasant tradition" on the packet. But *ribollita*, the Tuscan "reboiled" soup that is particularly cherished in Florence, is most definitely *not* one of the many dishes with a fake agrarian ancestry. It is the very epitome of "poor cuisine," the best-known member of a large family of bread soups and paps that have their origins in the Tuscan farmsteads. And a short history of *ribollita* is the best way to show how Italy's food culture was democratized during the country's rapid transformation into an industrial society in the 1950s and 1960s.

RIBOLLITA

Take some *cannellini* beans, soak them overnight, and then boil them in plenty of lightly salted water. Ladle out roughly half of the beans and purée them, making sure to keep the cooking water.

In a large pot, sweat some chopped onion in olive oil, then add other vegetables like celery, carrot, and garlic, followed by a potato and some tinned tomatoes, and then the first really essential and distinctive ingredients: equal proportions of roughly chopped savoy cabbage and *cavolo nero*—the "black cabbage" or dark kale that is used so much in Tuscany. Pork rind can be added, too, if desired, but most recipes stick to other vegetables like chard, leeks, etc.

After ten minutes of gentle softening, stir in the beans and their cooking water. Season with salt and pepper. The soup must then bubble quietly for two hours. Stir occasionally.

Add in a generous quantity of stale Tuscan bread in pieces. (Tuscan bread contains no salt.) Cook for 10 to 15 minutes more. Allow to stand for another ten minutes. Then serve with a deep swirl of olive oil that is peppery enough to catch gently at the back of the tongue.

This recipe is synthesized from a number of sources, but then any *ribollita* "recipe" is something of a misnomer. One set of instructions on how to make a Tuscan bread soup can only ever be a version of a practice that was carried out in a huge variety of ways in different families, depending on the available ingredients. The unglamorous core principle was nonetheless the same: adding stale bread to *minestrone*.

For centuries large areas of central Italian countryside, including much of Tuscany, were characterized by sharecropping, the contractual system in which the landowner split the fruits of agriculture equally with his peasant tenants. The proprietor supplied the land; the peasant supplied the labor. Sharecroppers lived a life of dawn-to-dusk toil, and were often exploited and cheated by the landowner and his bailiffs. But they rarely went hungry, and were markedly better off than the landless laborers of, say, the great southern estates. The sharecroppers' families tended to be very large and live close to the fields as one working unit, in the same smoke-blackened, crowded farmhouse as their animals. The male head of the household was subordinate to the will of landowner, whose approval was even needed for a peasant to marry. But within the household, the father-boss was invested with supreme authority by law, whether or not those under him were his relatives. It was he who distributed work and decided what to grow.

The hub of the sharecropping household was the senior woman, the *massaia* or housewife. She made sure that the women worked even harder than the men: rearing children, tending farmyard animals, fetching water, washing and darning—as well as working in the fields like the men. And of course, to women fell the task of preparing food, which was done on a large scale.

Ribollita originates in the simple, bulk cooking of the sharecropping farmsteads. As had always been the way in peasant homes, soup from a cauldron over the fire was at the heart of most meals. The cauldron would be constantly filled and refilled, boiled and reboiled. Self-sufficiency was the sharecropping norm—not even bread would be bought. Baking was done once a week to economize on firewood and time. The bread was made without salt, because salt, besides being expensive, attracts moisture that can turn bread moldy and inedible before the week is over. As baking day approached, dried bread would be used to bulk out the inevitable *minestrone*.

The economic miracle brought sharecropping to a rapid end. When tractors and weedkiller were introduced, the demand for labor fell, and with it the viability of family farms. In 1951 there were more than 2.2 million sharecroppers in Italy; twenty years later considerably less than a quarter of that number remained. Faced with a choice between a city life of scooters, cinema, and ice cream, or a rural life of physical labor and bread soup, young people from sharecropping families did not hesitate for long. In Tuscany, Umbria, and the Marche, countless farmsteads were abandoned. Eventually, they would be converted into holiday homes for wealthy Britons, or rural restaurants remodeled to fit to the "White Mill" ideal.

The end of sharecropping was the beginning of a period of breakneck change for many Tuscan families. In the space of a few years, they moved from a life of subsistence agriculture to a life of wage labor whose rhythms were set by money and the market. Families that were once extended work units shrank to nuclear size; they also became "long," in the sense that children arrived later in life, once economic independence had been obtained. A generation that had known poverty in its youth reared children who took abundance for granted.

Amid such wholesale change, a humble dish like *ribollita* seemed to represent a rare point of fixity and integrity. But of course *ribollita*, too, could not help but register the upheavals of modernity Tuscan-style. For example, that "deep swirl" of good olive oil to finish the dish would once upon a time have been at best a shallow C shape. For many sharecropping families, oil was a precious resource, and cooking with pig fat was more common. A contemporary bread soup would also be less likely to include pork rind, which no longer fits into the "Mediterranean diet." But the biggest change of all was that *ribollita* slowly became a *recipe*. In other words it became just one more option within a varied daily regimen that was rich in meat, fresh fish, and other foods that had been rarities in the days of sharecropping. It also became available in restaurants. No dish remains the same when you can choose whether to make it or not. One obvious sign of that change in status is the soup's very name: no one has been able to find the word *ribollita* in a written source published before 1960, when it appeared in a novel by Florence's Vasco Pratolini. Thus *ribollita* entered the national language only just before it came on to the menu.

Yet there is another important strand to the story of *ribollita*. For when the sharecroppers first migrated to Florence in the 1950s and 1960s, they found that *ribollita* had got there before them. In fact it had arrived in 1891, imported by a man in muttonchop whiskers:

TUSCAN PEASANT SOUP

Ingredients
400 g [about a pound] of stale dark bread
300g [10½ ounces] of white beans
150g [5¼ ounces] of oil
2 litres [8½ cups] of water
Half a medium savoy cabbage
The same amount, or more, of *cavolo nero*
A bunch of chard
A potato
A few pieces of pork rind or strips of fatty ham

Put the beans on to boil in the water with the pork rind, adding more water if they are in danger of drying out. While they are boiling, put the oil in a pan and add a *battuto* (sautéing mix) made from the following finely chopped ingredients: a quarter of a large onion, two cloves of garlic, two palm-length pieces of celery, and a handful of parsley. Cook until the *battuto* has colored, then add the other vegetables, roughly chopped. Season with salt and pepper, then add sieved tomatoes. Add the cooking liquid from the beans if the vegetables dry out. When the beans and pork rind are cooked, add a quarter of them to the soup. Purée the rest of the beans, mix them with the cooking liquid, and add to the soup. Mix, cook a little more, and then pour everything into a soup tureen where you have already placed the stale bread, thinly sliced. Wait for twenty minutes before eating.

Makes enough for six people. The soup is good hot, and even better cold.

The tone of the recipe is unmistakably Artusian: "This soup deserves to be called 'peasant' because it is so modest. Yet I'm convinced that, if made with the proper care, it will appeal to everyone, even gentlemen." History has certainly proved Pellegrino Artusi right. Bread soup lost none of its appeal after it was transplanted from the cauldron to the tureen.

Despite his concern for bourgeois dignity, Artusi was sanguine and open-minded enough to include other peasant dishes in *Science in the Kitchen and the Art of Eating Well*. Even maize-meal *polenta* is there, albeit in rich versions—served as an accompaniment to sausages, or made with creamy milk and shaped into fritters. Just as the pope's secret cook Bartolomeo Scappi had done centuries before, Artusi was granting peasant fare conditional access to his urban table, where it could bring variety and unadorned charm. In Artusi's case, such simple dishes were important for another reason: they made an earthy statement about Italian food that distinguished it from the rarefied, elaborate cuisine of France.

So in a sense, after the great exodus from the land during the economic miracle, *ribollita* became the meeting point of two food cultures defined by the cauldron and the tureen respectively. It fit with the nostalgia of upwardly mobile former peasants, and with the inverted snobbery of urban gastronomes. There could be no more democratic dish.

The culinary effects of Italy's postwar economic transformation are easy to summarize. For the best part of a millennium, an intimate but wholly unequal partnership between city and country shaped the history of eating in Italy. The city drew on the food resources produced by the varied landscapes beyond its walls; it traded those resources with other cities, and other countries, to increase the variety at its disposal. From the time of the medieval commune, Italy's cities created a glorious civilization of the table—often at the countryside's expense. The cities had the richest and most diverse cuisine, and the most powerful stories linking food and identity.

But with the economic miracle, that relationship was recast. The miracle heralded an urbanization of the whole country's diet. Wherever they lived, north or south, town or country, almost all Italians could sit down to the kinds of meals once reserved for wealthier city-dwellers. After the miracle, the story of Italian food remains very much a city story—but only because the whole country has been integrated into urban eating habits. Even *ribollita* is city food now.

18

Bologna, 1974

Mamma's Tortellini

"Everything You See, I Owe to Spaghetti"

Sophia Loren is a national monument in Italy; she was even, rather incongruously, chosen to carry the Olympic banner at the opening ceremony of the Turin Winter Games in 2006. Nonetheless, *la Loren*'s 1971 recipe collection, *In cucina con amore*, published in English as *Eat with Me*, says a great deal about the distinctive relationship between women and food in contemporary Italy. Sophia Loren set the pattern for a series of opulently proportioned beauties who have sought to incarnate some of the virtues of Italian cuisine. "Everything you see, I owe to spaghetti," she once quipped.

Loren became a star by exemplifying a spunky, spontaneous version of Italian womanhood, and food was integral to the image. She first became famous in Italy by playing what she herself describes as "an explosive, sexy, blowsy Neapolitan pizza girl" in Vittorio De Sica's *The Gold of Naples*, made in the same year as *An American in Rome*. Some later roles capitalized on the success of her *pizzaiola* persona, notably when she played a widowed fishmonger in *Scandal in Sorrento* in 1955. As Loren's life story became known, her hungry upbringing in Pozzuoli on the Bay of Naples added more authenticity to her aura.

But after she first went to America in 1957, her celebrity status at home came into conflict with the Sophia Loren created by Hollywood. Italian audiences were highly sensitive to America's misappropriation of its favorite cinematic assets, and to the stereotyping of their country that is often perpetrated by the dream factory. In 1958, one critic claimed that Hollywood had turned Loren into "a vaguely gypsy-like Mediterranean cliché." This was an extremely difficult time for her. In 1957 she had offended moral sensibilities in Italy by marrying her mentor and producer, Carlo Ponti: he was a divorcé and father of two, and his union with Loren was sealed in a hastily arranged, rather squalid proxy ceremony in Mexico. The Church issued a thinly disguised threat to excommunicate Loren, and the couple faced accusations of adultery

Sophia Loren poses with rococo charcuterie ensemble, early 1970s.
Through her love of food, Loren reconciled the divergent roles of spirited local girl, international sex symbol, aspirational icon, and mother.

and bigamy; the latter charge was so serious that Ponti would have been subject to arrest if he had been seen in public in Italy. To make matters worse, Loren's sister married Mussolini's son, and the star's driver ran over and killed a young man in chaotic scenes at the wedding.

Motherhood was the solution to Loren's difficulties, both on screen and off. Cinematic motherhood came first. In 1960 she gave the performance of her life in *Two Women*, Vittorio De Sica's harrowing story of a mother and her daughter in wartime Italy. Loren was originally penciled in to play the daughter, but she took the mother's part, drawing on her own memories of the war. Her character combined the sassiness and sensuality of her earlier trademark roles, but added a sensitive, nurturing dimension that came across particularly well in the film's many food scenes. She won the Academy Award for best actress, as well as a mantelpiece full of other prizes.

During the shooting of *Two Women*, a couple of leading press agents had begun to orchestrate a careful publicity campaign to rehabilitate Loren in Italy. "The aim," one of them explained, "was to reconcile Sophia with the Italian mammas and detach her from that terrible term: 'family-breaker.'" Stills were issued of her playing with children during a break in filming.

In the years following her Oscar triumph, Loren embarked on her own heartrending and protracted struggle to become a mother; she was devastated by two miscarriages. Her third pregnancy was carefully news-managed. To give herself the best possible chance of carrying the baby to term, Loren spent months on end in the Hotel Intercontinental in Geneva. Bulletins from her eighteenth-floor suite were eagerly devoured by the media, and generated such powerful sympathies for her that even the Catholic press had to concede she was due a little compassion. The whole country rejoiced when her first son was born in December 1968; the president of the republic sent a telegram of felicitations "in the name of the Italian people." Somehow she had managed to reconcile what in 1960s Italy was all but irreconcilable: she was both a sex goddess and a mother, both an unreachable vision of Hollywood stardom and a gutsy girl from Naples. Sophia Loren entered a period of undiluted public adoration (which lasted until 1979, when she created another image problem for herself by being arrested at Rome airport on charges of nonpayment of taxes, among other financial irregularities).

In cucina con amore is a product of the golden moment in Loren's life and career after the birth of her child in 1968. She is known to be a great cook, but *In cucina con amore* is not just a sum of her skill in the kitchen; it combines all the contradictory elements that made her so loved at the high plateau of her fame. There is glamour and sex appeal in large helpings, especially in the pictures. In one shot she poses in a loud kimono-style dress and caresses the tail of a stuffed pheasant that forms part of what can only be described as a rococo charcuterie ensemble. In another, sad to say, she becomes "a vaguely gypsy-like Mediterranean cliché" as she leans forward over some fruit and nuts in a low-cut bodice, large earrings, and ruffled hair.

Yet *In cucina con amore* is also the work of a mother, who is from as tough a background as any of her fans. As Loren explains in the preface, she perfected most of the recipes during her pregnancy, when she had passed the time in the Hotel Intercontinental cooking:

> This book is dearer to me than any successful film because it takes me back to the nerve-wracking days which came to a climax in the birth of Carlo, Jr., the greatest joy of my life. . . .
>
> My childhood poverty taught me the importance of finding, and inventing, new ways to cook and flavor the same cheap, essentially monotonous basic food. In that respect, grandmother left me a precious heritage. Thanks to her I know at least a dozen ways to cook eggplants, one of the cheapest and most plentiful foods in Italy, and I can perform miracles with a bony or third-rate, stringy piece of meat.

Thus *In cucina con amore* is designed to associate Italy's biggest star with the down-to-earth qualities that the country associated with its food. Loren's recipes are from many different regions—a national cuisine from a national icon—and range from the sweet and sour Sicilian eggplant dish, *caponata*, to a recipe for spaghetti with tomato sauce that is "handed down from mother to daughter in every Neapolitan household." Progressing up and around the peninsula, we move from Roman *bucatini all'amatriciana,* to Genoese *trenette al pesto,* then on to Milanese *risotto* and Bolognese *tagliatelle al ragù.* What unites all of these flavors, unsurprisingly, is Loren's respect for what is "genuine": "our age must fight for genuine food against dieting and frozen (or packaged) food," she counsels.

Sophia Loren's cookbook is also a record of a crucial period in the history of Italian women. In the late 1960s and early 1970s the deep social and cultural changes brought by the miracle suddenly broke to the political surface in a season of protest and militancy. Among the most important symptoms of change was the legalization of divorce in 1970; the law was resoundingly confirmed in a referendum in 1974. The following year, family law was amended to conform to the principle that a man and a woman were equal within marriage. Italian society had made a decisive move away from the traditional religious morality that had made Sophia Loren's screen presence crackle with illicit sexual promise, while simultaneously ostracizing her for her relationship with Carlo Ponti.

Yet the contradictions that found a magical unity in the Sophia Loren persona, contradictions between glamour and reality, between desire and motherhood, remained unresolved for the vast majority of Italian women. The country's increasing prosperity was having a paradoxical effect on their lives: on the one hand it was taking them away from the rural workforce and turning them into urban housewives and consumers; yet on the other it was educating them, drawing them out of the home, and giving them new roles in the labor market. The transition from peasant to housewife to working mother was often very rapid. The age of the classic *mamma* did not last long in a good many Italian families.

Changes in Italian media soon magnified these contradictions. And for that reason, *In cucina con amore* also foreshadows the extraordinary power that motherhood came to have in the marketing of Italian food. From the mid-1970s, the state television monopoly broke down, and privately owned commercial channels began to emerge. In the 1980s, these unregulated channels rose to dominate the airwaves with their mixture of American soap operas, game shows, scantily clad soubrettes, and enormous quantities of advertising that was far brasher and more intrusive than anything to which the country had ever been subjected. In the ad-land Italy of the 1980s, nothing could be eaten unless it was first made sacred by passing through a mother's hands; the most frequent scenario involved a smiling mother presenting the dish to her family at table. New, foreign goods in particular had to win *mamma's* approval, the essential guarantee that a product was good and genuine. "What's mayonnaise, *Mamma*?" a child asks in one campaign. "But you know it's Calvé," comes the reply. *Mamma* is still exalted by innumerable Italian food ads at home and abroad. Yet the irony is that *mamma* actually had a relatively short historical existence troubled by the competing pressures of children, work, home, and other people's expectations.

The pressures on mothers were such that something had to give. And in the 1980s what gave were *tortellini*.

Frog *Tortellini*

We have it on no less an authority than Sophia Loren that "there isn't a town or village of the Po valley which hasn't had the honor of bestowing its name on a special variation of those stuffed pasta called *cappelletti* (little hats), *tortellini*, *ravioli*, and so on." Her recipe for *tortellino* filling is wonderfully old-fashioned, containing calf's brain with butter, minced pork, *mortadella*, Parmesan, eggs, and a pinch of nutmeg. But at the very time when Sophia Loren was aligning herself with the down-home ethos of stuffed pasta, *tortellini* were poised to take over the world.

Tortellini and other filled pastas date back to the Middle Ages: they were in the Venetian manuscript *Book for Cook,* and in virtually every Italian recipe collection written thereafter. Over time, they became part of the rich traditions of festive eating of many parts of northern Italy. Celebrations involving food marked rites of passage in the lives of even humble families. Fresh homemade pasta was often produced for these rare, heavily ritualized moments of abundance. In parts of the Romagna, *passatelli* (the worm-shaped pasta made with bread crumbs) were an Easter dish. In the countryside near Ravenna, it was the custom to celebrate the safe arrival of a baby boy with *gnocchi*, and a baby girl with *lasagne*.

Tortellini belong to the same genre of celebratory specialties. For the northern Italians who could afford to make them often, *tortellini* used to be a Sunday lunch dish. With *tortellini*, families reaffirmed that all was well and everyone was in his place. They were a special treat and the filling also provided a way of putting leftovers to good use—the perfect demonstration of maternal magic. Thus the idea of a single, prescribed authentic recipe for such a dish would not have made much sense to the women who spent long hours making *tortellini*, and who passed their skills on to their daughters. Nor would the idea of buying *tortellini* from anyone they did not know and trust—for who knew what rubbish might be inside?

But where some people see a traditional eating habit, others see a market opportunity. In 1961, at the peak of the economic miracle, a twenty-four-year-old baker's son from near Verona in the Veneto region of northeastern Italy started making fresh pasta in a small workshop lent to him by his father-in-law. Giovanni Rana's business centered on meat *tortellini*. They would be made on Friday and Saturday so that they could be sold in local shops ready for Sunday lunch. To keep the machines and staff busy on other days, they made *fettuccine* and *gnocchi*, too.

The forty-five to sixty-five pounds of *tortellini* that Rana produced at this stage did not greatly distinguish him from the many other local producers, but if his beginnings were artisanal, his aims were industrial. Rana's business plan was based on an understanding of the changes that were afoot in women's lives. The ritual of *tortellini*-making was becoming just too time-consuming for mothers with jobs as well as kids and housework. Yet Sunday lunch had lost none of its symbolism. Indeed, as families became more dispersed, their union around the table once a week had taken on a new emotional force. If the lack-of-trust problem surrounding shop-bought *tortellini* could be resolved, a huge new market would open up.

Giovanni Rana solved the trust problem by never compromising on the quality of the ingredients in his fillings, and by building personal relationships with the shopkeepers who sold his pasta. Three years after setting up his business, he moved it to a factory ten times as big. In 1968, the year Sophia Loren had her first child, Rana introduced a pasteurization technique to extend the shelf life of his *tortellini* from three to ten days—they could now be sold much farther away from where they were made. In 1969 he began building another factory nearly seventy times the size of his original workshop. He recalls that he became "like a general in front of a map of Italy sticking little flags into the different provinces to show the ones covered by one of my sales representatives." By the end of the 1970s, the little flags reached as far south as Rome. Giovanni Rana had not just created a successful business, he had virtually invented a whole new market sector by bringing branding and industrial production methods to fresh pasta.

Thus far in the story of Rana pasta, the company's *tortellini* had been sold through small family outlets. Something odd happened to this kind of shop in Italy in the 1970s. Elsewhere in Europe, the number of small retailers decreased as supermarkets took over more and more of the food market, while in Italy the trend went in the opposite direction. By 1977 Italy had four times as many food shops as Germany, partly because of Italy's conservatism about food—women preferred the personal contact of the local market or small store—and because of the lack of space in many historic city centers. But the main reason was political: small traders and their families were a crucial reservoir of support for the Christian Democrat party, which therefore made sure that it did not pursue them too zealously when it came to paying taxes. The DC also helped the shopkeepers with a 1971 law that carefully stipulated a minimum permitted distance between two shops of a similar kind. No trading license would be granted to a proposed outlet if it encroached on the catchment area of another. Shopkeepers thus had their livelihood protected, but at the same time the local politicians gained greater power to dispense favors through the retail licenses. Big food manufacturers like Giovanni Rana also benefited because they could impose high wholesale prices on the weak, divided, small shopkeepers. Only consumers lost out, because they had to spend more time roving between stores and paid more for goods than did consumers in countries where supermarkets had a freer run at the market. Italy still displays the symptoms of its delayed supermarketization: in the mid-1990s, Italy had one-tenth of the number of France, and French food cost between 5 and 15 percent less.

Nevertheless, in the 1980s supermarkets did start to sell a larger share of Italy's food. Rana, as ever, responded to the change with great agility. He increased the shelf life of his *tortellini* further by selling them in packets filled with a mixture of carbon dioxide and nitrogen. The company lobbied politicians intensively until a law was passed that permitted the use of these gases. Once the new packs were available, sales teams worked closely with distributors to make sure that Rana products were positioned prominently in refrigerated cabinets.

The 1980s also saw advances intended to address the old problem of trust. Rana overhauled its *tortellini* packaging, adding pictures of ingredients, the label "Giovanni Rana's Classics," and the entrepreneur's own signature. This was a *personal* guarantee, a bond that directly linked the manufacturer and the shopper. Giovanni Rana believes that his surname added a touch of warts-and-all sincerity to the relationship, for *rana* in Italian means "frog." A new laboratory for quality control and product development further bolstered the brand's trustworthiness and the company's ability to innovate.

While Rana modernized, the growing number of supermarkets and the boom in television advertising were helping Italy shake off its Catholic and communist guilt about consumerism. The country discovered the pleasures of untrammelled commercial hedonism at table. Once more, Giovanni Rana's fresh pasta business benefited from the change in lifestyles. In fact Rana began actively to change eating habits: *tortellini* were being transformed from a Sunday treat into an everyday dish.

In the second half of the 1980s, Rana pasta's annual growth galloped at around the 20 percent mark. These profits began to attract the attention of the Italian food industry's big players, who at first tried to buy the company, and then launched their own fresh pasta brands. Giovanni Rana held them all off, and steadily increased his share of a rapidly expanding market, largely through a series of clever, nostalgic advertising campaigns showing an Italian family in what purports to be the old days: they live in the countryside, grow their own food, and eat homemade fresh pasta.

In the early 1990s, the company used Giovanni Rana himself on the small screen, and the kind features of the fifty-something baker's son from Cologna Veneta became one of the most recognizable faces in Italy. He came across like a favorite grandfather: many of these enormously successful ads contained a brief sequence of him napping contentedly in an armchair after he had, for example, presented a mother with a packet of pasta for her children.

The advertising campaigns capitalized on Giovanni Rana's personal trustworthiness to introduce consumers to some of the new products that his scientists were coming up with, such as a filling placed in layers that can be *seen* when you cut into the *tortellino* with a fork. Another novelty is the *Sfogliavelo*, a thinner pasta envelope that allows busy moms to shave valuable seconds off cooking times; *Sfogliavelo tortellini* are also sold in single-portion packets for the increasing number of Italians who live on their own, but who want the satisfaction of preparing their own dinner.

Naturally, as these products have taken off, Rana advertising has continued to stress the traditional family virtues of *tortellini*. In one typical commercial for *Sfogliavelo tortellini* from 2006, Rana visits a family in Piedmont on their extensive vineyard. A fresh-faced father leaps from his tractor to shake Giovanni Rana's hand. "Have you gone back to being a peasant?" the old entrepreneur jokes in the Veneto dialect. "I wish!" comes the reply in Piedmontese. "I work in a bank!" All together they spend a leisurely day bringing in the grape harvest before dinner, when mother serves the new Giovanni Rana *Sfogliavelo* filled with *brasato*—the braised beef that is one of the staples of Turinese cuisine. "The *brasato* is just like we make it here in Piedmont!" mother exclaims.

Sales of fresh pasta in Italy have recently stabilized, after three decades of constant growth. Thus, half a century after they reached their ceiling with *pasta secca*, Italians are now eating as many *tortellini* as they want. Giovanni Rana remains the leader in this mature market, with about one third of the business, and four pasta factories in northern Italy and one in Argentina. The *tortellini* fillings are pasteurized in bacteria-free environments at a minutely controlled temperature and humidity level. The company spends $20 million every year on research and development, and is constantly improving its product line with such novelties as potato *gnocchi* ready-filled with sauce, or *tortellini* with cheese and pears.

The company is expanding successfully in other European countries that have only recently developed a taste for fresh pasta. In Luxembourg more *tortellini* are eaten per head of population than anywhere else on earth, and 60 percent of them are made by Rana. Among the few European countries where Giovanni Rana's face is not known is the United Kingdom, where the all-powerful supermarket chains sell Rana-made pasta and *gnocchi* under their own names. But Rana is not content for the brand's distinctive identity to be excluded from Britain. The company is looking into developing fast-food outlets with automated cooking systems that can have filled pasta freshly cooked and ready for you to eat forty-five seconds after you walk through the door. If the initiative is successful, the medieval *tortellino* will be Italy's elegant riposte to the chicken nugget.

The Giovanni Rana story illustrates a great many things about recent Italian history. His business is typical of the family firms that became the engine of the Italian economy in the 1980s, and made the Veneto into one of the richest areas in Europe. His spectacular success is due, fundamentally, to two things: the way he has capitalized on profound changes in the food culture of Italian families; and his ability to innovate while simultaneously flattering Italians' conservatism at table, their obsession with eating what is good and genuine, and their cherished notion that food should be rural, traditional, and typical.

Whether Giovanni Rana is to be considered a hero or a villain of Italy's civilization of the table depends on your point of view and what you believe "traditional" and "genuine" mean. Thirty years ago, Sophia Loren gave an eloquent, typically optimistic summary of what the modern food industry was doing in kitchens the length and breadth of the country:

> We have at our disposal food, and very good food it is very often, from any part of the world, every day of the year. Manufacturers have solved for us the problem of time and labor in preparing meals. But at the same time, it strikes me that this boon of modern science and marketing can make us too lazy for our own good. . . . So when we speak of genuine food, we ought to rediscover the pleasure of cooking . . . , of creating some small masterpiece with our hands, however ephemeral it may be. . . . There was a time not so long ago when women regarded the kitchen stove as an emblem of slavery.

Today the slavery is over. So why not transform the chains into an
instrument of delight?

Most Italian women have not found it as easy as Sophia Loren did to
"transform the chains into an instrument of delight." The pressures of
consumerism have created anxiety as well as pleasure. Indeed, for one
group of people the gravity-defying rise of the fresh pasta industry has
been a cause for profound concern: Bologna's Learned Confraternity of
the Tortellino.

The producers of Italy's typical dishes have always been under
threat from imitators—as was Bologna's own *mortadella* sausage in
the seventeenth century. In recent years, as the food industry has colo-
nized ever greater areas of the Italian diet, food producers, shopkeepers, restaurateurs, and politicians have been compelled to stand guard
around many more famous specialties, including *tortellini*.

Tortellini are more strongly identified with Bologna than with
any other place in the country; they became a badge of the city in
the eighteenth century. *Tortellini alla bolognese* are a subtle, succulent delicacy—especially when served in the correct way, in capon
broth. But making them is hugely labor-intensive in proportion to
even these delicious rewards. The disks of almost diaphanous fresh
pasta require artful mixing, resting, and rolling. One recipe recommends that they measure exactly 3.7 centimeters across. The prescribed filling also consumes hours of preparation. It includes pork
loin, *prosciutto crudo* ("raw ham," usually known outside Italy as
Parma ham), egg, nutmeg, Parmesan cheese, and, of course, *mortadella*. The pork loin has to be left for two days in a mixture of salt,
pepper, rosemary, and garlic before being cooked in butter. Once all
the ingredients have been chopped very finely, the mixture is left to
stand for another twenty-four hours, then placed in chickpea-sized
dollops on the pasta. Each *tortellino* is then folded around the tip of
the index finger—rather as a waiter might fold a napkin around his
hand. Apparently this procedure works best if the relevant fingertip
is 18 millimeters in diameter. The result, for anyone patient enough
to follow these instructions to the letter, is a fat, flat, yellowish crown
the size of a small coin.

There is a story behind the sheer precision of these widely available instructions for making authentic Bolognese *tortellini*. On December 7, 1974, representatives from the city's Learned Confraternity of the Tortellino (founded 1965) went to the local Chamber of Commerce and solemnly deposited a legal deed that stipulated the correct *tortellino* filling recipe, which is outlined above. Two years earlier, the maximum width of *tagliatelle* (8 millimeters) had been set in administrative stone in the same fashion. In 1982 the recipe for *ragù* followed. The producers and restaurateurs who comprised the membership of the Learned Confraternity had risen to the defense of their typical dishes. Faced with the challenge of manufacturers like Giovanni Rana, Bolognese pastamakers wrapped the *tortellino* in the ancient flag of civic patriotism.

The Learned Confraternity of the Tortellino were pioneers. Today, the issue at the center of Italy's civilization of the table is the same problem that faced the confraternity: how to defend the core values of genuineness and typicality from the perceived threat of industrial food. One local dish, Genoa's *pesto* sauce, reveals just how fraught that issue now is, and how delicious are the stakes.

19

Genoa, 2001–2006

Faulty Basil

The word "sublime" is used too much in food writing. But good *pesto* gives the word back its richest meanings. When eating *pesto*, the olfactory senses are so pervaded by fragrance that solid food is exalted to a point fleetingly within reach of the spiritual realm. To champion this uplifting experience, the Pesto Confraternity was formed in Genoa in 1992—on the five hundredth anniversary of Columbus's "discovery" of America. The confraternity's Grand Master, and its Order of Paladins and Knights, wisely do not stipulate a specific *pesto* recipe—the precise quantity of each of the seven ingredients depends to some extent on taste, and to some extent on how aromatic the basil is. Nevertheless the Chancellor of the Confraternity was kind enough to send me the guideline amounts used in his own family. The explanatory notes are mine:

TRUE GENOESE *PESTO*

Ingredients
100g [3½ ounces] of basil leaves from Liguria
    (Some recipes stipulate that not less than
    25 percent of the contents of the *pesto*
    by weight must be basil. Ligurian basil is

noted for having none of the minty notes
to its taste that are found in other varieties.
50g of grated [1¾ ounces] *Parmigiano-
Reggiano* cheese
50g of grated [1¾ ounces] Sardinian
pecorino cheese
30g [1 ounce] of Italian pine nuts
(Other recipes suggest that walnuts may
be used instead. But they must be from
the Mediterranean area.)
1 large clove of garlic
A pinch of unmilled salt
Enough Ligurian extra-virgin olive oil to
dissolve the mixture

Equipment
Marble mortar and wooden pestle

Some authorities point out that the basil must be gently washed
in cold water, without crushing the leaves, and then left to dry
naturally. It is recommended that, before one begins, all of the
ingredients and the equipment be allowed to reach room temperature, and that the cheese be grated and everything else be
ready to hand to avoid any undue waiting that could impair the
pesto's flavor through oxidization.

A gentle and continuous rotating movement of the pestle in
the mortar is the best way to release all the essential oils in the
basil leaves' venules. Begin with the basil, garlic, and salt until
the leaves have produced a brilliant green liquor, then add the
pine nuts, cheese, and finally the oil.

The Genoese Pesto Consortium, based in the offices of
the Ligurian regional government, advises that the finished
pesto should have a maximum 82 percent fat content, and a pH
greater than 4.8.

From a historical perspective, this elevation of *pesto*-making into a precise, refined art is anything but traditional. During the First World War, as we read, Second Lieutenant Giuseppe Chioni yearned for a *pesto* that contained parsley, onion, and spices. Just as was the case with Bolognese *tortellini*, it would seem, local food lovers have retreated into an orthodoxy when faced with the threat of cheap, industrialized versions of their typical local dishes.

But in the new *pesto* orthodoxy there is one more absolutely fundamental requirement for genuine *pesto*; it lies at the center of the strange but instructive dramas that have surrounded Genoa's much-loved sauce since July 2001. The basil used, like the oil and the cheeses, must have the proper European Union DOP certificate, meaning *Denominazione di Origine Protetta*, or Protected Designation of Origin. DOP products derive their unique characteristics from the environment of a specific place. All phases of the production process must be carried out in the area set out in the EU regulations.

Like everything else about the European Union, DOP legislation is very boring but very important: quite simply, there is a huge amount of money at stake. At last count, Italy had 155 products that have qualified either for DOP status, or for the less tightly defined IGP (*Indicazione Geografica Protetta*—Protected Geographical Indication). They range from Traditional Modena Balsamic Vinegar DOP, to the Sicilian Blood Orange IGP; from San Daniele Ham DOP, to the Mortara Goose Salame IGP; from Gorgonzola Cheese DOP, to the Tuscan Sorana Bean IGP; from Campanian Buffalo-Milk Mozzarella DOP, to the Calabrian Clementine IGP. No other country can boast as many DOPs and IGPs. Europe's move toward quality produce aimed at elite consumers is particularly well suited to Italy's diverse, specialized, and historically prestigious agriculture. Together, those typical Italian products generate annual sales of just under $16 billion. In a world where consumers are ever more sensitive to the quality of produce, and where globalization has created immense downward pressures on the price of anonymous ingredients, the little blue and yellow badge that signals a DOP pedigree can be priceless. Typical products bring exceptional rewards.

But the path to the DOP El Dorado is beset with hazards. In a global age, producing an edible symbol of local identity is tough and confusing.

• • •

In July 2001, Genoa hosted the Group of Eight conference. The arrival of George Bush, Tony Blair, and the other leaders of the world's most economically powerful nations was an opportunity for the city to show itself off to the world—which obviously meant showing off its food. The Liguria region's sixteen Michelin-starred chefs were formed into teams of four to prepare two lunches and two dinners for the attending VIPs. A month before the conference was due to begin, the menus were forwarded to the Italian Foreign Ministry for approval. Two dishes were struck from the list. The first was rabbit, apparently because it was thought that British and North American people regard rabbits as domestic animals in the same category as dogs and cats. Astonishingly, the second dish to fall foul of the diplomatic advisers was the one of which Genoa is mostly justly proud: *pesto genovese*, replaced on the menu by a "basil sauce." And the crucial difference between this dish and the orthodox *pesto* recipe? No garlic.

To many people, taking the garlic out of *pesto* offered a ready metaphor for the way the city was sanitized in preparation for the G8: there were strict exclusion zones, and inhabitants were instructed to remove washing from the lines that stretch across its narrow streets. Quite why the order to switch to "basil sauce" was given is unclear. Perhaps it was because garlic's pungent smell would discourage delegates from getting intimate; perhaps it was because the Japanese found garlic particularly unpalatable. But in the political climate of the time, one possible explanation soon acquired the ring of certainty: Silvio Berlusconi had vetoed the symbol of the city's cuisine. The media magnate, then Italian prime minister, is notoriously averse to both garlic and onion. Antiglobalization protesters with a strong sense of local pride were in no doubt, and equipped themselves with bulbs of garlic to throw at Berlusconi during the conference.

Tragically, the violence in the streets at the G8 conference in Genoa turned out to be much more serious. On July 20 in Piazza Alimonda, twenty-three-year-old local boy Carlo Giuliani was killed by a shot from a twenty-year-old *carabiniere*'s pistol. The *carabiniere* in question was later acquitted of any wrongdoing. The following night police raided a school where more antiglobalization campaigners were sleeping. As a result of what went on in that school, twenty-eight police and medical personnel are currently on trial. The charges include allegations that they administered violent beatings and refused medical attention for the victims (some of whom had broken limbs), that they urinated on those they detained, that they sang fascist songs, and that they planted false evidence in the form of two Molotov cocktails. One of the accused has admitted bringing the Molotov cocktails into the school. Those on trial will almost certainly deny the other charges. As the pugnacious satirist Beppe Grillo commented bitterly at the time, "After the G8, Genoa isn't the same any more. *Pesto alla genovese* means something different now."

Beppe Grillo is perhaps the most famous living Genoese. And he has a particularly *Italian* kind of global fame. Barred from Italy's stiflingly conformist television system for years, the bearded Grillo tours the theater circuit tirelessly, and now runs one of the most popular blog sites in the world. *Time* magazine made Grillo one of its "European heroes" in 2005, calling him "that rare class clown who does his homework." The summer after the G8 tragedy, the meaning of *pesto* shifted once more, and Grillo again made a high-profile intervention.

In July 2002 the head of Liguria's regional government, transport entrepreneur Sandro Biasotti, announced that he and his family were boycotting products made by the Swiss multinational Nestlé. Nestlé owns Barilla, one of Italy's biggest food groups: they are the people who make Mulino Bianco biscuits and Barilla pasta. The Biasotti family boycott was a response to learning that Nestlé-Barilla had "copyrighted" two types of basil with the European Union, naming them "Pesto" and "Sanremo." Biasotti was making a striking populist gesture in favor of authentic local recipes made with authentic local ingredients.

Soon afterward, the *carabinieri* reported eight companies, including Nestlé-Barilla, for producing *pesto alla genovese* that contained nonlocal ingredients. No charges followed.

At this stage in the drama Beppe Grillo used an interview in the city's leading newspaper to pop a few pieties and highlight some of the paradoxes of globalization:

The basil that they pretend is grown in our greenhouses has been coming from Vietnam for years. Basil from Vietnam and garlic from

China. The battle has been lost. And I want basil to come from Vietnam—that way the poor peasants in that part of the world can earn something too. That's what globalization is. We can't think globally and act locally by setting up protectionist regimes. . . . I'd be happy if the Germans made Parmesan cheese. I bet they'd do it better.

The *pesto* war came to a peaceful conclusion at a summit between regional governor Biasotti and the head of Nestlé in Italy. Nestlé agreed to rename its basil, and to help smooth the path toward European Union DOP certification for both Ligurian basil and Genoese *pesto*. For their part, Biasotti and various local food interests agreed to try to help *genuine* Genoese *pesto* become a product that could be transported around the world by allowing tiny modifications in its preparation that would make for better preservation. *Pesto*, Biasotti announced, could now become "an ambassador for Liguria."

It seemed to work. In 2004, an American lifestyle guru defined *trofie* with *pesto* as Seattle's "it" pasta of the moment. (*Trofie* are handmade twists.) Ligurian basil obtained its precious DOP status in October of the same year. *Pesto* itself was still waiting for the certificate.

But less than a month later came a new threat. Scientists campaigning in support of using genetically modified organisms in agriculture cited research suggesting that basil plants below a height of about four inches contain a carcinogen, methyl eugenol. The media fast-forwarded to the most alarming possible conclusion: *pesto* gives you cancer. Green politicians, farmers' organizations, and other lobbies joined the inevitable fray.

As is often the case, the science was less dramatic than the sound-bite battle. Some young basil plants do contain methyl eugenol, it seems—they need it to protect themselves from insects. Ginger and nutmeg contain it, too. But basil is harvested after the methyl eugenol has gone, and in any case the carcinogenic effects have only been recorded in animals so far, and then after massive doses. Italy's leading oncologist declared that he loved *pesto* and would be happy to eat it even if was made with young leaves. But none of this stopped the conspiracy theories from circulating. Was the engineered-foods industry behind the scare story? Or did it serve the interests of Sicilian basil producers, whose plants are taller? Or perhaps the *pesto* lobby had suppressed the scientific truth? It is unclear whether all the confusion hit *pesto* sales.

June 2006 saw yet another new organization set up to protect the delicious green sauce: the Prà Basil Park. Many *genovesi* insist that the basil for *pesto* should only come from Prà, a small plain just west of Genoa. Most DOP Ligurian basil is grown in greenhouses in Prà. The Basil Park aimed to promote the local crop, defend its producers' interests, and generally get people to eat more genuine *pesto*. These are people who have invested years of their lives and a great deal of money in making the most fragrant basil possible. But they had their work cut out from the start: two months after the Basil Park was set up, exceptional summer heat generated a freak storm, and hailstones the size of golf balls smashed the Prà greenhouses. Eighty percent of the basil crop was destroyed. The *pesto*'s off, the world's media proclaimed, and global warming was to blame.

Pine nuts or walnuts. Garlic or no garlic. Vietnamese basil or Genoese basil. GMOs or natural crops. In Italy today, the question of what counts as an authentic dish makes for both local politics and global business. At the time of writing, Genoese *pesto* is still waiting optimistically for its DOP or IGP credentials.

Pesto is only one food of many that show how Italians today enjoy the same kind of privileges, and face the same kind of political dilemmas, that only the inhabitants of the Italian cities knew in the past. Once upon a time, peasants were, metaphorically at least, locked outside the walls. In fact Italy, along with the rich world in which Italian DOP and IGP products are sold, now belongs to a vast global city. But there is no need to look beyond Italy's borders to see the modern-day counterparts of the excluded peasants of old. In fact all that is required is to look a little farther down the menu, and order spaghetti with tomato sauce instead of *trofie* with *pesto*.

Puglia is the heel of the Italian boot, the region in the opposite corner of Italy to Liguria. The tomatoes grown near the Puglian city of Foggia go to factories in Naples, Caserta, and Salerno to be tinned or made into *passata* (sieved) and concentrate. They are sold to markets in Rome and Milan to make sauces and salads. During the same summer that Prà's basil suffered from the greenhouse effect, a courageous undercover journalist exposed conditions among thousands of migrants who pick those prized tomatoes. Men and women from Rumania, Bulgaria, Uganda, and Eritrea spend fourteen hours a day working for twenty or perhaps twenty-five dollars. They endure stifling heat, racial abuse, and discipline administered with fists or iron bars. They have to ask permission to speak. They have been raped and even murdered. Foremen, some with links to organized crime, exploit them further by levying fines for lateness, and charging extortionate sums for rank water, inedible food, unsafe transport, and subhuman accommodation without any water or electricity. When the time finally comes for the workers to be paid, the foremen will often tip off the police and have them arrested as illegal immigrants.

The international humanitarian organization Médecins Sans Frontières (Doctors Without Borders) exists to provide medical relief in areas stricken by famine, disaster, and war. In 2005 and 2006 they ran clinics for the seasonal farm workers in Puglia, Sicily, and Calabria. They found "gastrointestinal disorders, dermatological and respiratory diseases and musculoskeletal pathologies" all related to the harsh living and working conditions. These are the same fields where, only two or three generations ago, stunted Italian day laborers endured malaria and police brutality to work for starvation wages. The Médecins Sans Frontières report on the farms of southern Italy is called *The Fruits of Hypocrisy*. It could just as well have been called the *Fruits of Forgetting*. After a thousand years, Italy's civilization of the table still casts a shadow of human misery.

20

Turin, 2006

Peasants to the Rescue!

It is October 26, 2006. Farmers, fisherfolk, and food artisans—4,803 of them from all over the planet—have gathered at the Slow Food movement's Terra Madre conference in an immense glass and steel hangar built for the Winter Olympics in Turin. Slow Food began in 1986 as a society of left wing gourmets incensed by the arrival of a McDonald's hamburger restaurant in Rome's historic Piazza di Spagna. (The spirit of Alberto Sordi's *mack-a-rownee* scene is still strong.) Now twenty years later, Slow Food is the dynamic heart of Italy's civilization of the table. Based in the Piedmontese town of Bra, it has evolved into nothing less than a distinctively Italian plan for good food to save the world. *Terra Madre* means "Mother Earth." The press are calling it "the peasants' United Nations." But there is more sense of purpose here than the rather hippyish title suggests, or than the United Nations has ever mustered. Terra Madre's express goal is to overthrow the global market economy. This, as the Slow Food activists assert, is a revolution.

Yet if so, it is more full of incongruities than any revolution yet seen. Terra Madre is sponsored by Lufthansa airlines, Budget car rental, and every tier of local government in the Piedmont region. As the opening ceremony approaches, a camera crew shoots footage for a feature film about the event by one of Italy's leading directors. The scene they are recording has the mood of the departures zone at an international airport, except that people seem to be waiting to board tractors, fishing smacks, and donkeys as well as jumbo jets and helicopters. Savvy London gastro-entrepreneurs and sharp-dressed Italian politicians mingle with Andean llama herders, central Armenian beekeepers, Belgian microbrewers, Javanese prawn farmers, and bean growers from the mountains of Kyrgyzstan. Terra Madre would hardly be more diverse if all the personalities in the history of Italian food were milling around in there as well; if one could spot a medieval spice merchant chatting with a First World War POW, a papal chef comparing notes with a *lazzaro*, and a humanist scholar listening intently to a ragged transatlantic migrant.

Delegates gradually assemble on a stage as wide as a soccer field beneath two giant screens framed by banners in the yellow ochre and crimson of the Terra Madre logo. Sitting before them, among the hundreds of expectant guests and other delegates, are dozens of dignitaries, including the Italian head of state, the president of the republic.

Proceedings are opened by a choir of old ladies in loud blue floral pinafores, red leggings, and broad-brimmed straw hats. Their odd garb is unmistakable to any northern Italian whose memory stretches back before the economic miracle: they are rice-weeders. Every May, until herbicides made their labor redundant in the early 1960s, women like them would come in cattle trucks from all over the Po valley to spend forty days working in the paddy fields of Vercelli and Novara. In lines of eight to a dozen abreast, they would advance barefoot through the stinking water, tormented by flies and mosquitoes as they felt for weeds with their fingers. The songs they sang then are the same ones they are keening now: they tell of heartless foremen and tightfisted bosses, of exploitation and resistance. Their message is clear: the Slow Food revolution has its roots in Italy's peasant past. The choir hails from Novi, near Modena—in a province that has done very well out of the recent balsamic vinegar boom.

After the choir of rice-weeders comes Elgar. Bizarrely, to the British imperial-era tones of the "Pomp and Circumstance" March Opus 39 in D, the 150 flags of the participating nations are borne in by a stuttering relay of traditional costumes, like an agrarian World Cup. Under the flags of Senegal and Kenya march African peasant militants who have been flown to Turin at the expense of an airline and a car rental company.

When the grand parade has finished, the politicians begin the speech making: mayors, ministers, and governors all profess themselves great enthusiasts for the peasant revolution. But their rhetoric, as assertive as it is abstract and impenetrable, cannot survive translation from Italian into any of the seven other official languages. Across the great hall, minds wander and hands fiddle with earphones. Expectation has become distracted impatience.

Then, at last, to loud cheers and prolonged applause, the founder of the Slow Food movement advances to the microphone to explain what Slow Food and Terra Madre are all about. Bald and tanned, with hollow cheeks made starker by the spotlight, Carlo Petrini wears his beard cut close and his glasses at the tip of his long nose. The look is professorial; the effect is decidedly charismatic. And like all charismatic leaders, Petrini talks in broken phrases of us versus them, of bright-burning hopes set against grave perils, of decisive moments and redemptive choices:

> We produce enough food for 12 billion living souls, and there are only 6 billion 300 thousand of us on earth. Eight hundred million people suffer from malnutrition and hunger; one billion 700 million suffer from obesity. Madness! It is madness to continue asking more from the earth. Plundering resources and obeying the logic that says all consumption must be fast, abundant and wasteful: it's all reaching the end of the line. The end of the line. . . . What isn't made clear is just how complicit we are. Just how responsible as individual consumers in the so-called developed world. . . . We are complicit, we are involved. So you, the peasants of the so-called developing world, you have to show us the way. The way to an economy that can make consumption and agriculture *local* once more. . . .
>
> You, the American delegates from the green state of California, you are building the local economy by creating farmers' markets and bringing producers and consumers closer together. You, peasants from India, are creating the local economy by fighting the multinationals' domination of seed types. . . . Italy itself has chosen to

support typical products; it has chosen to support them as part of a system which also reinforces the strong fabric of local identities that attract tourists to our beautiful country. In doing these things, whether consciously or unconsciously, Italy is bringing to life a local economy. A local economy so strong that the market economy comes and copies good ideas from our typical products and even tries to take them away from us.

We must have the strength to give this economy back to the peasants. Because food must be good, clean and fair. *Good, clean* and *fair.*

Good, absolutely good: Who said that we are condemned to eating badly? . . . Italy's gastronomic memory used to have a name: hunger. But even so that memory was shaped by the wisdom of countless women; within a subsistence economy, these women created food masterpieces that were very simple, but good.

Clean: because food cannot be produced by putting ecosystems under strain, by ruining the environment, by destroying biodiversity.

And *fair*: because the peasants must be paid. If we want young people to stay on the land, to return to the land—here, in our countries—then they must be given dignity and rewards. They must be valued. No *civilized* country enslaves foreign laborers to produce tomatoes. No *civilized* country advances organic agriculture, as California is doing, by enslaving so many Mexican growers. . . .

Delegates from all over the world, allow me to pay homage to you by paraphrasing a great Piedmontese poet: if the world can endure, then the world will owe it to people like you. . . . People who have the future of the earth in their hands.

Enjoy Terra Madre, all of you.

The auditorium is rapt, and the message feels nerve-tinglingly relevant. Petrini has said these things many times before. Yet despite all Terra Madre's incongruities and the familiarity of his message, he communicates an urgent sense of possibility that is hard to resist. Slow Food is a movement wired directly into the most sensitive issues of our age.

At the heart of the Slow Food ideal is what Petrini calls a new gastronomy. Good taste, he argues, should no longer be about hedonism. The old gastronomy constantly sought to stimulate our taste buds with

Good, clean, and fair. The charismatic founder of the Slow Food movement, Carlo Petrini, expounds the values of a new gastronomy at the opening ceremony of Terra Madre, the so-called "peasant United Nations" in Turin, 2006.

endless novelties; it was about exorbitant consumption and instant gratification; it wanted more, more, more. The old gastronomy was sometimes sophisticated, but always blind. Like the guests at the Estes' Ferrara banquet in 1529, it ignored the suffering going on beyond the city walls. The old gastronomy, to use a much more ancient word, was a form of gluttony.

In an age when gluttony on a Renaissance duke's scale is available to almost the entire Western world, the old gastronomy cannot last. Food, Petrini argues, is connected to everything, from the economy to the environment. In our globalized age, what we eat has repercussions around the planet—repercussions we cannot pretend we do not see, for modern communications have brought them over the city walls, into our homes, and into our hands. People are being impoverished, and the planet is being ravaged, to support our gluttonous lifestyles. It is time for a new gastronomy.

For the Slow Food movement's adherents, having good taste should still mean cultivating our palates. In fact the delights available to truly discriminating food connoisseurs are now greater than ever. But the new gastronomy should also involve cultivating our powers of empathy and understanding. We must season the pleasure of eating with the joys of interpreting the world and making it a better place.

The new gastronomy's ambitions are global. But it begins with the simple gestures that have always bound us together while we eat: hospitality, wholesome food, good manners, and, above all, *time*. Slow Food is about giving us all the time to transform the biological matter of feeding, and the capitalist business of consuming, into something slower and more human.

That *something* does not really have a name in the English language. The Italian word for it is *commensalità*; it means "companionship at table." Used by Slow Food, it suggests that eating is a great reminder of our common humanity. But what *commensalità* also suggests is that no country other than Italy could have generated such a far-reaching food philosophy. There is so much about the Slow Food movement that has its roots in Italy: its stress on what is simple and genuine; its pleasure in typical foods that express a sense of place and identity; its historical memory of plenty cruelly juxtaposed with hunger; its underlying belief in the sheer importance of eating. Through the ideals of Slow Food, it would seem, the Italian civilization of the table is reaching out to embrace the world.

But as the applause for Petrini's speech fades, Terra Madre's incongruities loom once more in the mind: the contrast between its titanic aims and humble means; the attempt to yoke postmodern communications to premodern agriculture; the seemingly far-fetched dream of a common cause that will unite hedonistic First World consumers and hard-pressed Third World producers. This sense of strange contradictions persists on leaving the Terra Madre hangar and strolling a few yards through the exceptionally warm autumn sunshine to the Salone del Gusto—Slow Food's "Taste Show."

The Fiat automobile factory at Lingotto is the great Italian symbol of the postindustrial age. Once it was a manufacturing plant so big that it seemed to be a city in its own right—its front runs along the roadside for over a mile. In 1982 it was converted into a university, a shopping mall, and a series of vast exhibition spaces. The Slow Food taste show takes up no less than four of those exhibition spaces and has filled them with food stalls and miniature restaurants. It is the world's largest international urban food market. Signposts tell you the way to "Cheese Street," "Cereals Street," and "Fruit, Vegetables and Spices Street."

The initial impression is of the worst kind of sales-time frenzy. There is an insistent, exhausting din as tens of thousands of visitors, who have each paid twenty-seven dollars, jostle for cocktail-stick tasters of smoked fish, preserved eggplant, or bread dipped in olive oil. A twenty-minute tour of the taste show yields enough marketing leaflets to fill an oxcart. Long and eager lines form outside gleaming corporate stands as salespeople hand out free jars of pasta sauce, slices of *prosciutto*, or chunks of Parmesan. The whole of the fourth exhibition space is taken up by Slow Food's highly popular "Taste Workshops." Here anyone—or at least anyone with enough foresight to have booked days in advance— can hear internationally renowned experts explaining the finer points of everything from Chinese bamboo to Scottish beef.

There is history here, too. But among all the noise and color, it is never quite clear what is genuine tradition and what is White Mill kitsch.

The biggest crowds form before the stall run by one of Palermo's best pastry shops. Its products are disappearing as fast as they can be made: mini-*cannoli*, marzipan tomatoes and lemons, slices of *cassata*— the dessert with "more than ten centuries of history" behind it, according to the makers.

The provincial council of Ferrara has brought an ultramodern eatery to the taste show. Here a plasma screen projects images of the misty Po delta landscape as a chef with a microphone lectures diners about the dishes placed before them on plastic plates. The menu includes marinated Comacchio eel, smoked fillet of goose breast, and a wonderful pumpkin *risotto* whose creaminess is set off superbly by a spoonful of "Ancient Cristoforo da Messisbugo Condiment." A kind of cousin of balsamic vinegar, the condiment in question was concocted in 2000 and named after the Este dynasty's faithful steward by the enterprising proprietor of an *agriturismo*. Her aim, as explained in a beautifully produced leaflet, is a taste that conjures up the "history of the peasants who have loved, lived on, and worked our land." Messisbugo would have been flattered, but probably also mystified.

At the *mortadella* stall, visitors make repeat passes, unable to resist jabbing their cocktail sticks into the little cubes of pink meat. Meanwhile, a prominent Bolognese manufacturer gesticulates confidently as he gives an interview to a local television station. Amid the plastic vines and grapes of the display that surrounds him, magnificent string-bound sausages sit alongside framed copies of the cardinal-legate's 1661 proclamation against butchers who adulterate their *mortadelle*.

In a separate auditorium in one corner of the taste show, Mario Soldati's 1957 television documentary *In Search of Genuine Foods* is being projected to a new audience. In the opposite corner, a specially built wooden kiosk dispenses such typical Roman dishes as roast chestnuts, deep-fried salt cod, and *supplì* (rice balls with a crunchy coating and melting mozzarella center). The kiosk has STREET FOOD chalked in English down its sides.

The restaurant run by the Emilia-Romagna regional government serves only dishes adapted from *Science in the Kitchen and the Art of Eating Well*. Beside a giant poster of Pellegrino Artusi in his muttonchop whiskers, a leading politician poses for photographs. Artusi hated politicians almost as much as he hated priests.

Yet amid all the promotional hullabaloo, the Slow Food gospel of *good, clean*, and *fair* still manages to make itself heard. One of the movement's most pressing concerns is the way industrial agriculture ruthlessly promotes a few hyperproductive crops, such as maize and soya, at the expense of both biodiversity and gastronomic variety. Slow Food's Ark of Taste was launched in 1997 to catalogue the thousands of edible species and traditional products that are in danger of extinction. So pride of place among the taste show stalls goes to the Presidia. These are small bodies set up to guarantee a viable future for foods and species listed in the Ark of Taste—whether by bringing new marketing expertise, or by helping improve manufacturing standards. Slow Food's reasoning is that if we rediscover a taste for these vulnerable flavors, then we will nurture both them and the human ways of life that are intertwined with them.

There are 195 Italian Presidia. Among the tastes they protect are the distinctively buttery, toasted hazel flavor of a hard sheep's milk cheese or *pecorino* produced only near Osilo in Sardinia. And the aromatic hams and *salami* made from the tiny, hairy semiferal black pig from the Nebrodi mountains in eastern Sicily. And the small yellow-green *zolfino* bean; this early modern import from the Americas has almost disappeared from the markets and tables of Tuscany, where it is dressed with good olive oil and accompanies steak. And the Basilicata region's dark, oven-baked olives from Ferrandina, which are excellent dressed with garlic and lemon or orange zest.

There are ninety-one Presidia in the rest of the world. In the United States, for example, there are five such groups looking out for foods like Cape May oysters and the *manoomin* wild rice gathered by the Native American Anishinaabeg people—Slow Food gourmets describe its taste as "richly complex with subtle earthy notes of mushrooms and wood smoke." In the British Isles, Irish raw milk cheeses, Cornish pilchards, and artisan-made Somerset cheddar have their own appointed Slow Food guardians. Among the steep Himalayan terraces in the Indian state of Uttar Pradesh, four endangered varieties of basmati rice, including the exquisite *dehradhuni* with its hints of sandalwood, are shielded by a Presidium that includes more than 60,000 peasants. The basmati Presidium runs seed banks, supports organic agriculture, and promotes the rice on the international market. In 2005 Slow Food's Foundation for Biodiversity financed the purchase of a vacuum-packing machine for the growers.

The Slow Food taste show is like that: just when it seems easy to dismiss it all as a vast marketing operation, you come across an initiative so compelling in its mix of idealism and practical know-how that it is impossible not to be won over.

Judged by criteria of flavor and by these local initiatives, Slow Food has been a storming success. But its broader analysis and ultimate goals deserve more critical scrutiny. Is a thoroughgoing Slow Food revolution really the way, finally, to take the barbarism out of our food civilization? Economists would be skeptical about the movement's antiglobal market ethos. They would argue that many of the world's food problems are caused not by too *much* market rigor, but by too *little*: the most scandalous case being the subsidies that Western governments pay to their own farmers, and the resultant dumping of cut-price goods in the Third World. A related question arises from Beppe Grillo's Vietnamese basil growers. Is Europe's move to prestige goods with DOP and IGP status just another way of shutting off the developing world from the benefits of trade? Then there are the food scientists who argue that organic farming uses much more land than conventional agriculture—and more energy for plowing.

Petrini often endorses the view that Italian food history is best embodied in the peasantry. That is a highly selective and rather sentimental account. Good food has rarely been on the side of the poor, and much of the diversity that Slow Food seeks to protect was itself generated by specialization for urban markets. Petrini is also sniffy about fusion cuisine, and rather quiet about the ethnic foods that are such an exciting feature of the way many Western cities now eat. Thus he leaves unanswered the question of how Slow Food's "local economy" can accommodate the Moroccan couscous restaurants in Turin's San Salvario quarter, or the Sri Lankan spice stalls in the Piazza Vittorio market in Rome. And he forgets perhaps that Italian culinary culture would simply be unrecognizable without the long-range influence of the Arab world, the Americas, and France, and without the migration within and between its regions. All food, ultimately, is fusion food.

It would be unfair to imply that some of these objections have not occurred to the Slow Foodistas: the movement's literature is critical of unfair subsidies, for example. Nor could anyone who has been to Terra Madre dismiss the organization as antitechnological or antiscientific. Slow Food may have its incongruities, in short, but many of them are simply the incongruities of our age.

Slow Food has set a new example for the world's food conversation. We badly need more places where people from across the planet can take part in that conversation in the way they do at the Terra Madre conference, and through the Slow Food network. We also need that conversation to be based on better information. We need fewer folksy traditions, and much clearer labels. The food we eat must now tell us better stories about its history, where it has come from, the ingenuity and effort that have gone into making it, and what it has cost in human and environmental terms. Slow Food may think of itself as a peasant revolution, but in many ways it is an expression of Italy's long tradition of city eating, its civilization of the table. For what urban Italians have done again and again over the past thousand years is use food to create identities for themselves. As befits the inheritors of that tradition, Petrini and his followers are trying to pioneer a new identity, a global form of citizenship that takes the politics of food as seriously as its flavor.

Acknowledgments

It would have been impossible to write this book without an enormous amount of assistance. In fact so many people have helped me that I have almost certainly forgotten to mention some of them here. I hope they will accept my apologies in advance.

I am lucky enough to have two colleagues in the Italian Department at University College London whose expertise is only equaled by the generosity with which they shared it: Catherine Keen and Dilwyn Knox. Michael Broers, Helen Dixon, Ida Fazio, Donna Gabaccia, Giulio and Laura Lepschy, Duncan McConnell, Jonathan Morris, Stuart Oglethorpe, Brian Richardson, Martin Thom, and Stuart Woolf also provided highly valuable advice and information. I have learned a great deal from some of the extremely well-informed people who were patient enough to allow me to rehearse my ideas on them: the incomparable Matthew Fort, Giorgio Locatelli, Fiona Richmond, Jane Stewart-Smith, and Benedetta Vitali at the marvelous Zibibbo in Florence. Paul Ginsborg, Ayse Saraçgil, Giovanni Contini, and Giuseppina Caputo supplied endless food for thought during a memorable dinner in Florence. Giuseppina also passed on her grandfather's beautiful First World War recipe collection to me.

My colleagues in the Italian Department at UCL along with the Arts and Humanities Research Council deserve my gratitude for providing the time needed to complete my research and writing.

Roberta Chioni was kind enough to allow me access to her grandfather's wonderful cookbook from the First World War—the case for publishing it seems to me to be overwhelming. No houseguest can ever have been offered a more delicious or historically informative meal than the Artusian lunch of *passatelli*, *tortellini*, and rabbit fricassee that Iain Antony MacLeod and Marina Ardito prepared for me in Florence. Marina and her sister also guided me around the cuisine of Bologna, where the staff of the famous Diana restaurant allowed me into their kitchens to see the making of *tortellini*. Laura Bonamici, Federica Fornasier, Donatella Trotti, and Nicola Cipani were very articulate in their disgust. Sam Barnish and Anne Alwis deserve my thanks for their translations, respectively, of Cassiodorus and of the inscription on Theodoric's dining room floor. Cesarina Perrone, Alfredo Rubino, and Nino Rosolia explained some of the wonders of Sicilian cuisine to me in Marsala. Michele Nani and Marco Poltronieri were expert and entertaining guides to Ferrara and its food—Michele's parents introduced me to *salama da sugo* and other local delights. Laila Tentoni was enormously helpful during my visits to Forlimpopoli. Fabio Caffarena was a generous host at the Archivio Ligure della Scrittura Popolare in Genoa and offered me many precious insights. Mariella Console provided kind hospitality in Turin. John Irving was a beacon in the *Salone del Gusto* storm; he also introduced me to Mario Soldati's extraordinary documentary series and, with Geoff Andrews, helped me clarify my thinking about the Slow Food movement. Pietro Attilio Uslengo, *Cancelliere della Confraternita del Pesto*, supplied his family's own *pesto* recipe.

I relied heavily on many people who were patient and perceptive enough to read and comment on long sections of the typescript: Andrew Carrick, Robert Gordon, Radoyka Miljevic, Doug Taylor, Rob and Dave Webb. Two people, John Foot and Prue James, were nothing less than heroic in their devotion to the cause of improving my substance and style. Andy Jameson was a perceptive reader, and the ideal traveling companion for a trans-Apennine eating expedition; Andy's team at Basis also deserve my thanks for their impromptu focus group on the book jackets.

Several people have helped me hunt down sources: Molly Cygan in New York, Eddie Zengeni in Rome, Michael McDermott in London, Silvia Alessandri in Florence, and Melanie Baldo in Milan. Giampiera Arrigoni and Liliana Picciotto enabled me to get my hands on works by Fernanda Momigliano at short notice. Leading South American gourmand Tony Walters astounded me with the breadth of his knowledge and helped convince me that trying to write world history of Italian food was folly. Writing *Delizia!* would have been considerably harder had Elizabeth David not bequeathed her cookbook collection to the Warburg Institute. The staff in the British Library, particularly in Humanities 2, still deserve a big pay raise.

My sincere thanks are also due to my alchemical agent, Catherine Clarke; to my neighbor from staircase 16 Old Quad; to Josine Meijer for her help with the illustrations; and to the people at Hodder and Free Press, particularly my editors, Rupert Lancaster and Leslie Meredith, who have been perceptive and cheerful guides through the whole process.

While I was writing, Sarah Penny managed to take on the bulk of the care for our little boy, Elliot, while at the same time working full-time and redrafting a book that is much better than this one. She inspires me with love and disbelief in equal measure. *Delizia!* is dedicated to her, to Elliot, and to his forthcoming sibling.

Notes on Sources

Every reasonable effort has been made to acknowledge the ownership of the copyrighted material included in this volume. Any errors that may have occurred are inadvertent, and will be corrected in subsequent editions provided notification is sent to the author. All translations are the author's own, unless stated.

1. Tuscany: Don't Tell the Peasants . . .

3   "There were real processions. Hundreds of people came to visit the mill at weekends": translated from T. Biancolatte, "Il principio fu il mulino: Bianco," interview with Andrea Burchianti, www.kataweb.it/spec/articolo_speciale.jsp?ids=684850&id=684691.

2. Palermo, 1154: Pasta and the Planisphere

17   I have taken my translation of the title of al-Idrisi's book from A. Metcalfe, *Muslims and Christians in Norman Sicily*, London, 2003, p. 101.

18   "The Apulian and the Calabrian, the Sicilian and the African all serve me": H. T. Houben, *Roger II of Sicily: A Ruler Between East and West*, Cambridge, 2002, p. 83.

3. Milan, 1288: Power, Providence, and Parsnips

30   "There is a mountain": *Decameron*, VIII, 3.

42   "No one has bothered to count Milan's wars during the third quarter of the thirteenth century": L. Martines, *Power and Imagination: City-States in Renaissance Italy*, London, 2002, p. 96.

4. Venice, 1300s: Chinese Whispers

51   All quotations from *Book for Cook* are translated from the text in E. Faccioli (ed.), *Arte della cucina dal XIV al XIX secolo*, Milan, 1966, vol. 1, pp. 61–105.

5. Rome, 1468: Respectable Pleasure

63   "There are parts which look like thick woods, and wild beasts, hares, foxes, deer and even so it is said porcupines breed in caves": P. Partner, *Renaissance Rome, 1500–1559: A Portrait of a Society*, Berkeley, 1976.

67   I have followed Mary Ella Milham's dating of Platina's *Respectable Pleasure*, and her account of the text's relationship to Martino.

68   "There is no reason why we should prefer our ancestors' tastes to our own": this translation of Platina, like the others in this chapter, is taken from M. E. Milham (ed.), *Platina: On Right Pleasure and Good Health*, Tempe, Ariz., 1998.

75   "Paul II loved to have a great variety of dishes at his table": translation, slightly amended, of Platina, *The Lives of the Popes, from the time of our Saviour Jesus Christ to the Reign of Sixtus IV*, trans. Sir P. Rycaut, London, 1688, p. 416.

6. Ferrara, 1529: A Dynasty at Table

96   "Fish, birds, quadrupeds and other comestibles": translated from A. Frizzi, *Memorie per la storia di Ferrara*, vol. 4, Ferrara, 1848, p. 310.

97   The historian who refers to Renée's entourage as an "unscrupulous mafia" is E. Lanzoni, *Ferrara: Una città nella storia*, Ferrara, 1984, p. 315.

7. Rome, 1549–50: Bread and Water for Their Eminences

111   "The Cardinals are now on the one dish regime": translated from F. Petruccelli della Gattina, *Histoire diplomatique des conclaves*, Paris, 1864–65, vol. 2, p. 40.

118   "The biggest laugh in the world": quoted in Pastor, *History of the Popes*, vol. 13, p. 48n.

118   My account of the history of Roman offal dishes draws on G. Ciampi, "L'alimentazione popolare a Roma e nell'Agro romano," in Capatti et al. *L'alimentazione*.

8. Bologna, 1600s: The Game of Cockaigne

139   My account of the history of the word *mortadella* draws on V. Valente, "*Mortadella di Firenze*," *Lingua Nostra*, vol. 49, 1988.

141   The 1644 *mortadella* recipe is from V. Tanara, *L'economia del cittadino in villa*, Bologna, 1644.

143   Quotations from Labat are from his *Voyages du P. Labat de l'ordre des FF. Precheurs en Espagne et en Italie*, Paris, 1730, tome 2, p. 284.

143   The 1588 law against gaming is quoted from *Costume e società nei giochi a stampa di Giuseppe Maria Mitelli*, Perugia, 1988, p. 63.

9. Naples, late 1700s: *Maccheroni*-Eaters

146   This chapter draws particularly on Emilio Sereni's justly famous essay, "Note di storia dell'alimentazione nel Mezzogiorno: i napoletani da 'mangiafoglia' a 'mangiamaccheroni,'" in his collection of essays, *Terra nuova e buoi rossi*, Turin, 1981, as well as on Franco Benigno's brilliant recent research on the history of the *lazzaroni* begun in his *Specchi sulla rivoluzione: Conflitto e identità politica nell'Europa moderna*, Rome, 1999, and developed further in F. Benigno, "Trasformazioni discorsive e identità sociali: il caso dei *lazzari*," *Storica*, vol. 31, 2005.

146   The account of the Grand Tourists' attitudes to Italian food draws on and takes quotes from C. Chard, *Pleasure and Guilt on the Grand Tour*, Manchester, 1999. I have also quoted from A. Miller, *Letters from Italy, Describing the Manners, Customs, Antiquities, Paintings &c of that Country in the Years MDCCLXX and MDCCLXXI*, Dublin, 1776, 3 vols., vol. 2, p. 89.

147   My account of the development of British food is based on Stephen Mennell's *All Manners of Food: Eating and Taste in England and France from the Middle Ages to the Present*, Chicago, 1996. I also drew on this fascinating study in my paragraph on French food in the following chapter.

148   The quotation from Boswell comes from J. Boswell, *Boswell on the Grand Tour: Italy, Corsica, and France 1765–1766*, New York, 1955, p. 6.

148   The various quotations from Goethe are all from the Penguin edition of his *Italian Journey*.

150   "When a *lazzarone* has earned four or five coins to have some macaroni for the day": Joseph Thomas d'Espinchal, *Journal d'émigration*, Paris, 1912, p. 83.

155   "I do not know whether Naples does not surpass London for the insolence of the people": W. A. Mozart, *The Letters of Mozart and His Family*, E. Anderson (ed.), London, 1989.

161   "He seized it in his fingers, twisting and pulling it about, and cramming it voraciously into his mouth": M. Kelly, *Reminiscences*, London, 1975.

166   "The *lazzaroni*, these astonishing men, are heroes": translated from A. Consiglio, *Lazzari e Santa Fede*, Milan, 1936, p. 172.

10. Turin, 1846: *Viva l'Italia!*

171   The quotation from Valerio's toast comes from L. Valerio, *Carteggio (1825–1865)*, vol. 2 (1842–47). Turin, 1994, p. lxxi.

174   All quotations from Chapusot, including the banquet menu, come from F. Chapusot, *La cucina sana, economica ed elegante*, Bologna, 1990 (Turin, 1846).

178   "Turinese cuisine has a good reputation among gastronomists": P. Baricco, *Torino*, Turin, 1869, p. 42.

179 Focus groups on Italian tourists' attitudes to London pubs conducted by the author on behalf of Basis.

11. Naples, 1884: Pinocchio Hates Pizza

186 Dumas quoted from *Le Corricolo*, in *Oeuvres*, vol. 6, Brussels, 1843, pp. 561–62.

187 The letter from the royal household regarding pizza can be viewed at www.brandi.it/index3.html.

189 My account of the 1884 cholera epidemic, and of cholera's effects on its victims, is drawn from F. M. Snowden, *Naples in the Time of Cholera, 1884–1911*, Cambridge, U.K., 1995.

191 "'See Naples and die.' Well I do not know that one would necessarily die after merely seeing it": M. Twain, *The Innocents Abroad, or The New Pilgrims' Progress*, Hartford, Conn., 1869.

192 The Tuscan who entered the low city of Naples was Renato Fucini, and the quotation comes from R. Fucini, *Napoli a occhio nudo*, Turin, 1976, p. 29.

192 "A people steeped in ignorance and superstition, and overwhelmed by sorrow and fear": "Southern Italy," *The Times*, September 16, 1884.

193 "Almost crazy with enthusiasm for the King": "Plague scenes in Naples,"; *New York Times*, September 14, 1884.

194 The Neapolitan biographer of Queen Margherita is V. De Napoli, *L'eterna bellezza della Regina Margherita di Savoia*, Naples, 1894, quoted from p. 69.

12. Florence, 1891: Pellegrino Artusi

196 All quotations from Pellegrino Artusi, *La scienza in cucina e l'arte di mangiar bene*, come from the 1974 edition published by Einaudi, Turin.

201 The description of the Ferryman's carnival meal is quoted in R. Ragazzini, M. Casalini, R. Casalini, *Il Passatore: Le imprese brigantesche di Stefano Pelloni nella Romagna ottocentesca*, Cesena, 1998, p. 175.

202 The quotations from Artusi commenting on the events of his own life come from *Autobiografia*, Milan, 1993.

211 "We're stuck in front of these ovens almost the whole day": Domenico Amaducci, who ate with Artusi near the end of his life and wrote of the experience in "Incontro con Pellegrino Artusi," *Forum Popili*, 1961, p. 41.

13. Genoa, 1884–1918: Emigrants and Prisoners

226 The spaghetti with meatballs recipe comes from S. Gibbs Campbell, "Spaghetti for Americans," *Macaroni Journal*, October 15, 1929, reproduced with the kind permission of the National Pasta Association.

227 All quotations from the story of Marco Polo's sailing companion are from Anon., "A Saga of Cathay," *Macaroni Journal*, October 15, 1929, reproduced with the kind permission of the National Pasta Association.

230 "Consumption is up. The peasants are less sober—": V. Teti, "Emigrazione, alimentazione, culture popolari," in P. Bevilacqua, A. De Clementi, E. Franzina (eds.), *Storia dell'emigrazione italiana*, vol. 1, *Partenze*, Rome, 2001, p. 581.

233 "Desperation, hunger, guts tortured by hunger: continual wasting away": Gadda, *Giornale di Guerra e di prigionia*, in *Saggi giornali favole e altri scritti*, II, C. Vela et al. (eds.), Milan, 1992, p. 746. The other two quotes from hungry POWs are taken from Giovanna Procacci, *Soldati e prigionieri italiani nella Grande guerra*, Turin, 2000, pp. 303–4.

234 All quotations from the Chioni recipe book are reproduced with the kind permission of Roberta Chioni, the manuscript's owner.

234 "There are continual disputes over trifles: there are cries against injustice when an extra piece of potato falls into someone else's bowl": Procacci, *Soldati e prigionieri italiani nella Grande guerra*, p. 307.

14. Rome, 1925–38: Mussolini's Rustic Village

244 "Fascism declares that the materialistic conception": Mussolini, "La dottrina del fascismo," in *Scritti e discorsi di Benito Mussolini*, vol. 8, Milan, 1934, p. 79.

15. Turin, 1931: The Holy Palate Tavern

252 All descriptions of Futurist dishes are quoted from Marinetti and Fillìa, *La cucina futurista*, Milan, 1986 edition.

16. Milan, 1936: Housewives and Epicures

256 "Without leaving home and hearth their hands are working and their hearts beating for the Nation": quoted in P. R. Willson, "Cooking the Patriotic Omelette: Women and the Italian Fascist Ruralization Campaign," *European History Quarterly*, vol. 27, no. 4, 1997.

258 "Girls! Kindly mothers! Women of Italy!": F. Momigliano, *Vivere bene in tempi difficili: Come le donne affrontano le crisi economiche*, Milan, 1933, pp. 7–8. All other Momigliano quotations in this section of the chapter are from the same source.

263 "Jewish *risotto* is exquisite, and it can be appreciated by everyone, whatever faith they profess!": this and other quotations from F. Momigliano, *Mangiare all'italiana*, Milan, 1936.

263 My account of the history of Jewish cuisine in Italy draws on A. Toaff, *Mangiare alla giudia: La cucina ebraica in Italia dal Rinascimento all'età moderna*, Bologna, 2000.

265 "Forty years ago or so, eggplant and fennel were rarely seen": P. Artusi, *La scienza in cucina e l'arte di mangiar bene*, Turin, 1974, p. 363.

17. Rome, 1954: Miracle Food

280 "The heart of what we now consider the Mediterranean diet": A. Keys, "Mediterranean Diet and Public Health: Personal Reflections," *American Journal of Clinical Nutrition*, 61, 1995, p. 396.

288 The Artusi soup recipe in this chapter comes from *La scienza in cucina e l'arte di mangiar bene*. The other *ribollita* recipe I have synthesized from numerous sources, both printed and oral.

18. Bologna, 1974: *Mamma's Tortellini*

290 I would particularly like to thank Stephen Gundle for his advice on this chapter, which draws on his excellent essay on Sophia Loren for its account of the development of her persona.

293 "This book is dearer to me than any successful film": Sophia Loren, *Eat with Me*, London, 1972, p. 7.

297 "Like a general in front of a map of Italy": quoted in E. Invernizzi, *Pasta, amore e fantasia: La ricetta del successo del Pastificio Rana*, Milan, 2006, p. 31.

300 "We have at our disposal food, and very good food it is very often, from any part of the world, every day of the year": Loren, *Eat with Me*, p. 62.

19. Genoa 2001–2006: Faulty Basil

307 "The basil that they pretend is grown in our greenhouses." "Beppe Grillo: 'E' una battaglia persa,'" interview with Renzo Parodi in *Il Secolo XIX*, July 24, 2002.

20. Turin, 2006: Peasants to the Rescue!

313 "We produce enough food for 12 billion living souls, and there are only 6 billion 300 thousand of us on earth": Petrini's speech translated from the press release distributed at Terra Madre, 2006, and quoted with the kind permission of Slow Food, Bra.

Bibliography

Since the day I went to the White Mill, the greatest pleasure that this book has brought me has been simply talking. Italians love to talk about food. They talk about it at a length that initially seems stupefying to foreigners. The conversation began in the Italian cities of the Middle Ages. It is now also conducted in books and newspapers, on television, and via the Internet. Without the support of that ongoing discussion Italy's civilization of the table would quickly decline. So presenting its most articulate and informed passages was one of my most important aims in *Delizia!* That is why I owe such a great debt to the leading historians of Italian food.

There are several historians whose work I referred to constantly while researching and writing *Delizia!*, most notably Aldo Capatti and Massimo Montanari, who also deserve my particular thanks for being such good company at table. The work of Piero Camporesi and Bruno Laurioux has also been a constant source of stimulation.

As readers familiar with the work of the above scholars will know, the idea that cities offer the best viewpoint on the history of Italian food is not my invention, although *Delizia!* does push that thesis further than anyone has done before. Some of the sources I use were discovered by others; some of my arguments also echo the findings of the now-extensive research into Italian food history.

The following books are an essential starting point for anyone seeking to find out more about Italian food and its history. Although the authors' names do not appear in the text of *Delizia!*, I have learned a great deal from them.

P. Camporesi, *Alimentazione, folclore, società*, Parma, 1980.

P. Camporesi, "Introduzione," in P. Artusi, *La scienza in cucina e l'arte di mangiar bene*, Turin, 1974.

A. Capatti, A. De Bernardi, A. Varni (eds.), *Storia d'Italia. Annali 13. L'alimentazione*, Turin, 1998. (Individual essays are referenced below as coming from Capatti et al., *L'alimentazione*.)

A. Capatti and M. Montanari, *La cucina italiana: Storia di una cultura*, Laterza, 1999.

E. Faccioli (ed.), *Arte della cucina dal XIV al XIX secolo*, 2 vols., Milan, 1966.

J. L. Flandrin and M. Montanari (eds.), *Storia dell'alimentazione*, Rome-Bari, 1997. (Individual essays are referenced below as coming from Flandrin and Montanari, *Storia dell'alimentazione*.)

P. Meldini, "A tavola e in cucina," P. Melograni (ed.), *La famiglia italiana dall'Ottocento a oggi*, Rome-Bari, 1988.

M. Montanari, *La fame e l'abbondanza: Storia dell'alimentazione in Europa*, Rome-Bari, 1997.

M. Montanari, *Il cibo come cultura*, Rome-Bari, 2005.

S. Serventi and F. Sabban, *La pasta: Storia e cultura di un cibo universale*, Rome-Bari, 2000.

P. Sorcinelli, *Gli italiani e il cibo: Dalla polenta ai cracker*, Milan, 1999.

There is one work of reference that deserves to be mentioned here since it also constitutes an invaluable source of clues to the many obscure aspects of Italian food history: *Grande dizionario della lingua italiana*, S. Battaglia (ed.), Turin, 1961–2002.

1. Tuscany: Don't Tell the Peasants . . .

T. Biancolatte, "Il principio fu il mulino: Bianco," interview with Andrea Burchianti, www.kataweb.it/spec/articolo_speciale.jsp?ids=684850&id=684691.

W. Benjamin, "Theses on the Philosophy of History," in *Illuminations*, London, 1973.

G. Giusti and G. Capponi, *Dizionario dei proverbi italiani*, Milan, 1956.

A. Ivardi Ganapini and G. Gonizzi (eds.), *Barilla: Cento anni di pubblicità e comunicazione*, Milan, 1994.

D. Merlini, *Saggio di ricerche sulla satira contro il villano*, Turin, 1894.

G. Pittano, *Frase fatta capo ha: Dizionario dei modi di dire, proverbi e locuzioni*, Bologna, 1996.

"La svolta del Mulino Bianco," *La Repubblica*, October 16, 2005.

L. Vercelloni, "La modernità alimentare," in Capatti et al., *L'alimentazione*.

Mulino Bianco, www.ilmulinobianco.it.

Il Mulino delle Pile, www.agriturismoilmulino.com.

2. Palermo, 1154: Pasta and the Planisphere

D. Abulafia, "The End of Muslim Sicily," in D. Abulafia, *Commerce and Conquest in the Mediterranean, 1100–1500*, Aldershot, 1993.

D. Abulafia, "The Kingdom of Sicily under the Hohenstaufen and Angevins," in D. Abulafia (ed.), *The New Cambridge Medieval History*, vol. 5, c. 1198–c. 1300, Cambridge, U.K., 1999.

A. Ahmad, *A History of Islamic Sicily*, Edinburgh, 1975.

M. Amari, *L'Italia descritta nel "Libro del Re Ruggero,"* Rome, 1883.

M. Amari, *Storia dei musulmani di Sicilia*, Catania, 1933–39, vol. 3, part 3.

P. Amédée Jaubert, *Géographie d'édrisi: Traduite de l'arabe en français*, Paris, 1836 (vol. 1) and 1840 (vol. 2).

C. Battisti and G. Alessio, *Dizionario etimologico italiano*, Florence, 1951.

G. B. Cardona, "Marzapane," *Lingua Nostra*, 1969, 2.

G. Coria, *Profumi di Sicilia: Il libro della cucina siciliana*, Palermo, 1981.

M. Cortelazzo and P. Zolli, *Dizionario etimologico della lingua italiana*, Bologna, 1983.

N. Daniel, *The Arabs and Mediaeval Europe*, London, 1979.

A. Denti di Pirajno, *Il gastronomo educato*, Vicenza, 1964.

V. Di Giovanni, *La topografia antica di Palermo dal secolo X al XV*, 2 vols., Palermo, 1889 and 1890.

Abu al Qasim Muhammad ibn Hawqal, "Dal Kitab al masalik ecc." (*Libro delle vie e dei reami*), in M. Amari (ed.), *Bibioteca arabo-sicula*, vol. 1, Turin, 1880.

S. D. Goitein, "Sicily and Southern Italy in the Cairo Geniza documents," *Archivio Storico per la Sicilia Orientale*, vol. 1, 1971.

H. T. Houben, *Roger II of Sicily: A Ruler Between East and West*, Cambridge, U.K., 2002.

Idrisi, *La première géographie de l'Occident*, Paris, 1999.

La géographie d'Idrîsî: Un atlas du monde au XIIe siècle (CD), Paris, 2000.

D. Keene, "Towns and the Growth of Trade," in D. Luscombe and J. Riley-Smith (eds.), *The New Cambridge Medieval History*, vol. 4 *c. 1024–c. 1198*, Cambridge, U.K., 1999.

H. Kennedy, "Sicily and al-Andalus under Muslim Rule," in T. Reuter (ed.), *The New Cambridge Medieval History*, vol. 3, *c.900–c. 1024*, Cambridge, U.K., 1999.

I. Kratchkovsky, "Les géographes arabes des XIe et XIIe siècles en Occident," *Annales de l'Institut d'Etudes Orientales*, 1960–61.

R. S. Lopez, *The Commercial Revolution of the Middle Ages, 950–1350*, Cambridge, U.K., 1976.

M. Loria and S. Quadruppani, *Alla tavola di Yasmina: Sette storie e cinquanta ricette di Sicilia al profumo d'Arabia*, Milan, 2004.

G. A. Loud, "Southern Italy in the Eleventh Century" and "Norman Sicily in the Twelfth Century," both in D. Luscombe and J. Riley-Smith (eds.), *The New Cambridge Medieval History*, vol. 4, *c. 1024–c. 1198*, part 2, Cambridge, U.K., 2004.

A. Metcalfe, *Muslims and Christians in Norman Sicily*, London, 2003.

G. Oman, "al-Idrisi," in *Encyclopedia of Islam*, vol. 3, London, 1971.

G. Palermo Patera, *Palermo araba*, Palermo, 1991.

G. Pardi, "L'Italia nel XII secolo descritta da un geografo arabo," in *Memorie Geografiche*, supplement to *Rivista Geografica Italiana*, vol. 13, 1919.

F. B. Pegolotti, *La pratica della mercatura*, Cambridge, Mass., 1970.

G. B. Pellegrini, "MARTABANA-MARZAPANE," *Lingua Nostra*, 1976, pp. 3–4.

T. Peterson, "The Arab Influence on Western European Cooking," *Journal of Medieval History*, vol. 6, no.3, 1980.

G. Pitrè, *Spettacoli e feste popolari siciliane*, Palermo, 1881.

A. Prati, *Vocabolario etimologico italiano*, Milan, 1951.

O. Redon and B. Laurioux, "L'apparition et la diffusion des pâtes sèches en Italie (XIIIe–XVIe siècles)," in D. Garcia and D. Meeks (eds.), *Techniques et économie antiques et médiévales*, Paris, 1997.

O. Redon and B. Laurioux, "La constitution d'une nouvelle catégorie culinaire? Les pâtes dans les livres de cuisine italiens de la fin du Moyen Age," *Médiévales*, vols. 16–17, 1989.

B. Rosenberger, "La cucina araba e il suo apporto alla cucina europea," in Flandrin and Montanari, *Storia dell'alimentazione*.

B. Rosenberger, "Les pâtes dans le monde musulman," *Médiévales*, vols. 16–17, 1989.

L. Sada, *Spaghetti e compagni*, Bari, 1982.

N. Sapio Bartelletti, *La cucina siciliana nobile e popolare*, Milan, 1980.

J. Schacht and C. E. Bosworth (eds.), *The Legacy of Islam*, Oxford, 1974.

E. Valli, *La cucina siciliana*, Bologna, 1997.

A. Varvaro, *Vocabolario etimologico siciliano*, vol. 1, Palermo, 1986.

L. Zaouali, *L'Islam a tavola: Dal Medioevo a oggi*, Rome-Bari, 2004.

3. Milan, 1288: Power, Providence, and Parsnips

D'A. S. Avalle, "Bonvesin da la Riva," in *Dizionario Biografico degli Italiani*, vol. 12, Rome, 1970.

G. Boccaccio, *Decameron*, V. Branca (ed.), Florence, 1976.

Bonvesin da la Riva, "De quinquaginta curialitatibus ad mensam," in *Le opere volgari*, G. Contini (ed.), Rome, 1941.

Bonvesin da la Riva, "De quinquaginta curialitatibus ad mensam," in *Volgari scelti*, P. S. Diehl and R. Stefanini (eds.), New York, 1987.

Bonvesin da la Riva, *De magnalibus Mediolani: Meraviglie di Milano*, Milan, 1998.

A. Bosisio, "Milano e la sua coscienza cittadina nel Duecento," *La coscienza cittadina nei comuni italiani del Duecento*, Perugia, 1972.

"Consumi: Coldiretti, è il parmigiano il più rubato nei supermercati," *News Coldiretti*, no. 624, October 15, 2006, http://www.coldiretti.it/docindex/cncd/informazioni/624_06.html.

G. Contini (ed.), *Poeti del Duecento*, vol. 1, Milan-Naples, 1960.

T. Dean, "The Rise of the *Signori*," in D. Abulafia (ed.), *Italy in the Central Middle Ages*, Oxford, 2004.

G. Fasoli, "La coscienza civica nelle 'laudes civitatum,'" in *La coscienza cittadina nei comuni italiani del Duecento*, Perugia, 1972.

A. Frugoni and C. Frugoni, *Storia di un giorno in una città medievale*, Rome-Bari, 1997.

E. Guidoni, "Gli Umiliati e la cultura urbana lombarda," in *La città: Dal Medioevo al Rinascimento*, Bari, 1981.

P. J. Jones, *The Italian City-State: From Commune to Signoria*, Oxford, 1997.

L. Martines, *Power and Imagination: City-States in Renaissance Italy*, London, 2002.

F. Novati, "Sul libro Delle grandezze di Milano di Fra Bonvesin da Riva," *Reale Istituto Lombardo di Scienze e Lettere: Rendiconti*, vol. 28, 1895.

F. Novati (ed.), "De magnalibus urbis Mediolani," *Bullettino dell'Istituto Storico Italiano*, vol. 20, 1898.

E. Occhipinti, *Il contado Milanese nel secolo XIII*, Bologna, 1982.

D. Romagnoli, "Cortesia nella città: Un modello complesso: Note sull'etica Medievale delle buone maniere," in D. Romagnoli (ed.), *La città e la corte: Buone e cattive manierie tra Medioevo ed Età Moderna*, Milan, 1991.

F. Sachetti, *Il trecentonovelle*, Turin, 1970.

Storia di Milano, vol. 4, *Dalle lotte contro il Barbarossa al primo Signore (1152–1310)*, Milan, 1954.

4. Venice, 1300s: Chinese Whispers

A. Dalby, *Dangerous Tastes: The Story of Spices*, London, 2000.

J.-L. Flandrin, "Condimenti, cucina e dietetica tra XIV e XVI secold," in Flandrin and Montanari, *Storia dell'alimentazione*.

J.-L. Flandrin and O. Redon, "Les livres de cuisine italiens des XIV e XV siècles," *Archeologia Medievale*, vol. 8, 1981, "Problemi di storia dell'alimentazione nell'Italia medievale."

L. Frati (ed.), *Libro di cucina del secolo XIV*, Livorno, 1899.

C. Frugoni, *Medioevo sul naso: Occhiali, bottoni e altre invenzioni medievali*, Rome-Bari, 2001.

G. Ghirardini, *Cento antiche ricette di cucina veneziana*, Venice, 1970.

H. H. Hart, *Marco Polo: Venetian Adventurer*, Norman, Okla., 1967.

J. Larner, *Marco Polo and the Discovery of the World*, London, 1999.

B. Laurioux, "De l'usage des épices dans l'alimentation médiévale," in *Médiévales*, vol. 5, 1983.

B. Laurioux, "Modes culinaries et mutations du gout à la fin du Moyen Age," in *Artes Mechanicae en Europe médiévale*, Brussels, 1989.

B. Laurioux, "Cucine medievali (secoli XIV e XV)," in Flandrin and Montanari, *Storia dell'alimentazione*.

B. Laurioux, "Identità nazionali, peculiarità regionali e 'koinè' europea nella cucina del Medioevo," in M. Montanari (ed.), *Il mondo in cucina: Storia, identità, scambi*, Rome-Bari, 2002.

F. C. Lane, *Venice: A Maritime Republic*, Baltimore, 1973.

F. C. Lane, *Studies in Venetian Social and Economic History*, London, 1987.

G. Luzzatto, *Storia economica di Venezia dall'XI al XVI secolo*, Venice, 1961.

G. Maffioli, *La cucina veneziana*, Padua, 1982.

G. Maffioli, *La cucina veneziana*, Padua, 1995.

R. Lopez and I. Raymond (trans.), *Medieval Trade in the Mediterranean World*, New York, 2001.

P. G. Molmenti, *Storia di Venezia nella vita privata*, Turin, 1880.

L. Olschki, *L'Asia di Marco Polo*, Venezia, 1957.

G. Pinto, "Le fonti documentarie bassomedievali," in *Archeologia Medievale*, vol. 8, 1981, "Problemi di storia dell'alimentazione nell'Italia medievale."

M. Polo, *Milione*, E. Mazzali (ed.), Milan, 1982.

G. Rebora, *La cucina medievale italiana tra oriente ed occidente*, Genova, 1996.

O. Redon, F. Sabban, and S. Serventi, *A tavola nel Medioevo*, Rome-Bari, 2005.

C. Ruggini et al. (eds.), *Storia di Venezia: Dalle origini alla caduta della serenissima*, vol. 1. *Origini-età ducale*, Rome, 1992.

M. Salvatori de Zuliani, *A tola co i nostri veci: La cucina veneziana*, Milan, 1986.

A. Tenenti and C. Vivanti, "Le fin d'un grand système di navigation: Les galeres marchandes vénitiennes, xiv–xvi siècles," *Annales*, 1961.

5. Rome, 1468: Respectable Pleasure

C. Benporat, *Cucina italiana del Quattrocento*, Florence, 1996.

C. Benporat, *Feste e banchetti: Convivialità italiana fra Tre e Quattrocento*, Florence, 2001.

D. Caccamo, "Buonaccorsi, Filippo (Callimachus Experiens)," *Dizionario Biografico degli Italiani*, vol. 15, Rome, 1972.

A. Campana and P. Medioli Masotti (eds.), *Bartolomeo Sacchi: Il Platina (Piadena 1421–Roma 1481)*, Padua, 1986.

G. Chittolini, "Stati regionali e istituzioni ecclesiastiche nell'Italia centosettentrionale del Quattrocento," in G. Chittolini and G. Miccoli (eds.), *Storia d'Italia: Annali*, vol. 9, *La Chiesa e il potere politico*, Turin, 1986.

N. Clark, *Melozzo da Forlì: Pictor papalis*, London, 1990.

J. F. D'Amico, *Renaissance Humanism in Papal Rome: Humanists and Churchmen on the Eve of the Reformation*, Baltimore, 1983.

G. B. de Rossi, "L'accademia di P. Leto e le sue memorie scritte sulle pareti delle catacombe romane," *Bolletino di Archeologia Cristiana*, vol. 1, 1890.

E. Duffy, *Saints & Sinners: A History of the Popes*, New Haven, Conn., 1997.

A. J. Dunston, "Pope Paul II and the Humanists," *Journal of Religious History*, vol. 4, 1973.

E. Garin, *Prosatori latini del Quattrocento*, Milan, 1952.

R. Lanciani, *Ancient Rome in the Light of Recent Discoveries*, London, 1888.

B. Laurioux, "Cuisiner à l'antique: Apicius au Moyen Âge," *Médiévales*, vol. 26, 1994.

Martino of Como, *The Art of Cooking: The First Modern Cookery Book*, L. Ballerini (ed.), Berkeley, 2005.

P. Medioli Masotti, "L'Accademia Romana e la congiura del 1468," *Italia Medioevale e Umanistica*, vol. 25, 1982.

P. Medioli Masotti, "Callimaco, l'Accademia Romana e la congiura del 1468," in G. C. Garfagnini (ed.), *Callimaco Esperiente poeta e politico del '400*, Florence, 1987.

E. Garin, "L'accademia romana, Pomponio Leto e la congiura," in *Storia della letteratura italiana*, vol. 3, Garzanti, 1966.

R. J. Palermino, "The Roman Academy, the Catacombs, and the Conspiracy of 1468," *Archivum Historiae Pontificiae*, vol. 18, 1980.

P. Partner, *Renaissance Rome, 1500–1559: A Portrait of a Society*, Berkeley, 1976.

L. Pastor, *The History of the Popes*, vols. 3 and 4, London, 1949.

Platina, *The Lives of the Popes, from the time of our Saviour Jesus Christ to the Reign of Sixtus IV*, Sir P. Rycaut (trans.), London, 1688.

Platina, *The Lives of the Popes from the Time of our Saviour Jesus Christ to the Accession of Gregory VII*, 2 vols., W. Benham (trans.), London, 1888.

Platina, *Il piacere onesto e la buona salute*, Turin, 1985, with introduction by E. Faccioli.

Platina, *On Right Pleasure and Good Health*, M. E. Milham (trans. and ed.), Tempe, Ariz., 1998.

V. Zabughin, *Giulio Pomponio Leto: Saggio critico*, Rome, 1909–10.

6. Ferrara, 1529: A Dynasty at Table

N. Sapegno, "Ariosto, Ludovico," in *Dizionario biografico degli italiani*, vol. 4, Rome, 1962.

L. Ariosto, *La Cassaria*, in *Commedie*, Turin, 1976.

A tavola con il Principe: Materiali per una mostra su alimentazione e cultura nella Ferrara degli Estensi, Ferrara, 1988.

G. Boerio, *Dizionario del dialetto veneziano*, Venice, 1829.

P. Camporesi, "Alimentazione e cucina," in A. Berselli (ed.), *Storia della Emilia Romagna*, vol. 2, Bologna, 1977.

M. Catalano, *Vita di Ludovico Ariosto*, 2 vols. Geneva, 1930.

F. Cazzola, "La città e il pane: Produzioni agricole e consumi alimentari a Ferrara tra medioevo ed età moderna," in *A tavola con il Principe: Materiali per una mostra su alimentazione e cultura nella Ferrara degli Estensi*, Ferrara, 1988.

F. Cazzola, *La città, il principe, i contadini: Ricerche sull'economia ferrarese nel Rinascimento 1450–1630*, Ferrara, 2003.

L. Chiappini, *Gli estensi*, Varese, 1967.

L. Chiappini, *La corte estense alla metà del Cinquecento: I compendi di Cristoforo di Messisbugo*, Ferrara, 1984.

L. Chiappini, "Lo scalco ideale: Cristoforo da Messisbugo," in *A tavola con il Principe: Materiali per una mostra su alimentazione e cultura nella Ferrara degli Estensi*, Ferrara, 1988.

E. Faccioli, "Scenicità dei banchetti estensi," in *Il Rinascimento nelle corti padane*, Bologna, 1977.

B. Fontana, *Renata di Francia*, Rome, 1889.

A. Frizzi, *Memorie per la storia di Ferrara*, vol. 4, Ferrara, 1848.

W. L. Gundersheimer, *Ferrara: The Style of a Renaissance Despotism*, Princeton, 1973.

R. Iotti (ed.), *Gli Estensi: La Corte di Ferrara*, Modena, 1997.

E. Lanzoni, *Ferrara: Una città nella storia*, Ferrara, 1984.

G. Mantovano, "Il banchetto rinascimentale: Arte, magnificenza, potere," in *A tavola con il Principe: Materiali per una mostra su alimentazione e cultura nella Ferrara degli Estensi*, Ferrara, 1988.

L. Martines, *Power and Imagination: City-States in Renaissance Italy*, London, 2002.

C. da Messisbugo, *Banchetti: Compositioni di vivande, et apparecchio generale*, Ferrara, 1549.

C. da Messisbugo, *Banchetti composizioni di vivande e apparecchio generale*, Vicenza, 1960.

G. Pagagno and A. Quondam, *La corte e lo spazio: Ferrara estense*, 3 vols. Rome, 1982.

D. Pizzagalli, *La signora del Rinascimento*, Milan, 2002.

P. Prodi, "Il 'sovrano pontefice,'" in G. Chittolini and G. Miccoli (eds.), *Storia d'Italia: Annali*, vol. 9, *La Chiesa e il potere politico*, Turin, 1986.

A. Prosperi (ed.), *Storia di Ferrara*, vol. 6, *Il Rinascimento: Situazioni e personaggi*, Ferrara, 2000.

C. M. Rosenberg, *The Este Monuments and Urban Development in Renaissance Ferrara*, Cambridge, 1997.

A. Solerti, *Ferrara e la corte estense nella seconda metà del secolo decimosesto*, Città di Castello, 1900.

G. Vasari, *Le vite de' più eccellenti pittori scultori e architettori*, Florence, 1984.

Vocabolario veneziano e padovano co'termini, e modi corrispondenti toscani, Padua, 1775.

B. Zevi, *Biagio Rossetti: Architetto ferrarese, il primo urbanista moderno europeo*, Turin, 1960.

7. Rome, 1549–50: Bread and Water for Their Eminences

F. Baumgart and B. Biagetti, *Gli affreschi di Michelangelo nella Cappella Paolina in Vaticano*, Vatican City, 1934.

V. Bartoccetti, "Conclave," in *Enciclopedia Cattolica*, vol. 4, Vatican, 1950.

G. Ciampi, "L'alimentazione popolare a Roma e nell'Agro romano," in Capatti et al., *L'alimentazione*.

A. Dowling, "Conclave," in *Catholic Encyclopedia*, New York, 1908.

D. Hay, *Italy in the Age of the Renaissance*, London, 1989.

M. Heim, *Introduzione alla storia della Chiesa*, Turin, 2002.

L. Lector, *Le Conclave*, Paris, 1894.

M. Montanari, "La cucina scritta come fonte per lo studio della cucina orale," *Food & History*, vol. 1, 2003.

P. Partner, *Renaissance Rome, 1500–1559: A Portrait of a Society*, Berkeley, 1976.

L. Pastor, *The History of the Popes*, vols. 13–17, London, 1951.

F. Petruccelli della Gattina, *Histoire diplomatique des conclaves*, Paris, 1864–65, vol. 2, 1864.

F. Priscianese, *Del governo della corte d'un signore in Roma*, Città di Castello, 1883 (1543).

G. Riley, "The Gastronomic Michelangelo," G. Mars and V. Mars (eds.), *Food, Culture and History*, vol. 1, 1993.

B. Scappi, *Opera di Bartolomeo Scappi, cuoco secreto di Papa Pio Quinto*, Venice, 1570.

J. Di Schino and F. Luccichenti, *Bartolomeo Scappi cuoco nella Roma del Cinquecento*, Rome, 2004.

8. Bologna, 1600s: The Game of Cockaigne

M. Aureli, *Nuovo dizionario usuale tascabile del dialetto Bolognese*, Bologna, 1851.

P. Bellettini et al. (eds.), *Una città in piazza: Comunicazione e vita quotidiana a Bologna tra '500 e '600*, Bologna, 2000.

A. Bignardi, *Le campagne emiliane nel Rinascimento e nell'Età barocca*, Bologna, 1978.

P. Burke, *Popular Culture in Early Modern Europe*, London, 1978.

P. Camporesi, *La maschera di Bertoldo: G. C. Croce e la letteratura carnevalesca*, Turin, 1976.

P. Camporesi, *Rustici e buffoni*, Turin, 1991.

J. Bentini and M. Borella (eds.), *Il castello estense*, Ferrara, 2002.

G. Cocchiara, "Il Paese di Cuccagna: L'evasione della realtà nella fantasia popolare," in *Il Paese di Cuccagna e altri studi di folklore*, Turin, 1980.

P. Colliva, "Bologna dal XIV al XVIII secolo: 'Governo misto' o signoria senatoria?" in A. Berselli (ed.), *Storia della Emilia Romagna*, Imola, 1977.

Costume e società nei giochi a stampa di Giuseppe Maria Mitelli, Perugia, 1988.

G. C. Croce, "La festa della porchetta" (1597), in O. Guerrini, *La vita e le opere di Giulio Cesare Croce*, Bologna, 1879.

G. C. Croce, *Dialogo piacevolissimo fra li dua costumattissimi, e ben creati M. Asino, e M. Porco, sopra l'abondanza de meloni*, Bologna (no date).

G. C. Croce, *L'eccellenza et trionfo del porco*, Venice, 1605.

G. C. Croce, *Banchetto de' mal cibati. Comedia dell'Academico Frusto recitata da gli affamati nella città calamitosa alli 15 del mese dell'estrema miseria, l'anno dell'aspra, & insopportabile necessità*, Venice, 1608.

G. C. Croce, *Alfabeto de giuocatori in ottava rima: Opera morale*, Bologna, 1611.

G. C. Croce, *Canzone sopra la porcellina che si tra giù del Palazzo dell'Illustrissima Città di Bologna, per la Festa di S. Bartolomeo*, Bologna, 1622.

G. C. Croce, *Maridazzo di molte sorti d'herbe fatto in un'insalata del mese di maggio, nel quale si vede l'ingegno di ciascuna nel maritarsi*, Bologna, 1622.

G. C. Croce, *La vera regola per mantenersi magro con pochissima spesa*, Bologna, 1622.

G. C. Croce, *Il giocondo e florido convito fatto nelle sontuose nozze del raffanno, e della rapa*, Bologna, 1637.

G. C. Croce, *Le sottilissime astuzie di Bertoldo: Le piacevoli e ridicolose simplicità di Bertoldino*, Turin, 1978.

G. C. Croce, *Bertoldo e Bertoldino*, Milan, 1994.

U. Dallari, "Un'antica costumanza Bolognese (Festa di San Bartolomeo o della Porchetta)," *Atti e Memorie della R. Deputazione di Storia Patria per le Provincie di Romagna*, 3rd series, vol. 13, 1894–95.

L. Entio, *Il trionfo della porchetta overo Invitto generale à ciascuna persona à venire à vedere questo bellissimo Trionfo: Con una descrittione di tutto quello si fece in tal giorno l'anno passato 1627*, Bologna, 1628.

L. Frati, *La vita privata di Bologna dal secolo XIII al XVII*, Rome, 1968.

O. Guerrini, *La vita e le opere di Giulio Cesare Croce*, Bologna, 1879.

J.-B. Labat, *Voyages du P. Labat de l'ordre des FF. Precheurs en Espagne et en Italie*, Paris, 1730.

D. Mancini, "Giustizia in piazza: Appunti sulle esecuzioni capitali in Piazza Maggiore a Bologna durante l'età moderna," *Il Carrobbio*, 1985.

E. Maule, "La 'Festa della porchetta' a Bologna nel Seicento: Indagine su una festa barocca," *Il Carrobbio*, 1980.

G. M. Mitelli, *I 33 giochi del Mitelli*, Bergamo, 1976.

M. Montanari, "La città grassa," in P. Bellettini et al. (eds.), *Una città in piazza: Comunicazione e vita quotidiana a Bologna tra '500 e '600*, Bologna, 2000.

M. Montanari, "Bologna grassa: La costruzione di un mito," in M. Montanari (ed.), *Il mondo in cucina: Storia, identità, scambi*, Rome-Bari, 2002.

M. Montanari, *Bologna grassa: La costruzione di un mito*, Bologna, 2004.

C. Penuti, "Carestie ed epidemie," in A. Berselli (ed.), *Storia della Emilia Romagna*, Imola, 1977.

S. Pepys, *Diary*, R. Latham and N. Matthews (eds.), vol. 7, 1666, London, 1972.

P. Petroni, *Il libro della vera cucina Bolognese*, Florence, 1978.

G. Ricci, *Bologna*, Rome-Bari, 1980.

G. Roversi, "Il 'Testamento del porco': Note di storia gastronomica Bolognese," in *Strenna Storica Bolognese*, 1969.

M. C. Sartoni and A. Molinari Pradelli, *La cucina bolognese*, Rome, 1996.

P. Sostegno, "Dietro le quinte della Festa della Porchetta: Risvolti economici e organizzativi," *Il Carrobbio*, 1985.

H. Stehlé, "Jean-Baptiste LABAT (1663–1738)," in *Hommes et destins: Dictionnaire biographique d'Outre-Mer*, tome 2, vol. 2, Paris, 1977.

V. Tanara, *L'economia del cittadino in villa*, Bologna, 1644.

A. Trauzzi, "Bologna nelle opere di G. C. Croce," *Atti e Memorie della R. Deputazione di Storia Patria per le Provincie di Romagna*, 3rd series, vol. 23, 1905.

V. Valente, "Mortadella di *Firenze*," *Lingua Nostra*, vol. 49, 1988.

9. Naples, late 1700s: *Maccheroni*-Eaters

H. Acton, *The Bourbons of Naples (1734–1825)*, London, 1956.

L. Barletta, *Il carnevale del 1764 a Napoli: Protesta e integrazione in uno spazio urbano*, Naples, 1981.

F. Benigno, *Specchi sulla rivoluzione: Conflitto e identità politica nell'Europa moderna*, Rome, 1999.

F. Benigno, "Trasformazioni discorsive e identità sociali: Il caso dei *lazzari*," *Storica*, vol. 31, 2005.

J. Black, *Italy and the Grand Tour*, New Haven, Conn., 2003.

J. Boswell, *Boswell on the Grand Tour: Italy, Corsica, and France 1765–1766*, New York, 1955.

M. Calaresu, "Looking for Virgil's Tomb: The end of the Grand Tour and the Cosmopolitan Ideal in Europe," in J. Elsner and J.-P. Rubiés (eds.), *Voyages and Visions: Towards and Cultural History of Travel*, London, 1999.

J. Caròla Francesconi, *La cucina napoletana*, Naples, 1977.

I. Cavalcante, *La cucina teorico-pratica*, Naples, 1844.

E. Chaney, *The Evolution of the Grand Tour*, London, 1998.

C. Chard, "The Intensification of Italy: Food, Wine and the Foreign in Seventeenth-Century Travel Writing," in G. Mars and V. Mars (eds.), *Food, Culture and History*, London, 1993.

C. Chard, *Pleasure and Guilt on the Grand Tour*, Manchester, 1999.

A. Consiglio, *Lazzari e Santa Fede*, Milan, 1936.

V. Corrado, *Il cuoco galante*, Naples, 1773.

V. Corrado, *Tre opere di gastronomia*, L. Sada (ed.), Bari, 1976.

V. Corrado, *Del cibo pitagorico, ovvero erbaceo: Seguito dal Trattato delle patate*, Rome, 2001.

B. Croce, "I lazzari," *Archivio per lo studio delle tradizioni popolari*, vol. 14, 1895.

B. Croce, "Aneddoti su re Ferdinando IV di Napoli," in *Aneddoti di varia letteratura*, vol. 3, Naples, 1942.

N. E. Cunningham, Jr., *In Pursuit of Reason: The Life of Thomas Jefferson*, Baton Rouge, 1987.

M. Douglas, *Purity and Danger: An Analysis of the Concepts of Pollution and Taboo*, London, 1978.

J. T. d'Espinchal, *Journal d'émigration*, Paris, 1912.

I. Fazio, "I mercati regolati e la crisi settecentesca dei sistemi annonari italiani," *Studi Storici*, vol. 3, 1990.

A. Giraffi, *Masaniello: Rivoluzione di Napoli del 1647*, Brussels, 1844.

J. W. von Goethe, *Italian Journey*, London, 1982.

J. Gorani, *Memoires secrets et critiques des course, des gouvernements, et des moeurs des principaux états de l'Italie*, tome 1, Paris, 1793.

G. Green Shackelford, *Thomas Jefferson's Travels in Europe, 1784–1789*, Baltimore, 1995.

C. Hibbert, *The Grand Tour*, London, 1987.

R. Hudson (ed.), *The Grand Tour 1592–1796*, London, 1993.

T. Jefferson, *The Papers of Thomas Jefferson*, J. P. Boyd et al. (eds.), Princeton, 1950–, vols. 10, 11 and 14.

M. Kelly, *Reminiscences*, London, 1975.

A. Latini, *Lo scalco alla moderna, ovvero L'Arte di ben disporre li Conviti, Parte prima: In cui si tratta delle vivande di grasso*, Naples, 1692.

A. Latini, *Lo scalco alla moderna, ovvero L'Arte di ben disporre li Conviti, Parte seconda: Nella quale specialmente si tratta delle vivande di magro*, Naples, 1694.

A. Latini, *Autobiografia (1642–1696): La vita di uno scalco*, Rome, 1992.

H. Lynch Piozzi, *Observations and Reflections Made in the Course of a Journey Through France, Italy, and Germany*, Ann Arbor, 1967 (1789).

P. Macry, *Mercato e società nel regno di Napoli: Commercio del grano e politica economica del '700*, Naples, 1974.

P. J. Malouin, *Description et détails des arts du meûnier, du vermicellier, et du boulanger*, Paris, 1767.

A. Miller, *Letters from Italy, Describing the Manners, Customs, Antiquities, Paintings &c of that Country in the Years MDCCLXX and MDCCLXXI*, 3 vols., Dublin, 1776.

W. A. Mozart, *The Letters of Mozart and His Family*, E. Anderson (ed.), London, 1989.

A. Mozzillo, *Passaggio a Mezzogiorno: Napoli e il Sud nell'immaginario barocco e illuminista europeo*, Milan, 1993.

C. Petraccone, *Napoli dal '500 all '800: Problemi di storia demografica e sociale*, Naples, 1974.

D. Scafoglio, *La maschera della cuccagna: Spreco, rivolta e sacrificio nel Carnevale napoletano del 1764*, Naples, 1994.

E. Sereni, "Note di storia dell'alimentazione nel Mezzogiorno: i napoletani da 'mangiafoglia' a 'mangiamaccheroni,'" in *Terra nuova e buoi rossi*, Turin, 1981.

S. Sharp, *Letters from Italy: Describing the Customs and Manners of that Country in the years 1765, and 1766*, London, 1766.

A. Spagnoletti, *Storia del Regno delle Due Sicilie*, Bologna, 1997.

F. Venturi, "1764: Napoli nell'anno della fame," *Rivista Storica Italiana*, vol. 85, no. 2, 1973.

E. Zaniboni, *Alberghi italiani e viaggiatori stranieri: Sec. XII–XVIII*, Naples, 1921.

"World Directory of Pasta Shapes," http://www.professionalpasta.it/dir_1/go_1(1).htm.

10. Turin, 1846: *Viva l'Italia!*

R. Balzani, "Il banchetto patriottico: Una 'tradizione' risorgimentale forlivese," in F. Tarozzi and A. Varni (eds.), *Il tempo libero nell'Italia unita*, Bologna, 1992.

P. Baricco, *Torino*, Turin, 1869.

V. Bersezio, *Il Regno di Vittorio Emanuele II: Trent'anni di vita italiana*, Turin, 1978, book 2.

P. Camporesi, *Exotic Brew: The Art of Living in the Age of Enlightenment*, Cambridge, U.K., 1994 (trans. of *Il brodo indiano*, Milan, 1994).

F. Chapusot, *La cucina sana, economica ed elegante*, Bologna, 1990 (Turin, 1846).

Il cuoco piemontese ridotto all'ultimo gusto che insegna facilmente a cucinare qualunque sorta di vivande in grasso ed in magro; istruisce pure nella scelta e bontà d'ogni cosa appartenente alla cucina dando la spiegazione di tutti gli utensili necessarii a tale arte ed insegna il vero metodo per il pasticciere e confetturiere, i doveri di un maestro di casa, le minute per le provvisioni delle quattro stagioni, e la maniera di trinciare ogni sorta di cibi, 3rd ed., Florence, 1843.

Il cuoco piemontese perfezionato a Parigi, Bra, 1995 (Turin, 1766).

J. A. Davis, "Cultures of Interdiction: The Politics of Censorship in Italy from Napoleon to the Restoration," in D. Laven and L. Riall (eds.), *Napoleon's Legacy: Problems of Government in Restoration Europe*, Oxford, 2000.

A. Galante Garrone, "I giornali della Restaurazione, 1815–1847," in A. Galante Garrone and F. Della Peruta (eds.), *La stampa italiana del Risorgimento*, Rome-Bari, 1979.

V. La Chapelle, *Le Cuisinier moderne, qui apprend à donner toutes sortes de repas . . . Avec . . . des desseins de table . . . en taille-douce*, 2nd ed., The Hague, 1742.

F. La Varenne, *Le Cuisinier François*, Paris, 1651.

U. Levra (ed.), *Storia di Torino, VI, La città nel Risorgimento (1798–1864)*, Turin, 2000.

D. Mack Smith, *Cavour*, London, 1985.

F. Marin, *Les dons de Comus ou les délices de la table*, Paris, 1775.

V. Marone and L. Brangi, *I banchetti politici: Briciole di storia*, Naples, 1888.

F. Massialot, *Le cuisinier roïal et bourgeois: Qui apprend a ordonner toute sorte de repas, & la meilleure maniere des ragoûts les plus à la mode & les plus exquis: Ouvrage tres-utile dans les familles, & singulierement necessaire à tous maitres d'hôtel, & ecuïers de cuisine*, Paris, 1698.

P. Meldini, "A tavola e in cucina," in P. Melograni (ed.), *La famiglia italiana dall'Ottocento a oggi*, Rome-Bari, 1988.

S. Mennell, *All Manners of Food: Eating and Taste in England and France from the Middle Ages to the Present*, Chicago, 1996.

Menon, *La Cuisinière bourgeoise, suivie de l'office, à l'usage de tous ceux qui se mêlent de la dépense des maisons*, Brussels, 1775.

W. I. Miller, *The Anatomy of Disgust*, London, 1997.

A. Molinari Pradelli, *La cucina piemontese*, Rome, 1998.

F. Predari, *I primi vagiti della libertà italiana in Piemonte*, Milan, 1861.

F. Rizzi, *La coccarda e le campane: Comunità rurali e Repubblica Romana nel Lazio (1848–1849)*, Milan, 1988.

T. Spadaccino (ed.), *La Sicilia dei Marchesi e dei Monsù*, Palermo, 1992.

M. Thom, "Neither fish nor fowl? The Correspondence of Lorenzo Valerio, 1825–1849," *Modern Italy*, vol. 11, no. 3, 2006.

L. Tibone, *I piaceri della tavola: Cento menu raccontano la storia del Piemonte*, Turin, 1993.

L. Valerio, *Carteggio (1825–1865)*, vol. 2 *(1842–1847)*, Turin, 1994.

G. Vialardi, *A tavola con il Re: Trattato di gastronomia*, Turin, 2000.

11. Naples, 1884: Pinocchio Hates Pizza

A. Banti, *Matilde Serao*, Turin, 1965.

C. Battisti and G. Alessio, *Dizionario etimologico italiano*, vol. 4, Florence, 1954.

C. Brice, "'The King was pale': Italy's National-Popular Monarchy and the Construction of Disasters, 1882–1885," in J. Dickie, J. Foot, and F. Snowden (eds.), *Disastro! Disasters in Italy since 1860: Culture, Politics, Society*, New York, 2002.

D. L. Caglioti, *Il guadagno difficile: Commercianti napoletani nella seconda metà dell'Ottocento*, Bologna, 1994.

C. Carabba (ed.), *Napoli d'allora: Testimonianze di Matilde Serao e Edoardo Scarfoglio*, Milan, 1976.

I. Cavalcante, *La cucina teorico-pratica over il pranzo periodico di otto piatti al giorno cumulativamente col suo corrispondente riposto, e dettaglio approssimativo della spesa giornaliera, pratica di scalcare e servire in tavola finalmente Quattro settimane secondo le stagioni della cucina casareccia in dialetto napolitano*, 4th ed., Naples, 1844.

C. Collodi, *Il viaggio per l'Italia di Giannettino*, vol. 3, *L'Italia meridionale*, Florence, 1886.

C. Del Balzo, *Napoli e i napoletani*, Milan, 1885.

V. De Napoli, *L'eterna bellezza della Regina Margherita di Savoia*, Naples, 1894.

C. Duggan, *Francesco Crispi 1818–1901: From Nation to Nationalism*, Oxford, 2002.

A. Dumas, *Le Corricolo*, in *Oeuvres*, vol. 6, Brussels, 1843.

R. Fucini, *Napoli a occhio nudo*, Turin, 1976.

G. Gargano, *Vocabolario domestico napolitano-italiano*, Naples, 1841.

Guida pratica del dialetto napolitano, Naples, 1877.

C. Helstosky, *Garlic & Oil: Food and Politics in Italy*, Oxford, 2004.

E. Lémonon, *Naples: Notes historiques et socials*, Paris, 1911.

R. Minervini, *Storia della pizza*, Naples, 1973.

B. Puoti, *Vocabolario domestico napoletano e toscano*, Naples, 1841.

O. Roux, *La prima Regina d'Italia*, Milan, 1901.

M. Serao, *Il ventre di Napoli* (1884 ed.), Pisa, 1995.

F. M. Snowden, *Naples in the Time of Cholera, 1884–1911*, Cambridge, U.K., 1995.

M. Twain, *The Innocents Abroad, or The New Pilgrims' Progress*, Hartford, Conn., 1869.

J. White Mario, "The Poor in Naples," in *The Poor in Great Cities*, London, 1896.

"Lo sventramento di Napoli," *La Nazione*, June 16, 1889.

G. Vittori, *Margherita di Savoia*, Naples, 1891.

Vocabolario delle parole del dialetto napoletano, che più si scostano dal dialetto toscano, Naples, 1789.

Pizzeria Brandi, www.brandi.it/index3.html.

12. Florence, 1891: Pellegrino Artusi

Q. Antonelli, "Ricette di donne," *Primapersona: Percorsi autobiografici*, vol. 16, 2006.

P. Artusi, *La scienza in cucina e l'arte di mangiar bene*, Turin, 1974.

P. Artusi, *Osservazioni in appendice a trenta lettere di Giuseppe Giusti*, Florence, 1881.

P. Artusi, "Copia del testamento olofrafo di Pellegrino Artusi," *Forum Popili*, vol. 1, 1961.

P. Artusi, *Autobiografia*, Milan, 1993.

K. Baedeker, *Italy: Handbook for Travellers, Southern Italy and Sicily*, London, 1896.

E. Bottrigari, *Cronaca di Bologna*, Bologna, vol. 2., 1960.

S. Camerani, "Da Torino a Firenze," *Rassegna Storica Toscana*, 1966, vol. 1, "Firenze capitale."

M. Cattini, "Le Emilie agricole al momento dell'Unità," in R. Finzi (ed.), *Storia d'Italia: Le regioni dall'Unità a oggi: L'Emilia-Romagna*, Turin, 1997.

G. Conti, *Firenze vecchia*, Firenze, 1899.

R. Cremante, "Noterelle artusiane," *Studi e problemi di critica testuale*, vol. 4, no. 4, 1972.

E. De Amicis, "Alberto," in *Novelle*, Milan, 1879.

J. A. Dix, *A Winter in Madeira and a Summer in Spain and Florence*, New York, 1851.

S. Fei, *Nascita e sviluppo di Firenze città borghese*, Florence, 1971.

Firenze d'oggi, Florence, 1896.

S. C. Hughes, *Crime, Disorder and the Risorgimento: The Politics of Policing in Bologna*, Cambridge, 1994.

P. Mantegazza, *Igiene dell'amore*, Florence, 1896.

P. Mantegazza, *Igiene della bellezza*, Milan, 1912.

P. Mantegazza, *Le estasi umane*, Florence, 1939.

G. Manzoni, *Briganti in Romagna 1851–1853*, Imola, 1976.

G. Mori, "Dall'unità alla Guerra: Aggregazione e disgregazione di un'area regionale," in G. Mori (ed.), *Storia d'Italia: Le regioni dall'Unità a oggi: La Toscana*, Turin, 1986.

A. Pollarini (ed.), *La cucina bricconcella 1891/1991: Pellegrino Artusi e l'arte di mangiar bene cento anni dopo*, Bologna, 1991.

R. Ragazzini, M. Casalini, R. Casalini, *Il Passatore: Le imprese brigantesche di Stefano Pelloni nella Romagna ottocentesca*, Cesena, 1998.

L. Rossi Nissim, "Vita fiorentina," *Rassegna Storica Toscana*, 1966, vol. 1, "Firenze capitale."

F. Serantini, *Fatti memorabili della banda del Passatore in terra di Romagna*, Ravenna, 1973 (1929).

M. Sharman Crawford, *Life in Tuscany*, London, 1859.

M. Vannucci, *Firenze Ottocento*, Rome, 1992.

P. Zama, "Artusi, Pellegrino," *Dizionario biografico degli italiani*, vol. 4, Rome, 1962.

13. Genoa, 1884–1918: Emigrants and Prisoners

V. Agnetti, *La nuova cucina delle specialità regionali*, Milan, 1909.

Anon., "A Saga of Cathay," *Macaroni Journal*, October 15, 1929.

L. Avagliano, *L'emigrazione italiana*, Naples, 1976.

P. Bevilacqua, "Emigrazione transoceanica e mutamenti dell'alimentazione contadina calabrese fra Otto e Novecento," *Quaderni Storici*, vol. 47, 1981.

G. Bertone, "La patria in piroscafo: Il viaggio di Edmondo De Amicis," in E. De Amicis, *Sull'Oceano*, Reggio Emilia, 2005.

M. E. Bianchi Tonizzi, "L'industria dello zucchero in Italia dal blocco continentale alla vigilia della grande Guerra (1807–1914)," *Annali di Storia dell'Impresa*, vol. 4, 1988.

C. Bianco, *The Two Rosetos*, Bloomington, Ind., 1974.

C. Bianco, "Migration and Urbanization of a Traditional Culture: An Italian Experience," in R. M. Dorson (ed.), *Folklore in the Modern World*, The Hague, 1978.

F. Caffarena, "Prigionieri di un mito," *Slow Food*, vol. 4, 2004.

F. Caffarena, "Fame di casa, sapore di guerra," *Primapersona: Percorsi autobiografici*, vol. 16, 2006.

F. M. A. Cassiodorus, *Variae*, S. J. B. Barnish (trans. and ed.), Liverpool, 1992.

G. Casaccia, *Vocabolario genovese-italiano*, Genova, 1851.

G. Chioni with L. Marazza, *Arte Culinaria*, January–February 1918. Manuscript held in the Archivio Ligure della Scrittura Popolare, Genoa.

Z. Ciuffoletti and M. Degl'Innocenti, *L'emigrazione nella storia d'Italia, 1868–1975: Storia e documenti*, Florence, 1978.

P. Corti, "Emigrazione e consuetudini alimentari: L'esperienza di una catena migratoria," in Capatti et al., *L'alimentazione*.

E. De Amicis, *Sull'Oceano*, Como-Pavia, 1991.

H. R. Diner, *Hungering for America: Italian, Irish and Jewish Foodways in the Age of Migration*, Cambridge, Mass., 2001.

G. Fiorentino, *B98, 30 November 917*. Manuscript transcribed and annotated by Annarita Caputo. Kindly supplied to the author by Giuseppina Caputo.

G. Fiorentino, *Ricettario Gulieke n. 2, Celle—Gennaio 1918*. Manuscript transcribed and annotated by Annarita Caputo. Kindly supplied to the author by Giuseppina Caputo.

E. Franzina, *La grande emigrazione: L'esodo dei rurali dal Veneto durante il secolo XIX*, Venice, 1976.

E. Franzina, *Merica! Merica! Emigrazione e colonizzazione nelle lettere dei contadini veneti in America Latina 1876–1902*, Milan, 1979.

G. Frisoni, *Dizionario moderno genovese-italiano e italiano-genovese arricchito di una raccolta di mille proverbi liguri*, Genova, 1910.

D. Gabaccia, *We Are What We Eat: Ethnic Food and the Making of Americans*, Cambridge, Mass., 1998.

C. E. Gadda, *Giornale di Guerra e di prigionia*, in *Saggi giornali favole e altri scritti*, vol. 2, C. Vela et al. (eds.), Milan, 1992.

General Assembly of Pennsylvania, Senate Resolution, no. 64, 1989 (on Girolamo Guerrisi).

General Assembly of Pennsylvania, House Resolution, no. 98, 1989 (on Girolamo Guerrisi).

G. Ghirardini, "Gli scavi del palazzo di Teodorico a Ravenna," *Monumenti Antichi*, vol. 24, 1918.

E. Gibbon, *The History of the Decline and Fall of the Roman Empire*, vol. 4, London, 1997 (reprint of 1788 ed.).

S. Gibbs Campbell, "Spaghetti for Americans," *Macaroni Journal*, October 15, 1929.

A. Gibelli and P. Rugafiori (eds.), *La Liguria*, Turin, 1994.

A. Gibelli, "Dal porto al mondo con De Amicis," in E. De Amicis, *Sull'Oceano*, Reggio Emilia, 2005.

A. Gismondi, *Nuovo vocabolario genovese-italiano con rilievi sulla ortografia, pronuncia e qualche particolarità grammaticale*, Genova, 1955.

P. Heather, "The Western Empire, 425–76," in A. Cameron, B. Ward-Perkins, and M. Whitby, *The Cambridge Ancient History*, vol. 14, *Late Antiquity: Empire and Successors, AD 425–600*, Cambridge, U.K., 2000.

P. Heather, "Theodoric, King of Goths," *Early Medieval Europe*, vol. 4, 1995.

C. Helstosky, *Garlic & Oil: Food and Politics in Italy*, Oxford, 2004.

M. J. Johnson, "Toward a History of Theodoric's Building Program," *Dumbarton Oaks Papers*, vol. 42, 1988.

G. M. Lapolla, *Italian Cooking for the American Kitchen*, New York, 1953.

N. Malnate, *Della storia del porto di Genova: Dalle origini all'anno 1892*, Genoa, 1892.

S. Martelli, "Dal vecchio mondo al sogno americano," in P. Bevilacqua, A. De Clementi, and E. Franzina (eds.), *Storia dell'emigrazione italiana*, vol. 1, *Partenze*, Rome, 2001.

G. Massullo, "Economia delle rimesse," in P. Bevilacqua, A. De Clementi, and E. Franzina (eds.), *Storia dell'emigrazione italiana*, vol. 1, *Partenze*, Rome, 2001.

Ministero degli Affari Esteri, *Emigrazione e colonie: Rapporti dei RR. agenti diplomatici e consolari*, Rome, 1893.

Ministero degli Affari Esteri, Commissariato dell'Emigrazione, *Emigrazione e colonie: Raccolta di rapporti dei RR. agenti diplomatici e consolari*, vol. 3, *America*, Rome, 1909.

G. Olivieri, *Dizionario genovese-italiano*, Genova, 1851.

N. Orengo, "Il pesto," in *MicroMega, Il cibo e l'impegno*, supplement to issue 4, 2004.

E. Poleggi and G. Timossi, *Porto di Genova: Storia e attualità*, Genova, 1977.

G. Procacci, "The Disaster of Caporetto," in J. Dickie, J. Foot, and F. Snowden (eds.), *Disastro! Disasters in Italy since 1860: Culture, Politics, Society*, New York, 2002.

G. Procacci, *Soldati e prigionieri italiani nella Grande guerra*, Turin, 2000.

Ricettario di casa Fiorentino Caputo: Palma di Montechiaro: XX secolo. Manuscript transcribed and annotated by Annarita Caputo. Kindly supplied to the author by Giuseppina Caputo.

V. Teti, "La cucina calabrese è un'invenzione americana?" *I Viaggi di Erodoto*, vol. 12, 1991.

V. Teti, "Emigrazione, alimentazione, culture popolari," in P. Bevilacqua, A. De Clementi, and E. Franzina (eds.), *Storia dell'emigrazione italiana*, vol. 1, *Partenze*, Rome, 2001.

M. Tirabassi, "Bourgeois Men, Peasant Women: Rethinking Domestic Work and Morality in Italy," in D. Gabaccia and F. Iacovetta (eds.), *Women, Gender, and Transnational Lives: Italian Workers of the World*, Toronto, 2002.

La via delle Americhe: L'emigrazione ligure tra evento e racconto, Genova, 1989.

O. G. Von Simson, *Sacred Fortress: Byzantine Art and Statecraft in Ravenna*, Chicago, 1948.

The Adventures of Marco Polo, A. Mayo (dir.), 1938, United States.

14. Rome, 1925–38: Mussolini's Rustic Village

A. Capatti "Lingua, regioni e gastronomia dall'Unità alla seconda guerra mondiale," in Capatti et al., *L'alimentazione*.

J. S. Cohen, "Fascism and Agriculture in Italy: Policies and Consequences," *Economic History Review*, vol. 1, 1979.

"Il Duce inaugura al Circo Massimo la prima Mostra Nazionale del Dopolavoro tra imponenti manifestazioni di popolo," *La Tribuna*, May 25, 1938.

R. Giannetti and A. Rustichini, "Consumi operai e salari negli anni '20 in Italia," *Movimento Operaio e Socialista*, 1978.

D. Mack Smith, *Mussolini*, London, 1983.

A. Marescalchi, *Storia dell'alimentazione e dei piaceri della tavola*, Milan, 1942.

B. Mussolini, "La dottrina del fascismo," *Scritti e discorsi di Benito Mussolini*, vol. 8, Milan, 1934.

B. Mussolini, "Discorso dell'Ascensione" (May 26, 1927), in *Opera omnia*, vol. 23, Florence, 1957.

V. Sechi, "Taverne tipiche e cucine regionali alla mostra del dopolavoro," *L'Albergo in Italia*, July–August 1938.

P. Sorcinelli, "Identification Process at Work: Virtues of the Italian Working-Class Diet in the First Half of the Twentieth Century," in P. Scholliers (ed.), *Food, Drink and Identity: Cooking, Eating and Drinking in Europe Since the Middle Ages*, Oxford, 2001.

15. Turin, 1931: The Holy Palate Tavern

E. Crispolti, *Il secondo Futurismo: Torino 1923–1938*, Turin, 1961.

L. De Maria (ed.), *Marinetti e i futuristi*, Milan, 1994.

M. Gatta, "A tavola con Marinetti & Co.," www.mensamagazine.it/articolo .asp?id=652.

M. Gatta, "La Taverna del Santopalato: Primo, unico, vero covo gastronomico futurista," www.mensamagazine.it/articolo.asp?id=710.

F. T. Marinetti e Fillìa, *La cucina futurista*, Milan, 1986.

C. Salaris, *Storia del Futurismo*, Rome, 1985.

C. Salaris, *Cibo futurista: Dalla cucina nell'arte all'arte in cucina*, Rome, 2000.

16. Milan, 1936: Housewives and Epicures

R. Anau and E. Loewenthal, *Cucina ebraica*, Milan, 2000.

M. Belgrado Passigli, *Le ricette di casa mia: La cucina casher in una famiglia ebraica italiana*, Florence, 1993.

R. J. B. Bosworth, "The *Touring Club Italiano* and the Nationalization of the Italian Bourgeoisie," *European History Quarterly*, vol. 27, 1997.

A. Fulco Tedeschi, "100 candeline per la signora Fernanda," *Bollettino della Comunità Ebraica di Milano*, November 1989.

A. di Leone Leoni, "Gli ebrei a Ferrara nel XVI secolo," in A. Prosperi (ed.), *Storia di Ferrara*, vol. 6, *Il Rinascimento: Situazioni e personaggi*, Ferrara, 2000.

L. Levi, *Poesia nascosta: Seicento ricette di cucina ebraica in Italia*, Florence, 1931.

D. Limentani Pavoncello, *Dal 1880 ad oggi: La cucina ebraica della mia famiglia*, Rome, 1982.

E. Momigliano, *Storia tragica e grottesca del razzismo fascista*, Milan, 1946.

F. Momigliano, *Vivere bene in tempi difficili: Come le donne affrontano le crisi economiche*, Milan, 1933.

F. Momigliano, *La casa Savoia: Biografie, episodi narrati agli insegnanti delle scuole elementari*, Milan, 1933.

F. Momigliano, *Mangiare all'italiana: 100 maniere di cucinare i pesci, 100 buone e nutrienti minestre, 100 piatti di verdure e legumi, 200 ricette assortite di pollame, cacciagione, uova, salse e dolci. Molte ricette inedite*, Milan, 1936.

P. Monelli, *Il ghiottone errante: Viaggio gastronomico attraverso l'Italia*, Milan, 2005.

M. P. Moroni Salvatori, "Ragguaglio bibliografico sui ricettari del primo Novecento," in Capatti et al., *L'alimentazione*.

M. Sarfatti, "Gli ebrei negli anni del fascismo: Vicende, identità, persecuzione," in C. Vivanti (ed.), *Storia d'Italia: Annali 11; Gli ebrei in Italia*, vol. 2, *Dall'emancipazione a oggi*, Turin, 1997.

L. Tasca, "The 'Average Housewife' in Post–World War II Italy," *Journal of Women's History*, vol. 16, no. 2, 2004.

A. Toaff, *Mangiare alla giudia: La cucina ebraica in Italia dal Rinascimento all'età moderna*, Bologna, 2000.

Touring Club Italiano, *Guida Gastronomica d'Italia*, Milan, 1931.

P. R. Willson, "Cooking the Patriotic Omelette: Women and the Italian Fascist Ruralization Campaign," *European History Quarterly*, vol. 27, no. 4, 1997.

P. R. Willson, *Peasant Women and Politics in Fascist Italy: The Massaie Rurali*, London, 2002.

V. Zamagni, "L'evoluzione dei consumi fra tradizione e innovazione," in Capatti et al., *L'alimentazione*.

S. Zuccotti, *The Italians and the Holocaust: Persecution, Rescue and Survival*, London, 1987.

17. Rome, 1954: Miracle Food

S. Aphel Barzini, *Così mangiavamo: Cinquant'anni di storia italiana fra tavola e costume*, Rome, 2006.

F. Ceccarelli, *Lo stomaco della Repubblica: Cibo e potere in Italia dal 1945 al 2000*, Milan, 2000.

C. M. Counihan, *Around the Tuscan Table: Food, Family, and Gender in Twentieth-Century Florence*, New York, 2004.

G. Crainz, *Il miracolo italiano: Culture, identità, trasformazioni fra anni cinquanta e sessanta*, Rome, 2003.

P. Ginsborg, *A History of Contemporary Italy: Society and Politics 1943–1988*, London, 1990.

A. Grasso, *Storia della televisione italiana: I 50 anni della televisione*, Milan, 2004.

S. Gundle, "L'americanizzazione del quotidiano: Televisione e consumismo nell'Italia degli anni cinquanta," *Quaderni Storici*, vol. 62, no. 2, 1986.

J. Irving, "Soldati con la S maiuscola," in *Slow Food*, vol. 22, 2006.

A. Keys, "Field Studies in Italy, 1954," in A. Keys and P. D. White (eds.), *Cardiovascular Epidemiology*, New York, 1956.

A. Keys and M. Keys, *Eat Well and Stay Well*, London, 1960.

A. Keys and M. Keys, *How to Eat Well and Stay Well the Mediterranean Way*, New York, 1975.

A. Keys, *Seven Countries: A Multivariate Analysis of Death and Coronary Heart Disease*, Cambridge, Mass., 1980.

A. Keys, "Mediterranean Diet and Public Health: Personal Reflections," *American Journal of Clinical Nutrition*, vol. 61, 1995.

G. Pedrocco, "La conservazione del cibo: Dal sale all'industria agro-alimentare," in Capatti et al., *L'alimentazione*.

V. Pratolini, *Lo scialo: Una storia italiana*, Milan, 1960.

P. Quirino, "I consumi in Italia dall'Unità ad oggi," in R. Romano (ed.), *Storia dell'economia italiana*, vol. 3, *L'età contemporanea: Un paese nuovo*, Turin, 1991.

F. M. Snowden, *The Fascist Revolution in Tuscany, 1919–1922*, Cambridge, U.K., 1989.

M. Soldati, *Alla ricerca dei cibi genuini: Viaggio nella Valle del Po*, RAI, first transmitted 1957–58.

M. Soldati, *Da leccarsi i baffi: Memorabili viaggi in Italia alla scoperta del cibo e del vino genuino*, Rome, 2005.

F. Taddei, "Pane e olio: L'alimentazione dei mezzadri in Toscana," in *Il Risorgimento*, vol. 44, no. 2, 1992, "Alimentazione e trasformazioni sociali tra '800 e '900."

F. Taddei, "Il cibo nell'Italia mezzadrile fra Ottocento e Novecento," in Capatti et al., *L'alimentazione*.

L. Vercelloni, "La modernità alimentare," in Capatti et al., *L'alimentazione*.

P. D. White, "Clinical Studies in Italy, 1954," in A. Keys and P. D. White (eds.), *Cardiovascular Epidemiology*, New York, 1956.

Un americano a Roma (*An American in Rome*), (Steno, dir.), 1954, Italy.

18. Bologna, 1974: *Mamma's Tortellini*

P. Camporesi, "Il pane e la morte." "Cucina di città e cucina di campagna," "Alimentazione e rituali agrari," all in *Alimentazione, folclore, società*, Parma, 1980.

S. Gundle, "Hollywood Glamour and Mass Consumption in Postwar Italy," *Journal of Cold War Studies*, vol. 4, no. 3, 2002.

S. Gundle, "Sophia Loren, Italian Icon." *Historical Journal of Film, Radio and Television*, vol. 15, no. 3, 1995.

A. E. Hotchner, *Sophia: Living and Loving: Her Own Story*, London, 1979.

E. Invernizzi, *Pasta, amore e fantasia: La ricetta del successo del pastificio Rana*, Milan, 2006.

S. Loren, *In cucina con amore*, Milan, 1971.

S. Loren, *Eat with Me*, London, 1972.

F. Monteleone, *Storia della radio e della televisione in Italia: Società, politica, strategie, programmi, 1922–1992*, Venice, 1992.

L. Vercelloni, "La modernità alimentare," in A. Capatti et al. (eds.), *L'alimentazione*.

L'oro di Napoli (The Gold of Naples), (V. De Sica, dir.) 1954, Italy.

Pane, amore e . . . (Scandal in Sorrento), (D. Risi., dir.) 1956, France / Italy.

La ciociara (Two Women), (V. De Sica, dir.), 1960, Italy / France.

Giovanni Rana, http://www.rana.it/it/storia.php.

19. Genoa 2001–2006: Faulty Basil

D. Atkinson, D. Gibbs, and S. Reimer, "Quality Food, 'Authentic' Production, and Rural Development in Campania," working paper, University of Hull, February 2006.

C. Brambilla, "Cibi ogm, il sì degli scienziati 'Sicuri e senza rischi,'" *La Repubblica*, 4 November 2004.

E. Carloni, "Di pesto ce n'è uno solo," *Corriere della Sera*, September 19, 2002.

P. Crecchi, "Pesto, firmata la pace," *Il Secolo XIX*, August 30, 2002.

F. Gatti, "Io schiavo in Puglia," *L'Espresso*, September 1, 2006.

"Beppe Grillo: 'E' una battaglia persa,'" interview with R. Parodi in *Il Secolo XIX*, July 24, 2002.

J. Israely, "Seriously Funny," *Time*, October 10, 2005.

D. McDonnell, "The Genoa G8 and the Death of Carlo Giuliani," in S. Gundle and L. Rinaldi (eds.), *Assassinations, Murders and Mysteries in Modern Italy*, New York, forthcoming.

"Le inchieste in cucina: Origine ed evoluzione dei piatti tipici liguri," *CdPNews*, September 2006.

"Riconoscimento del Pesto Genovese a livello europeo? Aggiornamenti sull'evoluzione della pratica presentata al Consiglio d'Europa," *CdPNews*, March 2006.

F. Parasecoli, *Food Culture in Italy*, London, 2004.

M. Riva, "Pesto & Salute," personal communication from Marco Riva of the Università di Scienze Gastronomiche di Pollenzo-Bra.

"Slow Food replica agli scienziati 'Polenta e pesto contro gli ogm,'" *La Repubblica*, November 5, 2004.

"Tendenze recenti del mercato dei prodotti DOP e IGP in Italia," Slow Food press release, Terra Madre, 2006.

P. A. Uslengo, "Pesto genovese," personal communication from Pietro Attilio Uslengo, Cancelliere della Confraternita del Pesto.

"Veronesi: Pronto a mangiare il pesto anche se fatto con il basilico giovane," *Corriere della Sera*, November 4, 2004.

Denominazione di origine protetta: Disciplinare di produzione "Basilico genovese" and *Scoprire il sapore delle eccellenze dell'agro—alimentare genovese*, Camera di Commercio di Genova; www.ge.camcom.it / servizi / agricola_basilico_dop.asp.

Mangiare in Liguria, www.mangiareinliguria.it / consorziopestogenovese / pestogenovesedop.php.

Parco del Basilico di Genova Pra, http:/ / parco-basilico.provincia.genova.it.

Information about the Médecins Sans Frontières activity in Italy is available at www .msf.org.

20. Turin, 2006: Peasants to the Rescue!

W. Parkins and G. Craig, *Slow Living*, Oxford, 2006.

C. Petrini, "'Manifesto sul futuro dei semi' per sancire la libertà di coltivare," *La Stampa*, October 29, 2006.

C. Petrini, *Slow Food: Le ragioni del gusto*, Rome-Bari, 2003.

C. Petrini, *Slow Food Revolution: Da Arcigola a Terra madre: Una nuova cultura del cibo e della vita*, Milan, 2005.

C. Petrini, *Buono, pulito e giusto: Principî di nuova gastronomia*, Turin, 2005.

R. Rizzo "I contadini provano a salvare il mondo," *La Stampa*, October 27, 2006.

"Il Salone del Gusto: Torino, al Lingotto l'Onu dei contadini," *La Stampa*, October 27, 2006.

A. C. Sartirani, *Antico Condimento di Cristoforo da Messisbugo*, Agriturismo Oasi Naturale Le Pradine–Mirabello (Fe).

"I numeri di Terra Madre 2006," "Terra madre, un film documentario di Ermanno Olmi: A Torino le riprese durante Terra Madre," Slow Food press releases, Terra Madre / Salone del Gusto, 2006.

Terra Madre: 1600 comunità del cibo, Bra, 2006.

Sources consulted for the captions to the illustrations

D. Benati and E. Roccòmini, *Annibale Carracci*, Milan, 2006.

G. Buitoni, *Storia di un imprenditore*, Milan, 1972.

G. Gallo (ed.), *"Sulla bocca di tutti." Buitoni e Perugina una storia in breve*, Perugia, 1990.

Nizza & Morbelli, *I quattro moschettieri. Illustrazioni di Angelo Bioletto*, Perugia, 1935.

D. Posner, *Annibale Carracci. A Study in the Reform of Italian Painting Around 1590*, 2 vols, London, 1971.

Index

Page numbers in italics refer to illustrations.

About the Author

John Dickie lectures in Italian Studies at University College London, where he teaches courses on all aspects of Italian language and culture. He's won numerous grants and awards, notably the title of Commendatore dell'Ordine della Stella della Solidarietà Italiana, given by the president of the Italian Republic. His previous popular book, *Cosa Nostra*, sold more than 200,000 copies in the United Kingdom, and has been translated into twenty languages. He lives in London with his family.